For Micah –

Frommer's 97

To remember your 10th Birthday

San Francisco

*in San Francisco –
Oh what fun!
Love, Grampy &
Grandneve*

by Erika Lenkert and Matthew R. Poole

August 12, 13, 14, 2014

Macmillan • USA

ABOUT THE AUTHORS

A native San Franciscan, **Erika Lenkert** worked for HarperCollins before becoming a free-lance writer. She has contributed to dozens of travel guides and is currently seeking her fortune in both San Francisco and Hollywood. Her Siamese cats are along for the ride.

Combining the only three things he's good at—eating, sleeping, and criticizing—**Matthew R. Poole** has found a surprisingly prosperous career as a freelance travel writer. A native Northern Californian and author of nearly a dozen travel guides to California and Hawaii, he's looking forward to retiring at thirty but fears he won't be able to tell the difference. He currently lives in San Francisco and has no intention of writing a novel.

Erika and Matthew also contribute to Frommer's *California* and *California from $60 a Day* guides.

MACMILLAN TRAVEL

A Simon & Schuster Macmillan Company
1633 Broadway
New York, NY 10019

Find us online at **http://www.mgr.com/travel** or
on America Online at Keyword **Frommer's.**

ISBN 0-02-861105-5
ISSN 0899-3254

Editor: Douglas Stallings
Production Editor: Lori Cates
Design by Michele Laseau
Digital Cartography by Ortelius Design and John Decammillis
Maps copyright © by Simon & Schuster, Inc.

SPECIAL SALES

Bulk purchases (10+ copies) of Frommer's and selected Macmillan travel guides are available to corporations, organizations, mail-order catalogs, institutions, and charities at special discounts, and can be customized to suit individual needs. For more information write to Special Sales, Macmillan General Reference, 1633 Broadway, New York, NY 10019.

Manufactured in the United States of America

Contents

List of Maps

ACKNOWLEDGEMENTS

Matthew and Erica would like to thank Dawn Stranne, Meredith Post, Elaine Sosa, and Shirley Fong-Torres.

AN INVITATION TO THE READER

In researching this book, we discovered many wonderful places—hotels, restaurants, shops, and more. We're sure you'll find others. Please tell us about them, so we can share the information with your fellow travelers in upcoming editions. If you were disappointed with a recommendation, we'd love to know that, too. Please write to:

Erika Lenkert/Matthew R. Poole
Frommer's San Francisco '97
Macmillan Travel
1633 Broadway
New York, NY 10019

AN ADDITIONAL NOTE

Please be advised that travel information is subject to change at any time—and this is especially true of prices. We therefore suggest that you write or call ahead for confirmation when making your travel plans. The authors, editors, and publisher cannot be held responsible for the experiences of readers while traveling. Your safety is important to us, however, so we encourage you to stay alert and be aware of your surroundings. Keep a close eye on cameras, purses, and wallets, all favorite targets of thieves and pickpockets.

WHAT THE SYMBOLS MEAN

✪ **Frommer's Favorites**

Hotels, restaurants, attractions, and entertainment you should not miss.

⑤ **Super-Special Values**

Hotels and restaurants that offer great value for your money.

The following abbreviations are used for credit cards:

AE	American Express	EU	Eurocard
CB	Carte Blanche	JCB	Japan Credit Bank
DC	Diners Club	MC	MasterCard
DISC	Discover	V	Visa
ER	enRoute		

The San Francisco Experience

You are standing on the corner of Powell and Geary streets at San Francisco's famed Union Square, pausing a moment to catch your breath. Bags in hand bear the rewards of a memorable day of shopping. It's about four in the afternoon on a summer Sunday; a stiff, cool breeze from the west mocks the cloudless skies. Above the din and traffic you hear the clang of a bell, and moments later a cable car—precariously overloaded with wide-eyed tourists—approaches from behind, groaning its way up yet another steep hill. A steady stream of chattering pedestrians passes by, few of whom seem to speak English as a first language. Across the way a bellman hails a taxi for an older couple, both men dressed in black. Though the sun is out, glimmering skyscrapers block any hope of a warm ray. "Should've dressed warmer," you reply to a shiver as you head back to your hotel to get ready for dinner. As you round the corner, an old man selling flowers on the street corner smiles and hands you a rose—a fitting end to a thoroughly enjoyable day.

Welcome to San Francisco.

Consistently rated one of the top tourist destinations in the world, San Francisco is awash with multiple dimensions: Its famous, thrilling streets go up, and they go down; its multifarious citizens—along with their native culture, architecture, and cuisine—hail from San Antonio to Singapore; and its politics range from hyper-liberalism to an ever-encroaching wave of conservatism. Even something as mundane as fog takes on a new dimension as it creeps from the ocean and slowly envelops San Francisco in a resplendent blanket of mist.

The result is a wee bit o' heaven for everyone: In a city so multifaceted, so enamored with itself, it's truly hard not to find what you're looking for. Feel the cool blast of salt air as you stroll across the Golden Gate. Stuff yourself on a Chinatown dim sum. Browse the Haight for incense and crystals. Walk along the beach, pierce your nose, see a play, rent a Harley—the list is endless. Like an eternal world's fair, it's all happening in San Francisco, and everyone's invited.

There are, however, three things you should know before coming to San Francisco. First, don't call it 'Frisco. Locals are horribly proud of their city and are surprisingly tolerant of tourists, but even a hearty, "I sure love 'Frisco!" will undoubtedly be met with a cool reply. Second, dress warmly. Bob Hope once remarked that San

Francisco is the city of four seasons—every day. Temperatures can drop darn quick within minutes, so be prepared. And finally, arrive with an open mind. There are so many diverse cultures and lifestyles crammed within this tiny peninsula that exercising tolerance and politeness isn't just a courtesy but a necessity. San Francisco's a crazy city, no doubt, but we wouldn't want it any other way.

1 Frommer's Favorite San Francisco Experiences

- **Cafe-Hopping in North Beach:** One of the most pleasurable smells of San Francisco is the aroma of roasted coffee beans wafting down Columbus Avenue. Start the day with a cup of Viennese at Caffè Trieste (a haven for true San Francisco characters), followed by a walk in and around Washington Square, lunch at Mario's Bohemian Cigar Store (à la focaccia sandwiches), book browsing at City Lights, more coffee at Caffè Greco, and dinner at L'Osteria del Forno or Moose's. Finish off the day with a little flamenco dancing at La Bodega or a nightcap with Enrico Caruso on the jukebox at Tosca's.
- **A Walk Along the Coastal Trail:** Walk the forested coastal trail from the Cliff House to the Golden Gate Bridge, and you'll see why San Franciscans put up with living on a fault line. Start at the parking lot just above Cliff House and head north. On a clear day you'll have incredible views of the Marin Headlands, but even on foggy days it's worth the trek to scamper over old bunkers and relish the crisp, cool air. Dress warmly.
- **A Drive to Muir Woods, Stinson Beach, and Point Reyes:** If you have wheels, reserve a day for a trip across the Golden Gate. Take the Stinson Beach exit off Highway 101, spend a few hours gawking at the monolithic redwoods at Muir Woods (people, I'm telling you, this place is amazing), continue on to Stinson Beach for lunch at the Parkside Café, then head up the coast to the spectacular Point Reyes National Seashore. Rain or shine, it's a day trip you'll never forget.
- **An Adventure to Alcatraz:** Even if you loathe tourist attractions, you'll like Alcatraz. The rangers have done a fantastic job of preserving The Rock—enough to give you the heebie-jeebies just looking at it—and they give excellent guided tours (highly recommended). Heck, even the boat ride across the bay is worth the price, so don't miss this one.
- **A Stroll Through Chinatown:** Chinatown is a trip. We've been through it at least 100 times, and it's never failed to entertain us. Skip the crummy camera and luggage stores and head straight for the outdoor markets, where a cornucopia of the bizarre, unbelievable, and just plain weird sits in boxes for you to scrutinize (one day we saw an armadillo for sale, and it wasn't meant to be a pet). Better yet, take one of Shirley Fong's Wok Wiz tours of Chinatown for the full effect.
- **A Date in the Haight:** Though the flowers of power have wilted, the Haight is still, more or less, the Haight: a sort of resting home for aging hippies, dazed Deadheads, skate punks, and an assortment of rather pathetic young panhandlers. Think of it as visiting a "people" zoo as you walk down the rows of used clothing stores and leather shops, trying hard not to stare at that girl (at least we *think* it's a girl) with the pierced eyebrows and shaved head. End the mystery tour with a plate of mussels at Cha Cha Cha, one of San Francisco's top restaurants.
- **An Afternoon at the Marin Headlands:** San Francisco's backyard of sorts, the Marin Headlands are located just across the Golden Gate Bridge to the west and offer not only the best views of the city, but also a wealth of outdoor activities. Birdwatching, hiking, mountain biking, horseback riding, the list goes on, are all fair game at this glorious national park. Don't miss the Marine Mammal Center, a ward for injured or abandoned seals (cute little buggers) and sea lions.

Impressions

Of all cities in the United States I have seen, San Francisco is the most beautiful.
—Nikita S. Khrushchev

- **A Walk Across the Golden Gate Bridge:** Don your windbreaker and walking shoes and prepare for a wind-blasted, exhilarating walk across San Francisco's most famous landmark. It's simply one of those things you have to do at least once in your life.
- **A Cruise Through the Castro:** The most populated and festive street in the city is not just for gays and lesbians (though the best cruising in town is right here). While there are some great shops and cafes—particularly Café Flore for lunch—it's the people-watching that makes the trip a must. And if you have the time, catch a flick at the beautiful 1930s Spanish colonial movie palace, the Castro Theatre.
- **A Day in Golden Gate Park:** A day at Golden Gate Park is a day well spent. Its arboreal paths stretch from the Haight all the way to Ocean Beach, offering dozens of fun things to do along the way. Top sites are the Conservatory of Flowers, Japanese Tea Garden, Asian Art Museum, and the Steinhart Aquarium. The best time to go is Sunday, when portions of the park are closed to traffic (rent skates or a bike for the full effect). Toward the end of the day, head west to the beach and watch the sunset.
- **A Soul-Stirring Sunday Morning Service at Glide:** Preacher Cecil Williams turns church-going into a spiritual party that leaves you feeling elated, hopeful, and unified with the world. All walks of life attend the service, which focuses not on any particular religion, but on what we have in common as people. It's great fun, with plenty of singing and hand clapping.
- **An Early Morning Cable Car Ride:** Skip the boring California line and take the Powell-Hyde cable car down to Fisherman's Wharf—the ride is worth the wait. When you reach the top of Nob Hill, grab the rail in one hand and hold the camera with the other, because you're about to see a view of the bay that'll make you a believer. Oh, and don't call it a trolley.
- **A Visit to MOMA:** Ever since the new MOMA opened in 1995, its been the best place to go for a quick dose of culture. Start by touring the museum, then head straight for the gift shop (oftentimes more entertaining than the rotating exhibits). Have a light lunch at Caffè Museo, where the food is a vast improvement from most museums' mush, then finish the trip with a stroll through the Yerba Buena Gardens across from the museum.

2 The City Today

Shaken but not stirred by the Loma Prieta earthquake in 1989, San Francisco has witnessed a spectacular rebound in recent years. The seaside Embarcadero, once plagued by a horrendously ugly freeway overpass, has been revitalized by a multimillion-dollar facelift, complete with palm trees, a new trolley line, and wide cobblestone walkways. SoMa, the once shady neighborhood south of Market Street, has exploded with new development, including the world-class Museum of Modern Art, the beautiful Yerba Buena Gardens, and a slew of hip new clubs and cafes. Even the city's dress code has improved: Hit the clubs wearing jeans, sneakers, and a T-shirt and you may just be asked to leave (even dress-down Fridays have changed to dress-up Fridays). In short, it's hot to be hip these days in San Francisco: Black is back, cigars are in, the blues rule, pool is cool again, and the '50s are back with a vengeance.

And though it seems hard to believe that one man could turn a city around, since the day Willie Brown was voted into office as mayor of San Francisco, things have been looking up for the city's state of affairs. After giving just about every member of former mayor Frank Jordan's administration the boot, the legendary ex-speaker of the house for California's State Assembly has been administering steady doses of shock therapy to this proud but oft-troubled city. Public transportation, always a thorny issue with the people, has improved (one bus driver, with the help of family, went so far as to clean his entire bus overnight to honor the new mayor); homelessness is no longer a crime and shelters and work programs are on the rise; the city's beleaguered 911 system is back on track; and San Franciscans in general are starting to take a renewed pride in there city since "Da Mayor" started running the show.

All that glitters is not the Golden Gate, however. At the end of World War II, San Francisco was the largest and wealthiest city on the West Coast. Since then, it has been demoted to the fourth-largest city in California, home to only 750,000 people, less than 5% of the state's total. The industrial heart of the city has been knocked out and shipped off to less costly locations such as Oakland and Los Angeles, and increasingly San Francisco has had to fall back on tourism as a major source of revenue. If the process continues unabated, the city may someday become another Venice or (egad!) Las Vegas, whose only raison d'être will be pleasing its visitors like one vast Fisherman's Wharf—a frightening premonition. Then, of course, there are the typical big-city problems. Crime is up along with drug use, homelessness and panhandling have gotten way out of hand, and a nationwide resurgence in racism hasn't left San Francisco—once a bastion of free-thinkers—untouched. (One odd predicament is the increase in drivers who run red lights, which has plagued the city and created fearful, angry pedestrians and nasty fender benders.)

But as a whole, San Francisco is doing just fine these days. Its symphony is in the black, its convention halls are fully booked, levels in city coffers are on the rise, the mayor's fired up—even AIDS is on the decline. It's hard to think of a whole city as having its ups and downs, but after nearly a decade of getting thumped by the recession and poor management (among other things), San Francisco is on a definite upswing. Though it may never relive its heady days as the king of the West Coast, San Francisco will undoubtedly retain the title as most everyone's favorite California city. As one resident put it, "Anything but LA."

3 A Look at the Past

Dateline

- **1542** Juan Cabrillo sails up the California coast.
- **1579** Sir Francis Drake lands near San Francisco, missing the entrance to the bay.
- **1769** Members of the Spanish expedition led by Gaspar de Portolá become the first Europeans to see San Francisco Bay.
- **1775** The *San Carlos* is the first European ship to sail into San Francisco Bay.

continues

Born as an out-of-the-way backwater of colonial Spain and blessed with a harbor that would have been the envy of any of the great cities of Europe, San Francisco boasts a story that is as varied as the millions of people who have passed through its Golden Gate.

THE AGE OF DISCOVERY   After the "discovery" of the New World by Columbus in 1492, legends of the fertile land of California were discussed in the universities and taverns of Europe, even though no one really understood where the mythical land was. (Some evidence of arrivals in California by Chinese merchants hundreds of years before Columbus's landing has been unearthed, although few scholars are willing to draw definite conclusions.) The first documented visit by a European to northern California, however, was by the Portuguese explorer Joaño Cabrilho, who circumnavigated the southern tip of South America as far north as the Russian River in 1542. Nearly 40 years later, in 1579, Sir Francis Drake landed on the northern California coast, stopping for a time to repair his ships and to claim the territory for Queen Elizabeth I of England. He was followed several years later by another Portuguese, Sebastian Cermeño, "discoverer" of Punta de los Reyes (King's Point) in the mid-1590s. Ironically, all three adventurers completely missed the narrow entrance to San Francisco Bay, either because it was enshrouded in fog or, more likely, because they simply weren't looking for it. Believe it or not, the bay's entrance is nearly impossible to see from the open ocean.

It would be another two centuries before a European actually saw the bay that would later extend Spain's influence over much of the American West. Gaspar de Portolá, a soldier sent from Spain to meddle in a rather ugly conflict between the Jesuits and the Franciscans, accidentally stumbled upon the bay in 1769, en route to somewhere else, but then stoically plodded on to his original destination, Monterey Bay, more than 100 miles to the south. Six years later, Juan Ayala, while on a mapping expedition for the Spanish, actually sailed into San Francisco Bay, and immediately realized the enormous strategic importance of his find.

Colonization quickly followed. Juan Bautista de Anza and around 30 Spanish-speaking families marched through the deserts from Sonora, Mexico, arriving after many hardships at the northern tip of modern-day San Francisco in June 1776. They immediately claimed the peninsula for Spain. (Ironically, their claim of allegiance to Spain occurred only about a week before the 13 English-speaking colonies of North America's eastern seaboard, a continent away, declared their independence from Britain.) Their headquarters was an adobe fortress, the Presidio, built on the site of today's park with the same name. The settlers' church, built a mile to the south, was the first of five Spanish missions later developed around the edges of San Francisco Bay. Although the name of the church was officially *Nuestra Señora de Dolores,* it was dedicated to St. Francis of Assisi and nicknamed San Francisco by the Franciscan priests. Later, the name was applied to the entire bay.

- 1776 Captain Juan Bautista de Anza establishes a presidio (military fort); San Francisco de Asis Mission opens.
- 1821 Mexico wins independence from Spain and annexes California.
- 1835 The town of Yerba Buena develops around the port; the United States tries unsuccessfully to purchase San Francisco Bay from Mexico.
- 1846 Mexican-American War.
- 1847 Americans annex Yerba Buena and rename it San Francisco.
- 1848 Gold is discovered in Coloma, near Sacramento.
- 1849 In the year of the gold rush, San Francisco's population swells from about 800 to 25,000.
- 1851 Lawlessness becomes acute before attempts are made to curb it.
- 1869 The transcontinental railroad reaches San Francisco.
- 1873 Andrew S. Hallidie invents the cable car.
- 1906 The Great Earthquake strikes, and the resulting fire levels the city.
- 1915 The Panama Pacific International Exposition celebrates San Francisco's restoration and the completion of the Panama Canal.
- 1936 The Bay Bridge is built.
- 1937 The Golden Gate Bridge is completed.
- 1945 The United Nations Charter is drafted and adopted by the representatives of 50 countries meeting in San Francisco.
- 1950 The beat generation moves into the bars and cafes of North Beach.
- 1967 A free concert in Golden Gate Park attracts 20,000 people, ushering in

continues

the Summer of Love and the hippie era.

- **1974** BART's high-speed transit system opens the tunnel linking San Francisco with the East Bay.
- **1978** Harvey Milk, a city supervisor and America's first openly gay politician, is assassinated, along with Mayor George Moscone, by political rival Dan White.
- **1989** An earthquake registering 7.1 on the Richter scale hits San Francisco during a World Series baseball game, as 100 million watch on TV; the city quickly rebuilds.
- **1991** Fire rages through the Berkeley/Oakland hills, destroying 2,800 homes.
- **1993** Yerba Buena Center for the Arts opens.
- **1995** New San Francisco Museum of Modern Art opens.
- **1996** Former Assembly Speaker Willie Brown elected mayor of San Francisco.

In 1821, Mexico broke away from Spain, secularized the Spanish missions, and abandoned all interest in the Indian natives. Freed of Spanish restrictions, California's ports were suddenly opened to trade. The region around San Francisco Bay supplied large numbers of hides and tallow for transport around Cape Horn to the tanneries and factories of New England and New York. The prospects for prosperity persuaded an English-born sailor, William Richardson, to jump ship in 1822 and settle on the site of what is now San Francisco. To impress the commandante of the Presidio, whose daughter he loved, Richardson converted to Catholicism and established the beginnings of what would soon became a thriving trading post and colony. Richard named his trading post *Yerba Buena* (or "good herb") because of a species of wild mint that grew there, near the site of today's Montgomery Street. (The city's original name was recalled with endless mirth 120 years later during San Francisco's hippie era.) He conducted a profitable hide-trading business and eventually became harbormaster and the city's first merchant prince. By 1839, the place was a veritable town, with a mostly English-speaking populace and a saloon of dubious virtue.

Throughout the 19th century, armed hostilities between English-speaking settlers from the eastern seaboard and the Spanish-speaking colonies of Spain and Mexico erupted in places as widely scattered as Texas, Puerto Rico, and along the frequently shifting U.S.–Mexico border. In 1846, a group of U.S. Marines from the warship *Portsmouth* seized the sleepy main plaza of Yerba Buena, ran the U.S. flag up a pole, and declared California an American territory. The Presidio (occupied by about a dozen unmotivated Mexican soldiers) surrendered without a fuss. The first move the new, mostly Yankee citizenry made was to officially adopt the name of the bay as the name of their town.

THE GOLD RUSH The year 1848 was one of the most pivotal years in European history, with unrest sweeping through Europe, horrendous poverty in Ireland, and widespread disillusionment about the hopes for prosperity throughout Europe and the eastern coast of the United States. Stories about the golden port of San Francisco and the agrarian wealth of the American West filtered slowly east, attracting slow-moving groups of settlers. Ex-sailor Richard Henry Dana extolled the virtues of California in his best-selling novel *Two Years Before the Mast*, and helped fire the public's imagination about the territory's bounty, particularly that of the Bay Area.

The first overland party crossed the Sierra and arrived in California in 1841. San Francisco grew steadily, reaching a population of approximately 900 by April 1848, but nothing hinted at the population explosion that was to follow. Historian Barry Parr has referred to the California gold rush as the most extraordinary event to ever befall an American city in peacetime. In time, San Francisco's winning combination of raw materials, healthful climate, and freedom would have attracted thousands of settlers even without the lure of gold. But the gleam of the soft metal is said to have compressed 50 years of normal growth into less than six months. In 1848, the year gold was first discovered, the population of San Francisco jumped from under 1,000 to 26,000 in less than six months. As many as 100,000 more passed through San Francisco in the space of less than a year on their way to the rocky hinterlands where the gold was rumored to be.

If not for the discovery of some small particles of gold at a sawmill that he owned, Swiss-born John Augustus Sutter's legacy would have been far less flamboyant. Despite Sutter's wish to keep the discovery quiet, his employee, John Marshall, leaked word of the discovery to friends. It eventually appeared in local papers, and smart investors on the East Coast took immediate heed. The rush did not start, however, until Sam Brannan, a Mormon preacher and famous charlatan, ran through the streets of San Francisco shouting, "Gold! Gold in the American River!" (Brannan, incidentally, bought up all of the harbor-front real estate he could get, and cornered the market on shovels, pickaxes, and canned food, just before making the announcement that was heard around the world.)

A world on the brink of change responded almost frantically. The gold rush was on. Shop owners hung "Gone to the Diggings" signs in their windows. Flotillas of ships set sail from ports throughout Europe, South America, Australia, and the East Coast, sometimes nearly sinking with the weight of mining equipment. Townspeople from the Midwest headed overland, tent cities sprang up, and the sociology of a nation was transformed almost overnight. Not since the Crusades of the Middle Ages had so many people been mobilized in so short a period of time. Daily business stopped; ships arrived in San Francisco and were almost immediately deserted by their crews. News of the gold strike spread like a plague through every discontented hamlet in the known world. Although other settlements were closer to the gold strike, San Francisco was the famous name, and therefore, where the gold-diggers disembarked. Tent cities sprung up, demand for virtually everything skyrocketed, and although some miners actually found gold, smart merchants quickly discovered that more enduring hopes lay in servicing the needs of the thousands of miners who arrived ill-equipped and ignorant of the lay of the land. Prices soared. Miners, faced with staggeringly inflated prices for goods and services, barely scraped a profit after expenses. Most prospectors failed, many died of hardship, others committed suicide at the alarming rate of 1,000 a year. Yet despite the tragedies, graft, and vice associated with the gold rush, within mere months San Francisco was forever transformed from a tranquil Spanish settlement into a roaring, boisterous boomtown.

BOOMTOWN FEVER   By 1855, most of California's surface gold had already been panned out, leaving only the richer but deeper veins of ore, which individual miners couldn't retrieve without massive capital investments. Despite that, San Francisco had evolved into a vast commercial magnet, sucking into its warehouses and banks the staggering riches that overworked newcomers had dragged, ripped, and distilled from the rocks, fields, and forests of western North America.

Investment funds were being lavished on more than mining, however. Speculation on the newly established San Francisco stock exchange could make or destroy an investor in a single day, and several noteworthy writers (including Mark Twain) were among the young men forever influenced by the boomtown spirit. The American Civil War left California firmly in the Union camp, ready, willing, and able to receive hordes of disillusioned soldiers fed up with the internecine war-mongering of the eastern seaboard. In 1869, the transcontinental railway linked the eastern and western seaboards of the United States, ensuring the fortunes of the barons who controlled it. The railways, however, also shifted economic power bases as cheap manufactured goods from the east undercut the high prices hitherto charged for goods that sailed or steamed their way around the tip of South America. Ownership of the newly formed Central Pacific and Southern Pacific railroads was almost completely controlled by the "Big Four," all iron-willed capitalists—Leland Stanford, Mark Hopkins, Collis P. Huntington, and Charles Crocker—whose ruthlessness was legendary. (Much of the bone-crushing labor for their railway was executed by low-paid Chinese newcomers, most of whom arrived in overcrowded ships at San Francisco ports.) As the 19th century came to a close, civil unrest became more frequent as the monopolistic grip of the railways and robber barons became more obvious. Adding to the discontent were the uncounted thousands of Chinese immigrants, who fled starvation and unrest in Asia at rates rivaling those of the Italians, Poles, Irish, and British.

During the 1870s, the flood of profits from the Comstock Lode in western Nevada diminished to a trickle, a cycle of droughts wiped out part of California's agricultural bounty, and local industry struggled to survive against the flood of manufactured goods imported via railway from the well-established factories of the East Coast and Midwest. Often, discontented workers blamed their woes on the now-unwanted hordes of Chinese workers, who by preference and for mutual protection had congregated into teeming all-Asian communities.

Despite these downward cycles, the city enjoyed other bouts of prosperity around the turn of the century thanks to the Klondike gold rush in Alaska and the Spanish-American War. Long accustomed to making a buck off gold fever, San Francisco managed to position itself as a point of embarkation for supplies bound for Alaska. Also during this time emerged the Bank of America, which eventually evolved into the largest bank in the world. Founded in North Beach in 1904, Bank of America was the brainchild of Italian-born A. P. Giannini, who later funded part of the construction for a bridge that many critics said was preposterous: the Golden Gate.

THE GREAT FIRE   On the morning of April 18, 1906, San Francisco changed for all time. The city has never experienced an earthquake as destructive as the one that hit at 5:13am (scientists estimate its strength at 8.1 on the Richter scale). All but a handful of the city's 400,000 inhabitants lay fast asleep when the ground beneath the city went into a series of convulsions. As one eyewitness put it, "The earth was shaking . . . it was undulating, rolling like an ocean breaker." The quake ruptured every water main in the city, and simultaneously started a chain of fires that rapidly fused into one gigantic conflagration. The fire brigades were helpless, and for three days San Francisco burned.

Militia troops finally stopped the flames from advancing by dynamiting entire city blocks, but not before more than 28,000 buildings lay in ruins. Minor tremors lasted another three days. The final damage stretched across a path of destruction 450 miles long and 50 miles wide. In all, 497 city blocks were razed, or about one-third of the city. As Jack London wrote in a heartrending newspaper dispatch, "The city of San Francisco is no more." The earthquake and subsequent fire so decisively changed the city that post-1906 San Francisco bears little resemblance to the town before the quake. Out of the ashes rose a bigger, healthier, and more beautiful town, though latter-day urbanologists regret that the rebuilding that followed the San Francisco earthquake did not follow a more enlightened plan. So eager was the city to rebuild that the old, somewhat unimaginative gridiron plan was reinstated, despite the opportunities for more daring visions that the aftermath of the quake afforded.

In 1915, in celebration of the opening of the Panama Canal and to prove to the world that San Francisco was restored to it full glory, the city hosted the Panama

Pacific International Exhibition, a world's fair that exposed hundreds of thousands of visitors to the city's unique charms. The general frenzy of civic boosterism, however, reached its peak during the years just before World War I, when investments and civic pride might have reached an all-time high. Despite Prohibition, speak-easies did a thriving business in and around the city, and building sprees were as high-blown and lavish as the profits on the San Francisco stock exchange.

WORLD WAR II   The Japanese attack on Pearl Harbor on December 7, 1941, mobilized the United States into a massive war machine, with many shipyards strategically positioned along the Pacific Coast, including San Francisco. Within less than a year, several shipyards were producing up to one new warship per day, employing hundreds of thousands of people working in 24-hour shifts (the largest, Kaiser Shipyards in Richmond, employed more than 100,000 workers alone). In search of work and the excitement of life away from their villages and cornfields, workers flooded into the city from virtually everywhere, forcing an enormous boom in housing. Hundreds found themselves separated from their small towns for the first time in their lives and reveled in their newfound freedom.

After the hostilities ended, many soldiers remembered San Francisco as the site of their finest hours and returned to live there permanently. The economic prosperity of the postwar years enabled massive enlargements of the city, including freeways, housing developments, a booming financial district, and pockets of counterculture enthusiasts such as the beatniks, gays, and hippies.

THE 1950s: THE BEATS   San Francisco's reputation as a rollicking place where anything goes dates from the Barbary Coast days when gang warfare, prostitution, gambling, and drinking were major city pursuits, and citizens took law and order into their own hands. Its more modern role as a catalyst for social change and the avant-garde began in the 1950s when a group of young writers, philosophers, and poets challenged the materialism and conformity of American society by embracing anarchy and Eastern philosophy, expressing their notions in poetry. They adopted a uniform of jeans, sweater, sandals, and beret, called themselves beats, and hung out in North Beach where rents were low and cheap wine was plentiful. *San Francisco Chronicle* columnist Herb Caen, to whom they were totally alien, dubbed them *beatniks* in his column.

Allen Ginsberg, Gregory Corso, and Jack Kerouac had begun writing at Columbia University in New York, but it wasn't until they came west and hooked up with Lawrence Ferlinghetti, Kenneth Rexroth, Gary Snyder, and others that the movement gained national attention. The bible of the beats was Ginsberg's *Howl*, which he first read at the Six Gallery on October 13, 1955. By the time he finished reading Ginsberg was crying, the audience was chanting, and his fellow poets were announcing the arrival of an epic bard. Ferlinghetti published *Howl*, which was deemed obscene, in 1956. A trial followed, but the court found that the book had redeeming social value, thereby reaffirming the right of free expression. The other major work, Jack Kerouac's *On the Road*, was published in 1957, instantly becoming a best seller (he had written it as one long paragraph in 20 days in 1951). The freedom and sense of possibility that this book conveyed became the bellwether for a generation.

While the beats gave poetry readings and generated controversy, two clubs in North Beach were making waves, notably the hungry i and the Purple Onion, where everyone who was anyone or became anyone on the entertainment scene appeared— Mort Sahl, Dick Gregory, Lenny Bruce, Barbra Streisand, and Woody Allen all worked here. Maya Angelou appeared as a singer and dancer at the Purple Onion.

The cafes of North Beach were the center of bohemian life in the fifties: the Black Cat, Vesuvio's, Caffè Trieste and Caffè Tosca, and Enrico's Sidewalk Cafe. When the tour buses started rolling in, rents went up, and Broadway was turned into a sex club strip in the early 1960s. Thus ended an era, and the beats moved on. The alternative scene shifted to Berkeley and the Haight.

THE 1960s: THE HAIGHT   The torch of freedom had been passed from the beats and North Beach to Haight-Ashbury and the hippies, but it was a radically different torch. The hippies replaced the beats' angst, anarchy, negativism, nihilism, alcohol, and poetry with love, communalism, openness, drugs, rock music, and a back-to-nature philosophy. Although the scent of marijuana wafted everywhere—on the streets, in the cafes, in Golden Gate Park—the real drugs of choice were LSD (a tab of good acid cost $5) and other hallucinogenics. Timothy Leary experimented with its effects and exhorted youth to turn on, tune in, and drop out. Instead of hanging out in coffeehouses, the hippies went to concerts at the Fillmore or the Avalon Ballroom to dance. The first Family Dog Rock 'n' Roll Dance and Concert, "A Tribute to Dr. Strange," was given at the Longshoreman's Hall in fall 1965, featuring the Jefferson Airplane, the Marbles, the Great Society, and the Charlatans. At this event, the first major happening of the 1960s, Ginsberg led a snake dance through the crowd. In January 1966, the three-day Trips Festival, organized by rock promoter Bill Graham, was also held at the Longshoreman's Hall. The climax came with Ken Kesey and the Merry Pranksters Acid Test show, which used five movie screens, psychedelic visions, and the sounds of the Grateful Dead and Big Brother and the Holding Company. The "be-in" followed in the summer of 1966 at the polo grounds in Golden Gate Park, when an estimated 20,000 heard the Jefferson Airplane perform and Ginsberg chant, while the Hell's Angels acted as unofficial police. It was followed by the Summer of Love in 1967 as thousands of young people streamed into the city in search of drugs and sex.

The sixties Haight scene was very different from the fifties beat scene. The hippies were much younger than the beats had been, constituting the first youth movement to take over the nation. Ironically, they also became the first generation of young, independent, and moneyed consumers to be courted by corporations. Ultimately, the Haight and the hippie movement deteriorated from love and flowers into drugs and crime, drawing a fringe of crazies like Charles Manson and leaving only a legacy of sex, drugs, violence, and consumerism. As early as October 1967, the "Diggers," who had opened a free shop and soup kitchen in the Haight, symbolically buried the dream in a clay casket in Buena Vista Park.

The end of the Vietnam War and the resignation of President Nixon took the edge off politics. The last fling of the mentality that had driven the 1960s occurred in 1974 when Patty Hearst was kidnapped from her Berkeley apartment by the Symbionese Liberation Army and taken on a bank-robbing spree before surrendering in San Francisco.

THE 1970s: GAY RIGHTS   The homosexual community in San Francisco developed at the end of World War II, when thousands of military personnel were discharged back to the United States via San Francisco. A substantial number of those men were homosexual and decided to stay on in San Francisco. A gay community grew up along Polk Street between Sutter and California. Later, the larger community moved into the Castro, where it remains today.

The gay political protest movement is usually dated from the 1969 Stonewall raid that occurred in Greenwich Village. Although the political movement started in New York, California had already given birth to two major organizations for gay rights:

the Mattachine Society, founded in 1951 by Henry Hay in Los Angeles, and the Daughters of Bilitis, a lesbian organization founded in 1955 in San Francisco.

After Stonewall, the Committee for Homosexual Freedom was created in spring 1969 in San Francisco; a Gay Liberation Front chapter was organized at Berkeley. In fall 1969, Robert Patterson, a columnist for the *San Francisco Examiner,* referred to homosexuals as "semi males, drag darlings," and "women who aren't exactly women." On October 31 at noon a group began a peaceful picket of the *Examiner.* Peace reigned until someone threw a bag of printer's ink from an *Examiner* window. Someone wrote "Fuck the Examiner" on the wall, and the police moved in to clear the crowd, clubbing them as they went. The remaining pickets retreated to Glide Methodist Church and then marched on city hall. Unfortunately, the mayor was away. Unable to air their grievances, they started a sit-in that lasted until 5pm, when they were ordered to leave. Most did, but three remained and were arrested.

Later that year, an anti-Thanksgiving rally was staged at which gays protested against several national and local businesses: Western and Delta airlines, the former for firing lesbian stewardesses, the latter for refusing to sell a ticket to a young man wearing a Gay Power button; KFOG, for its antihomosexual broadcasting; and also some local gay bars for exploitation. On May 14, 1970, a group of gay and women's liberationists invaded the convention of the American Psychiatric Association in San Francisco to protest the reading of a paper on aversion therapy for homosexuals, forcing the meeting to adjourn.

The rage against intolerance was appearing on all fronts. At the National Gay Liberation conference held in August 1970 in the city, Charles Thorp, chairman of the San Francisco State Liberation Front, called for militancy and issued a challenge to come out with a rallying cry of "Blatant is beautiful." He also argued for the use of what he felt was the more positive, celebratory term *gay* instead of *homosexual,* and decried the fact that homosexuals were kept in their place at the three B's: the bars, the beaches, and the baths. As the movement grew in size and power, debates on strategy and tactics occurred, most dramatically between those who wanted to withdraw into separate ghettos and those who wanted to enter mainstream society. The most extreme proposal was made in California by Don Jackson, who proposed establishing a gay territory in California's Alpine County, about 10 miles south of Lake Tahoe. It would have had a totally gay administration, civil service, university, museum— everything. The residents of Alpine County were not pleased with the proposal. But before the situation turned really ugly, Jackson's idea was abandoned because of lack of support in the gay community. In the end, the movement would concentrate on integration and civil rights, not separatism. They would elect politicians who were sympathetic to their cause and celebrate their new identity by establishing National Gay Celebration Day and Gay Pride Week, the first of which was celebrated in June 1970 when 1,000 to 2,000 marched in New York, 1,000 in Los Angeles, and a few hundred in San Francisco.

By the mid-1970s, the gay community craved a more central role in San Francisco politics. Harvey Milk, owner of a camera store in the Castro, decided to run as an openly gay man for the board of supervisors. He won, becoming the first gay person to hold a major public office. He and liberal Mayor George Moscone developed a gay rights agenda, but in 1978 both were killed by former Supervisor Dan White, who shot them after Moscone refused his request for reinstatement. White, a Catholic and former police officer, had consistently opposed Milk's and Moscone's more liberal policies. At his trial, White successfully pleaded temporary insanity caused by additives in his fast-food diet. The media dubbed it a "Twinkie defense," but the murder charges against White were reduced to manslaughter. On that day, angry and grieving, the gay community rioted, overturning and burning police cars in a night of rage. To this day a candlelight memorial parade is held on November 27. Milk's martyrdom was both a political and a practical inspiration to gay candidates across the country.

The emphasis in the gay movement shifted abruptly in the 1980s when the AIDS epidemic struck the community. AIDS has had a dramatic impact on the Castro. While it's still a thriving and lively community, it's no longer the constant party that it once was. The hedonistic lifestyle that had played out in the discos, bars, baths, and streets changed as the seriousness of the epidemic sunk in and the number of deaths increased. Political efforts have shifted away from enfranchisement and toward demanding money for social services and research money to deal with the AIDS crisis. The gay community has developed its own organizations, such as Project Inform and Gay Men's Health Crisis, to publicize information about the disease, treatments available, and safe sex. Though new cases of AIDS within the gay community are on the decline in San Francisco, it still remains a serious problem.

THE 1980s: THE BIG ONE, PART 2   The eighties may have arrived in San Francisco with a whimper (compared to previous generations), but they went out with quite a bang. At 5:04pm on Tuesday, October 17, 1989, as more than 62,000 fans filled Candlestick Park for the third game of the World Series—and the San Francisco Bay Area commute moved into its heaviest flow—an earthquake of magnitude 7.1 struck. Within the next 20 seconds, 63 lives would be lost, $10 billion in damage would occur, and the entire Bay Area community would be reminded of their humble insignificance. Centered about 60 miles south of San Francisco within the Forest of Nisene Marks, the deadly temblor was felt as far away as San Diego and Nevada.

Though scientists had predicted an earthquake would hit on this section of the San Andreas Fault, certain structures that were built to withstand such an earthquake failed miserably. The most catastrophic event was the collapse of the elevated Cypress Street section of Interstate 880 in Oakland, where the upper level of the freeway literally pancaked the lower level, crushing everything with such force that cars were reduced to inches. Other structures heavily damaged included the San Francisco–Oakland Bay Bridge, shut down for months when a section of the roadbed collapsed; San Francisco's Marina district, where several multimillion-dollar homes collapsed on their weak, shifting bases of landfill and sand; and the Pacific Garden Mall in Santa Cruz, which was completely devastated.

President Bush declared a disaster area for the seven hardest-hit counties, where at least 3,700 people were reported injured and more than 12,000 were displaced. More than 18,000 homes were damaged and 963 others destroyed. Although fire raged within the city and water supply systems were damaged, the major fires sparked within the Marina district were brought under control within three hours, due mostly to the heroic efforts of San Francisco's firefighters.

After the rubble had finally settled, it was unanimously agreed that San Francisco and the Bay Area had pulled through miraculously well—particularly when compared to the more recent earthquake in Kobe, Japan, which killed thousands and displaced an entire city. After the quake, a feeling of esprit de corps swept the city as neighbors helped each other rebuild and donations poured in from all over the world. Though its been nearly a decade since, San Francisco is still feeling the effects of the quake, most noticeably during rush hour as commuters take a variety of detours to circumvent freeways that were damaged or destroyed and are still under construction.

That another "big one" will strike is inevitable: It's the price you pay for living on a fault line. But if there is ever a city that is prepared for a major shakedown, it's San Francisco.

4 Famous San Franciscans

Ansel Adams (1902–84)   Photographer. Born in San Francisco, Adams is most famous for his photographs of Yosemite and the Sierra. He organized the first college of art photography department at the California School of Fine Arts in 1946.

Willie Brown (b. 1934)   Current mayor of San Francisco. Formerly California Assembly speaker of the house, Brown's flamboyant style, lavish tastes, and masterful politicking led to his rapid rise as California's most powerful and outspoken democrat.

Dave Brubeck (b. 1920)   Pianist and jazz composer. Born in Concord, California, Brubeck led experimental jazz groups in San Francisco in the 1940s. In 1951 he organized a quartet with alto saxophonist Paul Desmond and went on to international fame in the 1950s and 1960s. Gerry Mulligan was also a member of the group. Brubeck's signature composition is *Take Five*.

Herb Caen (b. 1916)   Author, newspaper columnist. Caen, born in Sacramento, moved to San Francisco in 1936 to eventually become "Mr. San Francisco," having written his column for the *San Francisco Chronicle* for more than half a century. He dubbed the beats the beatniks and continues to report on the scene.

Francis Ford Coppola (b. 1939)   One of America's most successful contemporary filmmakers. Coppola is best known for *Apocalypse Now* and *The Godfather*. He continues to live in San Francisco, working from his office within the Columbus Tower in North Beach.

Joe DiMaggio (b. 1914)   One of the greatest baseball players of all time. He began his career with the San Francisco Seals before becoming the New York Yankees's star centerfielder. During the 1950s, he married Marilyn Monroe in San Francisco.

Dianne Feinstein (b. 1933)   Politician. Born in San Francisco and educated at nearby Stanford, Feinstein served as the city's mayor and is now a U.S. senator. A political "centrist," Feinstein is supportive of alternative lifestyles and reproductive rights.

Jerry Garcia (1942–95)   Rock and bluegrass musician. Garcia was best known as the lead guitarist and vocalist of the psychedelic rock band the Grateful Dead. Soon after his death the Grateful Dead disbanded and an era ended.

Danny Glover (b. 1947)   Actor. Graduate of San Francisco State University and Black Actors' Workshop of the American Conservatory Theatre, Glover's roles include the domineering husband in *The Color Purple* (1985) and Mel Gibson's partner in the Lethal Weapon movies. Continues to live in San Francisco.

Bill Graham (1931–92)   Music promoter. Before his death in a helicopter accident in 1992, Graham was one of the leading concert promoters in the country. Many of his first concerts were staged at the Fillmore Auditorium.

Dashiell Hammett (1894–1961)   Author. Drawing on his experience with the Pinkerton Detective Agency, Hammett penned hard-boiled detective novels, including *The Maltese Falcon* and *The Thin Man*. He was imprisoned for refusing to testify during the House Un-American Activities Committee "witch-hunts" in the 1950s.

William Randolph Hearst (1863–1951)   Media mogul. Famous for his opulent lifestyle and grand castle at San Simeon, Hearst was a publishing magnate, who as a young man worked for the *San Francisco Examiner.* He later acquired a string of successful radio stations, motion picture companies, and daily newspapers.

Chris Isaak (b. 1956)   Singer. San Francisco's swooning, surfing heartthrob, Isaak got his start playing in small clubs around the city. Hits include "Somebody's Crying," "Wicked Game," and "San Francisco Days." Currently lives in the Sunset District.

Janis Joplin (1943–70)   Rock star. One of the 1960s' most charismatic rock 'n' roll voices, Joplin moved from Texas at the age of 18 and began her career in San Francisco with Big Brother and the Holding Company. She died from an overdose of heroin in 1970.

Jack Kerouac (1922–69)   Author. The leader of the "beat generation," Kerouac was born in Lowell, Massachusetts, and came to San Francisco in the 1950s to write the beats' bible *On the Road.*

Maxine Hong Kingston (b. 1940)   Author. Kingston burst onto the literary scene with *The Woman Warrior* in 1976, following it with *China Men,* which won the National Book Award. *Tripmaster Monkey* (1989) won the PEN fiction award. A graduate of Berkeley, she returned there to teach in 1991.

Jack London (1876–1916)   Author. Born in the SoMa District (an area south of Market Street), London later moved to Oakland where he grew up, helping support his family by working on the waterfront. As a teenager he became an oyster pirate. A legendary figure, London was a hobo, factory worker, sailor, and prospector. Among the more than 40 books he wrote in his abbreviated life were *Call of the Wild* and *The Sea Wolf.*

Harvey Milk (1931–78)   Activist. Originally from Brooklyn, Milk owned a camera store at 575 Castro St. He ran for the board of supervisors in 1977, becoming the first openly gay person to hold a major public office. He was assassinated in 1978 in city hall along with Mayor George Moscone by Dan White. Milk is memorialized in Harvey Milk Plaza, and a candlelight parade is held every year in November to mark his death.

Joe Montana (b. 1956)   Retired 49ers quarterback. Considered one of the greatest quarterbacks of all time. Led the 49ers to four Super Bowl championships; voted most valuable player (MVP) in three.

Randy Shilts (1951–94)   Journalist. Shilts wrote for both the *San Francisco Examiner* and the *San Francisco Chronicle* and such gay publications as *The Advocate* and *Christopher Street.* He became famous for his biography of Harvey Milk, *The Mayor of Castro Street,* and also for his massive *And the Band Played On,* documenting the AIDS crisis. He died of AIDS.

Amy Tan (b. 1952)   Author. Born in Oakland to parents who emigrated from China. Her first book, *The Joy Luck Club,* became a best-seller and provides a moving portrait of life in San Francisco's Chinatown. Other books include *The Kitchen God's Wife.*

Hunter S. Thompson (b. 1939)   Gonzo journalist. A long-time political columnist for the *San Francisco Examiner,* Thompson is also the national affairs editor at

Rolling Stone, and author of several best-selling books including *Fear and Loathing in Las Vegas* and *Fear and Loathing on the Campaign Trail.*

Robin Williams (b. 1952)   Actor, comedian. A San Francisco local, Williams nurtured his career in comedy clubs along the west coast. National exposure as the extraterrestrial Mork from Ork led to a series of starring roles in such films as *Mrs. Doubtfire, Dead Poets Society,* and *The Birdcage.* Frequently seen dining at Stars.

5 Sounds of the 1960s

During its heyday in the 1950s and 1960s, San Francisco was the place to be for anyone who eschewed the conventional American lifestyle. From moody beatniks to political firebrands, the city was a vortex for poets, writers, actors, and a bewildering assortment of free thinkers and activists. Drawn by the city's already liberal views on life, liberty, and the pursuit of happiness, thousands of the country's youth—including some of America's most talented musicians—headed west to join the party. What culminated in the 1960s was San Francisco's hat trick of rock legends: It was able to lay claim to three of the rock era's most influential bands: the Grateful Dead, Big Brother and the Holding Company and Janis Joplin, and the Jefferson Airplane.

THE GRATEFUL DEAD   Easily the most influential band to be spawned from the 1960s' psychedelic movement was San Francisco's music guru, The Grateful Dead. Described as the "house band for the famous acid tests that transformed the City by the Bay into one endless freak-out," the Dead's music was played simultaneously on so many stereo systems (and at such high volumes) that the group almost seemed to have set the tone for one enormous, citywide jam session.

Though the group disbanded in 1995 after the death of its charismatic lead vocalist, Jerry Garcia, the group's devoted fans had already elevated the Grateful Dead to cult empire status. Tie-dyed "Deadheads" (many of whom followed the band on tour for decades) can still be found tripping within the Haight, reminiscing about the good old days when the group never traveled with a sound system weighing less than 23 tons. In fact, more than any other band produced during the 1960s, the Grateful Dead were best appreciated during live concerts, partly because of the love-in mood that frequently percolated through the acidic audiences. Many rock critics remember with nostalgia that the band's most cerebral and psychedelic music was produced in the 1960s in San Francisco, but in the 1980s and 1990s, permutations of their themes were marketed in repetitive, less threatening forms that delighted their aficionados and often baffled or bored virtually everyone else.

For better or for worse, the Grateful Dead was a musical benchmark, expressing in new ways the mood of San Francisco during one of its drug-infused and most creatively fertile periods. But the days of the Dancing Bear and peanut butter sandwiches will never be quite over: Working from a proven formula, thousands of bands around the world continue to propagate the Dead's rhythmical standards.

But reading about the Grateful Dead is like dancing to architecture: If you're looking for an album whose title best expresses the changing artistic premises of San Francisco and the ironies of the pop culture that developed here, look for its award-winning retrospective *What a Long Strange Trip It's Been* at any of the city's record stores.

BIG BROTHER AND THE HOLDING COMPANY AND JANIS JOPLIN

The wide-open moral and musical landscape of San Francisco was almost unnervingly fertile during the 1960s. Despite competition from endless numbers of less talented singers, Texas-born Janis Joplin formulated much of her vocal technique before audiences in San Francisco. Her breakthrough style was first acknowledged at the Monterey Jazz Festival in 1967. Audiences reached out to embrace a singer whose rasping, gravely, shrieking voice expressed the generational angst of thousands of onlookers. *Billboard* magazine characterized her sound as composed of equal portions of honey, Southern Comfort, and gall. She was backed up during her earliest years by Big Brother and the Holding Company, a group she eventually outgrew.

Warned by specialists that her vocal technique would ruin her larynx before she was 30, Janis shrieked, wailed, gasped, and staggered over a blues repertoire judged as the most raw and vivid ever performed. Promoters frantically struggled to market (and protect) Janis and her voice for future artistic endeavors but, alas, her talent was simply too huge for her to handle, the time and place too destructive for her raw-edged psyche. Her style is best described as "the desperate blues," partly because it never attained the emotional nonchalance of such other blues singers as Bessie Smith or Billie Holiday.

Parts of Janis's life were the subject of such lurid books as *Going Down with Janis,* and stories of her substance abuse, sexual escapades, and general raunchiness litter the emotional landscape of modern-day San Francisco. The star died of a heroin over-dose at the age of 27, a tragedy still mourned by her thousands of fans, who continue to refer to her by her nickname, "Pearl." Contemporary photographs taken shortly before her death show a ravaged body and a face partially concealed behind aviator's goggles, long hair, and a tough but brittle facade. Described as omnisexual—and completely comfortable with both male and female partners—she once (unexpect-edly) announced to a group of nightclub guests her evaluation of the sexual perfor-mance of two of the era's most visible male icons: Joe Namath (not particularly memorable) and Dick Cavett (absolutely fantastic). The audience (like audiences in concert halls around California) drank in the anecdotes that followed as "Gospel According to Janis."

JEFFERSON AIRPLANE   In the San Francisco suburbs of the late 1960s, hundreds of suburban bands dreamed of attaining stardom. Of the few that suc-ceeded, none expressed the love-in ethic of that time in San Francisco better than the soaring vocals and ferocious guitar-playing of Jefferson Airplane. Singers Grace Slick and Marty Balin—as well as bass guitar player Jack Cassady—were considered at the top of their profession by their peers and highly melodic even by orchestral standards. Most importantly, all members of the band, especially Paul Kantner and Jorma Kaukonen, were songwriters. Their fertile mix of musical styles and creative energies led to songs that still reverberate in the minds of anyone who owned an AM radio during the late 1960s. The intense and lonely songs such as "Somebody to Love" and "White Rabbit" became the musical anthems of at least one summer, as American youth emerged into a highly psychedelic kind of consciousness within the creatively catalytic setting of San Francisco.

Although in 1989 the group reassembled its scattered members for a swan song as Jefferson Starship, the output was considered a banal repetition of earlier themes, and the energy of those long-faded summers of San Francisco in the late 1960s was never recovered. But despite its decline in its later years, Jefferson Airplane is still considered a band inextricably linked to the Bay Area's historic and epoch-changing Summer of Love.

Planning a Trip to San Francisco

Regardless of whether you chart your vacation months in advance or travel on a whim, you'll need to do a little advance planning to make the most of your stay. This chapter will help you with all the logistics.

1 Visitor Information & Money

Visitors from outside the United States should also see Chapter 3, "For Foreign Visitors," for entry requirements and other pertinent information.

VISITOR INFORMATION

The **San Francisco Convention and Visitors Bureau,** P.O. Box 429097, San Francisco, CA 94142-9097 (☎ **415/391-2000**), is the best source for any kind of specialized information about the city. Even if you don't have a specific question, you may want to send them $2 for their 100-page magazine *The San Francisco Book,* which includes 50 pages of lodging information, a three-month calendar of events, city history, shopping and dining information, and several good, clear maps. The bureau only highlights members' establishments, so if they don't have what you're looking for, it doesn't mean it's nonexistent.

You can also get the latest on San Francisco at the following on-line addresses:

- *Bay Guardian,* free weekly's city page: http://www.sfbayguardian.com
- **Hotel accommodations,** reserve on-line: http://www.hotelres.com/
- **Q San Francisco,** for gays and lesbians: http://www.qsanfrancisco.com/
- **SF Gate,** the city's combined *Chronicle* and *Examiner* newspapers: http://www.sfgate.com

MONEY

In addition to the details below, foreign visitors should see Chapter 3, "For Foreign Visitors," for further information about money.

U.S. dollar traveler's checks are the safest, most negotiable way to carry currency. They are accepted by most restaurants, hotels, and shops, and can be exchanged for cash at banks and check-issuing

What Things Cost in San Francisco	U.S. $
Taxi from airport to city center	35.00
Bus fare to any destination within the city (adult)	1.00
Bus fare to any destination within the city (children and seniors)	.35
Double room at Campton Place Hotel (deluxe)	220.00
Double room at Savoy Hotel (moderate)	115.00
Double room at the Commodore International Hotel (inexpensive)	69.00
Lunch for one at Zinzino (moderate)	15.00
Lunch for one at Mario's Bohemian Cigar Store (inexpensive)	8.00
Dinner for one, without wine, at Fleur de Lys (deluxe)	85.00
Dinner for one, without wine, at Restaurant LuLu (moderate)	35.00
Dinner for one, without wine, at Cha Cha Cha (inexpensive)	20.00
Glass of beer	2.75
Coca-Cola	1.50
Cup of coffee	1.00
Admission to the top of Coit Tower	3.00
Movie ticket	7.50
Theater ticket	8–50.00

offices. **American Express** offices are open Monday through Friday from 9am to 5pm and on Saturday from 9am until 2pm. See "Fast Facts: San Francisco" in Chapter 4 for office locations.

Most banks have automated teller machines (ATMs), which accept cards connected to networks like **Cirrus** and **Plus.** You'll find them on almost every commercial street, or for specific locations call **800/424-7787** for the Cirrus network, **800/843-7587** for the Plus system.

Of course credit cards are almost as good as cash and are accepted in most establishments. Also, ATMs will make cash advances against MasterCard and Visa cards. American Express cardholders can write a personal check, guaranteed against their card, for up to $1,000 in cash at an American Express office. See "Fast Facts: San Francisco" in Chapter 4 for office addresses.

2 When to Go

If you're dreaming of convertibles, Frisbee on the beach, and tank-topped evenings, change your reservations and head to Los Angeles. Contrary to California's sunshine-and-bikini image, San Francisco weather is mild and can often be downright fickle—it's *nothing* like that of neighboring Southern California. While summer is the most popular time to visit, it's also often characterized by damp, foggy days, cold windy nights, and crowded tourist destinations. A good bet is to visit in spring, or better yet, autumn. Every September, right about the time San Franciscans mourn being gypped (or fogged) out of another summer, something wonderful happens: The thermostat rises, the skies clear, and the locals call in sick to work and head for the beach. It's what residents call "Indian summer." The city is also delightful during winter, when the opera and ballet seasons are in full swing, there are fewer tourists, many hotel prices are lower, and downtown bustles with holiday cheer.

CLIMATE

Northern California weather has been extraordinary recently. In the past two years, the Bay Area has experienced one sizzling and one nonexistent summer, one winter that ended in late June (and kept Tahoe's ski lifts open until August), a series of floods, and a storm whose 80-mile-per-hour winds blew century-old trees right out of the ground. However, San Francisco's temperate, marine climate *usually* means relatively mild weather year-round. In summer, temperatures rarely top 70°F, and the city's chilling fog rolls in most mornings and evenings. Even when autumn's heat occasionally stretches into the 80s and 90s, you should still dress in layers or by early evening you'll learn firsthand why sweatshirt sales are a great business at Fisherman's Wharf. In winter, the mercury seldom falls below freezing, and snow is almost unheard of, but that doesn't mean you won't be whimpering if you forgot to bring a coat. Still, compared to most of the States' varied weather conditions, San Francisco is consistently pleasant.

It's that beautifully fluffy, chilly, wet, heavy, and sweeping fog that makes the city's weather so precarious. Northern California's summer fog bank is produced by a rare combination of water, wind, and topography. It lies off the coast and is pulled in by rising air currents when the land heats up. Held back by coastal mountains along a 600-mile front, the low clouds seek out any passage they can find. And the access most readily available is the slot where the Pacific Ocean penetrates the continental wall—the Golden Gate.

San Francisco's Average Temperatures (°F) & Rainfall (in.)

	Jan	Feb	Mar	Apr	May	June	July	Aug	Sept	Oct	Nov	Dec
High	56	59	60	61	63	64	64	65	69	68	63	57
Low	46	48	49	49	51	53	53	54	56	55	52	47
Rain	4.5	2.8	2.6	1.5	0.4	0.2	0.1	0.1	0.2	1.1	2.5	3.5

SAN FRANCISCO CALENDAR OF EVENTS

January
- **San Francisco Sports and Boat Show,** Cow Palace. Draws thousands of boat enthusiasts over a nine-day period. Call Cow Palace Box Office (☎ 415/469-6065) for details. Mid-January.

February
✪ **Chinese New Year.** In 1997, the year of the ox, public celebrations will again spill onto every street in Chinatown. Festivities begin with the crowning of "Miss Chinatown USA" pageant parade, and climaxes a week later with a celebratory parade of marching bands, rolling floats, barrages of fireworks, and a block-long dragon writhing in and out of the crowds. Make your hotel reservations early.

Where: Chinatown. **When:** New Year is February 7; festivities go from February 15 to 23; New Year Parade is on February 22. **How:** Arrive early for a good viewing spot on Grant Avenue. For information call **415/982-3000.**

March

- **St. Patrick's Day Parade.** Almost everyone's honorarily Irish at this festive affair starting at 12:30pm at Market and Second streets and continuing past city hall. But the party doesn't stop there. Head down to the Embarcadero's Harrington's bar after work hours and celebrate with hundreds of the Irish-for-a-day as they gallivant amidst the closed-off streets and numerous pubs. Call **415/391-2000** for details. The Sunday before March 17.

- **San Francisco International Film Festival.** Started 40 years ago, this is one of America's oldest film festivals, featuring more than 100 films and videos from more than 30 countries. Tickets are relatively inexpensive, and screenings are very accessible to the general public. Entries include new films by beginning and established directors.

  Where: The AMC Kabuki 8 Cinemas, at Fillmore and Post streets and many other locations. **When:** mid-April through early May. **How:** For a schedule or information call **415/931-FILM.**

April

- **Cherry Blossom Festival,** Japantown. Meander through the arts and crafts and food booths aligning the blocked-off streets; watch traditional drumming, sumo wrestling, flower arranging, origami, or a parade celebrating the cherry blossom and Japanese culture. Mid- to late April.

May

- **Cinco de Mayo Celebration,** Mission District. This is the day the Latino community celebrates the victory of the Mexicans over the French at Puebla in 1862. Mariachi bands, dancers, food, and a parade fill the streets of the Mission. May 5.

- **Bay to Breakers Foot Race.** Even if you don't participate, you can't avoid this run from downtown to Ocean Beach that stops morning traffic throughout the city. Around 80,000 entrants gather—many dressed in wacky, innovative, and sometimes X-rated costumes—for the approximately $7^1/2$-mile run. If you're feeling lazy, join the throng of spectators who line the route in the form of sidewalk parties, bands, and cheerleaders of all ages to get a good dose of true San Francisco fun.

  Where: Golden Gate Park. **When:** Third Sunday of May. **How:** The event is sponsored by the *San Francisco Examiner* (☎ **415/777-7770**).

- **Black and White Ball.** At close to $200 per ticket, this fund-raiser for the San Francisco Symphony held every two years is not a budget evening. Still, anyone who's anyone attends, and with good reason—aside from New Year's this is one of the only events in San Francisco where you can don your full-length sequin gown or break out the old tuxedo and dance the night away giddy on complimentary wine and champagne, and enjoy more than 50 live music performances. Traditionally, festivities take place in the Civic Center, where traffic is blocked off and thousands of the city's elite saunter wine-in-hand to and from City Hall, the War Memorial Opera House, and other prestigious buildings and venue tents. Unfortunately, due to Civic Center earthquake restoration, this year's event will take place at the foot of Market Street in the Embarcadero area. Surrounding streets are still cordoned off and tents are still raised, but without the classic civic surroundings, the evening feels less majestic than in earlier years. Nonetheless, the munchies donated by local restaurants and corporate sponsors are piled high on buffet tables and it's still *the* event of the year (with thousands of attendees). Bring enough money to pay for hard alcohol (if you want it) and your taxi (which will take a lifetime to flag) and wear—you guessed it—black and white. For information call **415/431-5400.** May 10.

○ **Carnival.** The San Francisco Mission District's largest annual event, Carnival, is a two-day series of festivities that culminates with a parade on Mission Street over Memorial Day weekend. One of San Franciscans' favorite events, more than half a million spectators line the route, and the samba musicians and dancers continue to play on 14th Street, near Harrison, at the end of the march.

Where: Mission Street, between 14th and 24th streets, and Harrison Street, between 15th and 21st streets. **When:** Memorial Day Weekend. **How:** Just show up. Phone the Mission Economic and Cultural Association (☎ **415/826-1401**) for more information.

June

- **Union Street Fair,** along Union Street from Fillmore to Gough streets. Stalls sell arts, crafts, food, and drink. You'll also find a lot of great-looking young, yuppie cocktailers packing every bar and spilling out into the street. Music and entertainment are on a number of stages. Call **415/346-4446** for more information. First weekend of June.

- **Haight Street Fair.** Featuring alternative crafts, ethnic foods, rock bands, and a healthy number of hippies and young street kids whooping it up and slamming beers in front of the blaring rock 'n' roll stage. The fair usually extends along Haight between Stanyan and Ashbury streets. For details call **415/661-8025.** Usually the second Sunday in June.

- **Lesbian and Gay Freedom Day Parade,** Market Street. A prideful event drawing up to half a million participants. The parade's start and finish have been moved around in recent years to accommodate road construction, but traditionally it begins at Civic Center Plaza and ends with hundreds of food, art, and information booths and sound stages. Call **415/864-3733** for information. Usually the third or last weekend of June.

○ **Stern Grove Midsummer Music Festival.** Pack a picnic and head out early to join thousands who come here to lie in the grass and enjoy classical, jazz, and ethnic music and dance in the Grove at 19th Avenue and Sloat Boulevard. These free concerts are held every Sunday at 2pm. Either show up with a lawn chair or blanket, or clamor by phone to reserve one of the envied picnic tables—they're free, but they go quickly, so call Parks and Recreation one week before the performance on Monday morning at 9am at 415/666-7027 or 415/666-7035. There are food booths if you forget snacks, but you'll be dying to leave if you don't bring warm clothes—the Sunset district can be one of the coldest parts of the city. Call **415/252-6252** for listings. Mid-June through August.

July

- **Fourth of July Celebration and Fireworks.** This event can be somewhat of a joke, since more often than not, like everyone else, fog comes into the city on this day to join in the festivities. Sometimes it's almost impossible to view the million-dollar fireworks from Pier 39 on the northern waterfront. Still, it's a party and if the skies are clear, it's a damn good show.

- **San Francisco Marathon.** One of the largest marathons in the world. For entry information, contact the USA Track and Field Association (☎ **415/391-2123**). Usually second weekend in July.

- **Comedy Celebration Day,** at the Polo Field in Golden Gate Park. A free comedy marathon featuring dozens of local comedians. For information call **415/777-7120.** Usually last Sunday in July.

August

- **Renaissance Pleasure Faire.** An expensive but enjoyable festival takes place north of San Francisco and takes you back to Renaissance times—with games, plays, and arts and crafts and food booths. The fair, located in Black Point Forest, just east of Novato, opens the weekend before Labor Day and runs six to eight weekends and on Labor Day (☎ 1/800-52FAIRE).

September

- **San Francisco Fair.** There are no tractor pulls or monster trucks at San Francisco's rendition of an annual county fair. This sophisticated urban party is attended by thousands and includes restaurant and winery booths, street artists, fine artists, and high-quality local entertainment. The fair is held at the Fort Mason Center each Labor Day weekend. For information call **415/391-2000.**

- ✪ **San Francisco Blues Festival.** The largest outdoor blues music event on the West Coast celebrates its 25th anniversary in 1997 and will again feature both local and national musicians performing back-to-back during the three-day extravaganza.
  Where: On the grounds of Fort Mason. **When:** Usually in late September. **How:** You can charge tickets by phone through BASS Ticketmaster (☎ 510/762-2277). For schedule information call **415/826-6837.**

- **Castro Street Fair.** Celebrates life in the city's most famous gay neighborhood. Usually third weekend in September.

- ✪ **Sausalito Art Festival.** A juried exhibit of more than 180 artists. It is accompanied by music—provided by Bay Area jazz, rock, and blues performers—and international cuisine, enhanced by wines from some 50 different Napa and Sonoma producers. Parking is impossible; take the Red and White Fleet (☎ 415/546-2628) ferry from Fisherman's Wharf to the festival site.
  Where: Sausalito. **When:** Labor Day weekend, early September. **How:** For more information call **415/332-3555.**

October

- **Columbus Day Festivities.** The city's Italian community leads the festivities around Fisherman's Wharf celebrating Columbus's landing in America. The festival includes a parade along Columbus Avenue and sporting events, but for the most part, it's just a great excuse to hang out in North Beach and people-watch. For information call **415/434-1492.** Sunday before Columbus Day.

- **Exotic Erotic Halloween Ball.** Friday or Saturday night before Halloween, thousands come to the Concourse Exhibition Center dressed in costume, lingerie, and sometimes even less than that. It's a wild fantasy affair with bands, dancing, and costume contests; $35 per person. For information call **415/567-BALL.**

- **Halloween.** A big night in San Francisco. A fantastical parade is organized at Market and Castro, and a mixed gay/straight crowd revels in costumes of extraordinary imagination. October 31.

- **San Francisco Jazz Festival.** This festival presents eclectic programming in an array of fabulous jazz venues throughout the city. With close to two weeks of nightly entertainment and dozens of performers, the jazz festival is a hot ticket. Past events have featured Herbie Hancock, Dave Brubeck, the Modern Jazz Quartet, Wayne Shorter, and Bill Frisell. For information call **415/864-5449** or 800/627-5277. End of October, beginning of November.

December

- **The Nutcracker,** War Memorial Opera House. Performed annually by the San Francisco Ballet (☎ 415/776-1999). Tickets to this Tchaikovsky tradition should be purchased well in advance.

3 Safety

San Francisco, like any large city, has its fair share of crime, but unlike New York and Los Angeles, most folks here don't have firsthand horror stories. There are some areas where you need to exercise extra caution, particularly at night—notably the Tenderloin, the Western Addition, the Mission District, and around the Civic Center. In addition, there are a substantial number of homeless people throughout the city with concentrations in and around Union Square, the theater district, the Tenderloin, and Haight Street, so don't be alarmed if you're approached for spare change. Basically, just use common sense.

See "Fast Facts: San Francisco" in Chapter 4 for city-specific safety tips. For additional crime-prevention information, phone San Francisco SAFE (☎ **415/ 553-1984**).

4 Tips for Travelers with Special Needs

FOR PEOPLE WITH DISABILITIES

Most of San Francisco's major museums and tourist attractions are fitted with wheelchair ramps. In addition, many hotels offer special accommodations and services for wheelchair-bound and other visitors with disabilities. These include extralarge bathrooms and ramps for the wheelchair-bound and telecommunication devices for deaf people. The San Francisco Convention and Visitors Bureau (see section 1, "Visitor Information and Money," above) has the most up-to-date information.

Travelers in wheelchairs can secure special ramped taxis by calling **Yellow Cab** (☎ **415/626-2345**), which charges regular rates for the service. Disabled travelers may also obtain a free copy of the "MUNI Access Guide," published by the **San Francisco Municipal Railway,** Accessible Services, 949 Presidio Ave., San Francisco, CA 94115 (☎ **415/923-6142**). Call this number Monday through Friday from 8am to 5pm weekdays.

FOR GAY MEN & LESBIANS

If you head down to the Castro—an area surrounding Castro Street near Market Street that's predominantly a gay and lesbian community—you'll understand why the city is a mecca for gay and lesbian travelers. Since the 1970s, this unique part of town has remained the colorfully festive gay neighborhood teeming with "outed" city folk who meander the streets shopping, eating, partying, or simply cruising. If anyone feels like an outsider in this part of town, it's heterosexuals, who, although warmly welcomed in the community, may feel uncomfortable or downright threatened if they harbor any homophobia or aversion to being "cruised." For many San Franciscans, it's just a fun area (especially on Halloween) with some wonderful shops.

It is estimated that gays and lesbians form one-fourth to one-third of the population of San Francisco, so it's no surprise that in recent years clubs and bars catering to them have popped up all around town. Although lesbian interests are concentrated primarily in the East Bay (especially Oakland), a significant community resides in the Mission District, around 16th Street and Valencia.

Several local publications are dedicated to in-depth coverage of news, information, and listings of goings-on around town for gay men and lesbians. *Bay Area Reporter* has the most comprehensive listings, including a weekly calendar of events and is distributed free on Thursdays. It can be found stacked at the corner of 18th and Castro streets and at 9th and Harrison streets, as well as in bars, bookshops, and various stores around town. It may also be available in gay and lesbian bookstores else-where in the country.

Guides and Publications   Gay men and lesbians might like to get either of the guides specifically for San Francisco, *Betty and Pansy's Severe Queer Review of San Francisco* ($10.95) and *The Official San Francisco Gay Guide* ($10.95). For accom-modations, check with two international guides: *Odysseus* ($25) and *Inn Places* ($16). These books and others are available by mail from Giovanni's Room, 1145 Pine St., Philadelphia, PA 19107 (☎ 215/923-2960) and A Different Light bookstore, 489 Castro St., San Francisco, CA 94114 (☎ 415/431-0891). Other locations are in New York City (☎ 212/989-4850) and Los Angeles (☎ 310/854-6601).

Our World, 1104 N. Nova Rd., Ste. 251, Daytona Beach, FL 32117 (☎ 904/441-5367), is a magazine devoted to gay and lesbian travel worldwide. It costs $35 for 10 issues. *Out and About,* 8 W. 19th St., Ste. 401, New York, NY 10011 (☎ 800/929-2268), has been hailed for its "straight" reporting about gay travel. It profiles the best gay or gay-friendly hotels, restaurants, clubs, and other places, with coverage of destinations throughout the world. It costs $49 a year for 10 information-packed issues. *Out and About* aims for the more upscale gay or lesbian traveler and has been praised by everybody from *Travel and Leisure* to *The New York Times.* Both these publications are also available at most gay and lesbian book stores.

Organizations   The **International Gay Travel Association** (IGTA), P.O. Box 4974, Key West, FL 33041 (☎ 305/292-0217 or voice mailbox 800/448-8550), encourages gay and lesbian travel worldwide. With around 1,200 member agencies, it offers quarterly newsletters, marketing mailings, and a membership directory that is updated four times a year. Travel agents, who are IGTA members, will be tied into this organization's vast information resources, or you can E-mail them at **IGTA@aol.com** or visit their web site at **http://www.rainbow-mall.com.igta**

Travel Agencies   In California, a leading gay-friendly option for travel arrangements is **Above and Beyond,** 330 Townsend St., Ste. 107, San Francisco, CA 94107 (☎ 415/284-1666 or 800/397-2681).

Also in California, **Skylink Women's Travel,** 2953 Lincoln Blvd., Santa Monica, CA 90405 (☎ 310/452-0506 or 800/225-5759).

FOR WOMEN

Women's services are often lumped together in the lesbian category, but there are resources geared toward women without regard to sexuality. The **Bay Area Women and Children's Center,** 318 Leavenworth St. (☎ 415/474-2400), offers specialized services and city information to women. **The Women's Building,** 3543 18th St. (☎ 415/431-1180), is a Mission-area space housing feminist art shows and politi-cal events and offering classes in yoga, aerobics, movement, and tai chi chuan. The **Rape Crisis Hotline** (☎ 415/647-7273) is staffed 24 hours daily.

FOR SENIORS

Seniors regularly receive discounts at museums and attractions and on public trans-portation; such discounts, when available, are listed in this guide, under their appro-priate headings. Ask for discounts everywhere—at hotels, movie theaters, museums, restaurants, and attractions. You may be surprised how often you'll be offered reduced rates. When making airline reservations, ask about a senior discount, but find out if there is a cheaper promotional fare before committing yourself.

The **Senior Citizen Information Line** (☎ 415/626-1033) offers advice, refer-rals, and information on city services. The **Friendship Line for the Elderly** (☎ 415/752-3778) is a support, referral, and crisis-intervention service.

FOR FAMILIES

San Francisco is full of sightseeing opportunities and special activities geared toward children. See section 3, "Especially for Kids," in Chapter 7, "What to See and Do in San Francisco," for information and ideas for families. *Frommer's San Francisco with Kids* is a comprehensive guide geared specifically to families; it is available at bookstores.

5 Getting There

BY PLANE

THE MAJOR AIRLINES   San Francisco is serviced by the following major domestic airlines: **American Airlines,** 433 California St. and 51 O'Farrell St. (☎ 800/433-7300); **Delta Airlines,** 433 California St. and 124 Geary St. (☎ 800/221-1212); **Northwest Airlines,** 124 Geary St. and 433 California St. (☎ 800/225-2525); **Southwest Airlines,** at the airport (☎ 800/I-FLY-SWA); **TWA,** 595 Market St., Suite 2240, at the corner of 2nd Street (☎ 415/864-5731 or 800/221-2000); **United Airlines** (☎ 800/241-6522), 433 California St., 124 Geary, and Embarcadero One; and **USAir,** 433 California St. (☎ 800/428-4322).

FINDING THE BEST AIRFARE   Check your newspaper and call the airlines, asking for the lowest promotional or special fare available. Note, though, that the lowest-priced fares will often be nonrefundable, require advance purchase of one to three weeks and a certain length of stay, and carry penalties for changing dates of travel.

If you can be flexible, ask if you can secure a cheaper fare by staying an extra day or by flying midweek. Many airlines won't volunteer this information. At the time of this writing, the lowest round-trip fare on one airline from New York was $278, but you had to purchase seven days in advance, stay at least one Saturday night in San Francisco, and travel between 7pm and 5:59am. Otherwise the price was $338. From Chicago, the trip cost $321. From Los Angeles, fares ranged from $38 round-trip (21 days advance purchase) to $144 (seven days advance purchase). Of course fares change radically depending on the time of year and whether there's a sale going on. In business class, expect to pay about $1,250 one way from New York and $1,100 from Chicago. First class costs about $2,000 one way from New York and $1,700 from Chicago.

Don't overlook a **consolidator,** or "bucket shop," when hunting for low domestic fares. By negotiating directly with the airlines, the "buckets" can sell discounted tickets but they will also carry restrictions and penalties for changes or cancellation.

The lowest-priced bucket shops are usually local operations with low profiles and overheads. Look for their advertisements in the travel section or the classifieds of your local newspaper. Nationally advertised businesses are usually not as competitive as the smaller operations, but they have toll-free telephone numbers and are easily accessible. Try **Travac,** 989 Sixth Ave., New York, NY 10018 (☎ **212/563-3303** or 800/872-8800).

Discounted fares have pared the number of **charters,** but they are still available. Most charter operators advertise and sell their seats through travel agents, thus making these local professionals your best source of information for available flights. Before deciding to take a charter flight, check the restrictions on the ticket: You may be asked to purchase a tour package, to pay in advance, to be amenable if the day of departure is changed, to pay a service charge, to fly on an airline you're not familiar with (this usually is not the case), and to pay harsh penalties if you cancel but to be understanding if the charter doesn't fill up and is canceled up to 10 days before departure. Summer charters fill up more quickly than others and are almost sure to fly, but if you decide on a charter flight, seriously consider cancellation and baggage insurance.

Courier flights are primarily long-haul jobs and are usually not available on domestic flights. Companies that hire couriers use your luggage allowance for their business baggage; in return, you get a deeply discounted ticket. Flights are often offered at the last minute, and you may have to arrange a pretrip interview to make sure you're right for the job. **Now Voyager,** open Monday through Friday from 10am to 5pm, and Saturday from noon to 4:30pm (☎ 212/431-1616), flies from New York and sometimes has flights to San Francisco for as little as $199 round-trip. Now Voyager also offers noncourier discounted fares, so call the company even if you don't want to fly as a courier.

THE MAJOR AIRPORTS   Two major airports serve the Bay Area: San Francisco International and Oakland International.

San Francisco International Airport   San Francisco International Airport, located 14 miles south of downtown directly on U.S. 101, is served by almost four dozen major scheduled carriers. Travel time to downtown during commuter rush hours is about 40 minutes; at other times it's about 20 to 25 minutes.

The airport offers a toll-free hotline available weekdays from 8am to 5pm (PST) for information on ground transportation (☎ 800/736-2008). The line is answered by a real person who will provide you with a rundown of all your options for getting into the city from the airport. Each of the three main terminals also has a desk where you can get the same information.

A cab from the airport to downtown will cost $25 to $30, plus tip.

SFO Airporter buses (☎ 415/495-8404) depart from outside the lower-level baggage claim area to downtown San Francisco every 15 to 30 minutes from 6:20am to midnight. They stop at several Union Square–area hotels, including the Grand Hyatt, San Francisco Hilton, San Francisco Marriott, Westin St. Francis, Parc Fifty Five, Hyatt Regency, and Sheraton Palace. No reservations are needed. The cost is $9 one way, $15 round-trip; children two to 16 (accompanied by an adult) pay $5 each way, and children under two ride for free.

Other private shuttle companies offer door-to-door airport service, in which you share a van with a few other passengers. **SuperShuttle** (☎ 415/558-8500) will take you anywhere in the city, charging $10 per person to a hotel; $11 to a residence or business, plus $8 for each additional person; and $38 to charter an entire van for up to seven passengers. **Yellow Airport Shuttle** (☎ 415/282-7433) charges $10 per person. Each shuttle stops every 20 minutes or so and picks up passengers from the marked areas outside the terminals' upper level. Reservations are required for the return trip to the airport only and should be made one day before departure. Keep in mind that these shuttles demand they pick you up two hours before your flight, three during holidays.

The San Mateo County Transit system, **SamTrans** (☎ 415/508-6200 or 800/660-4287 within Northern California) runs two buses between the airport and the Transbay Terminal at First and Mission streets. The **7B** bus costs $1 and makes the trip in about 55 minutes. The **7F** bus costs $2 and takes only 35 minutes, but permits only one carry-on bag. Both buses run daily, every half-hour from about 6am to 7pm, then hourly until about midnight.

Oakland International Airport   Located about 5 miles south of downtown Oakland, at the Hagenberger Road exit of Calif. 17 (U.S. 880), Oakland International Airport (☎ 510/577-4000) is used primarily by passengers with East Bay destinations. Some San Franciscans, however, prefer this less-crowded, accessible airport when flying during busy periods.

Again, taxis from the airport to downtown San Francisco are expensive, costing approximately $45, plus tip.

If you make advance reservations, the **AM/PM Airporter,** P.O. Box 2902, Oakland, CA 94609 (☎ **510/547-2155**), will take you from the Oakland Airport to your hotel any time of the day or night. The price varies, depending on the number of passengers sharing the van, but is usually $35 to $45 or less per person; get a quote when you call.

The cheapest way to downtown San Francisco is to take the shuttle bus from the airport to BART (Bay Area Rapid Transit ☎ **510/464-6000**). The **AirBART** shuttle bus (☎ **510/562-8428**) runs about every 15 minutes Monday through Saturday from 6am to midnight, Sunday from 8:30am to midnight, stopping in front of Terminals 1 and 2 near the ground transportation signs. The cost is $2 for the 10-minute ride to BART's Coliseum terminal. **BART** fares vary, depending on your destination; the trip to downtown San Francisco costs $2.15 and takes 20 minutes once onboard. The entire excursion should take around 45 minutes.

RENTING A CAR   All the major companies operate in the city and have desks at the airports. Call their 800 numbers before leaving home and shop around for the best price. Currently you can secure a compact car for a week for about $150, including all taxes and other charges.

Most rental firms pad their profits by selling an additional loss/damage waiver (LDW), which usually costs an extra $9 or more per day. Before agreeing to this, check with your insurance carrier and credit card company. Many people don't realize that they are already covered by either one or both. If you're not, the LDW is a wise investment.

A minimum-age requirement—ranging from 19 to 25—is set by most rental agencies. Some also have a maximum-age limit. If you're concerned that these limits may affect you, ask about rental requirements at the time of booking to avoid problems later.

Some of the national car-rental companies operating in San Francisco include: **Alamo** (☎ 800/327-9633); **Avis** (☎ 800/331-1212); **Budget** (☎ 800/527-0700); **Dollar** (☎ 800/800-4000); **Hertz** (☎ 800/654-3131); **National** (☎ 800/227-7368); and **Thrifty** (☎ 800/367-2277).

In addition to the big chains, there are dozens of regional rental places in San Francisco, many of which offer lower rates. These include **A-One Rent-A-Car,** 434 O'Farrell St. (☎ 415/771-3977) and **Bay Area Rentals,** 229 Seventh St. (☎ 415/621-8989).

BY TRAIN

Traveling by train takes a long time and usually costs as much as, or more than, flying, but if you want to take a leisurely ride across America, rail may be a good option.

San Francisco-bound **Amtrak** (☎ **800/872-7245** or 800/USA-RAIL) trains leave daily from New York and cross the country via Chicago. The journey takes about 3 1/2 days, and seats sell quickly. At this writing, the lowest round-trip fare would cost anywhere from $266 to $529 from New York and from $246 to $479 from Chicago. These heavily restricted tickets are good for 45 to 180 days and allow up to three stops along the way, depending on your ticket.

Round-trip tickets from Los Angeles can be purchased for as little as $88 or as much as $150. Trains actually arrive in Emeryville, just north of Oakland, and connect with regularly scheduled buses to San Francisco's Ferry Building and CalTrain station in downtown San Francisco.

CalTrain (☎ 415/546-4461 or 800/660-4287) operates train services between San Francisco and the towns of the peninsula. The city depot is at 700 Fourth St., at Townsend Street.

BY BUS

Bus travel is an inexpensive and often flexible option. **Greyhound/Trailways** (☎ **800/231-2222**) operates to San Francisco from anywhere, and offers several money-saving multiday bus passes. Round-trip fares vary, depending on your point of origin, but few, if any, ever exceed $300. The main San Francisco bus station is the Transbay Terminal, 425 Mission St. at First Street. For information ☎ **800/231-2222**.

BY CAR

San Francisco is easily accessed by several major highways: Interstate 5, from the north, and U.S. 101, which cuts south-north through the peninsula from San Jose and across the Golden Gate Bridge to points north. If you drive from Los Angeles, you can either take the longer coastal route (437 miles and 11 hours) or the inland route (389 miles and eight hours). From Mendocino, it's 156 miles and four hours; from Sacramento it's 88 miles, $1^1/2$ hours; and from Yosemite it's 210 miles or four hours.

If you are driving and aren't already a member, then it's worth joining the **American Automobile Association (AAA)** (☎ **800/222-JOIN**), which charges $40 to $60 per year, depending on where you join, and provides roadside and other services to motorists.

Amoco Motor Club (☎ **800/334-3300**) is another recommended choice.

PACKAGES & TOURS

Tours and packages combining transportation, hotel accommodations, meals, and sightseeing are sometimes available to San Francisco. Sometimes it's worth signing onto a tour package just to secure the savings that operators can achieve by buying travel services in bulk. Often you'll pay much less than if you had organized the same trip independently, and you can always opt out of the preplanned activities. To find out what tours and packages are available to you, check the ads in the travel section of your newspaper or visit your travel agent. Before signing up, however, read the fine print carefully and do some homework.

Most of the airlines listed above, along with many other tour companies, offer both escorted tours and on-your-own packages. Discuss your options with a travel agent and compare the prices of each tour component with those in this guide.

However, before you sign up for a tour or a package that is not associated with a major airline, call travel agents and the local Better Business Bureau, and check with the consumer department of the **U.S. Tour Operators Association,** 211 E. 51st St., Ste. 12B, New York, NY 10022 (☎ **212/750-7371**).

For Foreign Visitors 3

The pervasiveness of American culture around the world may make you feel that you know the USA pretty well, but leaving your own country for the States still requires an additional degree of planning. This chapter will help prepare you for the more common problems (expected and unexpected) that San Francisco visitors may encounter.

1 Preparing for Your Trip

ENTRY REQUIREMENTS
DOCUMENT REGULATIONS

Citizens of the United Kingdom, New Zealand, Japan, and most Western European countries traveling with valid passports may not need a visa for fewer than 90 days of holiday or business travel to the United States, providing that they hold a round-trip or return ticket and enter the United States on an airline or cruise line participating in the visa-waiver program. Canadian citizens may enter the United States without visas; they need only proof of residence.

(Note that citizens of these visa-exempt countries who first enter the United States may then visit Mexico, Canada, Bermuda, and/or the Caribbean islands and then reenter the United States, by any mode of transportation, without needing a visa. Further information is available from any U.S. embassy or consulate.)

Citizens of countries other than those stipulated above, including citizens of Australia, must have two documents: a valid passport with an expiration date at least six months later than the scheduled end of the visit to the United States; and a tourist visa, available without charge from the nearest U.S. consulate.

To obtain a visa, the traveler must submit a completed application form (either in person or by mail) with a 1 1/2-inch-square photo and demonstrate binding ties to a residence abroad. Usually you can obtain a visa at once or within 24 hours, but it may take longer during the summer rush from June to August. If you cannot go in person, contact the nearest U.S. embassy or consulate for directions on applying by mail. Your travel agent or airline office may also be able to provide you with visa applications and instructions. The U.S. consulate or embassy that issues your visa will determine whether you will be issued a multiple- or single-entry visa and any restrictions

---

Travel Tip

Any questions you have about U.S. immigration policies or laws can be answered by calling San Francisco's *INS Ask Immigration System* at **415/705-4411.**

---

regarding the length of your stay. U.K. citizens can obtain up-to-date passport and visa information by calling the U.S. Embassy Visa Information Line at **0891/200-290** or the London Passport Office at **0171/271-3000** (for recorded information, call **0990/210-410**).

MEDICAL REQUIREMENTS

Unless you are arriving from an area known to be suffering from an epidemic, or have HIV/AIDS–related problems, no inoculations or vaccinations are required to enter the United States. Foreign visitors should be sure to hold a doctor's prescription for any controlled substances they are carrying.

CUSTOMS REQUIREMENTS

Every visitor over 21 years of age may bring in, free of duty, the following: (1) 1 liter of wine or hard liquor; (2) 200 cigarettes, 100 cigars (but *not* from Cuba), or 3 pounds of smoking tobacco; and (3) $400 worth of gifts. These exemptions are offered to travelers who spend at least 72 hours in the United States and who have not claimed them within the preceding six months. It is altogether forbidden to bring into the country foodstuffs (particularly cheese, fruit, cooked meats, and canned goods) and plants (vegetables, seeds, tropical plants, and the like). Foreign tourists may bring in or take out up to $10,000 in U.S. or foreign currency with no formalities; larger sums must be declared to U.S. Customs on entering or leaving. For more specific information regarding U.S. Customs, call the customs office at the San Francisco International Airport at **415/876-2816.**

INSURANCE

Although it is not required of travelers, health insurance is highly recommended. Unlike many European countries, the United States does not usually offer free or low-cost medical care to its citizens or visitors. Doctors and hospitals are expensive, and in most cases will require advance payment or proof of coverage before they render their services. Policies can cover everything from the loss or theft of your baggage and trip cancellation to the guarantee of bail in case you are arrested. Good policies will also cover costs of an accident, repatriation, or death. Such packages are sold by automobile clubs, as well as by insurance companies and travel agents.

Though lack of health insurance may prevent you from being admitted to a hospital in nonemergencies, don't worry about being left on a street corner to die: The American way is to fix you now and bill the heck out of you later.

INSURANCE FOR BRITISH TRAVELERS

Most big travel agents offer their own insurance, and will probably try to sell you their package when you book a holiday. Think before you sign. Britain's Consumers' Association recommends that you insist on seeing the policy and reading the fine print before buying travel insurance. The **Association of British Insurers** (☎ **0171/600-3333**) gives advice by phone and publishes the free *Holiday Insurance,* a guide to policy provisions and prices. You might also shop around for better deals: Try **Columbus Travel Insurance Ltd.** (☎ **0171/375-0011**) or, for students, **Campus Travel** (☎ **0171/730-3402**).

MONEY
CURRENCY

The U.S. monetary system is painfully simple: The most common bills (all ugly, all green) are the $1 (colloquially, a "buck"), $5, $10, and $20 denominations. There are also $2 bills (seldom encountered), $50 bills, and $100 bills (the last two are usually not welcome when paying for small purchases). Note that a newly redesigned $100 bill was introduced in mid-1996. Despite rumors to the contrary, the old-style bill is still legal tender.

There are six denominations of coins: 1¢ (1 cent, or a penny); 5¢ (5 cents, or a nickel); 10¢ (10 cents, or a dime); 25¢ (25 cents, or a quarter); 50¢ (50 cents, or a half dollar); and, prized by collectors, the rare $1 piece (the older, large silver dollar and the newer, small Susan B. Anthony coin).

TRAVELER'S CHECKS

Though traveler's checks are widely accepted, make sure that they are denominated in U.S. dollars, as foreign-currency checks are often difficult to exchange. The three most widely recognized traveler's checks—and least likely to be denied—are Visa, American Express, and Thomas Cook. Be sure to record the numbers of the checks, and keep that information separately should they get lost or stolen. San Francisco businesses are pretty good about taking traveler's checks, but you're better off cashing them in at a bank (in small amounts, of course) and paying in cash. Remember: You will need identification, such a driver's license or passport, to change a traveler's check.

CREDIT CARDS/ATMS

Most major credit cards are accepted at San Francisco's larger hotels, and Visa and MasterCard are accepted just about everywhere else. There are, however, a handful of stores and restaurants that do not take credit cards, so be sure to ask in advance. Most businesses display a sticker near their entrance to let you know which cards they accept. (Note: Often businesses require a minimum purchase price, usually around $10, to use a credit card.)

It is *strongly* recommended that you bring at least one major credit card. Hotels, car rental companies, and airlines usually require a credit card imprint as a deposit against expenses, and in an emergency a credit card can be priceless.

In downtown San Francisco, there is an automated teller machine (ATM) on just about every block. Most accept Visa, MasterCard, and American Express, as well as ATM cards from other U.S. banks. There is, of course, a small fee for each transaction, but in an emergency ATMs can come in real handy.

SAFETY
GENERAL SAFETY TIPS

While most San Francisco tourist areas are generally safe, there are a few neighborhoods you should leave out of your itinerary, such as the Tenderloin and Hunter's Point areas. Avoid deserted areas, especially at night, and don't go into any of the

---

Travel Tip

Strapped for cash? Call **Western Union** at **800/325-6000** for a recording listing the nearest branch, then call Mom.

parks at night unless there is a concert or similar occasion that attracts crowds (see "Fast Facts: San Francisco" in Chapter 4 for city-specific safety tips).

DRIVING SAFETY

Driving safety is important, too, especially given the recent killings of foreign tourists in Florida. Question your rental agency about personal safety and ask for a traveler-safety-tips brochure when you pick up your car. Obtain written directions—or a map with the route marked in red—from the agency showing how to get to your destination. And, if possible, arrive and depart during daylight hours.

Recently, more and more crime has involved cars and drivers. If you drive off a highway into a doubtful neighborhood, leave the area as quickly as possible. If you have an accident, even on the highway, stay in your car with the doors locked until you assess the situation, or until the police arrive. If you are bumped from behind on the street or are involved in a minor accident with no injuries and the situation appears to be suspicious, motion to the other driver to follow you. *Never* get out of your car in such situations. You can also keep a pre-made sign in your car that reads: Please Follow This Vehicle To Report The Accident. Show the sign to the other driver and go directly to the nearest police precinct, well-lighted service station, or 24-hour store.

2 Getting to the U.S.

In addition to the domestic American airlines listed in "Getting There" in Chapter 2, here are the domestic toll-free numbers of several international carriers: **Aer Lingus** (☎ 800/223-6537); **Air Canada** (☎ 800/776-3000); **British Airways** (☎ 800/247-9297); **Japan Airlines** (☎ 800/525-3663); **Qantas** (☎ 800/227-4500); **Scandinavian Airline (SAS)** (☎ 800/221-2350); and **Virgin Atlantic** (☎ 800/862-8621 or 415/616-3935. For the best rates, compare fares and be flexible with the dates and times of travel.

FROM THE UNITED KINGDOM AND IRELAND   Many airlines offer service from the United Kingdom or Ireland to the United States. If they do not have direct flights from London to San Francisco, they can book you straight through on a connecting flight. You can make reservations by calling the following numbers in London: **American Airlines** (☎ 0181/572-5555); **British Airways** (☎ 0345/222-111); **Continental Airlines** (☎ 4412/9377-6464); **Delta Airlines** (☎ 0800/414-767); **United Airlines** (☎ 0181/990-9900); and **Virgin Atlantic** (☎ 0293/747-747).

Residents of Ireland can call **Aer Lingus** (☎ 01/844-4747 in Dublin or 061/415-556 in Shannon).

If possible, try to book a direct flight. Airlines that offer direct flights from London include British Airways, United, and Virgin. See also "Getting There" in Chapter 2 for information on alternative low-cost fares.

FROM AUSTRALIA AND NEW ZEALAND   Qantas (☎ 008/177-767 in Australia) has direct flights from Sydney to San Francisco. You can also take **United** from Australia to San Francisco.

Air New Zealand (☎ 0800/737-000 in Auckland or 643/379-5200 in Christchurch) offers service to LAX in Los Angeles.

FROM CANADA Canadian readers might also consider **Air Canada** (in Canada ☎ 800/268-7240 or 800/361-8620), which offers direct service from Toronto, Montreal, Calgary, and Vancouver to San Francisco. Many American carriers also serve similar routes.

The visitor arriving by air, no matter what the port of entry, should cultivate patience and resignation before setting foot on U.S. soil. Getting through immigration control may take as long as two hours on some days, especially on summer weekends, so have your guidebook or something else to read. Add the time it takes to clear customs and you will see you should make a very generous allowance for delay in planning connections between international and domestic flights—figure on two to three hours at least.

In contrast, for the traveler arriving by car or rail from Canada, the border-crossing formalities have been streamlined to the vanishing point. And for the traveler by air from Canada, Bermuda, and some places in the Caribbean, you can sometimes go through Customs and Immigration at the point of departure, which is much quicker.

3 Getting Around the U.S.

BY PLANE Some large airlines (for example, Northwest and Delta) offer travelers on their transatlantic or transpacific flights special discount tickets under the name **Visit USA,** allowing travel between any U.S. destination at minimum rates. They are not on sale in the United States and must be purchased abroad in conjunction with your international ticket. See your travel agent or airline ticket office for full details, including terms and conditions.

BY TRAIN International visitors can also buy a **USA Railpass,** good for 15 or 30 days of unlimited travel on Amtrak (☎ 800/USA-RAIL). The pass is available through many foreign travel agents. Prices in 1996 for a 15-day pass were $245 off-peak, $355 peak; a 30-day pass cost $290 off-peak, $440 peak. (With a foreign passport, you can also buy passes at some Amtrak offices in the United States, including locations in San Francisco, Los Angeles, Chicago, New York, Miami, Boston, and Washington, D.C.) Reservations are generally required and should be made for each part of your trip as early as possible.

BY BUS Although ticket prices for short hops between cities are often the most economical form of public transit, bus travel in the United States can be both slow and uncomfortable, so this option is not for everyone (particularly when Amtrak, which is far more luxurious, offers similar rates). **Greyhound** (☎ 800/231-2222), the sole nationwide bus line, offers an **Ameripass** for unlimited travel for seven days (for $179), 15 days (for $289), 30 days (for $399), and 60 days (for $599). Passes must be purchased from a Greyhound terminal.

FAST FACTS: For the Foreign Traveler

Automobile Organizations If you plan on renting a car in the United States, you will probably not need the services of an additional automobile organization. If you are planning to buy or borrow a car, automobile association membership is recommended. The **American Automobile Association (AAA),** 150 Van Ness Ave.,

San Francisco, CA 94102 (☎ **415/565-7941**), is the country's largest auto club and supplies its members with maps, insurance, and, most important, emergency road service. The cost of joining runs from $55 for singles to $80 for families, but if you're a member of a foreign auto club with reciprocal arrangements, you can enjoy free AAA service in America. See "Getting There" in chapter 2 for more information.

Business Hours   See "Fast Facts: San Francisco" in Chapter 4.

Climate   See "When to Go" in Chapter 2.

Currency and Exchange   Foreign-exchange bureaus are rare in the United States, and most banks are not equipped to handle currency exchange. San Francisco's money-changing offices include the following: **Bank of America,** 345 Montgomery St. (☎ **415/622-2451**), open Monday through Friday from 9am to 6pm; and **Thomas Cook,** 75 Geary St. (☎ **415/362-3452**), open Monday through Friday from 9am to 5pm.

Drinking Laws   The legal age for purchase and consumption of alcoholic beverages is 21; proof of age is required and often requested at bars, nightclubs, and restaurants, so it's always a good idea to bring ID when you go out. In San Francisco, liquor is sold in supermarkets, grocery, and liquor stores daily from 6am to 2am. Licensed restaurants are permitted to sell alcohol during the same hours. Note that many eateries are licensed only for beer and wine.

A big no-no is having an open container of alcohol in your car or any public area that isn't zoned for alcohol consumption. The police can, and probably will, fine you on the spot. And nothing will ruin your trip faster than getting a DUI (driving under the influence), so don't even *think* about driving while intoxicated.

Electricity   U.S. wall outlets give power at 110–115 volts, 60 cycles, compared with 220 volts, 50 cycles, in most of Europe. In addition to a 100-volt transformer, small foreign appliances, such as hair dryers and shavers, will require a plug adapter (available at most hardware stores) with two flat, parallel pins.

Embassies and Consulates   All embassies are located in the nation's capital, Washington, D.C. In addition, several of the major English-speaking countries also have consulates in San Francisco or in Los Angeles.

The embassy of **Australia** is at 1601 Massachusetts Ave. NW, Washington, DC 20036 (☎ 202/797-3000); a consulate-general is at 1 Bush St., Suite 700, San Francisco, CA 94104 (☎ 415/362-6160). The embassy of **Canada** is at 501 Pennsylvania Ave. NW, Washington, DC 20001 (☎ 202/682-1740)); the nearest consulate is at 300 South Grand Ave., 10th Floor, California Plaza, Los Angeles, CA 90071 (☎ 213/346-2700. The embassy of the **Republic of Ireland** is at 2234 Massachusetts Ave. NW, Washington, DC 20008 (☎ 202/462-3939); a consulate is at 44 Montgomery St., Suite 3830, San Francisco, CA 94104 (☎ 415/392-4214). The embassy of **New Zealand** is at 37 Observatory Circle NW, Washington, DC 20008 (☎ 202/328-4848); the nearest consulate is at 12400 Wilshire Blvd., Suite 1150, Los Angeles, CA 90025 (☎ 310/207-1605). The embassy of the **United Kingdom** is at 3100 Massachusetts Ave. NW, Washington, DC 20008 (☎ 202/462-1340); the nearest consulate is at 1 Sansome St., Ste. 850, San Francisco, CA 94104 (☎ 415/981-3030).

If you are from another country, you can get the telephone number of your embassy by calling "Information" (directory assistance) in Washington, D.C. (☎ 202/555-1212).

Emergencies   You can call the police, an ambulance, or the fire department through the single emergency telephone number 911 from any phone or pay phone (no coins needed). If that doesn't work, another useful way of reporting an emergency is to call the telephone company operator by dialing 0 (zero, not the letter *O*).

Gasoline (Petrol)   Prices vary, but expect to pay anywhere between $1.25 and $1.55 for 1 U.S. gallon (about 3.8 liters) of "regular" unleaded gasoline (petrol). Higher-octane fuels are also available at most gas stations for slightly higher prices. Taxes are already included in the printed price.

Holidays   On the following legal national holidays, banks, government offices, post offices, and many stores, restaurants, and museums are closed: New Year's Day (January 1); Martin Luther King Jr. Day (third Monday in January); Presidents Day (third Monday in February); Memorial Day (last Monday in May); Independence Day (July 4); Labor Day (first Monday in September); Columbus Day (second Monday in October); Veterans Day (November 11); Thanksgiving Day (last Thursday in November); Christmas Day (December 25). Election Day, for national elections, falls on the Tuesday following the first Monday in November. It is a legal national holiday during a presidential election, which occurs every fourth year.

Legal Aid   Happily, foreign tourists rarely come into contact with the American legal system. If you are stopped for a minor driving infraction (speeding, for example), *never* attempt to pay the fine directly to a police officer; fines should be paid to the clerk of the court, and a receipt should be obtained. If you are accused of a more serious offense, it is wise to say and do nothing before consulting a lawyer. Under U.S. law, an arrested person is allowed one telephone call to a party of his or her choice. You may wish to contact your country's embassy or consulate (see above).

Mail   If you want to receive mail, but aren't exactly sure where you'll be, have it sent to you, in your name, c/o General Delivery (Poste Restante) at the main post office of the city or region you're visiting (call ☎ **415/284-0755** for information on the nearest post office). The addressee must pick it up in person and produce proof of identity (driver's license, credit card, passport). Most post offices will hold your mail up to one month, and are open from 8am to 6pm, Monday through Saturday.

Generally found at street intersections, mailboxes are blue and carry the inscription U.S. MAIL. If your mail is addressed to a U.S. destination, don't forget to add the five-figure ZIP Code after the two-letter abbreviation of the state to which the mail is addressed (CA for California).

Postal rates for overseas mail are as follows: A first-class letter of up to $1/2$ ounce costs 60¢ (46¢ Canada and 40¢ to Mexico); a first-class postcard costs 50¢ (40¢ to Canada and 35¢ Mexico); and a preprinted postal aerogramme costs 50¢.

Medical Emergencies   To call an ambulance, dial 911 from any phone. No coins are needed. For hospitals and other emergency information, see "Fast Facts: San Francisco" in Chapter 4.

Newspapers and Magazines   Many of San Francisco's newsstands offer a selection of foreign periodicals and newspapers, such as *The Economist, Le Monde,* and *Der Spiegel.* For information on local literature and specific newsstand locations, see "Fast Facts: San Francisco" in Chapter 4.

Post   See "Mail," above.

Radio/Television   There are five national television networks that are broadcast over the air: ABC (Channel 7), CBS (Channel 5), NBC (Channel 4), PBS (Channel 9), and Fox (Channel 2). More common in the United States, however, is cable television, which includes the national networks as well as 50 or so other cable stations, including the Cable News Network (CNN), ESPN (sports channel), and MTV. Most hotels offer a dozen cable stations to choose from, as well as pay-per-view movies. You'll also find a wide choice of local radio stations, each broadcasting particular kinds of talk shows and/or music—classical, country, jazz, rock, pop, gospel—punctuated by news broadcasts and frequent commercials.

Smoking   Heavy smokers are in for a tough time in San Francisco. There is no smoking allowed in public buildings, sports arenas, elevators, theaters, banks, lobbies, restaurants that don't have bars, offices, stores, and most small hotels and bed-and-breakfasts.

Taxes   In the United States there is no value-added tax (VAT) or other direct tax at a national level. Every state, as well as every city, is allowed to levy its own local sales tax on all purchases, including hotel and restaurant checks and airline tickets. Taxes are already included in the price of certain services, such as public transportation, cab fares, phone calls, and gasoline. The amount of sales tax varies from 4% to 10%, depending on the state and city, so when you are making major purchases, such as photographic equipment, clothing, or high-fidelity components, it can be a significant part of the cost.

In addition, many cities charge a separate "bed" or room tax on accommodations, above and beyond any sales tax.

For information on sales and room taxes in San Francisco, see "Fast Facts: San Francisco" in Chapter 4.

Telephone and Fax   Pay phones can be found almost everywhere—at street corners, in bars and restaurants, and in hotels. Outside the metropolitan area, however, public telephones are more difficult to find; stores and gas stations are your best bet.

Phones do not accept pennies and few will take anything larger than a quarter. Some public phones, especially those in airports and large hotels, accept credit cards, such as MasterCard, Visa, and American Express. Credit cards are especially handy for international calls; instructions are printed on the phone.

In San Francisco, local calls cost 20¢. For domestic long-distance calls or international calls, stock up with a supply of quarters; a recorded voice will instruct you when and in what quantity you should put them into the slot. For direct overseas calls, dial 011 first, then the country code (Australia, 61; Republic of Ireland, 353; New Zealand, 64; United Kingdom, 44) followed by the city code, and then the number you wish to call. To place a call to Canada or the Caribbean, just dial 1, the area code, and the number you wish to call.

Before calling from a hotel room, always ask the hotel phone operator if there are any telephone surcharges. These can sometimes be reduced by calling collect or by using a telephone charge card. Hotel charges, which can be exorbitant, may be avoided altogether by using a pay phone in the lobby.

Travel Tip

Don't mix up the toll-free *1-800* (or *1-888*) number prefix with the pay-per-call *1-900* prefix, which is usually attached to a phone-sex number that charges oodles per minute.

For "collect" (reversed-charge) calls and for "person-to-person" calls, dial 0 (zero, not the letter *O*) followed by the area code and the number you want; an operator or recording will then come on the line, and you should specify that you are calling collect or person-to-person, or both. If your operator-assisted call is international, just dial 0 and wait for the operator.

For local "information" (directory inquiries), dial 411; for long-distance information in Canada or the United States, dial 1, then the appropriate area code and 555-1212.

Like the telephone system, telegraph and telex services are provided by private corporations, such as ITT, MCI, and above all, Western Union. You can bring your telegram to a Western Union office or dictate it over the phone (☎ **800/325-6000**). You can also telegraph money, or have it telegraphed to you, very quickly. In San Francisco, a Western Union office, located near the Civic Center, is at 61 Gough St. at Market Street (☎ **415/621-2031**). There are several other locations around town, too; call **800/325-6000** for the one nearest you.

Most copy shops also offer fax services, charging about $1 per page.

Time   The United States is divided into four time zones (six, if Alaska and Hawaii are included). From east to west, these are Eastern Standard Time (EST), Central Standard Time (CST), Mountain Standard Time (MST), and Pacific Standard Time (PST). There are also Alaska Standard Time (AST) and Hawaii Standard Time (HST). San Francisco is on Pacific Standard Time, which is eight hours behind Greenwich Mean Time. Noon in New York City (EST) is 11am in Chicago (CST), 10am in Denver (MST), 9am in San Francisco (PST), 8am in Anchorage (AST), and 7am in Honolulu (HST).

Daylight-saving time is in effect from the first Sunday in April until 2am on the last Sunday in October, except in Arizona, Hawaii, part of Indiana, and Puerto Rico. Daylight saving time moves the clock one hour ahead of standard time.

Tipping   Service in America is some of the best in the world, and is rarely included in the price of anything. The amount you tip should depend on the service you have received. Good service warrants the following tips: bartenders, 15%; bellhops, $2 to $4; cab drivers, 15%; cafeterias and fast-food restaurants, no tip; chambermaids, $1 per person per day; checkroom attendants, 50¢ to $1 (unless there is a charge, then no tip); gas station attendants, no tip; hairdressers, 15% to 20%; parking valets, $1; redcaps (in airports and railroad stations), $2 to $4; restaurants and nightclubs, 15%.

Toilets   Public toilets can be hard to find. There are none on the streets (with the exception of a few new French stalls on Market Street), and few small stores will allow you access to their facilities. You can almost always find a toilet in restaurants and bars, but if you are not buying from them, you should ask first. Large hotels and fast-food restaurants are probably the best bet for good, clean facilities. Museums, department stores, shopping malls, and, in a pinch, gas stations all have public toilets.

4

Getting to Know San Francisco

Half the fun in becoming familiar with San Francisco is wandering around and haphazardly stumbling upon great shops, restaurants, and viewpoints that even locals may not know exist. But you'll find that although metropolitan, San Francisco is a small town and you won't feel like a stranger for long. If you get disoriented, just remember that downtown is east, Golden Gate Bridge is north, and even if you do get lost, you probably won't go too far since three sides of the city are surrounded by water. The most difficult challenge you'll have, if traveling by car, is mastering the maze of one-way streets. This chapter offers useful information on how to become better acquainted with the city.

1 Orientation

VISITOR INFORMATION

Once in the city, visit the **San Francisco Visitor Information Center,** on the lower level of Hallidie Plaza, 900 Market St., at Powell Street (☎ **415/391-2000**), for information, brochures, discount coupons, and advice on restaurants, sights, and events in the city. They can provide answers in German, Japanese, French, Italian, and Spanish, as well as English, of course. To find the office, descend the escalator at the cable-car turnaround.

Dial **415/391-2001** any time of day or night for a recorded message about current cultural, theater, music, sports, and other special events. This information is also available in German, French, Japanese, and Spanish.

Keep in mind that this service supports only members of the Convention and Visitors Bureau and is *very* tourist-oriented. While there's tons of information here, it's not representative of all the city has to offer. The office is open Monday through Friday from 9am to 5:30pm, on Saturday from 9am to 3pm, and on Sunday from 10am to 2pm. It's closed on Thanksgiving Day, Christmas Day, and New Year's Day.

Pick up a copy of **The Bay Guardian.** The city's free alternative paper lists all city happenings—their kiosks are located throughout the city and in most coffee shops.

For specialized information on Chinatown's shops and services, and on the city's Chinese community in general, contact the **Chinese Chamber of Commerce,** 730 Sacramento St., San

Francisco, CA 94108 (☎ **415/982-3000**), open Monday through Friday from 9am to 5pm.

The **Visitors Information Center of the Redwood Empire Association,** 2801 Leavenworth, San Francisco, CA 94103 (☎ **415/543-8334**), offers informative brochures and a very knowledgeable desk staff who are able to plan tours both in San Francisco and north of the city. Their annual 48-page *Redwood Empire Visitors' Guide* ($3 by mail, free in person) offers information on everything from San Francisco walking tours and museums, to visits to Marin County and Mendocino. The office is open Monday through Friday from 9am to 5pm.

CITY LAYOUT

San Francisco occupies the tip of a 32-mile-long peninsula between San Francisco Bay and the Pacific Ocean. Its land area measures about 46 square miles. Twin Peaks, in the geographic center of the city, is more than 900 feet high.

San Francisco may seem confusing at first, but it quickly becomes easy to negotiate. The city's downtown streets are arranged in a simple grid pattern, with the exception of Market Street and Columbus Avenue, which cut across the grid at right angles to each other. Hills appear to distort this pattern, however, and can seem disorienting. But as you learn your way around, these same hills will become your landmarks and reference points.

MAIN ARTERIES AND STREETS   Market Street is San Francisco's main thoroughfare. Most of the city's buses travel this route on their way to the Financial District from the outer neighborhoods to the west and south. The tall office buildings clustered downtown are at the northeast end of Market; one block beyond lie the Embarcadero and the Bay.

The Embarcadero curves along San Francisco Bay from south of the Bay Bridge to the northeast perimeter of the city and terminates at Fisherman's Wharf, the famous tourist-oriented pier. Aquatic Park, Fort Mason, and the Golden Gate National Recreation area are located farther on around the Bay, occupying the northernmost point of the peninsula.

From the eastern perimeter of Fort Mason, **Van Ness Avenue** runs due south, back to Market Street. The area we have just described forms a rough triangle, with Market Street as its southeastern boundary, the waterfront as its northern boundary, and Van Ness Avenue as its western boundary. Within this triangle lie most of the city's main tourist sights.

FINDING AN ADDRESS   Since most of the city's streets are laid out in a grid pattern, finding an address is easy when you know the nearest cross street. When asking for directions, find out the nearest cross street and the neighborhood in which your destination is located, but be careful not to confuse numerical avenues with numerical streets. Numerical avenues (Third Avenue, etc.) are found in the Richmond and Sunset districts in the western part of the city. Numerical streets (Third Street, etc.) are South of Market in the east and south parts of town.

NEIGHBORHOODS IN BRIEF

Union Square   Union Square is the commercial hub of the city. Most major hotels and department stores are crammed into the area surrounding the actual square (named for a series of violent pro-union mass demonstrations staged here on the eve of the Civil War), and there are a plethora of upscale boutiques, restaurants, and galleries tucked between the larger buildings.

Financial District   East of Union Square, this area bordered by the Embarcadero, Market, Third, Kearny, and Washington streets is the city's business district and

San Francisco at a Glance

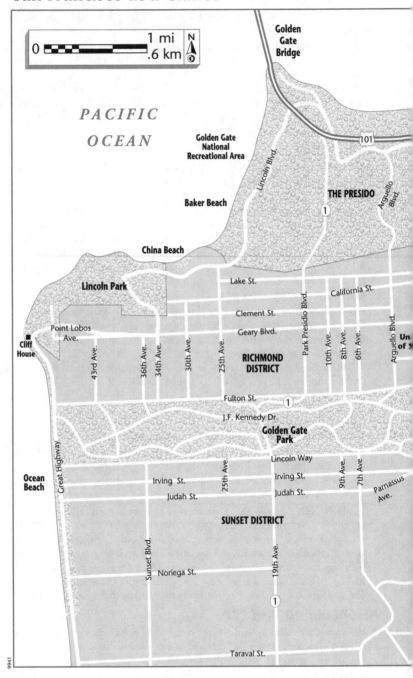

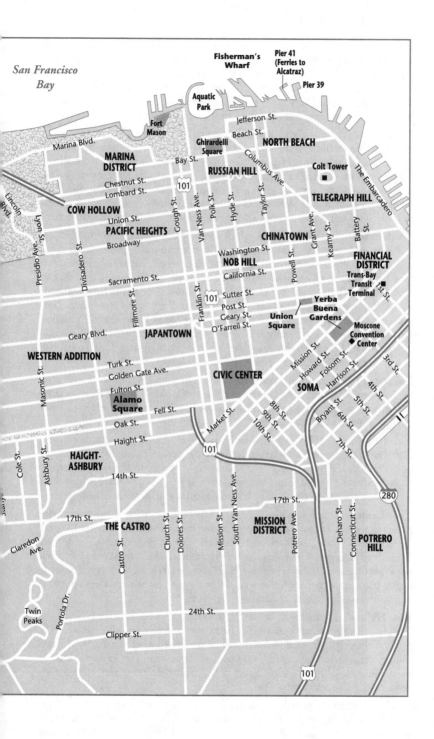

San Francisco
Bay

Fisherman's
Wharf

Pier 41
(Ferries to
Alcatraz)

Pier 39

Aquatic
Park

Fort
Mason

Jefferson St.

Ghirardelli
Square

Beach St.

NORTH BEACH

Marina Blvd.

MARINA
DISTRICT

Bay St.

RUSSIAN HILL

Coit Tower

Chestnut St.

Columbus Ave.

TELEGRAPH HILL

Lombard St.

101

Lincoln Blvd.

COW HOLLOW

Union St.

PACIFIC HEIGHTS

Broadway

Gough St.

Van Ness Ave.

Polk St.

Hyde St.

Taylor St.

CHINATOWN

Grant Ave.

Kearny St.

Battery St.

The Embarcadero

Presidio Ave.

Divisadero St.

Sacramento St.

Fillmore St.

Franklin St.

Washington St.

NOB HILL

California St.

Powell St.

FINANCIAL
DISTRICT

Trans-Bay
Transit
Terminal

1st St.

101

Sutter St.

Post St.

Geary St.

O'Farrell St.

Union
Square

Yerba
Buena
Gardens

Moscone
Convention
Center

Geary Blvd.

JAPANTOWN

WESTERN ADDITION

Masonic St.

Turk St.

Golden Gate Ave.

Fulton St.

Alamo
Square

Fell St.

CIVIC CENTER

Mission St.

Howard St.

Folsom St.

Harrison St.

SOMA

3rd St.

4th St.

5th St.

Oak St.

Bryant St.

6th St.

Cole St.

Ashbury St.

HAIGHT-
ASHBURY

Haight St.

101

Market St.

8th St.

9th St.

10th St.

7th St.

280

14th St.

17th St.

Claredon
Ave.

17th St.

THE CASTRO

Castro St.

Church St.

Dolores St.

Mission St.

South Van Ness Ave.

MISSION
DISTRICT

Potrero Ave.

Deharo St.

Connecticut St.

POTRERO
HILL

Twin
Peaks

Portola Dr.

24th St.

Clipper St.

101

41

stomping grounds for many major corporations. The pointy TransAmerica Pyramid, at Montgomery and Clay streets, is one of the district's most conspicuous architectural features. To its east stands the sprawling Embarcadero Center, an 8¹/₂-acre complex housing offices, shops, and restaurants. Farther east still is the World Trade Center, standing adjacent to the old Ferry Building, the city's pre-bridge transportation hub. Ferries to Sausalito and Larkspur still leave from this point.

Chinatown   The official entrance to Chinatown is marked by a large red and green gate on Grant Avenue at Bush Street. Beyond lies a 24-block labyrinth, bordered by Broadway, Bush, Kearny, and Stockton streets, filled with restaurants, markets, temples, and shops—and of course, a substantial percentage of San Francisco's Chinese residents. Chinatown is a great place for urban exploration all along Stockton, Grant, and Portsmouth Square, and the alleys that lead off them like Ross and Waverly. This area is jam-packed so don't even think about driving around here.

North Beach   The Italian quarter, which stretches from Montgomery and Jackson to Bay Street, is one of the best places in the city to grab a coffee, pull up a cafe chair, and do some serious people-watching. Night life is equally happening; restaurants, bars, and clubs along Columbus and Grant avenues bring folks from all over the Bay Area here to fight for a parking place and romp through the festive neighborhood. Down Columbus toward the Financial District are the remains of the city's Beat generation landmarks, including Ferlinghetti's City Lights Bookstore and Vesuvio's Bar. Broadway—a short strip of sex joints—cuts through the heart of the district. Telegraph Hill looms over the east side of North Beach, topped by Coit Tower, one of San Francisco's best vantage points.

Fisherman's Wharf   North Beach runs into Fisherman's Wharf, which was once the busy heart of the city's great harbor and waterfront industries. Today, it is a tacky tourist area with little if any authentic waterfront life, except for recreational boating and some friendly sea lions.

Nob Hill/Russian Hill   Bounded by Bush, Larkin, Pacific, and Stockton streets, Nob Hill is the genteel, well-heeled district of the city, still occupied by the major power brokers and the neighborhood businesses they frequent. Russian Hill extends from Pacific to Bay and from Polk to Mason. It is marked by steep streets, lush gardens, and high-rises occupied by both the monied and the more bohemian.

Civic Center   Although millions of dollars have been expended on brick sidewalks, ornate lampposts, and elaborate street plantings, the southwestern section of Market Street remains downright dilapidated. The Civic Center, at the "bottom" of Market Street, is an exception. This large complex of buildings includes the domed City Hall, the Opera House, Davies Symphony Hall, and the city's main library. The landscaped plaza connecting the buildings is the staging area for San Francisco's frequent demonstrations for or against just about everything.

Cow Hollow   Located west of Van Ness Avenue, between Russian Hill and the Presidio, this flat, grazable area supported 30 dairy farms in 1861. Today, Cow Hollow is largely residential and occupied by the city's Young and Yuppie. Its two primary commercial thoroughfares are Lombard Street, known for its many relatively inexpensive motels; and Union Street, a flourishing shopping sector filled with restaurants, pubs, cafes, and shops.

Marina District   Created on landfill for the Pan Pacific Exposition of 1915, the Marina boasts some of the best views of the Golden Gate, as well as plenty of grassy fields alongside the San Francisco Bay. Streets are lined with elegant Mediterranean-style homes and apartments, which are inhabited by the city's well-to-do singles and wealthy families. Here, too, is the Palace of Fine Arts, the Exploratorium, and Fort Mason Center. The main street is Chestnut between Franklin and Lyon, which is lined with shops, cafes, and boutiques. Because of its landfill foundation, the Marina was one of the city's hardest-hit districts in the 1989 quake.

Pacific Heights The ultra-elite, such as the Gettys and Danielle Steele—and those lucky enough to buy before the real estate boom—reside in the mansions and homes that make up Pacific Heights. When the rich meander out of their fortresses, they wander down to Union Street, a long stretch of boutiques, restaurants, cafes, and bars.

Japantown Bounded by Octavia, Fillmore, California, and Geary Boulevard, Japantown shelters only about 4% of the city's Japanese population, but it's still a cultural experience to explore these few square blocks and the shops and restaurants within them.

SoMa In recent years, high rents have forced residents and businesses into once desolate South of Market (dubbed "SoMa"). The area is still predominantly warehouses and industrial spaces, but now many of them are brimming with life. The area is officially demarcated by the Embarcadero, Highway 101, and Market Street, with the greatest concentrations of interest around Yerba Buena Center, along Folsom and Harrison streets between Steuart and Sixth, and Brannan and Market. Along the waterfront are an array of restaurants. Farther west, around Folsom between Seventh and Eleventh streets, is where much of the city's nightclubbing occurs.

Mission District The Mexican and Latin American populations, along with their cuisine, traditions, and art, make the Mission District a vibrant area to visit. Because some parts of the neighborhood are poor and sprinkled with the homeless, gangs, and drug addicts, many tourists duck into Mission Dolores, cruise by a few of the 200 amazing murals, and head back downtown. But there's plenty more to see in the Mission District. There's a substantial community of lesbians around Valencia Street, several alternative arts organizations, and most recently the ultimate in young hipster nightlife. New bars, clubs, and restaurants are popping up on Mission between 18th and 24th streets and Valencia at 16th Street. Don't be afraid to visit this area, but do use caution at night.

The Castro One of the liveliest streets in town, Castro is practically synonymous with San Francisco's gay community, even though technically it is only a street in the Noe Valley district. Located at the very end of Market Street, between 17th and 18th streets, Castro supports dozens of shops, restaurants, and bars catering to the gay community. Open-minded straight people are welcome, too.

Haight-Ashbury Part trendy, part nostalgic, part funky, the Haight, as it's most commonly known, was the soul of the psychedelic and free-loving 1960s and the center of the counterculture movement. Today, the neighborhood straddling upper Haight Street on the eastern border of Golden Gate Park is more gentrified, but the commercial area still harbors all walks of life. Leftover aged hippies mingle with grungy, begging street kids outside Ben and Jerry's ice cream (where they may still be talking about Jerry Garcia), nondescript marijuana dealers whisper "Buds" as shoppers pass, and most people walking down the street have glow-in-the-dark hair color. But you don't need to be a freak or wearing tie-dye to enjoy the Haight: The food, shops, and bars cover all tastes. From Haight, walk south on Cole Street, to a more peaceful and quaint neighborhood.

2 Getting Around

BY PUBLIC TRANSPORTATION

The **San Francisco Municipal Railway,** 949 Presidio Ave., better known as **Muni** (☎ 415/673-6864), operates the city's cable cars, buses, and Metro streetcars. Together, these three public transportation services crisscross the entire city, making San Francisco fully accessible to everyone. Buses and Metro streetcars cost $1 for adults, 35¢ for ages five to 17, and 35¢ for seniors over 65. Cable cars cost a whopping $2 ($1 for seniors from 9pm to midnight and from 6 to 7am). Needless to say, they're packed primarily with tourists. Exact change is required on all vehicles except cable cars. Fares quoted here are subject to change.

For detailed route information, phone Muni or consult the bus map at the front of the *Yellow Pages*. If you plan on making extensive use of public transportation, you may want to invest in a comprehensive route map ($2), sold at the San Francisco Visitor Information Center (see "Visitor Information" in "Orientation," above) and in many downtown retail outlets.

Muni **discount passes,** called "Passports," entitle holders to unlimited rides on buses, Metro streetcars, and cable cars. A Passport costs $6 for one day, and $10 or $15 for three or seven consecutive days. As a bonus, your passport also entitles you to admission discounts at 24 of the city's major attractions, including the M. H. De Young Memorial Museum, the Asian Art Museum, the California Academy of Sciences, and the Japanese Tea Garden (all in Golden Gate Park); the Museum of Modern Art; Coit Tower; the Exploratorium; the zoo; and the National Maritime Museum and Historic Ships (where you may visit the U.S.S. *Pampanito* and the S.S. *Jeremiah O'Brien*). Among the places where you can purchase a Passport are the San Francisco Visitors Information Center, the Holiday Inn Civic Center, and the TIX Bay Area booth at Union Square.

BY CABLE CAR   San Francisco's cable cars may not be the most practical means of transport, but these rolling historic landmarks sure are a fun ride. There are only three lines in the city and they're all condensed in the downtown area. The most scenic, and exciting, is the **Powell-Hyde line,** which follows a zigzag route from the corner of Powell and Market streets, over both Nob Hill and Russian Hill, to a turntable at gas-lit Victorian Square in front of Aquatic Park. The **Powell-Mason line** starts at the same intersection and climbs over Nob Hill before descending to Bay Street, just three blocks from Fisherman's Wharf. The least scenic is the **California Street line,** which begins at the foot of Market Street and runs a straight course through Chinatown and over Nob Hill to Van Ness Avenue. All riders must exit at the last stop and wait in line for the return trip. The cable car system operates from approximately 6:30am to 12:30am.

BY BUS   Buses reach almost every corner of San Francisco, and beyond—they travel over the bridges to Marin County and Oakland. Some buses are powered by overhead electric cables; others use conventional gas engines; and all are numbered and display their destinations on the front. Stops are designated by signs, curb markings, and yellow bands on adjacent utility poles, and most bus shelters exhibit Muni's transportation map and schedule. Many buses travel along Market Street or pass near Union Square and run from about 6am to midnight, after which there is infrequent all-night "Owl" service. If you can help it, for safety purposes avoid taking buses late at night.

Popular tourist routes are traveled by bus nos. 5, 7, and 71, all of which run to Golden Gate Park; 41 and 45, which travel along Union Street; and 30, which runs between Union Square and Ghirardelli Square.

BY METRO STREETCAR   Five of Muni's six Metro streetcar lines, designated J, K, L, M, and N, run underground downtown and on the street in the outer neighborhoods. The sleek railcars make the same stops as BART (see below) along Market Street, including Embarcadero Station (in the Financial District), Montgomery and Powell streets (both near Union Square), and the Civic Center (near City Hall). Past the Civic Center, the routes branch off in different directions: The J line will take you to Mission Dolores; the K, L, and M lines to Castro Street; and the N line parallels Golden Gate Park. Metros run about every 15 minutes—more frequently during rush hours. Service is offered Monday through Friday from 5am to 12:30am, on Saturday from 6am to 12:20am, and on Sunday from 8am to 12:20am.

The most recent streetcar addition is not a newcomer at all, but San Francisco's beloved rejuvenated 1930s streetcars. The beautiful green-and-cream colored F-Market line runs from downtown Market Street to the Castro and back. It's a quick and charming way to get up and downtown without any hassle.

BY BART   BART, an acronym for Bay Area Rapid Transit (☎ **415/992-2278**), is a futuristic-looking, high-speed rail network that connects San Francisco with the East Bay—Oakland, Richmond, Concord, and Fremont. Four stations are located along Market Street (see "By Metro Streetcar," above). Fares range from 90¢ to $3.55, depending on how far you go. Tickets are dispensed from machines in the stations and are magnetically encoded with a dollar amount. Computerized exits automatically deduct the correct fare. Children four and under ride free. Trains run every 15 to 20 minutes, Monday through Friday from 4am to midnight, on Saturday from 6am to midnight, and on Sunday from 8am to midnight.

A $2.5 billion, 33-mile BART extension, currently under construction, includes a southern line that is planned to extend all the way to San Francisco International Airport. It will open, presumably, in 1997.

BY TAXI

This isn't New York, so don't expect a taxi to suddenly appear right when you need one. If you're downtown during rush hours or leaving from a major hotel it won't be hard to hail a cab—just look for the lighted sign on the roof that indicates if one is free. Otherwise, it's a good idea to call one of the following companies to arrange a ride: **Veteran's Cab** (☎ 415/552-1300), **Desoto Cab Co.** (☎ 415/673-1414), **Luxor Cabs** (☎ 415/282-4141), **Yellow Cab** (☎ 415/626-2345), **City** (☎ 415/468-7200), and **Pacific** (☎415/986-7220). Rates are approximately $2 for the first mile and $1.80 for each mile thereafter.

BY CAR

You don't need a car to explore downtown San Francisco and in fact, in central areas, such as Chinatown, Union Square, and the Financial District, a car can be your worst nightmare. But if you want to venture outside of the city, driving is the best way to go. If you need to rent a car, see the car rental information in chapter 2. Before heading outside of the city, especially in winter, call for California road conditions (☎ **415/557-3755**).

PARKING   If you want to have a relaxing vacation here, don't even attempt to find street parking in Nob Hill, North Beach, Chinatown, by Fisherman's Wharf, and on

San Francisco Mass Transit

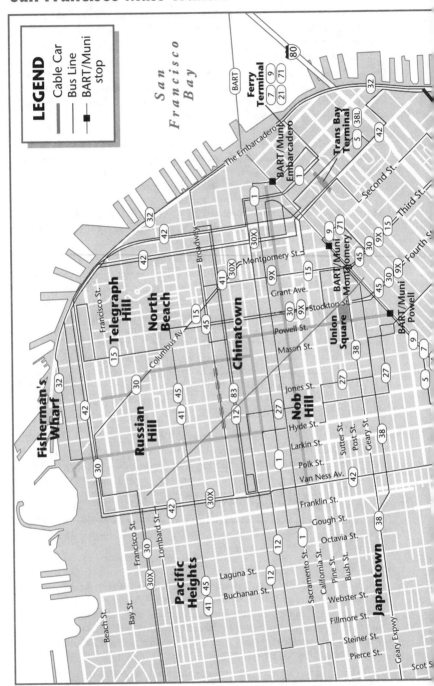

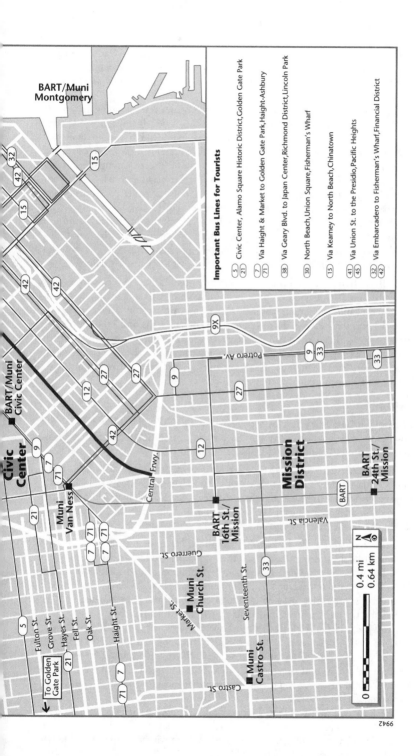

BART/Muni
Montgomery

Important Bus Lines for Tourists

(5) Civic Center, Alamo Square Historic District, Golden Gate Park

(21) Via Haight & Market to Golden Gate Park, Haight-Ashbury
(71)

(38) Via Geary Blvd. to Japan Center, Richmond District, Lincoln Park

(30) North Beach, Union Square, Fisherman's Wharf

(15) Via Kearney to North Beach, Chinatown

(41) Via Union St. to the Presidio, Pacific Heights
(45)

(32) Via Embarcadero to Fisherman's Wharf, Financial District
(42)

Civic Center

BART/Muni
Civic Center

Muni
Van Ness

Central Frwy.

Mission
District

BART
16th St./
Mission

BART
24th St./
Mission

Valencia St.

Guerrero St.

Muni Church St.

Market St.

Seventeenth St.

Muni Castro St.

Castro St.

Haight St.

Oak St.

Fell St.

Hayes St.

Grove St.

Fulton St.

To Golden
Gate Park

Potrero Av.

0   0.4 mi
0   0.64 km

N

9942

47

Telegraph Hill. Park in a garage or take a cab or a bus. If you do find street parking, pay attention to street signs that will explain when you can park and for how long. Be especially careful not to park in zones that are tow areas during rush hour.

Curb colors also indicate parking regulations. *Red* means no stopping or parking; *blue* is reserved for disabled drivers with a California-issued disabled plate or a placard; *white* means there's a five-minute limit; *green* indicates a 10-minute limit; and *yellow* and *yellow-black* curbs are for commercial vehicles only. Also, don't park at a bus stop or in front of a fire hydrant; and watch out for street-cleaning signs. If you violate the law, you may get a hefty ticket or your car may be towed. To get your car back, you must obtain a release from the nearest district police department, then go to the towing company to pick up the vehicle.

When parking on a hill, apply the hand brake, put the car in gear, and *curb your wheels*—toward the curb when facing downhill, away from the curb when facing uphill. Curbing your wheels will not only prevent a possible "runaway," but will also keep you from getting a ticket—an expensive fine that is aggressively enforced.

DRIVING RULES   California law requires that both drivers and passengers wear seat belts. You may turn right at a red light (unless otherwise indicated), after yielding to traffic and pedestrians, and after making a complete stop. Cable cars always have the right-of-way, as do pedestrians at intersections and crosswalks. Pay attention to signs and arrows on the streets and roadways or you may find yourself suddenly in a lane that requires exiting or turning when you really want to go straight ahead. What's more, San Francisco's many one-way streets can drive you in circles, but most road maps of the city indicate which way traffic flows.

BY FERRY

The **Golden Gate Ferry Service** fleet, Ferry Building (☎ **415/923-2000**), operates between the San Francisco Ferry Building, at the foot of Market Street, and downtown Sausalito (30 minutes) and Larkspur (45 minutes).

To/From Sausalito   Service to Sausalito is frequent, departing at reasonable intervals every day of the year except New Year's Day, Thanksgiving Day, and Christmas Day. Phone for exact schedule information. The ride takes a half hour and costs $4.25 for adults and $3.20 for kids aged 6 to 12. Senior and physically disabled passengers ride for $2.10; children five and under ride free.

To/From Larkspur   The Larkspur ferry is primarily a commuter service during the week, with frequent departures around the rush hours and limited service on weekends. Boats make the 13-mile trip in about 45 minutes and cost $2.50 for adults, $1.90 for kids aged 6 to 12, and $1.25 for seniors and physically disabled passengers; on weekends, prices rise to $4.25 for adults, $3.40 for young riders, and $2.10 for seniors and the physically disabled; children five and under ride free.

The **Blue and Gold Fleet,** Pier 39, Fisherman's Wharf (☎ **415/705-5444** or 510/522-3300), operates daily from the Ferry Building and Pier 39 to Oakland, Alameda, and Vallejo. Fares are $3.75 adult, $1.50 children, and $2.50 seniors to Oakland; $7.50, $4, and $6 respectively to Vallejo. This service will also take you to Marine World Africa USA on a package trip that includes boat, bus shuttle, and admission. Call for prices.

The **Red and White Fleet,** Pier 41 and 43$^1/_2$ (☎ **415/546-2700** or 800/229-2784) operates from Pier 43$^1/_2$ to Sausalito and Tiburon. Ferries also operate to Angel Island daily in summer and weekends only in winter. On weekdays ferries operate from Tiburon to the Ferry Building.

Round-trip fares to Angel Island are $9 adult and seniors, $8 children 12 to 18, $4.50 children 5 to 11, and free for children under five. Sausalito/Tiburon fares are $11 adults and seniors, $5.50 children. At press time, the Blue and Gold Fleet had just purchased the Red and White Fleet and schedule changes were yet to be determined. Call either number for updated schedules and fare changes.

FAST FACTS: San Francisco

Airport   See "Getting There" in Chapter 2.

American Express   For travel arrangements, traveler's checks, currency exchange, and other member services, American Express has an office at 295 California St., at Battery Street (☎ **415/536-2686**), and at 455 Market St., at 1st Street (☎ **415/536-2600**) in the Financial District, open Monday through Friday from 9am to 5pm and Saturday from 9am to 2pm. To report lost or stolen traveler's checks, call **800/221-7282.** For American Express Global Assist call **800/554-2639.**

Area Code   The area code for San Francisco and the peninsula is 415; Oakland, Berkeley, and much of the East Bay use the 510 area code. All phone numbers in this book are in San Francisco's 415 area code, but there's no need to dial it if you're within the city limits.

Baby-Sitters   Hotels can often recommend a baby-sitter or child-care service. If yours can't, try Temporary Tot Tending (☎ **415/355-7377** or 415/871-5790 after 6pm), which offers child care by licensed teachers by the hour for children from three weeks to 12 years of age. It's open Monday through Friday from 6am to 7pm (weekend service is available only during convention times).

Business Hours   Most banks are open Monday through Friday from 9am to 3pm. Several stay open until about 5pm at least one day a week. Many banks also feature ATMs for 24-hour banking (see section 1, "Visitor Information and Money," in Chapter 2).

Most stores are open Monday through Saturday from 10am to at least 6pm, with restricted hours on Sunday. But there are exceptions: Stores in Chinatown, Ghirardelli Square, and Pier 39 stay open much later during the tourist season; and large department stores, including Macy's and Nordstrom, keep late hours.

Most restaurants serve lunch from about 11:30am to 3pm and dinner from 5:30 to 10pm. You can sometimes get served later on weekends. Nightclubs and bars are usually open daily until 2am, when they are legally bound to stop serving alcohol.

Car Rentals   For car rental information, see Chapter 2.

Climate   See "When to Go," in Chapter 2.

Convention Center   The Moscone Convention Center, 774 Howard St. (☎ **415/974-4000**), between 3rd and 4th streets, was completed in 1981 and named for slain San Francisco mayor George Moscone. Part of a large revitalization project in the SoMa district, the center contains one of the world's largest column-free exhibition halls.

Dentist   In the event of a dental emergency, see your hotel concierge or contact the San Francisco Dental Society (☎ **415/421-1435**) for 24-hour referral to a specialist. The San Francisco Dental Office, 132 The Embarcadero (☎ **415/777-5115**), between Mission and Howard streets, offers emergency service and comprehensive dental care Monday and Friday from 8am to 4:30pm, Tuesday through Thursday from 10:30am to 7pm.

Doctor   Saint Francis Memorial Hospital, 900 Hyde St., between Bush and Pine streets on Nob Hill (☎ **415/353-6000**), provides urgent-care service 24 hours; no appointment is necessary. The hospital also operates a physician-referral service (☎ **415/353-6566**).

Driving Rules   See "Getting Around" earlier in this chapter.

Drugstores   There are Walgreens pharmacies all over town, including one at 135 Powell St. (☎ **415/391-4433**). The store is open Monday through Saturday from 8am to midnight and on Sunday from 9am to 9pm, but the pharmacy has more limited hours; Monday through Friday they're open from 8am to 8pm, Saturday from 9am to 5pm, and Sunday from 10am to 6pm. The branch on Divisadero Street at Lombard (☎ **415/931-6415**) has a 24-hour pharmacy. Merrill's Drug Center, 805 Market St. (☎ **415/781-1669**), is open Monday through Friday from 7am to 10pm and on Saturday and Sunday from 7:30am to 10pm, but the pharmacy is only open Monday through Friday from 9am to 7pm and is closed on weekends. Both chains accept MasterCard and Visa.

Earthquakes   There will always be earthquakes in California, most of which you'll never notice. However, in case of a significant shaker, there are a few basic precautionary measures you should know. When you are inside a building, seek cover; do not run outside. Stand under a doorway or against a wall and stay away from windows. If you exit a building after a substantial quake, use stairwells, not elevators. If you are in your car, pull over to the side of the road and stop—but not until you are away from bridges, overpasses, telephone poles, and power lines. Stay in your car. If you're out walking, stay outside and away from trees, power lines, and the sides of buildings. If you're in an area with tall buildings, find a doorway in which to stand.

Emergencies   Dial 911 for police, ambulance, or the fire department; no coins are needed from a public phone. Emergency hotlines include the Poison Control Center (☎ **800/523-2222**) and Rape Crisis (☎ **415/647-7273**).

Information   See "Visitor Information" earlier in this chapter.

Liquor Laws   Liquor and grocery stores, as well as some drugstores, can sell packaged alcoholic beverages between 6am and 2am. Most restaurants, nightclubs, and bars are licensed to serve alcoholic beverages during the same hours. The legal age for purchase and consumption is 21; proof of age is required.

Maps   See "City Layout" earlier in this chapter.

Newspapers and Magazines   The city's two main dailies are the *San Francisco Chronicle* and the *San Francisco Examiner;* both are distributed throughout the city. The two papers combine for a massive Sunday edition that includes a pink "Datebook" section, an excellent preview of the week's upcoming events. The free weekly *San Francisco Bay Guardian,* a tabloid of news and listings, is indispensable for night life information; it's widely distributed through street-corner dispensers and at city cafes and restaurants.

Of the many free tourist-oriented publications, the most widely read are *Key* and *San Francisco Guide.* Both of these handbook-size weeklies contain maps and information on current events. They can be found in most hotels and in shops and restaurants in the major tourist areas.

Pharmacies   See "Drugstores," above.

Police   For emergencies, dial 911 from any phone; no coins are needed. For other matters, call **415/553-0123.**

Post Office   There are dozens of post offices located all around the city. The closest office to Union Square is inside Macy's department store, 170 O'Farrell St. (☎ **415/956-3570**). You can pick up mail addressed to you, and marked "General Delivery" (Poste Restante), at the Civic Center Post Office Box Unit, P.O. Box 429991, San Francisco, CA 94142-9991 (☎ **415/441 8329**).

Safety   Few locals would recommend that you walk alone late at night in certain areas, particularly the Tenderloin, between Union Square and the Civic Center. Compared with similar areas in other cities, however, even this section of San Francisco is relatively tranquil. Other areas where you should be particularly alert are the Mission District, around 16th and Mission streets; the Fillmore area, around lower Haight Street; and the SoMa area south of Market Street. See "Safety" in Chapter 2 for additional safety tips.

Taxes   An 8.5% sales tax is added at the register for all goods and services purchased in San Francisco. The city hotel tax is a whopping 12%. There is no airport tax.

Taxis   See "Getting Around" earlier in this chapter.

Television   In addition to the cable stations, available in most hotels, all the major networks and several independent stations are represented. They include: Channel 2, KTVU (FOX); Channel 4, KRON (NBC); Channel 5, KPIX (CBS); Channel 7, KGO (ABC); and Channel 9, KQED (PBS).

Time Zone   San Francisco is in the Pacific Standard Time zone, which is eight hours behind Greenwich Mean Time and three hours behind Eastern Standard Time. To find out what time it is, call **415/767-8900.**

Transit Information   The San Francisco Municipal Railway, better known as Muni, operates the city's cable cars, buses, and Metro streetcars. For custom information call Muni at 415/673-6864 during the week between 7am and 5pm and on the weekends between 9am and 5pm. At other times, recorded information is available.

Useful Telephone Numbers   Tourist information (☎ 415/391-2001); highway conditions (☎ 415/557-3755); KFOG Entertainment Line (☎ 415/777-1045); KMEL's Movie Phone Line (☎ 415/777-FILM); Grateful Dead Hotline (☎ 415/457-6388); Morrison Planetarium Sky Line (☎ 415/750-7141).

Weather   Call 415/936-1212 to find out when the next fog bank is rolling in.

5 Accommodations

Whether you want a room with a view or just a room, San Francisco is more than accommodating for its 11 million annual guests. Most of the city's 180 hotels are concentrated around Union Square, but there are also some smaller independent gems scattered around town. When reading over your options, keep in mind that prices listed are hotel rack rates (the published rates) and you should always ask for special discounts or, even better, vacation packages. It's possible that you could get the room you want for $100 less than what's quoted here, except in summer when the hotels are packed and bargaining is close to impossible.

Hunting for hotels in San Francisco can be a tricky business, particularly if you're not a seasoned traveler. What you don't know—and the reservation agent may not tell you—may very well ruin your vacation, so keep the following pointers in mind when it comes time to book a room:

- Prices listed below do not include state and city taxes, which total 14%. Other hidden extras include parking fees and hefty surcharges—up to $1 per local call—for telephone use.
- San Francisco is Convention City, so if you wish to secure rooms at a particular hotel during high season, book well in advance.
- Be sure to have a credit card in hand when making a reservation, and don't be surprised if you're asked to pay for a least one night in advance (this doesn't happen often, though).
- Reservations are usually held until 6pm. If you don't tell the hotel you'll be arriving late, you may lose your room.
- Almost every hotel in San Francisco requires a credit card imprint for "incidentals" (and to prevent walkouts). If you don't have a credit card, then be sure to make special arrangements with the management *before* you hang up the phone, and take down names.

The hotels listed below are classified first by area and then by price, using the following categories: **Very Expensive:** more than $175 per night; **Expensive:** $130 to $175 per night; **Moderate:** $80 to $130 per night; and **Inexpensive:** less than $80 per night. These categories reflect the price of an average double room during the high season, which runs approximately from April through September. *Read each of the entries carefully:* Many hotels also offer rooms at rates

Reservation Services

Having reservations about your reservations? Then leave it up to the pros:

Bed and Breakfast California, P.O. Box 282910, San Francisco, CA 94128 (☎ 415/696-1690 or 800/872-4500; fax 415/696-1699), offers a selection of B&Bs ranging from $60 to $150 per night (two-night minimum). Accommodations range from simple rooms in private homes to luxurious, full-service carriage houses, houseboats, and Victorian homes.

San Francisco Hotel Reservation is a nifty World Wide Web site that allows Internet users to make their reservations on-line. Plug in at **http://www. hotelres.com.**

San Francisco Reservations, 22 Second St., San Francisco, CA 94105 (☎ 800/ 667-1550 or 415/227-1500), arranges reservations for more than 200 of San Francisco's hotels and often offers discounted rates. Ask about their Events and Hotel Packages that include VIP or discount admissions to various San Francisco museums.

above and below the price category that they have been assigned in this guidebook. Also note that we do not list single rates. However, some hotels, particularly more budget-oriented establishments, do offer lower rates for singles, so do inquire about these if you are traveling alone.

In general, hotel rates in San Francisco are rather inelastic; they don't vary much during the year because the city is so popular year-round. You should always ask about weekend discounts, corporate rates, and family plans; most larger hotels, and many smaller ones, offer them, but many establishments do not mention these discounts unless you make a specific inquiry. You will find no-smoking rooms available in all of the larger hotels and many of the smaller hotels; establishments that are entirely nonsmoking are listed as such. Nowadays, the best advice for smokers is to confirm a smoking-permitted room in advance.

Most larger hotels will also be able to accommodate guests confined to wheelchairs or those who have other special needs. Ask when you make a reservation to ensure that your hotel of choice will be able to accommodate your needs, especially if you are interested in a bed and breakfast.

1 Best Bets

- **Best for Families:** Kids like the **Westin St. Francis,** 335 Powell St. (☎ 415/ 397-7000), because all children under 12 are given a Kids Club hat on arrival and special sports bottles and complimentary refills in the restaurants, while their siblings three to seven are given dinosaur soaps and sponges and coloring books.
- **Best Romantic Rendezvous:** Secure a garden suite at the **Sherman House,** 2160 Green St. (☎ 415/563-3600), with French doors leading out onto a sunken garden terrace with gazebo and pond or the Paderewski suite with a fireplace in the bathroom. Honorable mentions include the **Archbishop's Mansion, Hotel Bohème,** and **Hotel Majestic.**
- **Best Modern Hotel: Hotel Milano,** 55 Fifth St. (☎ 415/543-8555), comes decked out in Italian modern style and the latest in electronic amenities. The lobby shows it all—curvaceous staircase, bold floor patterns, and a Calder mobile. Second place: **Hotel Diva.**

- **Best Historic Hotel:** The **Sheraton Palace Hotel,** 2 New Montgomery St. (☎ **415/392-8600**), the extravagant creation of banker Bonanza King Will Ralston in 1875, has one of the grandest rooms in the city: the Garden Court. Running a close second is the magnificent lobby at the **Fairmont Hotel** on Nob Hill.
- **Best Old-World Hotel:** Those who appreciate comfort, beautiful surroundings, absolute privacy, and unobtrusive service should choose **The Huntington,** 1075 California St. (☎ **415/474-5400**).
- **Best for the Culture Vulture: Inn at the Opera,** 333 Fulton St. (☎ **415/ 863-8400**), an intimate hotel frequented by musicians and other performing artists, is perfect for its location close to all the city's cultural icons, including the opera and Davies Symphony Hall. And the lounge and Act IV are intimate places for an after-show supper in the warm glow of firelight.
- **Best for Your Budget:** Sure, the rooms are small at **San Remo,** 2237 Mason St. (☎ **415/776-8688**), but the North Beach location, friendly staff, and low prices can't be beat. Besides, you're here to see the city, not your hotel room.
- **Best Moderately Priced Hotel: Petite Auberge,** 863 Bush St. (☎ **415/ 928-6000**), is a delightful rendering of a French country inn. The 26 rooms have attractive furnishings and lace curtains; the tiled breakfast room opens onto a small garden where guests enjoy afternoon tea and wine. If the Auberge is full, try the equally quaint **White Swan Inn** down the street.
- **Best Bed and Breakfast:** It's a tie between the **Union Street Inn,** 2229 Union St. (☎ **415/346-0424**), and **Bed and Breakfast Inn,** 4 Charlton Court (☎ **415/ 921-9784**). Both Union Street inns live up to the expectations of true B&B enthusiasts.
- **Best Funky Hotel: The Phoenix Inn,** 601 Eddy St. (☎ **415/776-1380**), wouldn't look out of place at Palm Springs. It's a favorite with the rock and movie set, including Sinead O'Connor, k.d. Lang, and the Red Hot Chili Peppers. Former flower children will prefer the 1960s-nostalgic **Red Victorian Bed and Breakfast Inn,** 1665 Haight St. (☎ **415/864-1978**).
- **Best Views:** From the rooms in the **Mandarin Oriental** (222 Sansome St. (☎ **415/885-0999**), all of which are on the 38th to the 48th floors, you not only have a great view of the city, you have a great view of the entire Bay Area. Pricey, though.
- **Best Service:** The small, luxurious **Campton Place,** 340 Stockton St. (☎ **415/ 781-5555**); the historic, eager-to-please **Ritz-Carlton,** 600 Stockton St. (☎ **415/ 296-7465**); the large, elegant **Clift,** 495 Geary St. (☎ **415/441-4621**); and the modern, pampering **Mandarin Oriental** all rate at the very top for service. Any one of these will deliver on this promise.
- **Best Dining Room:** Formal with its gilt pictures and warm wood paneling, the dining room at the **Ritz Carlton** has established itself as topnotch. Chef Danko combines the spices, ingredients, and techniques of several cuisines—Thai, Indian, Japanese, and Italian—to create a unique cuisine.

2 Union Square

VERY EXPENSIVE

Campton Place Hotel. 340 Stockton St. (between Post and Sutter sts.), San Francisco, CA 94108. ☎ **415/781-5555** or 800/235-4300. Fax 415/955-5536. 107 rms, 10 suites. A/C MINIBAR TV TEL. $220–$330 double; from $420 suite. Continental breakfast $12.50 extra. AE, CB, DC, MC, V. Parking $23. Cable car: Powell-Hyde and Powell-Mason lines (1 block west). Bus: 2, 3, 4, 30, or 45.

They don't miss a trick at this small, elegant luxury hotel. From the beautifully appointed guest rooms with extra-large beds and exquisite marble bathrooms to the bathrobes and top-notch toiletries, every necessity and whim is covered at Campton Place. The only downside: The rooms and hotel itself are cramped enough to make you wonder what you're forking over the big bucks for, but the superlative service almost makes up for it.

Dining/Entertainment: The Campton Place Restaurant, which serves three meals a day, is highly revered. The menu is contemporary American, with dishes like stuffed, braised oxtail and saffron-steamed sea bass, priced from $19 to $30.

Services: 24-hour room service, concierge, evening turndown, laundry/valet, complimentary overnight shoe shine, morning newspaper. Business services such as typing, translating, and faxing available by request at the front desk.

Facilities: Access to nearby health club.

The Clift Hotel. 495 Geary St. (at Taylor St., two blocks west of Union Square), San Francisco, CA 94102. ☎ **415/775-4700** or 800/437-8243 in the U.S. Fax 415/441-4621. 326 rms, 31 suites. A/C MINIBAR TV TEL. $255–$400 double; from $405 suite. Continental breakfast $12.50 extra. AE, CB, DC, MC, V. Parking $23. Cable car: Powell-Hyde and Powell-Mason lines (2 blocks east). Bus: 2, 3, 4, 30, 38, or 45.

One of San Francisco's top luxury hotels, the Clift went through some shaky times in recent years as ownership changed hands, but everything seems to be back on track—enough so to win both Five-Star and Five-Diamond awards for the tenth year in a row. Located in the city's Theater District, two blocks from Union Square, the Clift's staff excels at pampering its guests and even manages to be cordial to the droves of tourists who wander slack-jawed through the palatial lobby. The decor of the guest rooms leans toward old-fashioned, with high ceilings, elaborate moldings and woodwork, Georgian reproductions, and marble bathrooms with everything from hair dryers to plush terry-cloth robes. Thoughtful extras include padded hangers, individual climate controls, two-line telephones, and a scale in your dressing room. The windows also open—a nice touch for those guests who appreciate fresh air.

The Clift's "Young Travelers Program" provides traveling families with toys and games, diapers, bottles, children's books, and other amenities to help children and their parents feel at home. The hotel also accepts and pampers pets.

Dining/Entertainment: The French Room, open for breakfast, lunch, and dinner, specializes in seasonally appropriate California-French cuisine. The hotel's dramatic Redwood Room, which opened in 1933 and remains one of San Francisco's most opulent piano bars, has beautiful 22-foot-tall fluted redwood columns and is also famous for its Gustav Klimt murals. The lobby lounge serves cocktails daily and a traditional English tea Monday through Saturday.

Services: 24-hour room service, concierge, twice-daily maid service, overnight laundry and shoe polishing, one-hour pressing, evening turndown, complimentary in-room fax and computers.

Facilities: 24-hour business center, gift shop, extensive fitness facility.

Crowne Plaza Parc Fifty Five. 55 Cyril Magnin St. (at Market and North Fifth sts.), San Francisco, CA 94012. ☎ **415/392-8000** or 800/338-1338. Fax 415/403-6602. 978 rms, 31 suites. A/C TV TEL. $275 double; $300 Executive Club double; from $340 one-bedroom suite, from $525 two-bedroom suite. Extra person $15. Packages available. Continental breakfast $8 extra; buffet breakfast $11.75 extra. AE, CB, DC, DISC, MC, V. Parking $23. Cable car: Powell-Hyde and Powell-Mason lines (1 block north). All Market St. buses. Muni Metro: All Market St. trams.

This enormous and somewhat impersonal hotel just became part of the Crowne Plaza conglomerate. The rooms were being renovated when this book went to press, but we doubt there's a chance of sprucing up the labyrinth of a lobby enough to make

Accommodations Near Union Square and Nob Hill

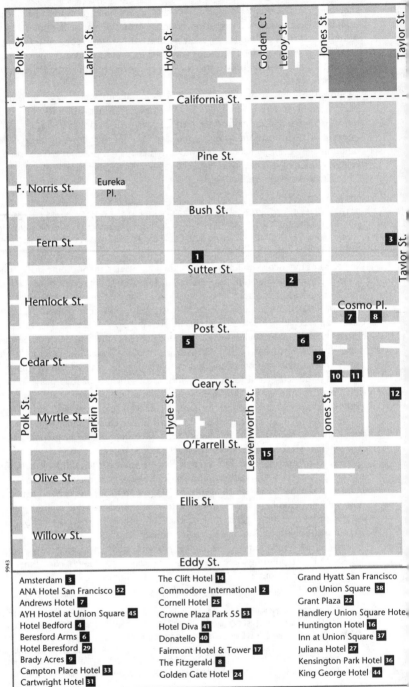

Polk St.
Larkin St.
Hyde St.
Golden Ct.
Leroy St.
Jones St.
Taylor St.

California St.

Pine St.

F. Norris St.
Eureka Pl.

Bush St.

Fern St.

3

Taylor St.

1

Sutter St.

2

Hemlock St.

Cosmo Pl.

7 **8**

Post St.

5

6

9

Cedar St.

10 **11**

Geary St.

12

Polk St.
Larkin St.
Hyde St.
Leavenworth St.
Jones St.

Myrtle St.

O'Farrell St.

15

Olive St.

Ellis St.

Willow St.

Eddy St.

9943

Amsterdam **3**	The Clift Hotel **14**	Grand Hyatt San Francisco
ANA Hotel San Francisco **52**	Commodore International **2**	on Union Square **38**
Andrews Hotel **7**	Cornell Hotel **25**	Grant Plaza **22**
AYH Hostel at Union Square **45**	Crowne Plaza Park 55 **53**	Handlery Union Square Hotel
Hotel Bedford **4**	Hotel Diva **41**	Huntington Hotel **16**
Beresford Arms **6**	Donatello **40**	Inn at Union Square **37**
Hotel Beresford **29**	Fairmont Hotel & Tower **17**	Juliana Hotel **27**
Brady Acres **9**	The Fitzgerald **8**	Kensington Park Hotel **36**
Campton Place Hotel **33**	Golden Gate Hotel **24**	King George Hotel **44**
Cartwright Hotel **31**		

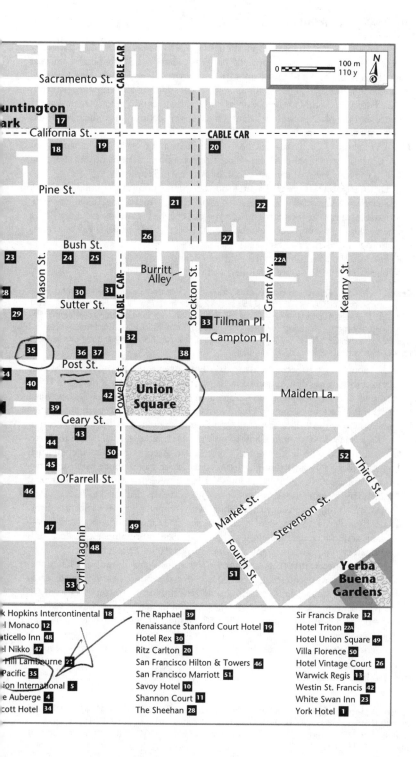

Sacramento St.

CABLE CAR

0 — 100 m
— 110 y

N

**untington
ark** **17**

California St. · – – – – – – **CABLE CAR** – – – – –

18 **19** **20**

Pine St.

21 **22**

26 **27**

Bush St.

23 Mason St. **24** **25**

Burritt
Alley

Stockton St.

Grant Av. **22A**

Kearny St.

28

30 **31** CABLE CAR

29

Sutter St.

33 Tillman Pl.

Campton Pl.

32

35

36 **37**

38

Post St.

34

40

42

**Union
Square**

Maiden La.

39

Powell St.

Geary St.

43

44

50

52 Third St.

45

O'Farrell St.

46

Market St.

Stevenson St.

47

49

Cyril Magnin

48

Fourth St.

51

**Yerba
Buena
Gardens**

53

k Hopkins Intercontinental **18**
l Monaco **12**
ticello Inn **48**
el Nikko **47**
Hill Lambourne **21**
Pacific **35**
ion International **5**
e Auberge **4**
cott Hotel **34**

The Raphael **39**
Renaissance Stanford Court Hotel **19**
Hotel Rex **30**
Ritz Carlton **20**
San Francisco Hilton & Towers **46**
San Francisco Marriott **51**
Savoy Hotel **10**
Shannon Court **11**
The Sheehan **28**

Sir Francis Drake **32**
Hotel Triton **22A**
Hotel Union Square **49**
Villa Florence **50**
Hotel Vintage Court **26**
Warwick Regis **13**
Westin St. Francis **42**
White Swan Inn **23**
York Hotel **1**

it warm and inviting. However, most guests don't come here to lounge, but rather to enjoy Parc Fifty Five's old standards: bay views, king-size beds, and bathrooms that include a phone, a well-lit makeup mirror, a shower massage, and a marble vanity. Claustrophobics take note: Windows don't open, and fresh air is supplied by vents. Parc Fifty Five is still largely a business hotel and will continue to cater to that clientele, but the place previously had a sterile feel to it, so it is hoped the new owners will bring it a little life.

The Executive Club occupies the top four floors and offers guests enhanced services, including personal check-in and concierge, continental breakfast, and afternoon hors d'oeuvres. Seven of the suites contain private whirlpool baths.

Dining/Entertainment: Located on the second floor is the hotel's premier restaurant, the Verandah, which serves innovative California cuisine. Rikyu serves traditional Japanese cuisine. In the atrium you can enjoy a leisurely drink at the Piazza Lounge while listening to contemporary and classical piano music. If you're a sports fan, drop in to Barley and Hops.

Services: 24-hour room service, concierge, laundry/valet.

Facilities: Business center, tour desk, car rental, health club.

Grand Hyatt San Francisco on Union Square. 345 Stockton St. (between Post and Sutter sts.), San Francisco, CA 94108. ☎ **415/398-1234** or 800/233-1234. Fax 415/391-1780. 663 rms, 30 suites. A/C MINIBAR TV TEL. $250–$280 double (doesn't include breakfast); $195–$285 Regency room (including continental breakfast); from $350 suite. Continental breakfast $14.50 extra. AE, CB, DC, JCB, MC, V. Parking $24. Cable car: Powell-Hyde and Powell-Mason lines (2 blocks west). Bus: 2, 3, 4, 30, 38, or 45.

If the thought of a 10-second walk to Saks Fifth Avenue makes you drool and your credit cards start to sweat, this hotel is the place for you. Not only is the grand Hyatt surrounded by all the downtown shopping, but it also boasts some of the best views in the area. The lobby is indeed *grand,* with Chinese artifacts and enormous ceramic vases, but sadly the well-kept rooms are little more than upscale basic with a corporate flare. They do have some elbow room and a small table and chairs, and the views from most of the 36 floors are truly spectacular. Accommodations include such amenities as TVs in the bathroom, first-run movies, and a telephone with computer-connection capability. Regency rooms are larger, and prices include continental breakfast and evening hors d'oeuvres. Three floors are also dedicated to Business Plan rooms, which contain private fax, telephone with computer hook-up, enhanced lighting, coffeemaker, iron and board, and hair dryer. They also include special services—24-hour access to compatible printer, photocopier, and office supplies, free local calls and credit card phone access, and daily newspaper. All for an additional $15.

Dining/Entertainment: The hotel's signature Plaza Restaurant has floor-to-ceiling windows overlooking Union Square. Breakfast, lunch, and dinner are served in a garden setting. Napper's Deli, an indoor/outdoor bistro, serves custom-cut sandwiches, seasonal salads, soups, and desserts; continental breakfasts are served here on weekends beginning at 8:30am. Club 36, on the 36th floor, serves cocktails with live jazz six nights a week and allows for a birds-eye view of downtown.

Services: Room service, concierge, free weekday morning town car service to the Financial District.

Facilities: Fitness center, tour desk, car-rental desk, fully equipped business center.

✪ **Hotel Monaco.** 501 Geary St. (at Taylor St.), San Francisco, CA 94102. ☎ **415/292-0100** or 800/214-4220. Fax 292-0111. 177 rooms, 24 suites. A/C MINIBAR TV TEL. From $170 double; from $295 suite. Call for discounted rates. AE, DC, DISC, JCB, MC, V. Parking $20. Bus: 2, 3, 4, 27, or 38.

This remodeled 1910 beaux arts building debuted in June 1995 and is the new diva of Union Square luxury hotels. For $24 million, the Kimpton Group did this place right—from the cozy main lobby with a two-story French inglenook fireplace to the guest rooms with canopy beds, Chinese-inspired armoires, bamboo writing desks, bold stripes, and vibrant color. Everything is brand-spanking new, in the best of taste, and as playful as it is serious. The decor, combined with the breathtaking neighboring restaurant, make this our favorite luxury hotel in the city. The only downside is that some rooms are too small.

Dining/Entertainment: The hotel's restaurant, the Grand Cafe, is the best room downtown. It is grand, in the true sense of the word, with sky-high ceilings, elaborate 1920s and 1930s style, and an amazing collection of local art. (See Chapter 6, "Dining," for complete information.)

Services: Computer, complimentary wine hour nightly, concierge, overnight shoeshine, valet/laundry, two-line phones, secretarial services.

Facilities: Health club with steam, sauna, and massage; meeting and banquet facilities.

Hotel Nikko. 222 Mason St. (at O'Farrell St.), San Francisco, CA 94102. ☎ **415/394-1111** or 800/645-5687. Fax 415/421-0455. 500 rms, 22 suites. A/C MINIBAR TV TEL. $225–$285 double; from $385 suite. AE, CB, DISC, JCB, MC, V. Parking $24. Cable car: Powell-Hyde and Powell-Mason. Bus: 2, 3, 4, 30, 38, or 45.

Part of Japan Airlines' international fleet of superluxury hotels, the 25-story Hotel Nikko combines the luxuries of both eastern and western cultures with heavenly results. Work out in the fitness center with your personal trainer, take a few laps in the glass-enclosed indoor swimming pool, rest in the Jacuzzi, Japanese sauna, or soaking tub, then top off the morning with a shiatsu massage before starting your day— what more could you ask for?

Ideally located near Union Square and the Theater District, the Nikko's penchant for pampering also carries on to the guest rooms, which feature top-of-the-line amenities such as two-line speaker phones with modem ports, blackout curtains, large windows with views of the city, and huge, marble bathrooms with separate tubs and showers. Suites include separate sitting areas, stereos, and entry halls (a Japanese tradition). Though the hotel's decor is a bit too staid for western tastes—simple furnishings and pearl gray tones predominate—the element of luxury ultimately prevails. Prices are steep, naturally, but the hotel's special "romance" packages ($129 per night with plenty of freebies) are perfect for special occasions.

Dining/Entertainment: The bistro-style Cafe 222 serves both California and Japanese cuisine for breakfast, lunch, and dinner. On the lobby level is a small sushi bar offering made-to-order sushi, as well as afternoon hors d'oeuvres and live music.

Services: 24-hour room service, twice-daily maid service, concierge, laundry/valet.

Facilities: Business center, swimming pool, fitness center, sauna, hot tub, shiatsu massage, tanning booth, gift and other shops.

Pan Pacific. 500 Post St. (at Mason St.), San Francisco, CA 94102. ☎ **415/771-8600.** Fax 415/398-0267. 300 rms, 29 suites. A/C MINIBAR TV TEL. $235–$335 double; from $375 suite. Continental breakfast $8 extra; American breakfast $14.25 extra. AE, DC, JCB, MC, V. Parking $24. Cable car: Powell Hyde and Powell Mason. Bus: 2,3,4, 30, 38, or 45.

If this were Hollywood, James Bond might hoodwink a villain here, magically drop down the skyrise's atrium, and disappear into the night. But all is quiet and intimate in the third-floor lobby, even though the skylight ceiling is another 18 floors up. The Pan Pacific is 21st century with Star Wars–like lighted corridors, artistically glitzy, enormous, and somehow romantic, all at the same time. The lobby's marble fountain with four dancing figures and its player piano set the mood for guests relaxing in front of the fireplace. The rooms are rather corporate, but in good taste, and immaculately clean and well stocked with all the luxurious extras, including lavish marble bathrooms with mini-TVs at the sink. Other amenities offered are in-room safes, three Touch-Tone phones, voice mail, and bathrobes. The hotel is also conveniently located close to Union Square.

Dining: The Pacific dining room serves breakfast, lunch, and dinner featuring California cuisine with Asian and French accents. See Chapter 6, "Dining," for details.

Services: 24-hour room service, concierge, laundry/valet, complimentary Rolls Royce transportation in the city.

Facilities: Business center

✪ **Prescott Hotel.** 545 Post St. (between Mason and Taylor sts.), San Francisco, CA 94102. ☎ **415/563-0303** or 800/283-7322. Fax 415/563-6831. 167 rms, 35 suites. A/C MINIBAR TV TEL. $175 double; $235 concierge-level double (including breakfast and evening cocktail reception); from $265 suite. AE, CB, DC, MC, V. Parking $21. Cable car: Powell-Hyde and Powell-Mason lines (1 block east). Bus: 2, 3, 4, 30, 38, or 45.

The Prescott has always been one of our favorite hotels in San Francisco. The staff treats you like royalty, the rooms are beautiful and immaculate, the location—one block from Union Square—is perfect, and room service is provided by one of the best restaurants in the city: Postrio. (In fact, it's not unheard of for visitors to check into the Prescott just to get preferred seating.)

Dark tones of green, plum, and burgundy blend well with the cherry wood furnishings within each of the soundproofed rooms; the view, alas, isn't so pleasant. All bathrooms are supplied with terry-cloth robes and hair dryers, though only the suites have whirlpool bathtubs. "Club Level" guests are pampered with free continental breakfast, evening cocktails, and exercise bicycles or rowing machines brought up to your room on request (all for only $20 extra per night).

Dining/Entertainment: The hotel provides preferred seating for guests at Postrio Restaurant. Be sure to make reservations when you book your room (see Chapter 6, "Dining," for complete information).

Services: Complimentary coffee and tea each morning, wine and hors d'oeuvres every evening in the living room, limousine service weekday mornings to the Financial District, concierge, twice-daily maid service, nightly turndown, same-day valet/laundry service, overnight shoe shine, room service from the Postrio.

Facilities: Access to off-premises health club, including swimming pool, free weights, and sauna.

San Francisco Hilton & Towers. 333 O'Farrell St. (between Mason and Taylor sts.), San Francisco, CA 94102. ☎ **415/771-1400** or 800/445-8667. Fax 415/771-1607. 1,614 rms, 180 suites. A/C MINIBAR TV TEL. $215–$260 double; from $310 suite. Children stay free in parents' room. Continental breakfast $10 extra. AE, CB, DC, DISC, MC, V. Parking $24. Cable car: Powell-Hyde and Powell-Mason lines (1 block east). Bus: 2, 3, 4, 30, 38, or 45.

Complete with bustling conventioneers, anxious smokers, and a line to register that resembles airport check-in, the Hilton's lobby is so enormous and busy it feels more like a convention hall than a hotel. It's the Hilton's three connecting buildings (the original 19-story main building, a 46-story tower topped by a panoramic restaurant, and a 23-story landmark with an additional 386 luxurious rooms and suites) that bring the swarms of visitors clamoring for a room. But even during quieter times, the sheer enormity of the place makes the Hilton somewhat overwhelming and its contents mysterious.

After you get past the sweeping grand lobby, jump on an elevator, and wind through endless corridors to your room, you'll find the mystique ends with common, corporate accommodations. Some rooms' floor-to-ceiling views may be memorable, but the decor definitely is not. Unless you're staying in one of the more luxurious abodes, the feel and decor here is impersonal and plain—perfect for the convention-eers, but not for a romantic weekend.

Dining/Entertainment: Cityscape, on the 46th floor, serves classic California cuisine with a breathtaking 360° view; the retractable skylight exposes the night sky in all its grandeur. Kiki of Tokyo offers Japanese cuisine. The Mason Street Deli serves breakfast and lunch, and Intermezzo offers Italian-style food to eat in or to go. An elegant sidewalk cafe, The Café on the Square, provides a spot for watching the passing parade.

Services: Room service (6am to midnight), concierge, laundry, shoe shine.

Facilities: Swimming pool, health club, business center, car rental, tour desk, shopping arcade. Towers-level accommodations offer upgraded services, including separate registration lounge with complimentary breakfast and hors d'oeuvres and daily newspaper.

San Francisco Marriott. 55 Fourth St. (between Market and Mission sts.), San Francisco, CA 94103. ☎ **415/896-1600** or 800/228-9290. Fax 415/442-0141. 1,366 rms, 134 suites. A/C MINIBAR TV TEL. $149–$189 standard double; $195–$265 concierge-level double; from $350 suite. Continental breakfast $6.95 extra. AE, CB, DC, JCB, MC, V. Parking $24. Cable car: Powell-Hyde and Powell-Mason lines (3 blocks west). All Market St. buses. Muni Metro: All Market St. trams.

Some call it a masterpiece, others liken it to the world's biggest parking meter. Regardless, the Marriott is one of the largest buildings in the city, making it a popular stopover for convention-goers and those looking for a room with a view. Fortunately, the controversy does not extend to the rooms, so expect pleasant accommodations with large bathrooms and beds and exceptional city vistas. Rooms on the concierge level are more spacious and provide a lengthy list of complimentary services, including continental breakfast, afternoon snacks and beverages, evening hors d'oeuvres and canapés, and an open honor bar. Upon arrival, enter from Fourth Street, between Market and Mission, to avoid a long trek to the registration area.

Dining/Entertainment: Kinoko is a Japanese teppanyaki restaurant and sushi bar. Allie's American Grill, facing the hotel's central fountain, has a breakfast bar and two buffets that prepare made-to-order omelets; there is also a varied lunch and dinner menu. You can choose between the Atrium Lounge and the View Lounge, which has a truly panoramic view of the bay and Golden Gate Bridge (assuming there's no fog) as well as live entertainment.

Facilities: Indoor pool and health club, business center, tour desk, car-rental, and gift shop.

Westin St. Francis. 335 Powell St. (between Geary and Post sts.), San Francisco, CA 94102. ☎ **415/397-7000** or 800/228-3000. Fax 415/774-0124. 1,192 rms, 83 suites. A/C MINIBAR TV TEL. Main building: $185–$305 double; from $225 suite. Tower: $265–$305 double; from $375 suite. Extra person $30. Continental breakfast $12.50 extra. AE, DC, DISC, JCB, MC, V. Parking $24. Cable car: Powell-Hyde and Powell-Mason lines (direct stop). Bus: 2, 3, 4, 30, 45, or 76.

At the turn of the century Charles T. Crocker and a few of his wealthy buddies decided that San Francisco needed a world-class hotel, and up went the St. Francis. Since then, hordes of VIPs have hung their hats and hosiery here, including Emperor Hirohito, Queen Elizabeth II, Mother Teresa, King Juan Carlos of Spain, the Shah of Iran, and all the U.S. presidents since Taft. In 1972 the 32-story Tower was added,

---

---

doubling the capacity and adding the requisite banquet and conference centers (as well as Club Oz, the hotel's rooftop dance club). The older rooms of the main building vary in size and have more old-world charm than the newer tower rooms, but the Tower is remarkable for its great views of the city once you rise above the 18th floor.

Though too massive to offer the personal service you get at the smaller deluxe hotels on Nob Hill, few other hotels in San Francisco can match the majestic aura of the St. Francis. We know it sounds corny, but the St. Francis is so intertwined with the city's past that it truly *is* San Francisco: Stroll through the vast, ornate lobby and you can feel 100 years of history oozing from its hand-carved redwood paneling. Even if you stay elsewhere, it's worth a visit if only to partake in high tea at the Compass Rose, one of San Francisco's most enduring and enjoyable traditions.

Dining/Entertainment: Club Oz, a popular dance club with a hefty cover on weekend nights, is open nightly. The lobby-level Dewey's, a sports bar, offers a do-it-yourself luncheon buffet, and burgers and pizzas at night. Dutch Kitchen, also on the lower level, offers a basic breakfast menu. The Compass Rose is open daily for lunch and afternoon tea (3 to 5pm), with live music, dancing, champagne, cocktails, and caviar tasting in the evening.

Services: 24-hour room service, voice mail, baby-sitting referral, Westin Kids Club (great for families), laundry.

Facilities: Fitness center, business center, tour and car rental desks, barber/beauty salon, gift shop.

EXPENSIVE

Donatello. 501 Post St. (at Mason Street), San Francisco, CA 94102. ☎ **415/441-7100** or 800/227-3184, or 800/792-9837 in California. Fax 415/885-8842. 91 rms, 3 suites. A/C TV TEL. $180–$215 double; from $275 suite. Additional person $25. Children under 12 stay free in parents' room. Continental breakfast $9 extra. AE, CB, DC, DISC, MC, V. Parking $16. Cable car: Powell-Hyde and Powell-Mason lines (2 blocks west). Bus: 2, 3, 4, 30, or 45.

If you're not looking for trendy or common corporate accommodations, but rather old-world class, book a room here. The Donatello is, in a word, dignified. The lobby is classy, with Italian marble and a serious staff. The rooms, which are some of the largest in the city, are airy and decorated with traditional dark-wood antiques, tapestries, and original art. Unfortunately, there's no great view from the extra-large windows, and some of the furnishings need to be updated, but each room comes with a dish of hard candies and bottled Italian water as well as guaranteed service from an attentive (though sometimes stuffy) staff. In-room amenities include extra-length beds, voice-mail phones, data ports, and terry-cloth bathrobes. Another plus is the roof-terrace lounge; too bad much of the view is blocked by surrounding buildings.

Dining/Entertainment: The intimate Zingari serves Italian cuisine at lunch and dinner; cocktails are available in the lounge.

Handlery Union Square Hotel. 351 Geary St. (between Mason and Powell sts.), San Francisco, CA 94102. ☎ **415/781-7800** or 800/843-4343. Fax 415/781-0269. 376 rms, 20 suites. A/C TV TEL. $130–$160 basic double; club section: from $160 double, from $220 suite. Extra person $10. AE, CB, DC, MC, V. Parking $15. Cable car: Powell-Hyde and Powell-Mason lines (direct stop). Bus: 2, 3, 4, 30, 38, or 45.

Think of the Handlery as place where Matlock would love to stay. A mere half a block from Union Square, the Handlery covers all bets by offering every amenity you could possibly need combined with completely nonoffensive (read: dull as Grandma's house) rooms. All the large, newly redecorated guest rooms come with the basic accouterments, including cable TV, coffeemaker, phone, and Nintendo system. An extra $10 per night buys you a membership to "The Club," which provides its members with a complimentary morning newspaper and turndown service, an extra dressing room, bathroom scale, robes, hair dryer, two phones, refrigerator, and—here's the clincher—an electric shoe polisher. Hip-hoppers can skip this one; it's the nuclear families and older folks that the Handlery caters to.

Services: Multilingual concierge staff, same-day laundry, baby-sitting.

Facilities: Heated outdoor swimming pool and sauna, barber shop, tour desk, gift shop.

✪ **Hotel Triton.** 342 Grant Ave. (at Bush St.), San Francisco, CA 94108. ☎ **415/394-0500** or 800/433-6611. Fax 415/394-0555. 140 rms, 7 suites. A/C MINIBAR TV TEL. $119–179 double; $199–279 suite. Continental breakfast $7.75 extra. AE, DC, DISC, MC, V. Parking $20. Cable car: Powell-Hyde and Powell-Mason lines (2 blocks west).

Executing a bold idea that was long overdue, hotelier magnate Bill Kimpton requisitioned a cadre of local artists and designers to "do their thing" to his latest acquisition, the Hotel Triton. The result was San Francisco's first three-star hotel to finally break the boring barrier. Described as vogue, chic, retro-futuristic, and even neo-Baroque, the Triton begs attention from the Daliesque lobby to the sumptuous designer suites à la Jerry Garcia, Wyland (the ocean artist), and Joe Boxer. Two dozen environmentally sensitive "EcoRooms"—biodegradable soaps, filtered water and air, all-natural linens—were also installed to please the tree-hugger in all of us. A mild caveat: Don't expect perfection; many of the rooms could use a little touching up here and there (stained curtains, chipped furniture), and service isn't as snappy as it could be. If you can live with this, and want to inject a little fun and style into your stay, then come join Dorothy and Toto for a trip far from Kansas.

Dining/Entertainment: Café de la Presse, a European-style newsstand and outdoor cafe, serves breakfast, lunch, and dinner. In the hotel lobby, complimentary coffee is served each morning and wine each evening.

Services: Room service, same-day laundry.

Facilities: Business center, exercise room.

Inn at Union Square. 440 Post St. (between Mason and Powell sts.), San Francisco, CA 94102. ☎ **415/397-3510** or 800/288-4346. Fax 415/989-0529. 23 rms, 7 suites. TV TEL. $130–$300 double. Rates include continental breakfast. AE, DC, JCB, MC, V. Parking $18. Cable car: Powell-Hyde and Powell-Mason lines. Bus: 2, 3, 4, 30, 38, or 45.

As narrow as an Amsterdam abode, the Inn at Union Square is a veritable antithesis to the big, impersonal hotels that surround Union Square. If you need plenty of elbow room, skip this one. But if you're looking for the type of inn whose staff knows the names of each guest and afternoon tea comes with crisp cucumber sandwiches, then read on. A half block west of the square, the seven-story inn makes up for its small stature by spoiling its guests with a pile of perks. Mornings start with breakfast served at your door along with *The New York Times,* followed by afternoon tea and evening hors d'oeuvres served in adorable little fireplace lounges at the end of each hall. The rooms, each handsomely and individually decorated with Georgian reproductions and floral fabrics, are smaller than average but infinitely more

Tom Sweeny, the head doorman at the Sir Francis Drake Hotel, is San Francisco's living historical monument. Dressed in traditional Beefeater attire (you can't miss those $1,400 duds), he's been the subject of countless snapshots for the past 18 years—an average 200 per day—and has shaken hands with every president since Jerry Ford.

appreciable than the cookie-cutter rooms of most larger hotels. Complete business services are available, as well as the use of a health club.

Juliana Hotel. 590 Bush St. (at Stockton St.), San Francisco, CA 94108. ☎ **415/392-2540** or 800/328-3880. Fax 415/391-8447. 84 rms, 22 suites. A/C MINIBAR TV TEL. $135–165 double; $169–179 junior suite; $179–189 executive suite. Special winter packages available. Continental breakfast $7.95 extra. AE, CB, DC, MC, V. Parking $16. Cable car: Powell-Hyde and Powell-Mason lines (1 block west). Bus: 2, 3, 4, 30, 38, or 45.

We love the lobby at this small, European-style hotel. With its rich, homey surroundings, English prints, and comfy couches facing a blazing fire, which is ensconced in brass and marble, it feels more like a rich friend's study than the entrance to a hotel. With the addition of daily papers hanging on a wooden rack, the Juliana has created a place that makes us want to kick up our feet and stay awhile. And with the complimentary coffee here by day and wine by night, there's no real reason to leave.

The rooms are light, spacious, and country-cute in a Laura Ashley kind of way, with floral drapes and bedspreads, white furnishings, and cozy, upholstered chairs. The bathroom, like the lobby, has homey touches like a large well-lit mirror, hair dryer, and a wicker basket holding soap and other house toiletries.

Services: Room service, laundry/valet, morning transport to the Financial District. Guests enjoy access to an off-premises health club.

Sir Francis Drake. 450 Powell St. (at Sutter St.), San Francisco, CA 94102. ☎ **415/392-7755** or 800/227-5480. Fax 415/677-9341. 412 rooms, 5 suites. A/C MINIBAR TV TEL. $149–$199 double; $185–$600 suite. AE, CB, DC, DISC, MC, V. Parking $23. Cable car: Powell-Hyde and Powell-Mason lines (direct stop). Bus: 2, 3, 4, 45, or 76.

It took a change of ownership and a multimillion-dollar restoration to save the Sir Francis Drake from becoming a Starbucks, but now this stately old queen is once again housing guests in grand fashion. Granted, this venerable septuagenarian is still showing signs of age (the owners admit there's still more work to be done), but the price of imperfection is certainly reflected in the room rate: a good $100 less per night than its Nob Hill cousins. The new Sir Francis Drake is a hotel for people who are willing to trade a chipped bathroom tile or oddly matched furniture for the opportunity to vacation in pseudo-grand fashion. Allow Tom Sweeny, the ever-ebullient (and legendary) Beefeater doorman, to handle your bags as you make your entrance into the elegant, captivating lobby. Sip cocktails at the superchic Starlight Lounge overlooking the city. Dine at Scala's Bistro, one of the hottest new restaurants in the city. In short, live like the king or queen of Union Square without all the pomp, circumstance, and credit card bills.

Dining/Entertainment: Scala Bistro at the lobby level serves excellent Italian cuisine in a stylish setting (see Chapter 6, "Dining," for complete information); Café Expresso, a small Parisian-style corner cafe, does an equally commendable job serving coffees, pastries, and sandwiches daily. The Starlight Room on the 21st floor offers cocktails, entertainment, and dancing nightly with a panoramic view of the city.

Services: Room service, business services, valet, concierge.

Facilities: Exercise room, extensive meeting facilities.

Villa Florence. 225 Powell St. (between Geary and O'Farrell sts.), San Francisco, CA 94102. ☎ **415/397-7700** or 800/553-4411. Fax 415/397-1006. 177 rms (36 suites). A/C MINIBAR TV TEL. $149–$159 double; $169–$179 junior suite; $249 deluxe suite. Continental breakfast $7.95 extra. AE, CB, DC, DISC, MC, V. Parking $18. Cable car: Powell-Hyde and Powell-Mason lines (direct stop). Bus: 2, 3, 4, 30, 38, or 45.

Located half a block south of Union Square and fronting the Powell Street cable car line, the seven-story Villa Florence is parked in one of the liveliest sections of the city (no need to drive, 'cause you're already here). While the aging rooms at the Villa Florence could use some redecorating—ubiquitous floral-print upholstery with an equally ubiquitous peach-colored theme just doesn't work anymore—amenities such as wonderfully comfortable beds and large bathrooms with hand-milled soap and hair dryers help even the score. But never mind the rooms: It's the hotel's restaurant that makes it a worthy contender among Union Square's medium-priced inns. As if the location alone weren't reason enough to book a room, adjoining the hotel is Kuleto's, one of San Francisco's most popular and stylish Italian restaurants (trust me, you'll want to make a reservation for dinner along with your room).

Hotel Vintage Court. 650 Bush St. (between Powell and Stockton sts.), San Francisco, CA 94108. ☎ **415/392-4666** or 800/654-1100. Fax 415/433-4065. 106 rms, 1 suite. A/C MINIBAR TV TEL. $119–$159 double; $275 penthouse suite. AE, CB, DC, DISC, MC, V. Parking $16. Cable car: Powell-Hyde and Powell-Mason lines (direct stop). Bus: 2, 3, 4, 30, 45, or 76.

Consistent personal service has prompted a loyal clientele at this European-style hotel located two blocks north of Union Square.

The lobby, accented with dark wood, deep green, and rose, is welcoming enough to actually spend a little time in, especially when the nightly complimentary California wines are being poured.

But the varietals don't stop at ground level. Each tidy room, renovated in 1995, is named after a winery and mimics a wine country excursion with its floral bed-spreads, matching drapes, and trellised wall-to-wall loop carpeting. Opus One, the deluxe, two-room penthouse suite, includes an original 1912 stained-glass skylight, a wood-burning fireplace, a whirlpool tub, a complete entertainment center, and panoramic views of the city.

The hotel's dining room, Masa's, serving traditional French fare, is one of the top restaurants in San Francisco (see Chapter 6, "Dining," for complete information). Services include free morning transportation to the Financial District, tour desk, and car-rental service. There is also access to an off-premises health club. Breakfast available in dining room.

✪ **White Swan Inn.** 845 Bush St. (between Taylor and Mason sts.), San Francisco, CA 94108. ☎ **415/775-1755.** Fax 415/775-5717. 23 rms, 3 suites. MINIBAR TV TEL. $145–$160 double; $195 romance suites; $250 two-room suite. Extra person $15. Rates include full breakfast. AE, MC, V. Parking $19. Cable car: California St. line (1 block north). Bus: 1, 2, 3, 4, 27, or 45.

From the moment you are buzzed in to this well-secured inn, you'll know you're not in a generic bed and breakfast. More than 50 teddy bears grace the lobby, and if that doesn't cure homesickness, complimentary homemade cookies, tea, and coffee will. The romantically homey rooms are warm and cozy—the perfect place to snuggle up with a good book. They're also quite big, with hardwood entryways, rich, dark wood furniture, working fireplaces, and an assortment of books tucked in nooks (in case you forgot one). The decor is English elegance at its best, if not to excess, with floral prints almost everywhere. Wine and hors d'oeuvres are served every evening. The Romance suites are not much better than regular rooms, just a little bigger with the addition of chocolates and champagne. Its location—2 1/2 blocks from Union

Square—makes this 1900s building a charming and serene choice with service and style to satisfy the most discriminating traveler. All guests enjoy access to an off-premises health club.

Dining/Entertainment: Each morning a generous breakfast is served in a common room just off a tiny garden. Afternoon tea is also served, with hors d'oeuvres, sherry, wine, and home-baked pastries. You can have your sherry in front of the fireplace while you browse through the books in the library. Note that there's no smoking.

Services: Concierge, laundry, evening turndown, morning newspaper, overnight shoe shine.

MODERATE

Andrews Hotel. 624 Post St. (between Jones and Taylor sts.), San Francisco, CA 94109. ☎ **415/563-6877** or 800/926-3739. Fax 415/928-6919. 43 rms, 5 suites. MINIBAR TV TEL. $86–$109 double; $119 petite suite. Rates include continental breakfast and evening wine. AE, DC, MC, V. Parking $15. Cable car: Powell-Hyde and Powell-Mason lines (3 blocks east). Bus: 2, 3, 4, 30, 38, or 45.

Two blocks west of Union Square, the Andrews was formerly a Turkish bath before its conversion in 1981. As is fitting with Euro-style hotels, the rooms are small but well maintained and comfortable; white lace curtains and fresh flowers in each room add a light touch. Some rooms have shower only, and bathrooms in general tend to be tiny, but for the location—a few blocks from Union Square—and price, the Andrews is a safe bet for an enjoyable stay in the city. An added bonus is the adjoining Fino Bar and Ristorante, which offers complimentary wine to its hotel guests in the evening.

ⓢ Hotel Bedford. 761 Post St. (between Leavenworth and Jones sts.), San Francisco, CA 94109. ☎ 415/673-6040 or 800/227-5642. Fax 415/563-6739. 137 rms, 7 suites. MINIBAR TV TEL. $109–$129 double; from $175 suite. Continental breakfast $8.50 extra. AE, CB, DC, JCB, MC, V. Parking $18. Cable car: Powell-Hyde and Powell-Mason lines (4 blocks east). Bus: 2, 3, 4, or 27.

For the price and location (three blocks from Union Square) the Bedford offers a darn good deal. You won't be paying for lavish furniture, but you will find clean, large, sunny rooms, not to mention an incredibly enthusiastic, attentive, and professional staff. Each accommodation is well furnished with king, queen, or two double beds, VCR, writing desk, and armchair. Many rooms have priceless views of the city.

The hotel's Wedgewood Lounge is a small, beautiful mahogany bar opposite the registration desk. Canvas Café, an enormous eatery located behind the lobby, is under separate management. Services include room service (for breakfast only), valet parking, and complimentary wine in the lobby each evening from 5 to 6pm. There's a video library, and free morning limousine service to the Financial District.

Beresford Arms. 701 Post St. (at Jones St.), San Francisco, CA 94109. ☎ **415/673-2600** or 800/533-6533. Fax 415/474-0449. 92 rms, 52 suites. MINIBAR TV TEL. $99 double; $115 Jacuzzi suite; $150 parlor suite. Rates include continental breakfast. Extra person $10. Children under 12 stay free in parents' room. Senior-citizen discount available. AE, CB, DC, DISC, MC, V. Parking $15. Cable car: Powell-Hyde line (three blocks east). Bus: 2, 3, 4, 27, or 38.

Every time we visit the Beresford Arms, its lobby always seems filled with happy, chatty Europeans. Maybe it's the Jacuzzi whirlpool bathtubs and bidets that keep them smiling, or the "Manager's Social Hour" with free wine and snacks. The price is fair, too: $115 for a large, reasonably attractive (though a bit old-fashioned) suite with a choice of wet bar or fully equipped kitchen—a key for families. Modest business services are available, as is valet or self-parking. The hotel's location, sandwiched between the Theater District and Union Square in a quieter section of San Francisco, is ideal for car-free visitors.

Hotel Beresford. 635 Sutter St. (near Mason St.), San Francisco, CA 94102. ☎ **415/ 673-9900** or 800/533-6533. Fax 415/474-0449. 114 rms. MINIBAR TV TEL. $99–$104 double. Rates include continental breakfast. Extra person $5. Children under 12 stay free in parents' room. Senior-citizen discounts available. Ask for special rates. AE, CB, DC, DISC, MC, V. Parking $15. Cable car: Powell-Hyde line (1 block east). Bus: 2, 3, 4, 30, 38, or 45.

Small and friendly, the seven-floor Hotel Beresford is a decent, moderately priced choice near Union Square. Rooms have a mish-mash of furniture and stocked fridges; some even have Jacuzzi tubs. Everything's well kept, but don't expect much more than a clean place to rest.

The White Horse restaurant, an attractive replica of an old English pub, serves a complimentary continental breakfast, as well as lunch and dinner.

Cartwright Hotel. 524 Sutter St. (at Powell St.), San Francisco, CA 94102. ☎ **415/421-2865** or 800/227-3844. Fax 415/421-2345. 111 rms, 5 suites. TV TEL. $99–$139 double or twin; $179–$229 family suite sleeping four. Rates include continental breakfast and afternoon tea. AE, CB, DC, DISC, MC, V. Parking $16. Cable car: Powell-Hyde and Powell-Mason lines (direct stop). Bus: 2, 3, 4, 30, or 45.

Diametrically opposed to the hip-hop, happenin' Hotel Triton down the street, the Cartwright Hotel is geared toward the "older, mature traveler" (as hotel marketers like to put it). The hotel management takes pride in its reputation for offering clean, comfortable rooms at fair prices, which explains why most of its guests have been repeat customers for a *long* time. Remarkably quiet despite its convenient location near one of the busiest downtown corners, the eight-story hotel looks not unlike it did some 80 years ago when it first opened. High-quality antiques collected during its decades of faithful service furnish the lobby, as well as each of the individually decorated rooms. A nice perk usually reserved for fancier hotels is the fully equipped bathrooms, all of which have tubs, shower massages, thick fluffy towels, and terry-cloth robes. Tip: Request a room with a view of the backyard; they're the quietest. Guests have access to a nearby health club; complimentary wine, tea, and cookies are served in the small library adjacent to the lobby from 5 to 6pm.

✪ **Commodore International.** 825 Sutter St. (at Jones St.), San Francisco, CA 94109. ☎ **415/923-6800** or 800/338-6848. Fax 415/923-6804. 113 rms. TV TEL. $69–$89 double or twin. AE, DC, MC, V. Parking $12. Bus: 2, 3, 4, 27, or 76.

If you're looking to pump a little fun and fantasy into your vacation, this is the place. Before its new owners revamped the aging Commodore from top to bottom, it—well, okay, it sucked. Then along came San Francisco hotelier Chip Conley who, pumped with his success in transforming the Phoenix Hotel into a rocker's retreat, instantly recognized this dilapidated eyesore's potential, added it to his collection, then let his hip-hop decor designers do their magic. The result? One groovy hotel. Stealing the show is the Red Room, a Big Apple–style bar and lounge that reflects no other spectrum but ruby red (you gotta see this one). The stylish lobby comes in a close second, followed by the adjoining Titanic Café, a cute little diner serving buckwheat griddlecakes and dragon fire salads. Appealing to the masses, Chip left the first four floors as standard no-frills—though quite clean and comfortable—rooms, while deckinging out the top two floors in Neo-Deco overtones (well worth the extra $10 per night).

Cornell Hotel. 715 Bush St. (between Powell and Mason sts.), San Francisco, CA 94108. ☎ **415/421-3154** or 800/232-9698. Fax 415/399-1442. 60 rms. TV TEL. $85–$105 double. Rates include full breakfast (except Sundays, when it's continental). Weekly room package including seven breakfasts and five dinners, $600 double. AE, CB, DC, MC, V. Parking $12. Cable car: Powell-Hyde and Powell-Mason lines. Bus: 2, 3, 4, 30, or 45.

It's the quirks that make this hotel more charming than many in its price range. You'll be greeted by Rameau, the house golden retriever, when you enter this small French-style hotel. Pass the office, where a few faces will glance up in your direction and smile, and embark on a ride in the old-fashioned elevator to get to your room. Each floor is dedicated to a French painter and is decorated with reproductions. Rooms are all plain and comfortable, with a desk and chairs, and individually decorated in a bland, modern style. No smoking is allowed in any of them. A full breakfast is included in the cavernlike provincial basement dining room, Jeanne d'Arc, and Union Square is a few blocks away.

✪ **Hotel Diva.** 440 Geary St. (between Mason and Taylor sts.), San Francisco, CA 94102. ☎ **415/885-0200** or 800/553-1900. Fax 415/346-6613. 98 rms, 12 suites. A/C TV TEL. $119 double; $139 junior suite, $300 villa suite. Rates include continental breakfast. AE, DC, DISC, JCB, MC, V. Parking $17. Bus: 38 or 38L.

Appropriately named, the Diva is the prima donna of San Francisco's modern hotels and one of our favorites. A showbiz darling when it opened in 1985, the Diva won "Best Hotel Design" by *Interiors Magazine* for its sleek, ultramodern interiors. A stunning profusion of curvaceous glass, marble, and steel mark the Euro-tech lobby, while the rooms, each spotless and neat, are softened with utterly fashionable "Italian Modern" furnishings. Nary a beat is missed with the toys and services either: VCRs (with discreet video vending machine), Nintendo, pay-per-view, valet parking, room service, complimentary room-delivered breakfast, and on-site fitness and business centers complete the package. Insider tip: Reserve one of the rooms ending in "09," which come with extra-large bathrooms with vanity mirrors and makeup tables.

The Fitzgerald. 620 Post St. (between Powell and Mason sts.), San Francisco, CA 94109. ☎ **415/775-8100** or 800/334-6835. Fax 415/775-1278. 42 rms, 5 suites. TV TEL. $79–$115 double. Rates include continental breakfast. Extra person $10. Lower rates in winter. AE, DISC, JCB, MC, V. Parking $15. Bus: 2, 3, 4, or 27.

If you think the guy at the front desk looks cramped in his nook of a lobby, wait till you get to your room. The Fitzgerald's 47 guest accommodations may be outfitted with new furniture that's accented with bright bedspreads and patterned carpet, but some of the rooms are really small (one that we saw had a dresser less than a foot from the bed). Ask for a larger room. If you can live without a sizable closet (read tiny), the price, breakfast, and newness of this hotel make it a good value.

Suites, some of which are located on no-smoking floors, include an additional sitting room furnished with a fold-out couch.

Breakfasts include home-baked breads, scones, muffins, juice, tea, and coffee. A nearby off-premises swimming pool is available free for guests' use.

Kensington Park Hotel. 450 Post St. (between Powell and Mason sts.), San Francisco, CA 94102. ☎ **415/788-6400** or 800/553-1900. Fax 415/399-9484. 82 rms, 2 suites. TV TEL. $115 double; $350 suite. Rates include continental breakfast. 50% discount for postmidnight check-in. Extra person $10. AE, CB, DC, MC, V. Parking $16. Cable car: Powell-Hyde and Powell-Mason lines (2 blocks east).

The Kensington caught us by surprise. We were expecting another boutique hotel with bland decor and wrinkles from age. What we found was a cheery, eager-to-please staff, tasteful accommodations, and extra efforts that showed the hotel really cared about its guests. Rooms are reminiscent of old England, with traditional ornate mahogany furnishings, beautiful damask fabrics, and enormous armoires—far more attractive than most hotel furnishings. Bathrooms may be small, but they're sweetly appointed in brass and marble. As for the views, ask for an upper corner room, and you'll be getting far beyond your money's worth. Additional services include complimentary coffee and croissants, available on each floor every morning from 7 to 10am; complimentary tea, sherry, and cookies every afternoon; and a complimentary piano-accompanied wine hour on Thursdays. If you really want the full treatment, book the Royal Suite, which contains a canopy bed, fireplace, and Jacuzzi. Guests have access to an off-premises health club.

The hotel offers 50% off-rack rates to guests who arrive after midnight. (No advance reservations are accepted, and the offer is restricted to a one-night maximum.)

Services: Room service, concierge, same-day laundry, morning newspaper, complimentary morning limo to the Financial District; fax and secretarial services also available.

King George Hotel. 334 Mason St. (between Geary and O'Farrell sts.), San Francisco, CA 94102. ☎ **415/781-5050** or 800/288-6005. Fax 415/391-6976. 138 rms, 2 suites. TV TEL. $125 double; $205 suite. Special-value packages available seasonally. Continental breakfast $5.75 extra. AE, CB, DC, DISC, JCB, MC, V. Parking $16.50. Cable car: Powell-Hyde and Powell-Mason lines (1 block west). Bus: 2, 3, 4, 30, 38, or 45.

Built in 1914 for the Panama-Pacific Exhibition when rooms went for $1 per night, the King George has fared well over the years, continuing to draw a mostly European clientele. The location—surrounded by cable car lines, the theater district, Union Square, and dozens of restaurants—is superb, and the rooms are surprisingly quiet for such a busy location. Though the decor is a bit old-fashioned, every room is meticulously neat and clean with full private baths and large beds. A big hit since it started a few years back is the hotel's English afternoon tea, served above the lobby Monday through Saturday from 3 to 6:30pm.

Services include 24-hour room service, concierge, laundry/valet, and business center.

Monticello Inn. 127 Ellis St. (between Mason and Powell sts.), San Francisco, CA 94102. ☎ **415/392-8800** or 800/669-7777. Fax 415/398-2650. 91 rms, 36 suites. A/C TV TEL. From $99 double; from $129 suite. Rates include continental breakfast, afternoon tea, and evening wine. Extra person $10. AE, CB, DC, DISC, MC, V. Parking $16. Cable car: Powell-Hyde and Powell-Mason lines (direct stop). Muni Metro: All Market St. metros. All Market St. buses.

Okay, we'll admit it: We didn't know Monticello was the estate of Thomas Jefferson, and we also didn't know that the Monticello mansion is on the tail side of the nickel (Tom's noggin is on the front.) Why the history lesson? In addition to the moniker, "Monticello" is also the hotel's theme. Federal style decor, Chippendale furnishings, grandfather clocks, Revolutionary War paintings, a toasty, brass-mantled fireplace, and various other old stuff scattered around the lobby attempt to create a colonial milieu. Though it makes for a pleasant entrance, unfortunately the period effect doesn't quite follow through to the rooms. Though the rooms are comfortable, spacious, and reasonably attractive, the stark blue carpets and floral upholstery don't have the same faux-Federal theme (certainly the homely air conditioners recessed into the walls don't help). If you can live with this, however, you'll be quite content here. The service is wonderful, the downtown location is primo, parking comes with in-out privileges, and there's even free access to a great fitness club around the block.

Dining/Entertainment: The hotel's restaurant, Puccini and Pinetti, features modern Italian cuisine; it's located next door, at the corner of Ellis and Cyril Magnin streets (see Chapter 6, "Dining," for complete information).

Services: Same-day laundry, valet service, limousine service to Financial District.

✪ **Petite Auberge.** 863 Bush St. (between Taylor and Mason sts.), San Francisco, CA 94108. ☎ **415/928-6000.** Fax 415/775-5717. 26 rms. TV TEL. $110–160 double; $220 petite suite. Rates include continental breakfast. AE, DC, MC, V. Parking $17. Cable car: Powell-Hyde and Powell-Mason lines. Bus: 2, 3, 4, 30, 38, or 45.

The Petite Auberge is so pathetically cute we can't stand it. We want to say it's overdone, that any hotel filled with teddy bears is absurd, but we can't. Bribed each year with a chocolate chip cookie from their never-empty platter, we make our rounds through the rooms and ruefully admit to ourselves that we're just going to have to use that word we loath to hear: *adorable.*

Nobody does French country like the Petite Auberge. Hand-crafted armoires, delicate lace curtains, cozy little fireplaces, adorable (there's that word again) little antiques and knickknacks—no hotel in Provence ever had it this good. Honeymooners should splurge on the Petite suite, which has its own private entrance, deck, spa tub, refrigerator, and coffeemaker. The breakfast room, with its mural of a country market scene, terra-cotta tile floors, French country decor, and gold-yellow tablecloths, opens onto a small garden where California wines and tea are served in the afternoon.

✪ **The Raphael.** 386 Geary St. (at Mason St.), San Francisco, CA 94102. ☎ **415/986-2000** or 800/821-5343. Fax 415/397-2447. 150 rms, 2 suites. A/C TV TEL. $109–$139 double; $160–$225 suite. Additional person $10. Corporate and weekend discounts available. Continental breakfast $8.29 extra. AE, CB, DC, DISC, MC, V. Parking $16. Cable car: Powell-Hyde and Powell-Mason lines (2 blocks east). Bus: 2, 3, 4, 30, 38, or 45.

From the old-style lobby and stained-glass–capped elevators to the mishmash of furniture in each room, this place has the feeling it's been around forever. The staff is amazingly friendly and helpful, and the price for the location (one block from Union Square) can't be beat. Unfortunately, the most exciting spaces are the hallways; they're decorated in fabulously funky colors and patterns, and each door is hand painted, playful, and distinct. The rooms are less artistic, but do offer an eclectic collection of period reproductions, plenty of space, two phones, makeup mirrors, and hair dryers. Small extra touches include a rose on arrival and complimentary coffee each morning in the lobby. Considering the price, space, and service, this is a darn good deal. Services offered include 24-hour room service, twice-daily maid service, laundry/valet, and nightly turndown.

Hotel Rex. 562 Sutter St. (between Powell and Mason sts), San Francisco, CA 94102. ☎ **415/433-4434** or 800/433-4434. Fax 415/433-3695. 94 rms, 2 suites. MINIBAR TV TEL. $115–$160 double; $225 suite. AE, CB, DC, MC, V. Parking $14. Cable car: Powell-Hyde and Powell-Mason lines (1 block east). Bus: 2, 3, 4, 30, 38, or 45.

Joie De Vivre, the most creative hotel group in the city, recently acquired this historic building (formerly the Orchard Hotel), which is situated near several fine galleries, theaters, and restaurants. They've kept some of the hotel's imported furnishings, and it will remain a European boutique hotel, but they have given the lobby and rooms a half-million-dollar facelift, adding a decorative flair that makes their hotels among the most popular in town. The clublike lobby lounge is modeled after a 1920s library and is, like all their properties, cleverly stylish. Joie de Vivre is positioning the Rex as a hotel for the arts and literary community (not unlike the Algonquin Hotel in New York City), and in that spirit an antiquarian bookstore adjoins the lobby.

The renovated rooms, which are all above average in size, feature telephones with voice mail and data port and a new electronic key card system. If you have one of the rooms in the back, you'll look out over a shady, peaceful courtyard (that's something you won't get in New York City). Attention to the details makes Hotel Rex one of the better choices in this price range downtown.

Services: Room service, concierge, same-day laundry/dry cleaning, complimentary newspaper, and complimentary evening wine hour.

Facilities: Access to an off-premises health club across the street.

✪ **Savoy Hotel.** 580 Geary St. (between Taylor and Jones sts.), San Francisco, CA 94102. ☎ **415/441-2700** or 800/227-4223. Fax 415/441-2700. 70 rms, 13 suites. MINIBAR TV TEL. $115–$125 double; from $155 suite. Ask about package, government, senior, and corporate rates. Rates include continental breakfast. AE, CB, DC, DISC, MC, V. Parking $16. Bus: 2, 3, 4, 27, or 38.

Both travelers and *Travel and Leisure* agree that the Savoy is an excellent, and affordable, small hotel a few blocks off Union Square. The medium-size rooms are cozy French provincial, with 18th-century period furnishings, featherbeds, and goosedown pillows—plus modern conveniences such as remote-control color TVs and hair dryers. Other perks include: triple sheets, turndown service, full-length mirrors, and two-line telephones. Guests also enjoy concierge service and overnight shoe-shine free of charge. Rates include complimentary late-afternoon sherry and tea and continental breakfast, served in the Brasserie Savoy, a seafood restaurant that brings even the locals downtown for dinner (see Chapter 6, "Dining," for complete details).

The Shannon Court. 550 Geary St. (between Jones and Taylor sts.), San Francisco, CA 94102. ☎ **415/775-5000** or 800/821-0493. Fax 415/928-6813. 168 rms, 5 suites. TV TEL. $105–$120 double or twin; from $200 suite. Extra person $10. Senior, government, AAA, group, and promotional rates. Continental breakfast $6.50 extra. AE, CB, DC, MC, V. Parking $14. Cable car: Powell-Hyde and Powell-Mason lines (3 blocks east). Bus: 2, 3, 4, 30, 38, or 45.

The Shannon Court's 1929 landmark building maintains its original Spanish flavor, with gracefully curved arches, white stucco walls, and highly polished brass fixtures in the lobby. When you head off for your room, however, the cheery atmosphere disappears in the dark, cold hallways. But don't turn and head for nearest motel yet. You'll be pleasantly surprised at how large, quiet (especially in the back portion of the building), and sunny the rooms are. Decor is classic old-hotel style, and most rooms have either a sitting area or an extended bathroom. Extras include a small unstocked fridge, and many rooms have couches and writing desks. The hotel's five suites are on the 16th floor; two have rooftop terraces. Although the rooms were renovated in 1989, the building is almost 70 years old, so expect to see a little age.

Complimentary morning coffee and afternoon tea are available in the lobby.

The City of Paris restaurant, a favorite with the theater crowd, adjoins the hotel and is open daily from 7am to midnight; aside from decent fare at affordable prices, there's also an oyster bar, a good wine list, and a full bar that remains open until 2am.

Warwick Regis. 490 Geary St. (between Mason and Taylor sts.), San Francisco, CA 94102. ☎ **415/928-7900** or 800/827-3447. Fax 415/441-8788. 40 rms, 40 suites. A/C MINIBAR TV TEL. $110–$150 double. Rates include continental breakfast. AE, DC, DISC, MC, V. Parking $18. Cable car: Powell-Hyde and Powell Mason lines. Bus: 2, 3, 4, 27 or 38.

Louis XVI may have been a rotten monarch, but he certainly had taste. Fashioned in the style of pre-Revolutionary France (ca. 18th century), the Warwick is awash with pristine French and English antiques, Italian marble, chandeliers, four-poster beds, hand-carved headboards, and the like. The result is an expensive-looking hotel that, for all its pleasantries and perks, is surprisingly affordable when compared to its Union Square contemporaries (singles are as low as $95). Honeymooners should splurge on the Fireplace rooms with canopy beds—ooh la la! Amenities include 24-hour room and concierge service, twice-daily maid service, complimentary shoeshine and newspaper, and valet parking. Adjoining the lobby is fashionable La Scene Café, the perfect place to start your day with a latte and end it with a nightcap.

York Hotel. 940 Sutter St. (between Hyde and Leavenworth sts.), San Francisco, CA 94109. ☎ **415/885-6800.** Fax 415/885-2115. 91 rms, 5 suites. MINIBAR TV TEL. $112–$120 double; from $210 suite. Rates include continental breakfast. Extra person $10. AE, DC, DISC, JCB, MC, V. Parking $14. Bus: 2, 3 or 4.

If this place is gives you déjà vu, it's because this hotel is where Kim Novak stayed in Alfred Hitchcock's classic flick *Vertigo*. Of course that was a long time ago and things have changed some. The hotel was renovated this year and, though far from glamorous, the rooms are clean, basic, and provide a few extra amenities, which include in-room coffeemakers, walk-in closets, and voice mail. Services available include laundry/valet, a limo to downtown, a complimentary newspaper, and a wine hour. The hotel has a fitness center and a bar, but its most charming feature is the Plush Room, a small cabaret-theater where you might catch some of San Francisco's finest talent.

INEXPENSIVE

Amsterdam Hotel. 749 Taylor St. (between Sutter and Bush sts.), San Francisco, CA 94108 ☎ **415/673-3277** or 800/637-3444. Fax 415/673-0453. 30 rms. TV TEL. $75–$79 double (including continental breakfast). AE, MC, V. Parking $13. Bus: 2, 3, 4 or 76.

This hotel is one strange place. The lobby feels like that of a cheap motel, and the rooms, though some are decorated with oak furnishings, are a mixture of old and new, tasteful and cheesy. The owners continue to remodel with Jacuzzi tubs, new drapes and carpet, and marble or black lacquer bathrooms, but it's clear there's no interior designer leading the way. The value is decent, though, and if you can race past the strange disinfectant odor in the breakfast room, there's a small dining patio out back where you can enjoy your continental breakfast.

AYH Hostel at Union Square. 312 Mason St. (between Geary and O'Farrell sts.), San Francisco, CA 94102. ☎ **415/788-5604.** 230 beds. $15 per person for Hostelling International members, $18 for nonmembers; $7 for persons under 18 when accompanied by a parent. Maximum stay 14 nights per year. MC, V. No parking on premises. A public parking lot on Mission between 4th and 5th sts. charges $12 per 24-hour period. Cable car: Powell-Mason line. Bus: 7B or 38.

For less than $20 per night you can relive college dorm life in an old San Francisco–style building right in the heart of Union Square. Occupying five sparsely decorated floors, rooms here are simple and clean, each with two or three bunkbeds, its own sink, and a closet; best of all, you can lock your door and take the key with you. Although most rooms share hallway baths, a few have private facilities. Suite rooms are reserved for families. Freshly painted hallways are adorned with laminated posters, and there are several common rooms, including a reading room, a smoking room, and a large kitchen with lots of tables, chairs, and refrigerator space. There are laundry facilities nearby, and a helpful information desk offering tour reservations and sightseeing trips. The hostel is open 24 hours and reservations are essential during the summer. Persons under 18 may not stay without a parent unless they have a notarized letter, and then they must pay the adult rate.

Brady Acres. 649 Jones St. (between Geary and Post sts.), San Francisco, CA 94102. ☎ **415/929-8033** or 800/627-2396. Fax 415/441-8033. 25 rms. MINIBAR TV TEL. $60–$85 double per day. Available only by the week Oct–Apr; call for daily availability. MC, V. Parking garage nearby. Bus: 2, 3, 4, 27, or 38.

Inside this small, four-story brick building is a penny-pincher's dream come true. Enter through a black-and-gold door, and you'll find everything you need to keep costs to a minimum. The small but very clean rooms have microwave oven, small refrigerator, toaster, and coffeemaker; hair dryer and alarm clock; direct-dial phone (with free local calls) and an answering machine; color TVs and VCR. Baths are newly renovated, and a coin-operated washer and dryer are located in the basement, along with free laundry soap and irons. Owner Deborah Liane Brady and her staff are usually on hand to offer friendly, personal service, making this option all in all an unbeatable deal. Keep in mind that during the high season, you can only rent by the week.

Golden Gate Hotel. 775 Bush St. (between Powell and Mason sts.), San Francisco, CA 94108. ☎ **415/392-3702** or 800/835-1118. Fax 415/392-6202. 23 rms (14 with bath). TV. $65–$69 double without bath, $95–109 double with bath. Rates include continental breakfast. AE, CB, DC, MC, V. Parking $12. Cable car: Powell-Hyde and Powell-Mason lines (1 block east). Bus: 2, 3, 4, 30, 38, or 45.

Among San Francisco's small hotels occupying historic turn-of-the-century buildings are some real gems, and the Golden Gate Hotel is one of them. It's two blocks north of Union Square and two blocks down (literally) from the crest of Nob Hill, with cable car stops at the corner for easy access to Fisherman's Wharf and Chinatown (the city's theaters and best restaurants are also within walking distance). But the best thing about the Golden Gate Hotel is that this is a family run establishment: John and Renate Kenaston are hospitable innkeepers who take obvious pleasure in making their guests comfortable. Each individually decorated room has handsome antique furnishings (plenty of wicker) from the early 1900s, quilted bedspreads, and fresh flowers (request a room with the claw-foot tub if you enjoy a good, hot soak). Most, but not all, rooms have phones, and complimentary afternoon tea is served daily from 4 to 7pm.

Grant Plaza Hotel. 465 Grant Ave. (at the corner of Pine St.), San Francisco, CA 94108. ☎ **415/434-3883** or 800/472-6899. Fax 415/434-3886. 72 rms. TV TEL. $42–$65 double. MC, V. Parking $9.50. Cable car: Powell-Hyde and Powell-Mason lines (2 blocks west).

You won't find any free little bottles of shampoo here. What you will find are cheap accommodations and basic—and we mean *basic*—rooms right in the middle of Union Square/Chinatown action. The pattern-crazy lobby isn't easy on the eye, but it's mostly a thoroughfare anyway, so who could care? Many of the small rooms in this six-story building overlook Chinatown's main street. Corner rooms on higher floors are both larger and brighter. Expect little more than a soap dispenser in the small shower and bathroom. The Grant Plaza offers nothing more than decent value, but for 50 bucks, what do you expect? Note that no visitors are permitted in the rooms after 11pm and no breakfast is served.

The Sheehan. 620 Sutter St. (near Mason St.), San Francisco, CA 94102. ☎ **415/775-6500** or 800/848-1529. Fax 415/775-3271. 68 rms (58 with bath). TV TEL. $62–$72 double without bath, $75–$105 double with bath. Rates include continental breakfast. AE, CB, DC, MC, V. Parking $14. Cable car: Powell-Hyde and Powell-Mason lines (2 blocks east). Bus: 2, 3, 4, 30, 38, or 45.

Formerly a YWCA hotel, the Sheehan is dirt-cheap considering its location is two blocks from Union Square. Of course, this isn't the Ritz—some walls could use a little paint and there are plenty of areas that would benefit from a little TLC. However, rooms are clean and simply furnished, come with cable color TV, and the bathrooms are brand new. The hotel has a clean, pleasant lobby; a comfortable tea room open for light lunches and afternoon tea; and an indoor, heated lap-pool and workout area.

3 Nob Hill

VERY EXPENSIVE

Fairmont Hotel & Tower. 950 Mason St. (at California St.), San Francisco, CA 94108. ☎ **415/772-5000** or 800/527-4727. Fax 415/772-5013. 538 rms, 62 suites. A/C MINIBAR TV TEL. Main building: $199–$299 double; from $620 suite. Tower: $239–$300 double; from $500 suite. Extra person $30. Continental breakfast $9.95 extra. AE, CB, DC, DISC, MC, V. Parking $25. Cable car: California St. line (direct stop).

The granddaddy of Nob Hill's elite cadre of ritzy hotels, the Fairmont wins top honors for the most awe-inspiring lobby in San Francisco. Even if you're not staying at the Fairmont, it's worth a side trip to gape at its massive, marble Corinthian columns, vaulted ceilings, velvet chairs, gilded mirrors, and spectacular wraparound staircase. Unfortunately, such ostentation doesn't carry over to the guest rooms, which are surprisingly ordinary (aside from the spectacular views from the top floors). In addition to the expected luxuries, guests will appreciate such details as goose-down pillows, electric shoe buffers, bath scales, large walk-in closets, and multiline phones with private voice mail.

Dining/Entertainment: Masons serves contemporary California cuisine, with live music Tuesday through Sunday. Bella Voce Ristorante features Italian American cuisine served by staff who occasionally pause for an aria or Broadway selection. The Crown offers deli lunches, dinner buffets, and Sunday brunch, with a panoramic view of the Bay Area. The Tonga Restaurant and Hurricane Bar offer Chinese and Polynesian specialties in a tropical ambience, as well as dancing and a generous happy hour. Afternoon tea is served daily in the hotel's lobby.

Services: 24-hour room service, twice-daily maid service, evening turndown, laundry/valet, 24-hour concierge, complimentary shoeshine, baby-sitting services, doctor on-call, complimentary morning limousine to the Financial District.

Facilities: Health club, business center, barbershop, beauty salon, pharmacy, shopping arcade.

Huntington Hotel. 1075 California St. (between Mason and Taylor sts.), San Francisco, CA 94108. ☎ **415/474-5400** or 800/227-4683, 800/652-1539 in California. Fax 415/474-6227. 110 rms, 30 suites. MINIBAR TV TEL. $190–$240 double; from $290–$790 suite. Special packages available. Continental breakfast $9.95. AE, CB, DC, MC, V. Parking $19.50. Cable car: California St. line (direct stop). Bus: 1.

One of the kings of Nob Hill, the stately Huntington Hotel has long been a favorite retreat for Hollywood stars and political VIPs who desire privacy and security. Family owned since 1924—an extreme rarity among large hotels—the Huntington eschews pomp and circumstance; absolute privacy and unobtrusive service are its mainstay. Though the lobby, decorated in a grand 19th-century style, is rather petite, the guest rooms are quite large and feature Brunschwig and Fils fabrics and bed coverings, French-style furnishings, and views of the city. The lavish suites, so opulent as to be featured in *Architectural Digest*, are individually decorated with custom-made and antique furnishings. Prices are steep, as you would expect, but special offers such as the Romance Package ($195 per couple, including free champagne,

Hotel Trivia

For nearly a century the most popular place for visitors to rendezvous in San Francisco has been under the magnificent hand-carved grandfather clock in the lobby of the Westin St. Francis Hotel.

sherry, and limousine service) make the Huntington worth considering for a special occasion.

Dining/Entertainment: The Big Four restaurant offers expensive seasonal continental cuisine in of the city's most handsome dining rooms. Live piano music plays nightly in the lounge.

Services: Room service, concierge, complimentary limousine to the Financial District and Union Square, overnight shoe shine, laundry, evening turndown, complimentary morning newspaper, complimentary formal tea or sherry service upon arrival.

Facilities: Access to off-premises health club and spa.

Mark Hopkins Intercontinental. 1 Nob Hill (at California and Mason sts.), San Francisco, CA 94108. ☎ **415/392-3434** or 800/327-0200. Fax 415/421-3302. 390 rms, 28 suites. A/C MINIBAR TV TEL. $180–$230 double; from $375 suite. Continental breakfast $9.50 extra. AE, CB, DC, MC, V. Parking $23. Cable car: California St. line (direct stop). Bus: 1.

Built in 1926 on the spot where railroad millionaire Mark Hopkins's turreted mansion once stood, the 19-story Mark Hopkins gained global fame during World War II when it was considered de rigueur for Pacific-bound servicemen to toast their goodbye to the States in the Top of the Mark cocktail lounge. Nowadays the hotel caters mostly to convention-bound corporate executives who can afford the high rates. Each neoclassical room comes with all the fancy amenities you would expect from a world-class hotel, including custom furniture, plush fabrics, sumptuous baths, and extraordinary views of the city. (Tip: The even-numbered rooms on the higher floor overlook the Golden Gate.) A minor caveat with the hotel is that it has only three guest elevators, making a quick trip up to your room difficult during busy periods.

Dining/Entertainment: The plush and decidedly formal Nob Hill Restaurant offers international cuisine with a California flair nightly (as well as continental buffet breakfast each morning), while the Nob Hill Terrace, adjacent to the lobby, serves lunch, afternoon tea, cocktails, and dinner daily. The world-renowned Top of the Mark lounge serves cocktails from 4pm to 1:30pm daily, Sunday brunch 10am to 2pm, and dancing to live music Wednesday through Saturday nights.

Services: 24-hour room service, concierge, evening turndown, overnight shoe shine, laundry, limousine, valet parking, and multilingual guest relations.

Facilities: Business center, health club, Executive Club floor, car-rental desk.

✪ **Ritz Carlton.** 600 Stockton St. (between Pine and California sts.), San Francisco, CA 94108. ☎ **415/296-7465** or 800/241-3333. Fax 415/296-0288. 292 rms, 44 suites. A/C MINIBAR TV TEL. $275 double; $395 club-level double; from $575 suite. Weekend discounts and packages available. Continental breakfast $14.50 extra; breakfast buffet $18.50 extra; Sunday brunch $42. AE, CB, DC, DISC, MC, V. Parking $27. Cable car: Powell-Hyde and Powell-Mason lines (direct stop).

Ranked among the top hotels in the world by readers of *Conde Nast Traveler* (as well as *the* top hotel in the city), the Ritz-Carlton has been the benchmark of San Francisco's luxury hotels since it opened in 1991. A Nob Hill landmark, this former Metropolitan Insurance headquarters stood vacant for years until the Ritz-Carlton company acquired it and embarked on a massive four-year renovation. The interior was completely gutted and restored with fine furnishings, fabrics, and artworks, including a pair of Louis XVI French blue marble-covered urns with gilt mounts, and 19th-century Waterford candelabras. The rooms offer every possible amenity and service: Italian-marble bathrooms with double sinks, telephone, and name-brand toiletries, plush terry bathrobes, and an in-room safe. The more expensive rooms

---

Hotel Trivia

The Ritz Carlton's bar holds claim to the country's largest collection of single-malt scotches. Prices range from $7.25 to $66 per glass.

---

take advantage of the hotel's location—the south slope of Nob Hill—and have good views of the city. Club rooms, located on the eighth and ninth floors, have a dedicated concierge, separate elevator-key access, and complimentary meals throughout the day.

Dining/Entertainment: The Ritz Carlton Dining Room, voted among the nation's top restaurants by several magazines, serves dinner Monday through Saturday (see Chapter 6, "Dining," for complete information). The Terrace Restaurant, less formal than the dining room, offers Mediterranean cuisine and outdoor dining in the courtyard. The lobby lounge offers afternoon tea and cocktails and sushi daily with low-key live entertainment from 3pm to 1am. Sunday brunch is easily one of the best in town.

Services: 24-hour room service, same-day valet, concierge, child care, complimentary morning newspaper, and shoeshine.

Facilities: Business center, an outstanding fitness center with pool, gift boutique, car-rental desk, VCR and video library.

Renaissance Stanford Court Hotel. 905 California St. (at Powell St.), San Francisco, CA 94108. ☎ **415/989-3500,** 800/227-4736, or 800/622-0957 in California. Fax 415/391-0513. 375 rms, 18 suites, A/C TV TEL. $205–$295 double; from $450 suite. Extra person 18 or over, $30. Continental breakfast $10.50 extra; American breakfast $16.50 extra. AE, CB, DC, DISC, MC, V. Parking $24. Cable car: Powell-Hyde and Powell-Mason lines (direct stop). Bus: 1.

The Stanford Court has maintained a long and discreet reputation as one of San Francisco's most exclusive, and expensive, hotels. Holding company with the Ritz, Fairmont, Mark Hopkins, and Huntington hotels atop Nob Hill, it was originally the mansion of Leland Stanford, whose legacy lives on in the many portraits and biographies that adorn the rooms. Frequented mostly by corporate executives, the rooms at first come across as austere and antiquated compared to most other top-dollar business hotels, but the quality and comfort of the furnishings are so superior that you're forced to admit there's simply no room for improvement. The Stanford Court also prides itself on its impeccable service; a nice touch is the complimentary tray of tea or coffee placed outside your door upon your request. The lobby, furnished in a 19th-century theme with Baccarat chandeliers, French antiques, and a gorgeous stained-glass dome, makes for a grand entrance, though the aroma of cigars emanating from the lounge tends to detract from the experience.

Many of the guest rooms have partially canopied beds, and all have writing desks, extremely comfortable beds, and oak armoires that conceal aging but adequate television sets. Bathrooms include mini-TV, telephone, heated towel racks, overhead heat lamps, and make-up mirrors.

Dining/Entertainment: Fournou's Ovens, the hotel's award-winning restaurant, features contemporary American cuisine in a romantic multilevel setting.

Services: Concierge, 24-hour room service, 24-hour laundry/valet, complimentary chauffeured car service to downtown destinations, complimentary morning newspaper and coffee or tea, evening turndown service, complimentary overnight shoeshine, baby-sitter on call.

Facilities: Fitness center; state-of-the-art business center.

EXPENSIVE

Nob Hill Lambourne. 725 Pine St. (between Powell and Stockton sts.), San Francisco, CA 94108. ☎ **415/433-2287** or 800/274-8466. 9 rms, 11 suites. A/C MINIBAR TV TEL. $155 double; $175–$250 suite. Rates include continental breakfast. AE, CB, DC, DISC, MC, V. Parking $20 valet. Cable car: California St. line (1 block north).

One of San Francisco's top "business-boutique" hotels, the Nob Hill Lambourne bills itself as an urban spa, offering on-site massages, facials, body scrubs, aromatherapy, waxing, manicures, pedicures, and yoga lessons to ease corporate-level stress. Even without this "hook," the Lambourne deserves a top-of-the-class rating. Sporting one of San Francisco's most stylish interiors, the hotel flaunts the comfort and quality of its contemporary French design. Top-quality, hand-sewn mattresses and goose-down comforters are complemented by a host of in-room accouterments that include fax machines, VCRs, stereos, kitchenettes, and coffeemakers. Bathrooms contain over-sized tubs and hair dryers, as well as an "honor bar" of goodies like geranium and orange bath oil, herbal lip balm, and jasmine moisturizer, sold for $6 to $10 each. Suites include an additional sitting room, plus a choice of treadmill, Lifecycle, or rowing machine. On Friday and Saturday, all guests are invited to enjoy complimentary wine and hors d'oeuvres and a 15-minute neck and shoulder massage.

Services: Evening turndown, business services.
Facilities: Spa treatment room.

4 Financial District

VERY EXPENSIVE

ANA Hotel San Francisco. 50 Third St. (between Market and Mission sts.), San Francisco, CA 94103. ☎ **415/974-6400** or 800/262-4683. Fax 415/495-6152. 641 rms, 26 suites. A/C MINIBAR TV TEL. $220–$250 double; from $380 suite. Continental breakfast $8.75 extra. AE, DC, DISC, JCB, MC, V. Parking $23. All Market St. buses. Muni Metro: All Market St. trams.

The hotel's large number of rooms and fine location—just one block south of Market Street, and one block from the Moscone Convention Center—makes the ANA attractive to both groups and business travelers. Separate check-in facilities for conventioneers keep the main lobby clear and welcoming for independent guests.

Rooms have floor-to-ceiling windows and are well outfitted with three telephones (with voice mail and data port for computer modem connection). Corner suites look across the Bay Bridge and to Candlestick ("3COM") Park, and Executive Level rooms include continental breakfast and evening hors d'oeuvres.

Dining/Entertainment: Café Fifty-Three serves three meals daily, plus a special Sunday brunch and offers garden terrace seating. The adjacent lobby bar serves cocktails, wine, beer, and appetizers.

Services: Room service, concierge, twice-daily maid service, laundry/valet.

Facilities: Fitness center, business center, complimentary use of nearby tennis club, gift shop.

Hyatt Regency San Francisco. 5 Embarcadero Center, San Francisco, CA 94111. ☎ **415/788-1234** or 800/233-1234. Fax 415/398-2567. 805 rms, 45 suites. TV TEL. $205–$230 double; from $350 suite. Continental breakfast $6.95 extra. AE, CB, DC, MC, V. Parking $25. Muni Metro: All Market St. trams. All Market St. buses.

The Hyatt Regency, a convention favorite, rises from the edge of the Embarcadero Center at the foot of Market Street. The structure, with a 1970s, gray concrete, bunkerlike facade, is shaped like a vertical triangle, serrated with long rows of jutting balconies. The 17-floor atrium lobby, illuminated by museum-quality theater

Accommodations Around Town

Albion House Inn **15**
Archbishop's Mansion **13**
Atherton Hotel **32**
Bed & Breakfast Inn **6**
Best Western Miyako Inn **11**
Black Stallion Inn **39**
Bock's Bed & Breakfast **37**
Hotel Bohème **23**
Castillo Inn **16**
Chelsea Motor Inn **3**
Cow Hollow Motor Inn & Suites **2**
Dolores Park Inn **39**
Essex Hotel **31**
Harbor Court **27**
Herb 'n Inn **38**
Holiday Lodge & Garden Hotel **24**
Hotel Griffon **27**
House o' Chicks **16**
Hyatt Regency San Francisco **26**
The Inn at the Opera **14**
Inn on Castro **18**
Jackson Court **8**
Hotel Majestic **10**
The Mansions **9**
Mandarin Oriental **25**
Hotel Milano **29**
Miyako Hotel **12**
New Abigail Hotel **34**
Pied à Terre **7**
Phoenix Inn **33**
Queen Anne Hotel **10**
Red Victorian Bed & Breakfast Inn **36**
San Francisco International Hostel **1**
San Remo **21**
Sheraton at Fisherman's Wharf **19**
Sheraton Palace **28**
Sherman House **5**
Stanyan Park Hotel **35**
Super 8 Hotel **30**
Tuscan Inn **20**
24 Henry **16**
Union Street Inn **4**
Washington Square Inn **22**
The Willows Inn **17**

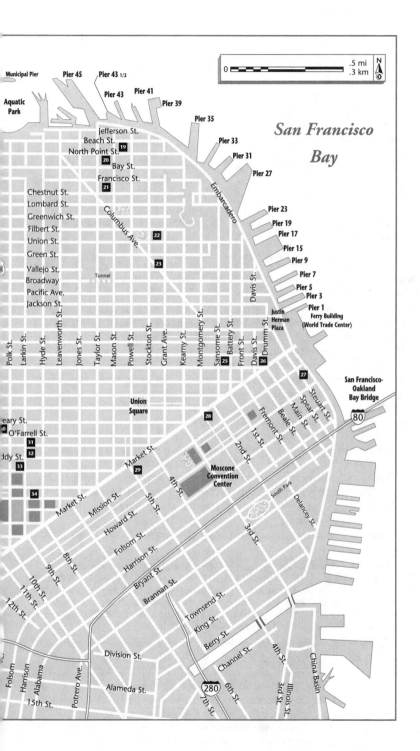

Municipal Pier

Pier 45

Pier 43 1/2

Aquatic Park

Pier 43

Pier 41

Pier 39

Pier 35

San Francisco Bay

Pier 33

Jefferson St.

Beach St.

North Point St. **19**

20 Bay St.

Francisco St.

21

Pier 31

Pier 27

Chestnut St.

Lombard St.

Greenwich St.

Filbert St.

Union St.

Green St.

Vallejo St.

Broadway

Pacific Ave.

Jackson St.

Columbus Ave.

Embarcadero

Pier 23

Pier 19

Pier 17

Pier 15

Pier 9

Pier 7

Pier 5

Pier 3

Pier 1

22

23

Tunnel

Davis St.

Justin Herman Plaza

Ferry Building (World Trade Center)

Polk St.

Larkin St.

Hyde St.

Leavenworth St.

Jones St.

Taylor St.

Mason St.

Powell St.

Stockton St.

Grant Ave.

Kearny St.

Montgomery St.

Sansome St.

Battery St.

Front St.

Davis St.

Drumm St.

25

26

27

San Francisco-Oakland Bay Bridge

80

Union Square

28

eary St.

O'Farrell St.

31

32

ddy St.

33

Stewart St.

Spear St.

Main St.

Beale St.

Fremont St.

1st St.

2nd St.

34

Market St.

29

4th St.

Moscone Convention Center

Market St.

Mission St.

Howard St.

Folsom St.

Harrison St.

Bryant St.

Brannan St.

5th St.

3rd St.

South Park

Delancey St.

8th St.

9th St.

10th St.

11th St.

12th St.

Folsom

Harrison

Alabama

15th St.

Potrero Ave.

Division St.

Alameda St.

280

7th St.

6th St.

Channel St.

Townsend St.

King St.

Berry St.

4th St.

3rd St.

Illinois St.

China Basin

0   .5 mi
     .3 km

N

79

lighting, features flowing water and a simulated environment of California grasslands and wildflowers. The hotel was totally renovated in 1993.

Rooms are comfortably furnished. Each also has a voice-mail telephone and computer ports for modems. Some rooms have tea- and coffeemaking facilities, and private fax machines are available free upon request. Rooms with two double beds also include a sofa, easy chair, and cocktail table. The hotel's 16th and 17th floors house the Regency Club, with 102 larger guest rooms, private bar-lounges and games rooms, complimentary continental breakfast, after-dinner cordials, and private concierge.

Dining/Entertainment: The Eclipse Café serves three meals daily; the Thirteen-Views Bar seats about 200 and is open for morning coffee and evening cocktails. The Equinox, a revolving rooftop restaurant and bar offers 360° city views.

Services: 24-hour room service, concierge, laundry, overnight shoeshine.

Facilities: Business center, access to off-premises health club, swimming pool, tennis courts.

Mandarin Oriental. 222 Sansome St. (between Pine and California sts.), San Francisco, CA 94104. ☎ **415/885-0999.** 800/622-0404. Fax 415/433-0289. 154 rms, 4 suites. A/C MINIBAR TV TEL. $285–$330 double; from $405 junior suite. Continental breakfast $12.95 extra. AE, DC, JCB, MC, V. Parking $21. Muni Metro: Montgomery. All Market Street buses.

If we were seeking respite from researching this guide, we'd probably head straight here, jump into a Jacuzzi, and from 48 floors up relax and admire the city we love most. We'd choose this hotel because all the rooms are located between the 38th and 48th floors of a downtown high-rise, which allows each of the large accommodations extraordinary panoramic views of the bay and city. Not all rooms have tub-side views, but they do have luxurious marble bathrooms stocked with a natural loofah, a large selection of English toiletries, terry and cotton cloth robes, hair dryer, makeup mirror, and silk slippers. The rooms are less opulent, with a kind of reserved-contemporary decor of light colors, Asian accents, and handsome furnishings, which includes a spacious desk and sitting area. Since high rates make this mostly a business hotel, additional amenities include three two-line phones with fax hookups, as well as TVs with on-command video access to more than 80 movies.

Dining: Silks is a serene dining room that has won rave reviews melding California and Asian ingredients. See Chapter 6, "Dining," for complete details.

Services: 24-hour room service, complimentary newspaper and shoeshine, concierge, laundry/valet.

Facilities: Business center, brand-new fitness center with cardio, Nautilus, and free weights.

Sheraton Palace Hotel. 2 New Montgomery St. (at Market St.), San Francisco, CA 94105. ☎ **415/392-8600** or 800/325-3535. Fax 415/543-0671. 517 rms, 33 suites. A/C MINIBARS TV TEL. $295–$355 double; from $650 suite. Additional person $25. Children under 18 sharing existing bedding stay free in parents' room. Weekend rates and packages available. Continental breakfast $13.50 extra; deluxe continental $15.75 extra. AE, DC, DISC, JCB, MC, V. Parking $20. Muni Metro: All Market St. trams. All Market St. buses.

The original 1875 Palace was one of the world's largest and most luxurious hotels, and every time you walk through the doors, you'll be reminded how incredibly majestic old luxury really is. The hotel was rebuilt after the 1906 quake and renovated in 1989, but the most spectacular attribute here is still the old regal lobby and the Garden Court, a San Francisco landmark that has been restored to its original 1909 grandeur. The court is flanked by a double row of massive Italian-marble, Ionic columns and dangles 10 huge chandeliers. The real heart-stopper, however, is the 80,000-pane stained-glass ceiling. Regrettably, the rooms have that standardized, chain-hotel appearance. The on-site, fourth-floor health club features a skylight-covered lap pool, whirlpool, sauna, and exercise room.

Dining/Entertainment: The Garden Court serves American cuisine, afternoon tea Monday through Saturday, and drinks Monday through Saturday nights. On major holidays, the Court serves a $52 brunch worth indulging in. Maxfields's Restaurant, a traditional San Francisco grill, has turn-of-the-century charm and is open daily for lunch and dinner. Kyo-ya is an authentic Japanese restaurant with a separate street entrance. The Pied Piper Bar is named after the $2.5 million Maxfield Parrish mural that dominates the room.

Services: 24-hour room service, concierge, evening turndown, laundry/valet.

Facilities: Business service center, health club, lobby-level shops.

EXPENSIVE

✪ **Hotel Milano.** 55 Fifth St. (between Market and Mission sts.), San Francisco, CA 94103. ☎ **415/543-8555** or 800/398-7555 in the U. S. Fax 415/543-5843. 108 rms. A/C MINIBAR TV TEL. $129–$189 double; extra person $20. Continental breakfast $6 extra. AE, MC, V, AE, DC, JCB, MC, V. Parking $19. All Market St. buses.

Contemporary Italian design, simple and elegantly streamlined rooms, and its central location make Hotel Milano a popular choice for tourists and business people alike. The hotel also has a film production facility and private screening room to entice the film industry. But corporate travelers also resonate to the guest rooms, which feature everything a business executive could want, from fax/computer modem hookups to a Nintendo game system. Other features include in-room safe and soundproof windows. Some have spa tub, bidet, double lavatories, and television with VCR.

Dining: Just off the lobby is the renowned Chef Michel Richard's Bistro M serving breakfast, lunch, and dinner in an equally moderne setting.

Services: Room service, concierge, laundry/valet.

Facilities: Fitness center and spa with steam and sauna, business center.

5 Japan Center & Environs

EXPENSIVE

The Archbishop's Mansion. 1000 Fulton St. (at Steiner St.), San Francisco, CA 94117. ☎ **415/563-7872** or 800/543-5820. 15 rms. TEL TV. $129–$385 double. Rates include continental breakfast. AE, MC, V. Free parking. Bus: 19, 31, or 38.

One thing is for certain: The Archbishop who built this 1904 belle epoque beauty was no Puritan. Drippingly romantic, the Archbishop's Mansion is one of the most opulent and fabulously adorned B&Bs you could possibly hope to stay in. The Don Giovanni suite—larger than most San Francisco houses—comes with a huge, angel-encrusted four-poster bed imported from a French castle, a palatial fireplace, elaborately embroidered linens, and a seven-head shower that you'll never want to leave. Slightly closer to earth is the Carmen suite, which has a deadly romantic combination of claw-foot bathtub fronting a toasty, wood-burning fireplace. In the morning, breakfast is delivered to the guest rooms, and in the evenings complimentary wine is served in the elegant parlor.

Services: Laundry/valet, concierge, limousine service, complimentary morning newspaper.

Hotel Majestic. 1500 Sutter St. (between Octavia and Gough sts.), San Francisco, CA 94109. ☎ **415/441-1100** or 800/869-8966. Fax 415/673-7331. 51 rms, 9 suites. TV TEL. $135–$170 double; from $260 suite. Group, government, corporate, and relocation rates available. Continental breakfast $8.50 extra. AE, DC, MC, V. Parking $14.

Tourists and business travelers adore The Majestic because it covers every professional need while retaining the ambience of a luxurious old-world hotel. It was built in 1902 and thankfully retains its original integrity—the lobby alone will sweep guests into another era with an overabundance of tapestries, tasseled brocades, Corinthian columns, and intricate, lavish detail.

Rooms are furnished with French and English antiques, the centerpiece of each being a large four-poster canopy bed; you'll also find custom-made, mirrored armoires and antique reproductions. Conveniences include a full-size, well-lit desk and clock-radio; extra bathroom amenities include bath robes. Some rooms also have fireplaces.

Dining/Entertainment: Café Majestic and Bar serves California and continental cuisine in a romantic setting and continues to intrigue a local clientele. Cocktails are offered in the adjacent bar complete with French mahogany bar.

Services: Room service, laundry/valet, concierge, complimentary newspaper, and afternoon sherry.

The Mansions. 2220 Sacramento St. (between Laguna and Buchanan sts.), San Francisco, CA 94115. ☎ **415/929-9444.** 21 rms, 5 suites. TV TEL. $169 double; from $199 suite. Rates include continental breakfast. AE, DC, DISC, MC, V. Parking $10. Bus: 1, 3, or 83.

Bob Pritikin's inn is one of San Francisco's most unusual and eclectic hideaways, attracting the likes of Robin Williams and Barbra Streisand. Set in a terraced garden adorned with sculptures, The Mansions is actually two historic buildings, connected by an interior corridor. Their total and often theatrical originality is reflected in Pritikin's philosophy that "the Mansions is only as good as its last performance."

Guests are greeted by a host in Victorian attire and offered a glass of wine or sherry upon check-in. Each room is different, but most units look out on a rose or sculpture garden, and all are furnished with well-chosen Victorian antiques. All have fresh flowers and TVs (delivered on request). Each unit is named for a famous San Franciscan and includes a wall mural depicting that person's story. The ultimate indulgence is the opulent Empress Josephine Room. There's even an all-glass Garden Room, partly done in spectacular stained glass. Breakfast includes English crumpets, English-style banger sausages, fruit, fresh-squeezed orange juice, coffee, and more.

Dining/Entertainment: The Victorian Cabaret Theater stages nightly performances by virtuoso pianist Claudia the Ghost, playing requests with invisible fingers. Some nights, she performs extraordinary feats of magic, and Pritikin, "America's foremost saw player," also entertains. There's also a game room with billiard tables.

Miyako Hotel. 1625 Post St. (at Laguna St.), San Francisco, CA 94115. ☎ **415/922-3200** or 800/533-4567. Fax 415/921-0417. 207 rms, 11 suites. A/C TV TEL. $139–$199 double or twin; from $299 suite. Children 12 and under stay free in parents' room. Continental breakfast $7.50 extra; breakfast buffet $12.50 extra. AE, CB, DC, MC, V. Parking $15. Bus: 38 Geary.

Japantown's Miyako is a tranquil alternative to staying downtown (and it's only about a mile away). The 15-story tower and five-story Garden Wing overlook the Japan Center, which is home to the city's largest complex of Japanese shops, restaurants, and a huge movie complex, but the hotel manages to maintain a feeling peace and quiet you'd expect somewhere much more remote. Rooms are Zenlike with East-meets-West decor; the western-style (don't think cowboy) rooms are fine, but romantics and adventurers should opt for the traditional-style Japanese rooms with tatami mats and futons, yukatas (cotton robes), a tokonoma (alcove for displaying art), and Shoji screens that slide away to frame views of the city. Two luxury suites have redwood saunas and deep-tub Japanese baths.

Dining/Entertainment: Yo Yo Tsumami Bistro, the hotel's restaurant, offers fantastic food, including "Tsumami," Japanese-style cocktail food, in a wonderfully warm, attractive dining room. See Chapter 6, "Dining," for complete details.

Services: Room service, concierge, evening turndown, overnight shoe shine, shiatsu massage.

Facilities: Business center, access to an off-premises health club, car-rental desk.

MODERATE

Best Western Miyako Inn. 1800 Sutter St. (at Buchanan St.), San Francisco CA 94115. ☎ **415/921-4000.** Fax 415/923-1064. 123 rms, 2 suites. A/C TV TEL. $95–$103 double; $160 suite. Continental breakfast $8 extra. AE, DC, JCB, MC, V. Parking $7.50. Bus: 2, 3, 4 or 22.

Located in the heart of Japantown, this hotel has typically modern but unremarkable rooms except for the 60 that have steam baths. Facilities include a restaurant.

Queen Anne Hotel. 1590 Sutter St. (between Gough and Octavia sts.), San Francisco, CA 94109. ☎ **415/441-2828** or 800/227-3970. Fax 415/775-5212. 45 rms, 4 suites. TV TEL. $99–$150 double; $175 suite. Extra person $10. Rates include continental breakfast. AE, DC, MC, V. Parking $12. Bus: 2, 3, or 4.

The majestic 1890 Victorian, which was once a grooming school for upper-class young women, is today a stunning hotel. Restored in 1981 and renovated in 1995, the four-story building remains true to its heritage and emulates San Francisco's golden days. Walk under rich, red drapery to the immaculate and lavish "grand salon" lobby complete with English oak-paneling and period antiques. Rooms follow suit with antiques—armoires, marble-top dressers, and other Victorian pieces. Some have corner turret bay windows that look out on tree-lined streets, as well as separate parlor areas and wet bars; others have cozy reading nooks and fireplaces. All rooms have a telephone in the bathroom, a computer hook-up, and refrigerator. Guests can relax in the parlor, with fluted columns and an impressive floor-to-ceiling fireplace, or in the hotel library. There's a complimentary continental breakfast. Services include room service, concierge, morning newspaper, and complimentary afternoon tea and sherry. There's also access to an off-premises health club with a lap pool. If you're not partial to Union Square, this hotel comes highly recommended.

6 Civic Center

EXPENSIVE

The Inn at the Opera. 333 Fulton St. (at Franklin St.), San Francisco, CA 94102. ☎ **415/863-8400** or 800/325-2708. Fax 415/861-0821. 30 rms, 18 suites. MINIBAR TV TEL. $125–$185 double; from $200 suite. Extra person $15. Rates include European buffet breakfast. AE, MC, V. Parking $19. Bus: 5, 21, 47, or 49.

Judging from its mild-mannered facade and offbeat location behind the Opera House, few would ever guess that The Inn at the Opera is one of San Francisco's, if not California's, finest small hotels. From the minute you walk in through the mullioned front door to a lobby decorated with silk and damask, upholstered antique chairs, hand-painted French screen, and a plush Oriental rug, you know you're about to be spoiled with sumptuousness. But don't take our word for it; Luciano Pavarotti, Placido Domingo, Mikhail Baryshnikov, and dozens of other stars of the stage throw their slumber parties here regularly, requisitioning the inn's luxurious restaurant and lounge, Act IV, along with a floor or two of rooms. Queen-size beds with huge stuffed pillows are standard in each pastel-hued guest room, along with elegant furnishings, wet bars, microwave ovens, refrigerators, and bouquets of fresh flowers. Baths include hair dryers, scales, terry-cloth robes, and French milled soaps. The larger rooms and suites are especially recommended for those who need elbow room; typical of small hotels, the least expensive "standard" rooms are short on space.

Dining/Entertainment: Act IV Restaurant, the hotel's fine dining room, provides an intimate setting for dinner, while the adjacent lounge with its leather chairs, glowing fire, and soft piano music is a favorite city meeting place (see Chapter 6, "Dining," for complete information).

Services: 24-hour room service, concierge, laundry/valet, evening turndown, complimentary light pressing and overnight shoeshine, staff physician, complimentary limousine service to the Financial District, and morning newspaper.

Facilities: Business center.

MODERATE

Abigail Hotel. 246 McAllister St. (between Hyde and Larkin sts.), San Francisco, CA 94102. ☎ **415/861-9728** or 800/243-6510. Fax 415/861-5848. 59 rms, 1 suite. TV TEL. $84 double; $129 suite. Extra person $10. Rates include continental breakfast. AE, CB, DC, MC, V. Parking $12. Muni Metro: All Market St. trams. All Market St. buses.

The Abigail is one of San Francisco's rare sleeper hotels: Though it doesn't get much press, this is one the better medium-priced hotels in the city. Built in 1925 to house celebrities performing at the world renowned Fox Theater, what the Abigail lacks in luxury is more than made up in charm. The rooms, while on the small side, are clean, cute, and comfortably furnished with cozy antiques and down comforters. Morning coffee, pastries, and complimentary newspapers greet you in the beautiful faux-marble lobby designed by Shawn Hall, while lunch and dinner are served downstairs in the hot new "organic" restaurant, the Millennium (see Chapter 6, "Dining," for complete information). Access to a nearby health club, as well as laundry and massage services, are available upon request.

Phoenix Inn. 601 Eddy St. (at Larkin St.), San Francisco, CA 94109. ☎ **415/776-1380** or 800/248-9466. Fax 415/885-3109. 42 rms, 2 suites. TV TEL. $89–$109 double; $135–$149 suite. Rates include continental breakfast. AE, DC, MC, V. Free parking. Bus: 19, 31, or 38.

If you'd like to tell your friends back home that you've stayed in the same as Linda Ronstadt, Arlo Guthrie, and the Red Hot Chili Peppers, this is the place. Situated on the fringes of San Francisco's less-then-pleasant Tenderloin District, this retro 1950s-style hotel has been described by *People* as the hippest hotel in town, a gathering place for visiting rock musicians, writers, and filmmakers who crave a dose of Southern California—hence the palm trees and pastel colors—on their trips to San Francisco. The focal point of the Palm Springs–style hotel is a small, heated outdoor pool adorned with a paisley mural by artist Francis Forlenza and ensconced by a modern-sculpture garden.

The rooms, while far from plush, are comfortably equipped with bamboo furnishings, potted plants, and original local art. In addition to the usual amenities, the inn's own closed-circuit channel shows films exclusively made in or about San Francisco. Services include an on-site massage therapist, concierge, laundry/valet, room service, and—whoo hoo!—free parking. Adjoining the hotel is Miss Pearl's Jam House restaurant/club, featuring spicy island cuisine and the reggae sounds to go with it (see Chapter 6, "Dining," for complete information).

7 Pacific Heights/Cow Hollow

VERY EXPENSIVE

Sherman House. 2160 Green St. (between Webster and Fillmore sts.), San Francisco, CA 94123. ☎ **415/563-3600** or 800/424-5777. Fax 415/563-1882. 8 rms, 6 suites. TV TEL. $200–$400 double; from $600 suite. Continental breakfast $14 extra. AE, CB, DC, MC, V. Parking $16. Cable car: Powell-Hyde line. Bus: 22, 41, or 45.

How expensive is a night at the Sherman House? Put it this way: If you have to ask, you can't afford it. Built in 1876 by philanthropist/music publisher Leander Sherman, this magnificent Pacific Heights Victorian doubled as his home and playhouse for such guest stars as Enrico Caruso, Lillian Russell, and Victor Herbert. After years of neglect, it took four years and a small fortune to restore the estate to its original splendor. Today the Sherman House sets the standard in San Francisco for privacy, personal service, and sumptuous furnishings. All rooms are individually decorated with authentic antiques in French Second Empire, Biedermeier, or English Jacobean style and contain queen-size canopy featherbeds along with ultra-rich tapestry fabrics and down comforters; all except one have fireplaces. Rooms also feature both TVs and stereos, and black granite bathrooms complete with bathrobes and whirlpool baths. The English-style Hyde Park room offers a fine Bay view from its cushioned window seat. The Jacobean-style Paderewski suite was formerly the Billiards room, and it retains the dark wainscoting and beamed ceiling. The least expensive room (number 203) is a twin furnished with English antiques but lacks a fireplace. The most expensive suite is the Thomas Church Garden suite, which consists of two rooms with one and a half baths, with an adjoining sunken garden terrace with gazebo and pond.

Dining: The dining room has a very fine reputation, but because of a zoning dispute, it has recently lost its license to serve food to non-guests and is now open only to residents; this change may affect the standards. Currently a fixed-price menu, without wine, is available for $70. Although the price is steep, the meal is quite elaborate. A limited à la carte menu is also available; main courses run from $27 to $30.

Services: Room service, butler who will discreetly unpack luggage, concierge, massage, personalized shopping, private chauffeuring.

Facilities: Business center.

EXPENSIVE

Jackson Court. 2198 Jackson St. (at Buchanan St.) San Francisco, CA 94115. ☎ **415/929-7670.** 10 rms. TV TEL. $122–$170 double. Rates include continental breakfast. AE, MC, V. Parking on street only.

The Jackson Court, a stately three-story brownstone Victorian mansion, is located in one of San Francisco's most exclusive neighborhoods, Pacific Heights. Its only fault—that it's far from the action—is also its blessing: if you crave a blissfully quiet vacation while swathed in elegant surroundings, this is the place. Each room is individually furnished with superior-quality antique furnishings; two have wood-burning fireplaces (de rigueur in the winter). The Blue Room, for example, features a brass and porcelain bed, Renaissance-style sofa, and inviting window seat, while the Garden Suite has handcrafted wood paneling and a large picture window looking out at the private garden patio. After breakfast, spend the day browsing the shops along nearby Union and Fillmore sts., then return in time for afternoon tea.

Pied à Terre. 2424 Washington St. (at Webster St.), San Francisco, CA 94123. ☎ **415/929-8033** or 800/627-2396. 3 apts. A/C TV TEL. $110–$200 double. Weekly rates available. Parking on street only. Cable car: Powell-Hyde Park or Powell-Mason lines. Bus: 2, 3, 4, 27, or 38.

If you want to live like the locals—the rich locals—then we can make no better suggestion than the Pied à Terre apartments. The fully equipped rentals are superbly located in Pacific Heights, between Alta Plaza and Lafayette parks, just a block from the upper Fillmore shopping area. One apartment is a studio suitable for two, with sunny bay windows, love seat, wardrobe, and mini kitchen (no stove). Two larger apartments have two bedrooms, a living room, two fireplaces, and a gourmet kitchen complete with dishwasher, gas range, large refrigerator, and microwave oven. Adjacent dining areas have room enough for up to eight guests, and free laundry facilities are available.

Union Street Inn. 2229 Union St. (between Fillmore and Steiner sts.), San Francisco, CA 94123. ☎ **415/346-0424.** Fax 415/922-8046. 5 rms, 1 cottage. TV TEL. $125–$175 standard double; $225 cottage. Rates include breakfast, hors d'oeuvres, and evening beverages. AE, MC, V. Parking $10. Bus: 22, 41, 45, or 47.

Who would have guessed that one of the most delightful B&Bs in California would be in San Francisco? This two-story Edwardian may front the perpetually busy (and trendy) Union Street, but it's quiet as a church on the inside. All individually decorated rooms are comfortably furnished with canopied or brass beds with down comforters, fresh flowers, bay windows (beg for one with a view of the garden), and private baths (some with Jacuzzi tubs). Breakfast (fresh-baked croissants, with jams, fresh-squeezed orange juice, fruit, and coffee) is served either in the parlor, in your room, or on an outdoor terrace overlooking a lovely English garden. The ultimate honeymoon retreat is the private carriage house behind the inn, but any room at this warm, friendly inn is guaranteed to please.

MODERATE

Bed & Breakfast Inn. 4 Charlton Court (off Union St., between Buchanan and Laguna sts.), San Francisco, CA 94123. ☎ **415/921-9784.** 11 rms (4 with shared bath), 2 suites. $70–$90 double without bath; $115–$140 double with bath; $190–$275 suite. Rates include continental breakfast. No credit cards. Parking $10 a day at nearby garage. Bus: 41 or 45.

San Francisco's first bed-and-breakfast is composed of a trio of Victorian houses all gussied up in English country style, hidden in a cul-de-sac just off Union Street. While it doesn't have quite the casual ambience of neighboring Union Street Inn, the Bed & Breakfast Inn is loaded with charm. Each room is uniquely decorated with family antiques, original art, and a profusion of fresh flowers. The Garden Suite—highly recommended for families or groups of four—comes with a fully stocked kitchen, a living room with fireplace, two bedrooms, two bathrooms (one with a Jacuzzi tub), a study, and French doors leading out into the garden. Breakfast (freshly baked croissants; orange juice; and coffee, tea, or cocoa) is either brought to your room on a tray with flowers and a morning newspaper, or served in a sunny Victorian breakfast room with antique china.

Chelsea Motor Inn. 2095 Lombard St. (between Fillmore and Webster sts.), San Francisco, CA 94123. ☎ **415/563-5600.** Fax 415/346-9127. 60 rms. A/C TV TEL. $83–$95 double. AE, CB, DC, MC, V. Free parking. Bus: 22, 28, 30, or 76.

An establishment on the "motel strip" that stretches from the Golden Gate Bridge to Van Ness Avenue, the Chelsea Motor Inn is perfectly located for a stroll along Union Street. Expect generic, clean motel accommodations, with coffee makers in each room. No breakfast is offered.

Hotel Trivia

The Clift Hotel charged a mere $2 per night when it first opened in 1915. The price for a room now? Try $250.

Holiday Lodge & Garden Hotel. 1901 Van Ness Ave. (between Clay and Washington sts.), San Francisco, CA 94109. ☎ **415/776-4469.** Fax 415/474-7046. 75 rms (12 with kitchenettes), 2 suites. TV TEL. $99–$109 double; $119 double with kitchenette; $125–$135 suites. AE, DC, DISC, MC, V. Free parking. Cable car: Powell-Hyde line. Bus: 42, 47, or 49.

Decorated in what could be called tropical contemporary style, the focal point of the property is the outdoor heated pool and courtyard. The modern rooms were recarpeted in 1996 and contain a TV with HBO. Kids are welcomed with coloring books, crayons, board games, and rubber ducks for the tub. No breakfast is offered, but there's complimentary coffee in the lobby. Services offered include room service (from a local restaurant delivery service), concierge, laundry/valet, and massage.

INEXPENSIVE

Cow Hollow Motor Inn & Suites. 2190 Lombard St. (between Steiner and Fillmore sts.), San Francisco, CA 94123. ☎ **415/921-5800.** Fax 415/922-8515. 117 rms, 12 suites. A/C TV TEL. $80 double, $7 extra per person; from $175 suite. Extra person $10. AE, DC, MC, V. Free parking. Bus: 28, 43, or 76.

If you're less interested in being downtown and more into playing in and around the beautiful bay-front Marina, check out this modest brick hotel smack in the middle of busy Lombard Street. There's no fancy theme here, but each room comes loaded with such amenities as cable TV, free local phone calls, free covered parking, and in-room coffeemakers. All the rooms were renovated in 1996, so you'll be sure to sleep on a nice firm mattress surrounded by clean, new carpeting and drapes.

San Francisco International Hostel. Fort Mason, Building 240 Fort Mason, San Francisco, CA 94123. ☎ **415/771-7277.** Fax 415/771-1468. 155 beds. $13–$15. MC, V. Reservations up 24 hours in advance.

Unbelievable but true, you can get front-row bay views for a mere $13 to $15 nightly. The hostel is on national park property, provides dorm-style accommodations for 155 guests, and offers easy access to the Marina's shops and restaurants. Rooms sleep three to four persons, and communal space includes a fireplace, pool table, kitchen, dining room, coffee bar, complimentary movies, laundry facilities, and free parking.

8 Haight-Ashbury

MODERATE

Red Victorian Bed & Breakfast Inn. 1665 Haight St. (between Cole and Belvedere sts.), San Francisco, CA 94117. ☎ **415/864-1978.** 18 rms (4 with bath), 1 suite. TEL. $76–$110 double without bath, $120–$126 double with bath; $200 suite. Rates decrease based on length of stay. Extra person $15. Rates include continental breakfast and afternoon tea. MC, V. Guarded parking lot nearby. Muni Metro: N line. Bus: 7, 66, 71, or 73.

Do you wish you were still in the sixties? If you'd like to relive them, the Red Vic, located in the heart of Haight, will give you a few memorable flashbacks. Owner Sami Sunchild, a confessed former flower child, runs this hotel and meditation center that honors the Summer of Love and Golden Gate Park. Rooms are inspired by San Francisco's sights and history and are decorated accordingly, psychedelic posters and all. The Flower Child Room has a sun on the ceiling and a rainbow on the wall, while the bed sports a hand-crocheted shawl headboard. The Peacock Suite, though pricey, is one funky and colorful room, with red beads, a canopy bed, and multicolored patterns throughout. The clincher is its bedroom bathtub that has a circular pass-through looking into the sitting area. Four guest rooms have private baths; the remaining accommodations share four bathrooms down the hall. In general, rooms and baths are clean, and the furnishings eccentric. This hotel is not for everybody, but if you're into it, it's pretty groovy. Rates for longer stays are a great deal. No smoking is allowed in the rooms.

A continental breakfast is served every morning in the Inn's Global Village Center and Gallery, a storefront gift shop.

Stanyan Park Hotel. 750 Stanyan St. (at Waller St.), San Francisco, CA 94117. ☎ **415/751-1000.** Fax 415/668-5454. 30 rms, 6 suites. TV TEL. $85–$105 double; from $135 suite. Rates include continental breakfast. Extra person $20. AE, CB, DC, DISC, MC, V. Parking $5. Muni Metro: N line. Bus: 7, 33, 71, or 73.

This small inn across from Golden Gate Park has operated as a hotel under a variety of names since 1904. Today it's a charming, three-story establishment decorated with antique furnishings, Victorian wallpaper, and pastel quilts, curtains, and carpets. Tub/shower baths come complete with massaging shower head, shampoos, and fancy soaps.

There are one- and two-bedroom suites. Each has a full kitchen, and formal dining and living rooms, and can sleep up to six comfortably; they're ideal for families. Complimentary tea and cookies are served each afternoon.

⑤ The Herb'n Inn. 535 Ashbury St. (between Page and Haight sts.), San Francisco, CA 94117. ☎ **415/553-8542.** Fax 415/553-8541. 4 rms. TV (upon request). $60–$75 double, two-night minimum. MC, V. Parking with advance notice. Bus: 6,7, 33, 43, 66 or 71.

For those of you who want to immerse yourself in the sights and sounds of San Francisco's legendary Haight-Ashbury District without compromising on high-quality (and low-cost) accommodations, there's The Herb'n Inn. Run by sister/brother duo Pam and Bruce Brennan—who know the history and highlights of the Haight better than anyone—this modernized Victorian inn consists of four attractive guest rooms, a huge country-style kitchen, a sunny back garden, and the beginnings of Bruce's Psychedelic History Museum (a.k.a. the dining room). Top choice among the guest rooms is the Cilantro Room, which, besides being the largest, has the only private bath and a view of the garden—all for only $10 extra per night. The Tarragon Room has two small beds and private deck (optimal for smokers, who aren't allowed to fire up inside the house), while the large Coriander Room faces the near mythical intersection of Haight and Ashbury streets, where there's always *something* going on. A hearty full breakfast—waffles, crepes, popovers, potato pancakes—is included, as well as office services (including fowarded e-mail), personal city tours à la Bruce, and plenty of free advice on how to spend your day in the city. Kids and lesbian/gay couples are welcome.

9 North Beach/Fisherman's Wharf

EXPENSIVE

The Sheraton at Fisherman's Wharf. 2500 Mason St. (between Beach and North Point sts.), San Francisco, CA 94133. ☎ **415/362-5500** or 800/325-3535. Fax 415/956-5275. 517 rms, 7 suites. A/C TV TEL. $135–$200 double; from $375 suite. Extra person $20. Continental breakfast $7.95 extra. AE, CB, DC, DISC, MC, V. Parking $12. Cable car: Powell-Mason line (1 block east, two blocks south). Bus: 15, 32, or 42.

Built in the mid-1970s, this modern, three-story hotel isn't the most visually appealing of hotels (even their brochure doesn't show it from the outside), but it offers the reliable comforts of a Sheraton within San Francisco's most popular tourist area. In 1995 the hotel spent $4 million renovating the rooms and adding a Corporate Floor catering exclusively to business travelers.

Dining/Entertainment: Chanen's is a Victorian-style cafe serving breakfast, lunch, and dinner. Live jazz is played several nights a week along with cocktails and assorted appetizers.

Services: Room service, concierge, evening turndown.

Facilities: Outdoor heated swimming pool, access to nearby health club, business center, hair salon, car-rental desk, travel desk.

Tuscan Inn. 425 North Point St. (at Mason St.), San Francisco, CA 94133. ☎ **415/561-1100** or 800/648-4626. Fax 415/561-1199. 209 rms, 12 suites. A/C MINIBAR TV TEL. $165–$188 double; $208–$228 suite. Rates include evening fireside wine reception. AE, DC, DISC, MC, V. Parking $13. Cable Car: Powell-Mason line. Bus: 42, 15 or 32.

The Tuscan Inn is, in our opinion, the best hotel at Fisherman's Wharf. Like an island of respectability in a sea of touristy schlock, the Tuscan exudes a level of style and comfort far beyond its neighboring competitors. Splurge on valet parking—cheaper than the wharf's outrageously priced garages—then saunter your way toward the plush lobby warmed by a grand fireplace. Even the rooms, each equipped with writing desks, armchairs, and handsome burgundy floral-print bedspreads, are a cut above. The only caveat is the lack of scenic views; a small price to pay for a good hotel in a great location.

Dining: The adjoining Café Pescatore, open for breakfast, lunch, and dinner, serves standard Italian fare in an airy, partial alfresco setting. (See Chapter 6, "Dining" for complete information).

Services: Concierge, valet parking, room service, laundry service, voice mail.

MODERATE

Hotel Bohème. 444 Columbus St., (between Vallejo and Green sts.), San Francisco, CA 94133 ☎ **415/433-9111.** Fax 415/362-6292. 15 rms. TV, TEL. $115 double. AE, DISC, DC, MC, V. Parking $20 at nearby public garage. Cable Car: Powell-Mason line. Bus: 12, 15, 30, 41, 45, or 83.

Although located on the busiest strip in North Beach, this recently renovated hotel's style and demeanor are more reminiscent of a prestigious home in upscale Nob Hill. The rooms are small but hopelessly romantic, with gauze-draped canopies and walls artistically accented with lavender, sage green, black, and pumpkin. It's a few steps to some of the greatest cafes, restaurants, bars, and shops in the city, and Chinatown and Union Square are within walking distance.

Washington Square Inn. 1660 Stockton St. (between Filbert and Union sts.), San Francisco, CA 94133. ☎ **415/981-4220** or 800/388-0220. Fax 415/397-7242. 16 rms (5 with shared bath). TEL. $85–$95 with shared bath; $95–$165 with private bath; $180 with park view. Rates include continental breakfast. AE, DC, DISC, JCB, MC, V. Parking $17. Bus: 15, 30, 39, or 45.

Reminiscent of a traditional English inn right down to the cucumber sandwiches served during afternoon tea, this small, comely bed-and-breakfast is ideal for older couples who prefer a more quiet, subdued environment than the commotion of downtown San Francisco. It's located across from Washington Square in the North Beach District—a coffee-craver's haven—and within walking distance of Fisherman's Wharf and Chinatown. Each room is decorated in English floral fabrics with quality European furnishings and plenty of fresh flowers; a few rooms share baths. A continental breakfast is included, as are afternoon tea, wine, and hors d'oeuvres.

INEXPENSIVE

San Remo. 2237 Mason St. (at Chestnut St.) San Francisco, CA 94133. ☎ **415/776-8688** or 800-352-REMO. Fax 415/776-2811. 59 rms (none with bath), 1 suite. $55–$65 double; $85 suite. AE, DC, MC, V. Parking $8. Cable car: Powell-Mason line. Bus: 15, 22, or 30.

This small, European-style pension is one of the best budget hotels in San Francisco. Located in a quiet North Beach neighborhood and within walking distance of Fisherman's Wharf, the San Remo originally served as a boardinghouse for dock workers displaced by the great fire of 1906. As a result, the rooms are small and bathrooms shared, but all is forgiven when it comes time to pay the bill. Rooms are decorated in a cozy country style with brass and iron beds, oak, maple, or pine armoires, and wicker furnishings; most have ceiling fans. The shared bathrooms, each one immaculately clean, feature claw-foot tubs and brass pull-chain toilets with oak tanks and brass fixtures. If the penthouse is available, book it: you won't find a more romantic place to stay in San Francisco for so little money.

10 South of Market

EXPENSIVE

Harbor Court. 165 Steuart St. (between Mission and Howard sts.), San Francisco, CA 94105. ☎ **415/882-1300** or 800/346-0555 in the U.S. Fax 415/882-1313. 130 rms. A/C MINIBAR TV TEL. $160–$295 double. Continental breakfast $6.95 extra. AE, DC, MC, V. Parking $17. Muni Metro: Embarcadero. Bus: 14, 32 or 80x.

When the Embarcadero Freeway was torn down after the Big One in 1989, one the major benefactors was the Harbor Court Hotel: Its backyard view went from a wall of cement to a dazzling view of the Bay Bridge (be sure to request a bay-view room, which is only $20 extra). Located just off the Embarcadero at the edge of the Financial District, this former YMCA books a lot of corporate travelers, but anyone who prefers stylish, high-quality accommodations—half-canopy beds, large armoires, writing desks, sound-proof windows—with a superb view and lively scene will be perfectly content here. A major bonus for health nuts is the free use of the adjoining top-quality fitness club with indoor, Olympic-size swimming pool. In the evening the hotel's dark, velvety restaurant, Harry Denton's, transforms into the Financial District's hot spot for hungry singles.

Hotel Griffon. 155 Steuart St. (between Mission and Howard sts.), San Francisco, CA 94105. ☎ **415/495-2100** or 800/321-2201. Fax 415/495-3522. 62 rms, 5 penthouse suites. A/C MINIBAR TV TEL. $165–$195 double; $275 penthouse suite. Rates include continental breakfast and newspaper. AE, DC, DISC, MC, V. Parking $15. All Market St. buses.

After dumping a cool $10 million on a complete rehab in 1989, the Hotel Griffon emerged as a top contender among San Francisco's small hotels. Ideally situated on San Francisco's historic waterfront and only steps from the heart of the Financial District, the Griffon is impeccably outfitted with contemporary features such as whitewashed brick walls, lofty ceilings, marble vanities, window seats, cherrywood

Hotel Trivia

Fitness magazine recently named the Embarcadero YMCA as one of the top 10 Hotel Health Clubs in the United States.

furniture, and art deco–style lamps (really, this place is smooth). Be sure to request a Bay View room overlooking the Bay Bridge—it's well worth the extra $20—and inquire about the excellent weekend packages the hotel occasionally offers.

Dining/Entertainment: Rôti, which has evolved into a prime lunch spot for the nearby Financial District, occupies one side of the lobby, offering California-style food prepared on spit roasts and wood-burning ovens, and served from an open kitchen. The dining room and mezzanine contain rich wood accents and a view of the San Francisco Bay and Bay Bridge.

Services: Room service, laundry/valet, concierge.

Facilities: Access to nearby health club.

11 Gay & Lesbian Hotels

Most of the previously recommended hotels are undoubtedly "gay friendly," but San Francisco also has a number of hotels catering primarily to gay men and lesbians.

Atherton Hotel. 685 Ellis St. (at Larkin St.), San Francisco, CA 94109. ☎ **415/474-5720** or 800/227-3608 in the U.S. Fax 415/474-8256. 75 rms. TV TEL. $59–$99 double. Continental breakfast $6 extra. AE, MC, DC, V. Bus: 19, 38, or 72.

Close to many gay clubs and restaurants in the more risqué section of Polk Street, this European-style hotel serves an equal mixture of gay and straight visitors. Totally refurbished in 1995 and 1996, it offers basic accommodation and each of the well-furnished bedrooms is complete with a private bath and shower.

Dining/Entertainment: The hotel's Abbey Room Bar is a relaxing place for a drink and perhaps a friendly conversation with a stranger. The hotel's Atherton Grill serves breakfast or lunch but only from Monday through Friday. Over the weekend a champagne brunch is featured here, attended by many gays who live in the nearby area.

Services: Complimentary weekday morning limo service. Staff will help acquire theater tickets or book city or wine country tours.

Black Stallion Inn. 635 Castro St. (between 19th and 20th sts.), San Francisco, CA 94114. ☎ **415/863-0131.** 7 rooms, 1 suite. $95 double; $110 suite. Ask about weekday and weekend specials. Breakfast included. AE, DISC, MC, V. Limited parking $10. Muni Metro: F, K, L, or M. Bus: 24.

Out and About Magazine warns that this self-proclaimed "only leather/Levi/Western bed and breakfast" is very sexually focused. Inside the black-colored Victorian are eight minimalist rooms, a communal lounge with TV and VCR, and a dining area. There's also a sundeck with lounge chairs and barbecue. The ground floor, a separate business, is a private, late-night "social club."

Bock's Bed & Breakfast. 1448 Willard St., San Francisco, CA 94117. ☎ **415/664-6842.** Fax 415/664-1109. 3 rms (1 with bath). TV TEL. $60 double without bath; $75 double with bath. Rates include continental breakfast. No credit cards. Bus: 6, 43, or N-Metro.

This 1906 restored Edwardian-style residence lies only two blocks from Golden Gate Park. It's a "secret address," a little urban getaway with lovely city views. Each room has its own private entrance and is well maintained. Guests may use the communal refrigerator, but may not smoke on the premises.

Castillo Inn. 48 Henry St., San Francisco, CA 94114. ☎ **415/864-5111** or 800/865-5112. Fax 415/641-1321. 4 rms (none with bath). $70 double; $160 suite. Suite rate negotiable depending on season and number of guests. Rates include American breakfast. MC, V. Muni Metro: F, K, L, M. Bus: 8, 22, 24 or 37.

Just two minutes from the heart of the Castro District, this charming little house provides a safe, quiet, and clean environment for its clientele. Catering mostly to gay men (though anyone is welcome), the Castillo makes its clientele feel at home while away. Hardwood floors decorated with throw rugs aid in the warmth. Bedrooms are small yet cozy, and phone messages via phone mail are collected at the front desk. The Castillo also provides the shared usage of a large refrigerator and microwave oven in the kitchen. One enormous, two-bedroom suite that sleeps four comfortably has a full kitchen, two TVs, VCR, parking, and a deck. On Friday and Saturday nights, a two-night minimum stay is required.

Dolores Park Inn. c/o Bernie H. Vielwerth, 3641 17th St., San Francisco, CA 94114. ☎ **415/ 621-0482.** Fax is the same; please call before faxing. 4 rms (none with bath), 1 suite (with kitchenette). TV. $89 double; $165 suite. Rates include full breakfast. MC, V, DC. Muni Metro: F, J, K, L, or M. Bus: 22 or 24.

The Dolores Park Inn has been awarded for being one of the best B&Bs in the city five years running. Conveniently located in the Castro, it's easy walking distance to many gay shops and clubs and a quick jaunt to downtown. Each bedroom is individually decorated with beautiful antiques and a queen-size bed. Celebrities (Tom Cruise, members of the *Sister Act* cast, Robert Downey Jr., and others) have stayed here to avoid hype. The owner takes special care in providing a warm, hospitable, and romantic environment with helpful service. The suite has a 20-foot sundeck looking up at Twin Peaks and a four-poster bed. A two-night minimum stay is required, and there is no smoking.

Essex Hotel. 684 Ellis St. (between Larkin and Hyde sts.), San Francisco, CA 49109. ☎ **415/ 474-4664** or 800/453-7739 in the U.S., 800/443-7739 in Canada. Fax 415/441-1800. 100 rms. TV TEL. $69 double. AE, MC, V.

When guests enter the Essex Hotel, they are immediately greeted by a member of Jean Chaban's hand-picked and trained staff, polished marble floors, fresh-cut flowers, ornate plaster ceilings, and French antiques. Bedrooms offer traditional, clean, and safe lodgings, which are among the more reasonably priced in the area. The staff, or perhaps Jean Chaban himself, is always available to help guests with any request and seem to truly care about the safety and welfare of their clientele. Because some of the staff are fluent in French and German, European gays frequent this hotel. No breakfast is served.

House O' Chicks. 2162 15th St., San Francisco, CA (at Noe and Market sts.) 94114. ☎ **415/ 861-9849.** 2 rms. $75 double (shared bath). Weekly and monthly rates. No credit cards.

If you're into communal living, House O' Chicks is the place for you. Two women who own and live in the 1890s Victorian, European-style house rent rooms to lesbian travelers and offer a homey environment in the Castro District. There's a communal kitchen, living room, and dining room, well-stocked library, and plenty of women's art throughout. The sunny Annie Sprinkle room is showered with Annie's original art (she stays here, too!), a TV with VCR, and an altar to Annie. The darker, more tranquil Kimono room has a stereo, altar, and meditation area. This is a private home, so do not simply arrive. You must call in advance.

Inn on Castro. 321 Castro St., San Francisco, CA 94114 (at Market St.) ☎ **415/861-0321.** 6 rms, 2 suites. TEL. $85–$120; suites $120. Rates include full breakfast and evening brandy. AE, MC, V. Castro St. metro.

One of the better choices in the Castro, a half block away from all the action, is this Edwardian-style inn decorated with contemporary furnishings, original modern art, and fresh flowers throughout. Almost all rooms have private baths and direct-dial phones and color TV available upon request. Most rooms share a small back patio, and the suite has its own private outdoor sitting area.

24 Henry. 24 Henry St., San Francisco, CA 94114 (at Noe). ☎ **415/864-5686** or 800/ 900-5686. Fax 415/864-0406. 5 rms (4 with bath), 5 suites. $75–$90 double; $95 suite, $25 extra person. Rates include continental breakfast. AE, MC, V. Muni Metro: J, F, K, L, M, or N. Bus: 8, 22, 37.

Its Castro location is not the only thing that makes 24 Henry a good choice for gay travelers. The building, a 123-year-old Victorian on a serene side street, is quite charming. The five guest rooms have high ceilings, are adorned with period furniture, and have private phone lines with voice mail. Guests tired of tromping around the neighborhood can watch TV or read in the double parlor (where breakfast is also served). The apartment suites sleep three comfortably and include parlors, separate entrances, phones, and TVs; two have a full kitchen. All rooms are nonsmoking.

The Willows Inn. 710 14th St. (between Church and Market sts.), San Francisco, CA 94114. ☎ **415/431-4770.** Fax 415/431-5295. 10 rms (none with bath), 1 suite. $86–$96 double; $105–$125 suite. Rates include continental breakfast. AE, DISC, MC, V. Limited on-street parking. Subway: Church Street Station (across the street). Bus: 8, 22, or 37.

Right in the heart of the gay Castro District, The Willows Inn employs a staff eager to greet and attend to visitors to San Francisco. The inn's willow furnishings, antiques, and Laura Ashley prints add a touch of romantic elegance. After a long and eventful day of sightseeing and shopping, followed by a night of dancing and cruising, you will be tucked in with a "sherry and chocolate turn-down." The staff will appear the next morning with your personalized breakfast delivered with a freshly cut flower and the morning newspaper. The place has simple elegance and quality and is eagerly sought out by discriminating gay visitors to San Francisco. Extra amenities include direct-dial phones, alarm-clock radios, and kimono bathrobes.

6 Dining

Restaurants are to San Franciscans as bagels are to New Yorkers: indispensable. At last count, city residents had more than 3,300 reasons to avoid cooking at home, and actually spent more money on dining out than those of any other city in the nation.

As one of the world's cultural crossroads, San Francisco is blessed with a cornucopia of cuisines. Afghan, Cajun, Burmese, Jewish, Moroccan, Persian, Cambodian, Vegan—whatever you're in the mood for tonight, this town has got it covered. All you need is money, reservations, and an adventurous palate, because half the fun of visiting San Francisco is the rare opportunity to sample the flavors of the world in one fell swoop.

While dining in San Francisco is almost always a hassle-free experience, there are a few things you should keep in mind your next time out:

- If you want a table at the expensive restaurants with the best reputations, you will probably need to book six to eight weeks ahead for weekends and several weeks ahead for a table during the week.
- If there's a long wait for a free table, ask if you can order at the bar, which is often faster and more fun.
- Don't leave *anything* valuable in your car while dining (particularly in or near high-crime areas), and only give the valet the key to your car, *not* your room or house key.
- Remember: It is against the law to smoke in any restaurant in San Francisco that has no bar; otherwise, smoking is allowed only in the bar area.

The restaurants below are divided first by area, then by price, using the following guide: **expensive,** more than $45 per person; **moderate,** $25 to $45 per person; **inexpensive,** less than $25 per person. These categories reflect the price of the majority of dinner menu items and include an appetizer, main course, coffee, dessert, tax, and tip.

1 Best Bets

- **Best for Cutting a Deal:** Nob Hill elite and local politicians pitch their proposals at **Moose's,** 1652 Stockton St. (☎ 415/989-7800), where well-prepared food and the high-profile atmosphere put everyone in the mood to negotiate.

- **Best Romantic Spot:** Anyone could be seduced at **Fleur de Lys,** 777 Sutter St. (☎ **415/673-7779**), under the rich burgundy-tented canopy that swathes the elegant room in romance. Lots of question-popping here, too.
- **Best for a Celebration:** Great food, a full bar, and a lively atmosphere are the three key ingredients that make **Boulevard,** 1 Mission St. (☎ **415/543-6084**), the place to shout "hooray for me!"
- **Best Decor: Cypress Club,** 500 Jackson St. (☎ **415/296-8555**), is a fantasy supper room that cost a couple of million. Gilt banquettes, gilt columns, and billowing fabrics set the nostalgic scene. The food is pricey, but an evening here will transport you to another, more glamorous era.
- **Best Wine List:** Owners of the small **PlumpJack Café,** 3127 Fillmore St. (☎ **415/563-4755**), also operate one of the city's best wine stores of the same name. The list, which consists of California wines, is expertly picked and offers more than 80 bottles and 33 selections by the glass. And it's reasonably priced.
- **Best Desserts: Stars,** 150 Redwood Alley (☎ **415/861-7827**), publishes a full-page listing of desserts that are luscious in the extreme. Among them, savor the signature chocolate soufflé pastry layered with chocolate ganache and served with champagne sabayon, or the banana nut torte filled with pralines and sliced bananas and frosted with white chocolate buttercream and a dark chocolate glaze. Devilish enough?
- **Best Value:** Nowhere else in town will you find such heaping plates of fresh pasta at penny-pinching prices than **Pasta Pomodoro,** 655 Union St. (☎ **415/ 399-0300**).
- **Best Brunch:** On Sunday, the brunch at the **Ritz-Carlton,** 600 Stockton St. (☎ **415/296-7465**), will set your eyes popping and your feet tapping. Strut around to the lavish buffets featuring sushi, caviar, freshly made blinis, and more traditional egg dishes. A jazz trio brings joy to it all.
- **Best Newcomers: Charles Nob Hill,** 1250 Jones St. (☎ **415/771-5400**), **Scala's Bistro,** 432 Powell St. (at Sutter St.) (☎ **415/395-8555**); **Rumpus,** One Tillman Pl. (☎ **415/421-2300**); **42 Degrees,** 235 16th St. (☎ **415/777-5558**); and **Zinzino,** 2355 Chestnut St. (☎ **415/346-6623**), have all hit the ground running. No matter which one you choose, you just can't loose.
- **Best Bistro:** Casual and comfortable, **Fringale,** 570 Fourth St. (☎ **415/ 543-0573**), offers some of the best moderately priced French food in the city. Start with a scrumptious galette and finish with the crème brûlée with vanilla bean. The middle's all yours.
- **Best Dim Sum:** Downtown and Chinatown dim-sum restaurants may be more centrally located, but that's all they've got on the **Hong Kong Flower Lounge,** 5322 Geary Blvd. (☎ **415/668-8998**), which serves up the best shark fin soup, seafood dumplings, and salt-fried shrimp this side of China.
- **Best Vegetarian:** For the food, the view of the Golden Gate, and the redwood booths, go to **Greens,** Building A, Fort Mason Center (☎ **415/771-6222**). If you want to experience how rich and varied vegetables can taste, then this is the place to sample an extraordinary five-course tasting menu.
- **Best Singles Scene:** The wait for dinner may be eternal at **Restaurant Lulu,** 816 Folsom St. (☎ **415/495-5775**), but the flirtatious scene at the bar will make any single hope being seated takes even a little bit longer.
- **Best Party Scene:** Throw back a few glasses of sangria with your tapas at **Cha Cha Cha,** 1801 Haight St. (☎ **415/386-5758**), and you'll quickly be swinging with the rest of the crowd.

2 Restaurants by Cuisine

AMERICAN

Balboa Café (Pacific Heights/
  Cow Hollow, *M*)
Boulevard (South of Market, *E*)
Cypress Club (North Beach, *E*)
Doidge's (Pacific Heights/
  Cow Hollow, *I*)
Dottie's True Blue Café
  (Union Square, *I*)
Family Inn Coffee Shop
  (Union Square, *I*)
Fly Trap (South of Market, *M*)
Fog City Diner (Around Town, *M*)
Hamburger Mary's (South of
  Market, *I*)
Hard Rock Café (Around Town, *I*)
Harris' (Pacific Heights/Cow
  Hollow, *E*)
John's Grill (Union Square, *M*)
Mel's Diner (Pacific Heights/
  Cow Hollow, *I*)
One Market (Financial District, *E*)
Patio Café (Gay Restaurants, *I*)
Planet Hollywood (Union Square, *I*)
Postrio (Union Square, *E*)
Salmagundi (Union Square, *I*)
Sears Fine Foods (Union Square, *I*)
Tommy's Joynt (Around Town, *I*)
Without Reservation
  (Gay Restaurants, *I*)
Woodward's Garden (Around
  Town, *I*)

AMERICAN/FRENCH

Universal Café (Mission
  District, *I*)

ASIAN/ITALIAN

Oritalia (Pacific Heights/
  Cow Hollow, *M*)

CALIFORNIA

Act IV (Civic Center, *E*)
Bix (North Beach, *E*)
Café Flore (Gay Restaurants, *I*)
Gordon Biersch Brewery (Around
  Town, *M*)
Hawthorn Lane (South of Market, *E*)

Moose's (North Beach, *E*)
"No Name" (Gay Restaurants, *I*)
Rumpus (Union Square, *M*)
Stars (Civic Center, *E*)
Val 21 (Mission District, *M*)

CALIFORNIA/ASIAN

Pacific (Union Square, *E*)
Silks (Financial District, *E*)

CALIFORNIA/AUSTRIAN

Hyde Street Bistro (Around
  Town, *M*)

CALIFORNIA/CHINESE

China Moon Café (Union
  Square, *M*)

CALIFORNIA/FRENCH

The Big Four (Around Town, *E*)
Brasserie Savoy (Union Square, *M*)
Ritz-Carlton Dining Room
  (Around Town, *E*)

CAJUN/CREOLE

The Elite Café (Pacific Heights/
  Cow Hollow, *M*)

CALIFORNIA/MEDITERRANEAN

PlumpJack Café (Pacific Heights/
  Cow Hollow, *M*)

CARIBBEAN

Cha Cha Cha (Haight-Ashbury, *I*)
Miss Pearl's Jam House (Civic
  Center, *M*)

CHINESE

Betelnut (Pacific Heights/
  Cow Hollow, *M*)
Brandy Ho's Hunan Food
  (Chinatown, *M*)
Harbor Village (Financial
  District, *E*)
Hong Kong Flower Lounge (Around
  Town, *I*)
House of Nanking (Chinatown, *I*)
The Mandarin (Fisherman's
  Wharf, *M*)

Key to Abbreviations: *E*= Expensive; *I*=Inexpensive; *M*=Moderate; *VE*=Very Expensive

Sam Wo (Chinatown, *I*)
Tommy Toy's (Financial
  District, *E*)
Yank Sing (Financial District, *M*)

CHINESE/DIM SUM

Hong Kong Flower Lounge
  (Around Town, *I*)
Yank Sing (Financial District, *M*)

CONTINENTAL

Cliff House (Around Town, *M*)
Carnelian Room (Financial
  District, *E*)
Grand Cafe (Union Square, *M*)
Jack's (Financial District, *M*)
Lulu (South of Market, *M*)
Rubicon (Financial District, *E*)
White Horse Tavern (Union
  Square, *M*)

CREPES

Crepes on Cole (Haight-Ashbury, *I*)

FRENCH

Alain Rondelli (Around Town, *E*)
Café Claude (Union Square, *M*)
Charles Nob Hill (Around
  Town, *E*)
City of Paris (Union Square, *M*)
Fleur de Lys (Union Square, *E*)
Flying Saucer (Mission
  District, *M*)
Fringale Restaurant (South of
  Market, *M*)
La Folie (Pacific Heights/
  Cow Hollow, *E*)
Masa's (Union Square, *E*)
South Park Café (South of
  Market, *I*)

FRENCH/ITALIAN

Bizou (South of Market, *M*)
Scala's Bistro (Union Square, *M*)

FRENCH/JAPANESE

Yo Yo Tsumami Bistro (Japan
  Center and Environs, *M*)

INDIAN

Gaylord's (Fisherman's Wharf, *M*)
North India Restaurant (Pacific
  Heights/Cow Hollow, *M*)

INTERNATIONAL

World Wrapps (Pacific Heights/
  Cow Hollow, *I*)

ITALIAN

A. Sabella's (Fisherman's Wharf, *E*)
Cafe Pescatore (Fisherman's
  Wharf, *M*)
Cafe Riggio (Around Town, *M*)
Caffè Freddy's (North Beach, *I*)
Caffè Lutia Pietia (Gay
  Restaurants, *I*)
Caffè Sport (North Beach, *E*)
Fino (Union Square, *M*)
Gira Polli (North Beach, *I*)
Il Fornio (Around Town, *M*)
Kuleto's (Union Square, *M*)
L'Osteria del Forno
  (North Beach, *I*)
Mario's Bohemian Cigar Store
  (North Beach, *I*)
North Beach Restaurant
  (North Beach, *M*)
Pane e Vino (Pacific Heights/
  Cow Hollow, *M*)
Pasta Pomodoro (North Beach, *I*)
Puccinni and Pinetti
  (Union Square, *M*)
Prego (Pacific Heights/
  Cow Hollow, *M*)
Stinking Rose (North Beach, *M*)
Tommaso's (North Beach, *M*)
Zinzino (Pacific Heights/
  Cow Hollow, *M*)

ITALIAN/ARGENTINEAN

Il Pollaio (North Beach, *I*)

JAPANESE

Flying Kamikazes (Pacific Heights/
  Cow Hollow, *M*)
Kabuto Sushi (Around Town, *M*)
Kyo-Ya (South of Market, *E*)
Osome (Pacific Heights/Cow
  Hollow, *M*)
Sanppo (Japan Center and
  Environs, *I*)

MEDITERRANEAN

Enrico's (North Beach, *M*)
42 Degrees (Around Town, *M*)
Zuni Café (Civic Center, *M*)

MEDITERRANEAN/AMERICAN

Splendido (Financial District, *M*)

MEDITERRANEAN/ITALIAN

Little City Antipasta Bar (North Beach, *M*)

MEXICAN

Café Marimba (Pacific Heights/Cow Hollow, *M*)

La Canasta (Pacific Heights/Cow Hollow, *I*)

Sweet Heat (Pacific Heights/Cow Hollow, *I*)

Zona Rosa (Haight-Ashbury, *I*)

PERSIAN/MIDDLE EASTERN

Maykadeh (North Beach, *E*)

PIZZA

Marcello's (Around Town, *I*)

SEAFOOD

A. Sabella's (Fisherman's Wharf, *E*)

Alioto's (Fisherman's Warf, *E*)

Aqua (Financial District, *E*)

Hayes Street Grill (Civic Center, *M*)

Sam's Grill and Seafood Restaurant (Financial District, *M*)

Scott's Seafood Grill and Bar (Financial District, *E*)

Swan Oyster Depot (Around Town, *I*)

Tadich Grill (Financial District, *M*)

SINGAPOREAN

Straits Café (Around Town, *I*)

SOUPS/SALADS/SANDWICHES

Mad Magda's Russian Tearoom and Café (Gay Restaurants, *I*)

SUSHI

Flying Kamikazes (Pacific Heights/Cow Hollow, *M*)

Kabuto Sushi (Around Town, *M*)

Kyo-Ya (South of Market, *E*)

THAI

Cha Am (South of Market, *M*)

Khan Toke Thai House (Around Town, *M*)

Manora's (South of Market, *I*)

VEGAN

Millenium (Civic Center, *M*)

VEGETARIAN

Greens Restaurant, Fort Mason (Pacific Heights/Cow Hollow, *M*)

VIETNAMESE

Tú Lan (Union Square, *I*)

3 Union Square

EXPENSIVE

✪ **Fleur de Lys.** 777 Sutter St. (at Jones St.). ☎ **415/673-7779.** Reservations recommended. Main courses $27–$35.50; five-course tasting menu $65; four-course vegetarian menu $50. AE, CB, DC, MC, V. Mon–Thurs 6–10pm, Fri–Sat 5:30–10:30pm. Bus: 2, 3, 4, 27, or 38. FRENCH.

Imagine a large version of Jeannie's (as in *I Dream of Jeannie*) live-in bottle; dark, cozy, with 700 yards of rich red floor-to-ceiling hand-painted fabric enclosing the room in lavish intimacy. Throw in dimly lit French candelabras, an extraordinary sculptural floral centerpiece, and about 20 tables filled with well-dressed diners. Welcome to one of the most renowned dining rooms in San Francisco. Fleur de Lys does everything seriously, from its foie gras starter to its petit fours after dinner. And with Chef Hubert Keller (who was President Clinton's first guest chef at the White House) in the kitchen, it's impossible to go wrong. You can order à la carte from the five-course tasting menu or from the four-course vegetarian menu. Start with the knockout blue potato chips with cauliflower purée and caviar. Try any of the "symphony" of appetizers, which include crispy sweetbreads with rock shrimp mousseline, citrus and peppercorn vinaigrette, and Beluga caviar with celery root blinis. Venture on to a main course, which might include herb-crusted salmon with mushrooms and spinach noodle pie or lamb loin with black truffles. Desserts are artistic creations and might feature chocolate-mousse mice or swans with meringue wings and raspberry coulis. A selection of 300 French and California wines makes this an all-around dining fantasy.

✪ **Masa's.** In the Hotel Vintage Court, 648 Bush St. (at Stockton St.). ☎ **415/989-7154.** Reservations required; accepted up to 21 days in advance. Main courses $30–$38.50; fixed-price dinner $68–$75. AE, CB, DC, DISC, MC, V. Tues–Sat 6–9:30pm. Closed first week in Jan and 4th week in July. Cable Car: Powell-Mason and Powell-Hyde lines. Bus: 2, 3, 4, 30, or 45. FRENCH.

After the death of founder Masataha Kobayashi in 1984, local gourmets questioned the future of Masa's—but no more. Chef Julian Serrano's brilliant cuisine matched with a flawless wine list and exemplary (even unpretentious) service has solidified Masa's reputation as one of the country's great French outposts.

Either fixed price or à la carte, dinner is a memorable expense-be-damned experience from start to finish. If you wish, you can simply leave the decisions up to the kitchen. Serrano's passion for using only the highest quality ingredients accounts for the restaurant's four-star ranking—and budget-busting prices. A typical dinner may begin with the Sonoma foie gras in a Madeira truffle sauce, or poached lobster with potatoes, fried leek, and a truffle vinaigrette. Main entrées may include medallions of New Zealand fallow deer with zinfandel sauce and caramelized green apples, or the Atlantic black bass with a saffron sauce. Dessert, as you would imagine, is heavenly.

Pacific. 500 Post St. (at Mason St. in the Pan Pacific Hotel). ☎ **415/771-8600.** Reservations recommended for dinner. Main courses $3.50–$13 breakfast, $8–$11.50 lunch, $17–$24 dinner. AE, DC, MC, V. Mon–Fri 6:30am–9:30pm, Sat–Sun 7am–10pm; Sat–Sun brunch 10am–2:30pm. Cable Car: Powell-Mason. Bus: 2, 3, 4, or 76. CALIFORNIA/ASIAN.

It's surprising how few people have heard about Pacific, especially considering that it has some veritable superstar chefs in its kitchen—including ex-Masa chef Taka Kawai, who now runs the show, and a wizard of a pastry chef who previously worked for Prince Ranier of Monaco. Combine this with professional yet unpretentious table service, a beautiful, marble-rich, mezzanine-level dining room, and a phenomenal wine selection, and what you end up with is a memorable dining experience.

On our last visit, we started with the fresh Sonoma foie gras sauté with braised daikon and shimeji mushrooms—which literally melted in our mouths—and the tournedos of lobster accompanied by an array of fresh root vegetables. Both were flawless. The tender rack of lamb, which came with garlic mashed potatoes and ratatouille flan, was equally good, as was the duck breast layered with a wild berry sauce and delectable little corn crepes. If you really want to have some fun, allow the sommelier to choose a suitable glass of wine to accompany each dish. A little secret: Lunch offers similar service and selections at nearly half the price.

✪ **Postrio.** 545 Post St. (between Mason and Taylor sts.). ☎ **415/776-7825.** Reservations required. Main courses $6–$15 breakfast, $14–$15 lunch, $20–$26 dinner. AE, CB, DC, DISC, MC, V. Mon–Fri 7–10am, 11:30am–2pm, and 5:30–10:30pm; Sat–Sun 9am–2pm; bar daily 11:30am–2am. Cable Car: Powell-Mason and Powell-Hyde lines. Bus: 2, 3, 4, or 38. AMERICAN.

They say the higher you climb, the longer it takes to fall, and that's certainly the case with Postrio. Ever since chefs Anne and David Gingrass left the kitchen to start their own enterprise, rumors have been flying that San Francisco's top restaurant isn't what it used to be (poor execution from the line tops the list). If its owners are crying, however, they're crying all the way to the bank, because it's a rare night when the kitchen doesn't perform to a full house.

Dining Near Union Square & the Financial District

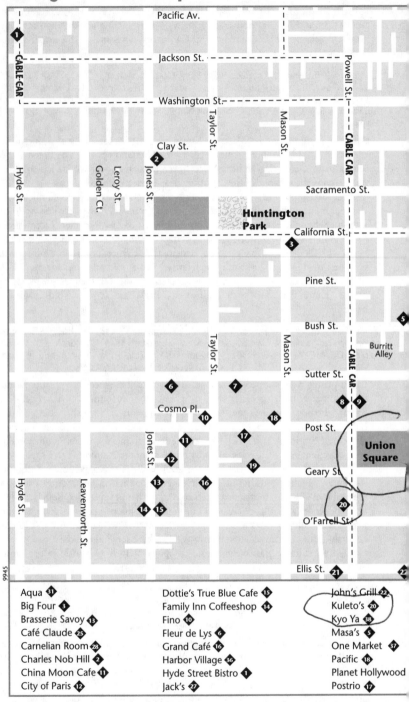

Aqua **31**
Big Four **3**
Brasserie Savoy **13**
Café Claude **25**
Carnelian Room **28**
Charles Nob Hill **2**
China Moon Cafe **11**
City of Paris **12**

Dottie's True Blue Cafe **15**
Family Inn Coffeeshop **14**
Fino **10**
Fleur de Lys **6**
Grand Café **16**
Harbor Village **36**
Hyde Street Bistro **1**
Jack's **27**

John's Grill **22**
Kuleto's **20**
Kyo Ya **38**
Masa's **5**
One Market **37**
Pacific **18**
Planet Hollywood
Postrio **17**

0 ▣▣▣ 100 m
        110 y

N

BLE CAR

Grant Av.
Columbus Ave.
Kearny St.
Montgomery St.
Sansome St.
Battery St.
Front St.
Davis St.
Drumm St.

Claude Ln.

man
Pl.
mpton Pl.

Maiden La.

Market St.
1st St.
Fremont St.
Beale St.

Market St.
New Montgomery St.
2nd St.
Mission St.

Third St.

Howard St.

Folsom St.

101

Eating, however, is only half the reason one comes to Postrio. After squeezing through the perpetually swinging bar—which, in its own right, dishes out excellent tapas and pizzas from a wood-burning oven in the corner—guests are forced to make a grand entrance down the antebellum staircase to the cavernous dining room below (it's everyone's 15 seconds of fame, so make sure your fly is zipped). Pure Hollywood, for sure, but fun.

The menu, prepared by brothers Mitchell and Steven Rosenthal, combines Italian, Asian, French, and California styles with mixed results. When we last visited Postrio, the sautéed salmon, for example, was a bit overcooked, but the accompanying plum glaze, wasabi mashed potatoes, and miso vinaigrette were outstanding. Again with the grilled squab: It lacked flavor, but the accompaniment—a sweet potato foie gras spring roll—was pure genius. The desserts, each artistically sculpted by pastry chef Janet Rikala, were the highlight of the evening. Despite the prime-time rush, service was friendly and infallible, as was the presentation.

MODERATE

✪ **Brasserie Savoy.** In the Savoy Hotel, 580 Geary St. (at Jones St.) ☎ **415/474-8686.** Reservations recommended. Main courses $11–$17. AE, DC, DISC, JCB, MC, V. Daily 6:30–11am and 5:30–10pm. Bus: 2, 3, 4, 27, or 38. CALIFORNIA/FRENCH.

If you're headed to the theater or are just looking for a good meal downtown, Brasserie Savoy is an excellent option. The atmosphere is French bistro, with a bright, busy dining room, black and white marble floors, and tables with beige and black leather, and woven chairs. The food is consistent, affordable, and delicious. Choices may include beef tenderloin with port sauce and green peppercorn butter, or duck breast with mille-feuille of potato and mushrooms served with a date purée and coffee sauce. On the lighter side, the crawfish risotto with red and green peppers, scallions, celery, and chive lemongrass butter is a perfect dish. Among the appetizers, the napoleon of braised rabbit with red onions, mushrooms, kalamata olives, and anise tuiles is a preferred choice, if it's offered, or any one of several freshly made salads. To finish, try the innovative crème brûlée.

Café Claude. 7 Claude Lane. ☎ **415/392-3505.** Reservations accepted. Main courses $5–$13. AE, MC, V. Mon–Fri 8am–10:30pm, Sat 10am–10:30pm. Cable Car: Powell-Hyde and Powell-Mason lines. FRENCH.

Euro-transplants love Café Claude, a crowded and lively restaurant tucked in a narrow lane near Union Square. Seemingly everything—every table, every spoon, every saltshaker, and every waiter—is imported from France. There is usually live jazz on Tuesdays and Thursdays after 7pm and Fridays and Saturdays after 11pm; outdoor seating is available when weather permits. With prices topping out at about $11 for main courses such as poussin rôti or the poisson du jour (fish of the day), Café Claude is a good value.

✪ **China Moon Café.** 639 Post St. (between Jones and Taylor sts.). ☎ **415/775-4789.** Main courses $15–$18.50. AE, DC, MC, V. Daily 5:30–10pm. Cable Car: Powell St. Bus: 2, 3, 4, 27, or 38. CALIFORNIA/CHINESE.

Chinese-food lovers are in for a treat at the landmark art deco coffee shop of China Moon. Painted in colors inspired by a 1989 Matisse exhibition, China Moon offers innovative and extraordinary Chinese cuisine prepared at the window-front kitchen. Sit at the candle-lit counter for a good view or slide into a booth for more intimate dining, then pore over the mouth-watering menu (it changes monthly but favorites are always available with some variation). Chopsticks in hand, pluck up a flavor-bursting spring roll, perhaps one filled with curried pork, fresh chiles, and glass noodles, then plunge it into its dipping sauce guaranteed to make your tongue dance. Then get a little loose—if it's available, pick up a duck-filled steamed lotus bun with your fingers, dab it in the rich, gingery plum sauce, and pop it into your mouth for another taste tango. You won't want to miss the pot-browned noodle pillow, which may be topped with chicken, oyster mushrooms, green chard, sunchokes, and, yes, accompanied by yet another wonderfully flavored sauce. For dessert, housemade ginger ice cream bathing in chocolate sauce keeps customers begging for more. If you can't live without learning the secrets of China Moon's kitchen, you can purchase owner Barbara Tropp's two cookbooks here. Keep in mind that portions are on the small side —you're paying for quality, not quantity.

City of Paris. 101 Shannon Alley (at Geary St.). ☎ **415/441-4442.** Main courses $6–$18. AE, MC, V. Tues–Sun 11:30am–2pm; daily 5:30–11pm. Cable Car: Powell St. FRENCH.

Named after the venerable Union Square department store that is now a Neiman Marcus, this popular Parisian-style bistro offers somewhat upscale dining without the usual outrageous prices of similar haute restaurants in the neighborhood. It's a bit tough to find, hidden up a small alley off Geary Street, but it's worth the effort— particularly for the rotisserie chicken or rack of lamb grilled enticingly behind the glimmering open kitchen. Service is a little shaky, and things tend to get noisy when the theater lets out, but otherwise the City of Paris is highly recommended for an informal night on the town.

Fino. 624 Post St. (between Taylor and Jones sts.). ☎ **415/928-2080.** Reservations recommended. Main courses $9–$17. AE, DC, MC, V. Daily 5:30–10pm. Cable Car: Powell-Mason and Powell-Hyde lines. ITALIAN.

Fino may not serve the best Italian food in the city, but it's certainly in the running for the most *romantic* Italian restaurant in the city. Beyond the arched windows and carved mahogany bar is a small, intimate dining room swathed in dark woods and bronze and warmed by a beautiful marble fireplace. Among the specialties are the contadina, an Italian stir-fry pasta with fresh vegetables, the salmon Palermo, prepared with olives, capers, spinach, and tomatoes in a creamy tomato sauce, and the zuppa di pesci (fish soup) filled with prawns, clams, scallops, salmon, and calamari. For dessert, try the chocolate raspberry crème brûlée; finish the evening with a snifter of brandy at the bar.

Grand Cafe. 501 Geary St. (at Taylor St.). ☎ **415/292-0101.** Reservations accepted. Main courses $9.25–$16. AE, DC, MC, V. 7am–3pm daily; Sun–Thurs 5–10pm, cafe menu until 1am; Fri–Sat 5–11pm, cafe menu until 2am. Bus: 2, 3, 4, 27, or 38. CONTINENTAL.

The Grand Cafe is hands down the most amazing room in the Union Square area. The cocktail area is swank and packed with a good-looking crowd, but walk back to the enormous but cozy dining area if you really want to be impressed. It's an architecturally restored, turn-of-the-century grand ballroom with 30-foot ceilings and an aura of old Europe interlaced with art nouveau and art deco. From every angle you'll see incredibly playful commissioned local art, which includes a towering bunny sculpture that you really must see for yourself. Though off to a shaky start in 1995, the fare is ambitious as well. Signature appetizers include a rich polenta soufflé served on a wild mushroom ragout with fonduta, and grilled eggplant napoleon. Move on to a main course, such as the lobster and shrimp ravioli in sorrel cream sauce or grilled Delmonico steak au poivre verte with pommes frites (steak with green pepper and french fries). The food, though not the absolute best in town, is very good, and the atmosphere and prices make it a worthwhile place to check out.

John's Grill. 63 Ellis St. (at Stockton St.). ☎ **415/986-DASH.** Reservations accepted. Main courses $12–$25. AE, DC, DISC, MC, V. Mon–Sat 11am–10pm, Sun 5–10pm. Cable Car: Powell-Mason, Powell-Hyde. Muni Metro: All Market St. trams. Bus: 38 or any Market St. AMERICAN.

John's Grill was one of Dashiell Hammett's regular hangouts in the 1920s, and the restaurant has been cashing in on that connection ever since. You may recall that in *The Maltese Falcon,* Sam Spade stops here for chops, a baked potato, and sliced tomatoes, before setting out on a wild-goose chase after the mysterious Brigid O'Shaughnessy. The real mystery, however, is why people still come here. We've eaten here three times, and on each occasion the food was ill-prepared and oversauced (as well as overpriced), and the service was atrociously unprofessional. Sam Spade buffs are better off just stopping in for a drink at the memorabilia-filled bar and lounge, which looks much the same as it did in Hammett's day.

Kuleto's. 221 Powell St. (between Geary and O'Farrell sts., in the Villa Florence Hotel). ☎ **415/397-7720.** Reservations recommended. Breakfast $3–$8; main courses $8–$18. AE, CB, DC, DISC, MC, V. Mon–Fri 7–10:30am, Sat and Sun 8–10:30am; daily 11:30am–11pm. Cable Car: Powell-Mason, Powell-Hyde. Muni Metro: Powell. Bus: 2, 3, 4, or 38. ITALIAN.

Story has it the owners of this popular downtown bistro were so delighted with the design of their new restaurant that they named it after the architect, Pat Kuleto. Whatever the reason, Kuleto's is truly a beautiful place filled with beautiful people who are here to see and be seen (don't come underdressed). The best plan of action is to skip the wait for a table, muscle a seat at the antipasto bar, and fill up on appetizers (which are often better than the entrées). For a main course, try the penne pasta drenched in a tangy lamb sausage marinara sauce, the clam linguini (generously overloaded with fresh clams), or any of the fresh fish specials grilled over hardwoods. If you don't arrive by 6pm, expect to wait—this place fills up mucha fasta.

Puccini & Pinetti. 129 Ellis St. (at Cyril Magnin). ☎ **415/392-5500.** Reservations recommended. Main courses $5–$13. AE, CB, DC, DISC, MC, V. Daily 11:30am–3:30pm; Sun–Thurs 5 –10pm, Fri–Sat 5–11pm. Cable Car: Powell-Mason. Bus: 27 or 38. ITALIAN.

It takes some buco bravado to open an Italian restaurant in San Francisco, but partners Bob Puccini and Steve Pinetti obviously did their homework, because this trendy little trattoria has been packed since the day it opened. The formula isn't exactly unique: good food at great prices. What really makes it work, though, is the upbeat, casual ambience, colorful decor, and live music Monday through Friday nights—sort of like crashing a catered party.

The menu doesn't take any chances. Italian standbys—pastas, salads, wood-fired pizzas, grilled meats—dominate the menu. The grilled salmon with sautéed spinach has been well received, along with the stuffed, oven-roasted portobello mushroom antipasti and fresh-baked focaccia sandwiches. The creamy tiramisu makes for a proper finish.

✪ **Rumpus.** 1 Tillman Place (off Grant Ave., between Sutter and Post sts.). ☎ **415/421-2300.** Reservations recommended. Main courses $11.95–$16.95. AE, DC, MC, V. Mon–Sat 11:30am–2:30pm, Sun–Thurs 5:30–10pm, Fri–Sat 5:30–11pm. CALIFORNIA.

Impressions

[San Francisco is] the city that knows how.

—President William Howard Taft

[San Francisco is] the city that knows chow.

—Trader Vic, Restaurateur

Tucked into a small cul-de-sac off Grant Avenue, you'll find Rumpus, a fantastic new restaurant serving well-prepared California fare at reasonable prices. The perfect place for a business lunch, shopping break, or dinner with friends, Rumpus is architecturally playful, colorful, and buzzing with conversation. Like most "in" restaurants in town, ahi tuna tartare is on the starters list. It is, however, wonderfully fresh, savory, and spiced with wasabi caviar. The pan-roasted chicken's crispy and flavorful crust is almost as delightful as the perfectly cooked chicken and mashed potatoes beneath it; and the quality cut of New York steak comes with a sweet-potato mash. If nothing else, make sure to stop in here for one of the best desserts we've ever had: the puddinglike chocolate brioche cake.

✪ **Scala's Bistro.** 432 Powell St. (at Sutter St.). ☎ **415/395-8555.** Reservations recommended. Breakfast $6–$9; lunch and dinner main courses $8–$17. AE, CB, DC, DISC, MC, V. Mon–Sun 6:30am–12am. Cable Car: Powell-Hyde. Bus: 2, 3, 4, 30, 45, or 76. FRENCH/ ITALIAN.

We had heard so much hype about the new Scala's Bistro that we were sure it wouldn't live up to our expectations. Let's just say we were happily mistaken. Firmly entrenched at the base of the refurbished Sir Francis Drake Hotel, this latest venture by husband and wife team Giovanni (the host) and Donna (the chef) Scala is one of the best new restaurants in the city. The Parisian-bistro/old-world atmosphere blends just the right balance of elegance and informality, which means it's perfectly okay to have some fun here (and apparently most people do).

Drawing from her success at Bistro Don Giovanni in Napa, Donna has put together a fantastic array of Italian and French dishes that are priced surprisingly low. Start with the Earth and Surf calamari appetizer (better than anything I've sampled along the Mediterranean) or the grilled portobello mushrooms. The Golden Beet salad and Anchor Steam mussels are also good bets, as is the Cipolla Pazza: hot Italian sausage spaghetti served in a roasted onion. Generous portions of the moist, rich duck leg confit will satisfy hungry appetites, but if you can only order one thing, make it Scala's signature dish: the seared salmon. Resting on a bed of creamy buttermilk mashed potatoes and ensconced with a tomato, chive, and white wine sauce, it's one of the best salmon dishes I've ever tasted. Finish with the creamy Bostini cream pie, a dreamy combo of vanilla custard and orange chiffon cake with a warm chocolate glaze.

White Horse Tavern. In The Beresford Hotel, 635 Sutter St. (between Mason and Taylor sts.). ☎ **415/673-9900.** Main courses $10.95–$14.95. AE, DC, MC, V. Tues–Sat 5:30–10:30pm. Bus: 2, 3, 4, 30, 38, or 45. CONTINENTAL.

Entering the White Horse Tavern is like going through a time/dimension warp to merrie olde England. A traditional English pub right down to the corned beef and cabbage, this small, quaint downtown fixture is usually frequented by older folk staying at the adjacent Beresford and Cartwright hotels. The food is also on the traditional side, featuring such steadfast selections as loin lamb chops with mint sauce, a stuffed pork chop served with apple sauce, and the classic prime rib and potato. It's far from exciting, but portions are substantial and prices are more than fair. The adorable little bar adjacent the dining area is the perfect spot for a predinner cocktail.

INEXPENSIVE

Dottie's True Blue Café. 522 Jones St. (at O'Farrell St.). ☎ **415/885-2767.** Reservations not accepted. Breakfast $4–$7; main courses $4.25–$7. DISC, MC, V. Wed–Mon 7:30am–2pm. Cable Car: Powell-Mason line. Bus: 2, 3, 4, 27, or 38. AMERICAN.

This family owned breakfast restaurant in the Pacific Bay Inn has only 10 tables and a handful of counter stools. A traditional coffee shop (with the exception of an espresso machine), Dottie's serves standard American morning fare (French toast, pancakes, bacon and eggs, omelets, and the like) delivered to blue-and-white checkerboard tablecloths on rugged, diner-quality plates. Whatever you order arrives with homemade bread, muffins, or scones. There are also daily specials and vegetarian dishes.

Family Inn Coffee Shop. 505 Jones St. (at O'Farrell St.). ☎ **415/771-5995.** Main courses $4–$6. No credit cards. Tues–Fri 7am–6pm, Sat 7am–4:30pm. Bus: 2, 3, 4, or 38. AMERICAN.

If you want a really inexpensive, hearty meal, it's hard to top the Family Inn. The menu varies daily, but homemade soups are featured at lunch, along with a special main course served with mashed potatoes, a vegetable, bread, and dessert that costs less than $5. It's not the least bit fancy—just counter seats in front of a hard-working kitchen—but the food is wholesome, good, and the price is right.

Planet Hollywood. 2 Stockton St. (at Market St.). ☎ 415/421-7827. Reservations not accepted except for parties of 20 or more. $7.75–$18.95. AE, DC, DISC, MC, V. Daily 11am–1am. Bus: 38 or any Market St. bus or Muni Metro. AMERICAN.

You won't find any locals here (or movie stars, for that matter), but for some reason tourists can't help but flock to Planet Hollywood. Similar to the Hard Rock, this is a themed restaurant chain that, instead of music, exhibits movie memorabilia. Expect long lines to get in, plenty of fellow tourists, and an affordable menu featuring salads, sandwiches, pastas, burgers, pizzas, fajitas, and a few grilled meat items.

Salmagundi. 442 Geary St. (between Mason and Taylor sts.). ☎ **415/441-0894.** Soups and salads $3.50–$8.50. AE, MC, V. Tues–Sat 11am–11pm, Sun–Mon 11am–9pm. Cable Car: Powell-Mason and Powell-Hyde lines. Bus: 2, 3, 4, or 38. AMERICAN.

If you're pinching pennies on this trip, there's no better deal on a meal in Union Square than at Salmagundi. Bright, pleasant, and sparkling clean, this cafeteria-style restaurant offers a variety of soups, salads, sandwiches, and the occasional special. Among the more unusual soup choices are English country cheddar, Hungarian goulash, North Beach minestrone, Barbary Coast bouillabaisse, and Ukrainian beef borscht. Seats in the rear look out onto a tiny garden.

Sears Fine Foods. 439 Powell St. (between Post and Sutter sts.). ☎ **415/986-1160.** Reservations not accepted. Breakfast $3–$8; salads and soups $1.80–$8; main courses $5–$10. No credit cards. Wed–Sun 6:30am–3:30pm. Cable Car: Powell-Mason and Powell-Hyde lines. Bus: 2, 3, 4, or 38. AMERICAN.

Sears would be the perfect place to breakfast on the way to work, but you can't always guarantee you'll get in the door before 9am. It's not just another pink-tabled diner run by motherly matrons, it's an institution, famous for its crispy, dark-brown waffles, light sourdough French toast, and Swedish dollar-sized pancakes. As the story goes, Sears was founded in 1938 by Ben Sears, a retired clown. It was his Swedish wife Hilbur, however, who was responsible for the legendary pancakes, which are still whipped up according to her family's secret recipe.

✪ Tú Lan. 8 Sixth St. (at Market St.). ☎415/626-0927. $3.50–$7. No credit cards. Mon–Sat 11am–9pm. Muni metro: F, J, K, L, M, N. Cable Cars: Powell-Mason and Powell-Hyde lines. Bus: 6, 7, 27, 31, 66, or 71. VIETNAMESE.

If you can handle walking down Sixth Street past the winos, weirdoes, and street stench and you don't need a beautiful dining room to make you appreciate your meal, you won't find better (or cheaper) Vietnamese food than that of Tú Lan. Even Julia Child (whose face graces the greasy old menus) has been known to pull up a chair at this shack of a restaurant to feast on such goodies as imperial rolls on a bed of rice noodles, lettuce, peanuts, and mint (under $5). Take pity on the poor waiter, who never seems to bring water no matter how many times you ask; he's been working here forever, he's the only server, and the place is always packed. For the price, this has been one of our all-time favorite restaurants for more than a decade.

4 Financial District

EXPENSIVE

✪ **Aqua.** 252 California St. (between Battery and Front sts.). ☎ **415/956-9662.** Reservations recommended. Main courses $26–$32; six-course tasting menu $65; vegetarian tasting menu $45. AE, DC, MC, V. Mon–Fri 11:30am–2pm; Mon–Sat 5:30–10:30pm. All Market St. buses. SEAFOOD.

Without question, Aqua is San Francisco's finest seafood restaurant, light years beyond the genre of shrimp cocktails and lemon-butter sauce. Chef Michael Mina dazzles his customers with a bewildering juxtaposition of earth and sea. The salmon, for example, is first glazed in ginger, then spiced with sweet orange marmalade that contrasts perfectly with the sour reduction sauce of braised red cabbage. The Atlantic cod has a similar twist: lightly seared and fully flavored with a tangy cabernet reduction, then accompanied by a wonderful caramelized onion risotto. Mina's passion for exotic mushrooms pervades most dishes, for taste as well as for show (Mina is, to a fault, amazingly adept at the art of presentation). Desserts are equally impressive, particularly the spiced pumpkin brioche with cream cheese ice cream, and the chocolate tasting plate—a feast for the eyes as well as the palate. Steep prices prevent most people from making a regular appearance, but for special occasions or billable lunches, Aqua is highly recommended.

Carnelian Room. 555 California St. (at Montgomery St.). ☎ **415/433-7500.** Reservations recommended. Main courses $25–$55, $24.50 adult brunch, $12 children. AE, CB, DC, DISC, MC, V. Mon–Sun 6pm–10pm; Sun 10am–2:30pm Brunch. Cable Car: California. Bus: 1, 15, 9, or 42. CONTINENTAL.

By day, the Carnelian Room is the exclusive Banker's Club, accessible only to members or by invitation, but at night anyone with a big enough bankroll can dine among the clouds. Soaring 52 stories above San Francisco's Financial District on the top floor of the Bank of America building, the Carnelian Room is a definite contender for "Best View." Dark oak paneling, brass railings, and huge picture windows reek with romanticism, particularly if you're fortunate enough to get a window table. Though the menu is definitely upscale, it tends to cater to old-style banker's tastes: expensive meat dishes—New Yorks, tenderloins, rack of lamb, pork loin, veal—with rich, thick sauces dominate the menu. A wine cellar of some 36,000 bottles all but guarantees the proper vintage to accompany your meal.

Harbor Village. 4 Embarcadero Center, lobby level (at Drumm St. between Sacramento and Clay sts.). ☎ **415/781-8833.** Reservations recommended. Main courses $9–$32. AE, DC, MC, V. Mon–Fri 11am–2:30pm, Sat 10:30am–2:30pm, Sun 10am–2:30pm; daily 5:30–9:30pm. Bus: 15, 45, or 76. CHINESE.

Voted best Chinese restaurant in San Francisco by *San Francisco* magazine, this is one of the city's most upscale Chinese restaurants, which serves primarily Cantonese dishes along with spicy Szechuan specials.

A courteous staff can guide you through the extensive menu, which includes some 30 seafood dishes alone, such as striped bass steamed with ginger and scallions. If you've never had shark fin soup, this is the place to try it. Unique appetizers include shredded spicy chicken and minced squab in lettuce cups. Stir-fried garlic prawns, beggar's chicken cooked in a clay pot, and sizzling beef in black-pepper sauce are

Dining Around Town

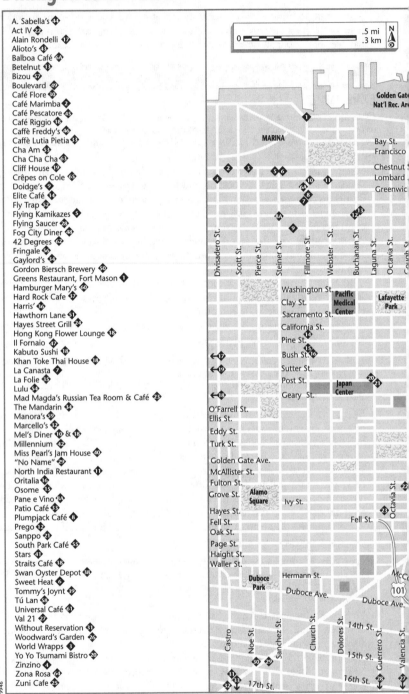

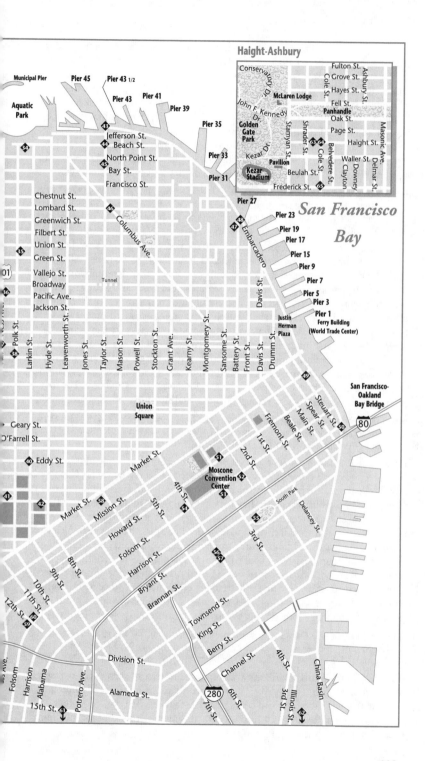

Haight-Ashbury

Conservatory Dr.
Fulton St.
Grove St.
Cole St.
Hayes St.
Ashbury St.
McLaren Lodge
Fell St.
Panhandle
John F. Kennedy Dr.
Oak St.
Golden Gate Park
Page St.
Stanyan St.
Shrader St.
Cole St.
Belvedere St.
Haight St.
Masonic Ave.
Kezar Dr.
Waller St.
Downey
Clayton
Delmar St.
Pavilion
Beulah St.
Kezar Stadium
Frederick St.

Municipal Pier
Pier 45
Pier 43 1/2
Pier 43
Pier 41
Pier 39
Aquatic Park
Pier 35
Jefferson St.
Beach St.
North Point St.
Pier 33
Bay St.
Pier 31
Francisco St.
Pier 27

San Francisco Bay

Chestnut St.
Lombard St.
Greenwich St.
Filbert St.
Union St.
Green St.
Columbus Ave.
Pier 23
Pier 19
Pier 17
Vallejo St.
Broadway
Pacific Ave.
Jackson St.
Embarcadero
Pier 15
Pier 9
Pier 7
Pier 5
Pier 3
Pier 1
Tunnel
Davis St.
Justin Herman Plaza
Ferry Building (World Trade Center)

Polk St.
Larkin St.
Hyde St.
Leavenworth St.
Jones St.
Taylor St.
Mason St.
Powell St.
Stockton St.
Grant Ave.
Kearny St.
Montgomery St.
Sansome St.
Battery St.
Front St.
Davis St.
Drumm St.

Union Square

San Francisco-Oakland Bay Bridge

Geary St.
O'Farrell St.

Eddy St.
Steuart St.
Spear St.
Main St.
Beale St.
Fremont St.
1st St.
Market St.
Market St.
Mission St.
Howard St.
4th St.
5th St.
2nd St.
80

Moscone Convention Center
Folsom St.
South Park
Delancey St.
8th St.
Harrison St.
3rd St.
9th St.
Bryant St.
10th St.
Brannan St.
11th St.
12th St.
Townsend St.
King St.
Berry St.
Channel St.
4th St.
China Basin
Division St.
280
Alameda St.
Folsom
Harrison
Alabama
Potrero Ave.
15th St.
7th St.
6th St.
Illinois St.
3rd St.

excellent main-course choices. Dim sum lunch is served daily (from 11am weekdays, 10:30am on Saturday and 10am on Sunday) and is definitely worth trying (although the Hong Kong Flower Lounge is better if you don't mind venturing to the Richmond District). The wait staff brings trays full of steaming hot appetizers (they will happily explain what they are) from which you can choose what you like. Try the Shanghai-style steamed pork dumplings flavored with ginger and scallions, the rice-paper dumplings filled with sweet shrimp, taro cake, or the curried beef wonton.

The restaurant offers validated parking at all the Embarcadero Center garages (located at the foot of Clay Street). It'll cost you a few dollars during weekdays, but it's free after 5pm Monday through Friday and all day on weekends and holidays.

One Market. 1 Market St. (at Steuart across from Justin Herman Plaza). ☎ **415/777-5577.** Reservations recommended. Main courses $18–$22. AE, DC, MC, V. Mon–Fri 11:30am–2pm, Sun 10am–2pm; Mon–Thurs 5:30–9:30pm, Fri 5:30–10pm, Sat 5–10pm, Sun 5–9pm. All Market St. buses. AMERICAN.

The enormous restaurant's decor, which is both cosmopolitan and folk-artsy, has been recently fine-tuned to complement renowned chef Bradley Ogden's farm-fresh menu. Amidst tapestry, banquettes, mahogany, and slate floors, there's seating for 170 in the main dining area. The bar, which features gold walls and sponge-painted mustard columns, displays a prominent colorful mural of a market scene. The menu changes frequently to reflect the freshest local ingredients and may start with Skookum and Fanny Bay oysters with homemade cocktail sauce and chili malt vinegar dressing and an array of oak-baked flatbread dishes. Main courses might include pan-roasted sea bass with smoked bacon, cabbage broth, and red wine onions or a Yankee pot roast with mashed red potatoes and root veggies. A corporate crowd convenes from 5 to 7pm weeknights for the $1 oysters and beer. The room picks up with live jazz Tuesday through Saturday and also during the Sunday brunch.

Rubicon. 558 Sacramento St. (between Sansome and Montgomery sts.). ☎ **415/434-4100.** Reservations recommended. Main courses $19–$24. AE, MC, V. Mon–Fri 11:30am–2:30pm; Mon–Sat 5:30–10:30pm. Bus 15 or 41. CONTINENTAL.

Opened in 1994, Rubicon won instant publicity because of the fame of its owners, film director Francis Ford Coppola and actor Robert DeNiro. Named for Coppola's Napa Valley wine, Rubicon features a contemporary and somewhat stiff dining room frequented by big-business power-lunchers and an upscale, middle-aged crowd.

The menu changes frequently. Favorites among the 10 or so appetizers include the ahi tuna carpaccio with radish vinaigrette, sautéed foie gras with sautéed sunchokes and tamarind glaze, and house-cured salmon with crisp potato chips and lemon vinaigrette. About eight main courses are available that might include a sautéed salmon with savoy cabbage, pearl onions, smoked bacon, and red wine sauce; loin of lamb with potato and celery root galette and chervil sauce; or Muscovy duck breast with braised turnips and tat soi honey coriander sauce. Finish with the pecan date tart with blood-orange sorbet or the bittersweet chocolate and peppermint gâteau.

Scott's Seafood Grill & Bar. 3 Embarcadero Center, 3rd Floor. ☎ **415/981-0622.** Reservations recommended. Main courses $12–$34. AE, CB, DC, DISC, MC, V. Mon–Thurs 11am–10pm, Fri–Sat 11am–11pm, Sun 4:30–9:30pm. Bus: 15, 45, or 76. SEAFOOD.

Although Scott's Seafood Grill is a California chain, each site allows the managers to cater to the local market, and apparently, Scott's knows its Financial District clientele well enough to keep them coming back for more. The large, gray, stone and brass dining room features well-spaced tables; in summer people opt for the dining terrace with its umbrella-topped tables.

Creamy clam chowder, seafood salads, and pan-fried sole are Scott's signature lunch dishes. Dinners extend the choices to about a dozen or so different fish dishes— blackened seared ahi tuna with Cajun rémoulade; broiled mahimahi with soy, ginger, and mustard glaze; fisherman's stew with freshly caught Dungeness crab; or the most expensive item on the menu, the broiled Australian lobster tail. An extraspecial dish is the local sand dabs grilled with lemon caper butter.

Silks. In the Mandarin Oriental Hotel, 222 Sansome St. (between Pine and California sts.). ☎ **415/885-0999.** Reservations recommended. 2-course meal $32; 3 courses $39; 4 courses $47. AE, DC, MC, V. Mon–Fri 7–11:30am, 11:30am–2pm; nightly 6–9:30pm. Bus: 2, 38, or 42. CALIFORNIA/ASIAN.

Though the atmosphere is rather somber with burnt reds and golden ambers, modern, free-form sculptures and local artworks, it's still regarded as one of the better dining rooms in the city. The menu changes quarterly, melds California and Asian ingredients and styles, and is offered in two, three, or four courses. If available, start with the three-tuna tartare sampler with lime and caviar; the seared, wrapped nori and crispy spring rolls; or the pan-seared striped bass with roasted fennel ravioli, and carrot and ginger consommé. Main courses may include coriander-crusted tuna with soba noodles; Asian-marinated lamb loin and spicy satay; and the signature grilled yakitori quail with sweet potato purée, star anise, and foie gras wontons. Follow with such desserts as banana cake with slices of caramelized bananas and two kinds of ice cream.

Tommy Toy's. 655 Montgomery St. (at Columbus Ave. and Washington St.). ☎ **415/ 397-4888.** Main courses $16.95–$28.50. Fixed-price dinner $45. AE, DC, JCB, MC, V. Mon– Fri 11:30am–2:30pm; daily 6–9:30pm. CHINESE.

Chinese food is to San Franciscans what pizza is to college students. It's fast, delicious, and cheap. But Tommy Toy's turned Chinese from a take-out affair to a dress-up affair when he created an opulent, dark, and unmistakably Asian fine dining environment that cost a cool $1.5 million. The dining room, created after the 19th-century empress dowager's reading room, is accented with dimly lit candelabras and ancient paintings. Most evenings, the restaurant is crowded with tourists and some locals who come for the five-course fixed-price meal, which usually includes minced squab in lettuce leaves, lobster bisque soup served in a coconut and topped with puffed pastry, a whole lobster in black bean sauce, duck served with plum sauce, medallions of beef, and finally a light dessert of peach mousse. The à la carte menu flaunts vanilla prawns and other such delicacies. On the two occasions we've been here, once the food was very good, the next time it was just okay, and both times, the portions were substantial. Our only issue with Tommy Toy's is that if we were to throw down around $50 for a feast, we would do it at La Folie, Fleur de Lys, or Allain Rondelli where the food is remarkably special. But if you want romantic Chinese, this is as good as it gets.

MODERATE

Jack's. 615 Sacramento St. (at Montgomery St.). ☎ **415/986-9854.** Reservations recommended. Main courses $8–$19; fixed-price dinner $19.50. AE, MC, V. Mon–Fri 11:30am–9:30pm, Sat 5–9:30pm. Bus: 1, 15, or 41. CONTINENTAL.

Founded in 1864, this San Francisco institution claims a devoted, faithful following that expect things just as they were for the last visit. From the wooden Thonet chairs and worn tile floors down to the sure-footed waiters, everything looks as it might have a century ago.

Choices run the gamut: oysters, foie gras, and caviar to start; roast turkey with cranberry dressing, omelets, pastas, and steaks and grills for main courses. The real specialty, however, is the rex sole meunière. Four-course fixed-price dinners are served from 5 to 9pm—a very good buy.

Sam's Grill & Seafood Restaurant. 374 Bush St. (between Montgomery and Kearny sts.). ☎ **415/421-0594.** Reservations accepted for dinner and for 5 or more at lunch. Main courses $10–$20. AE, DC, MC, V. Mon–Fri 11am–9pm. Bus: 15, 45, or 76. SEAFOOD.

Power-lunching at Sam's is a San Francisco tradition, and they've been doing a brisk business with Financial District types for what seems like forever (they opened in 1867). The entrance, which holds a polished, small mahogany bar, opens onto a main dining room with high-backed booths. It's noisy at midday, but if privacy is your primary concern, choose one of the individually curtained booths that line the corridor to the left of the main dining room.

For lunch, consider the clam chowder, a charcoal-broiled filet of fish, and a dessert of French pancakes anisette. Shellfish, steak, and veal dishes round out the dinner menu.

Splendido. 4 Embarcadero Center (at Clay and Drum sts.). ☎ **415/986-3222.** Reservations accepted. Main courses $14–$23. AE, DC, DISC, MC, V. Mon–Fri 11:30am–2:30pm; daily 5:30–10pm. Bus: 15, 45, or 76. MEDITERRANEAN/AMERICAN.

Warm olive wood, flickering candles, rustic stone walls, hand-painted tiles, and hand-hewn beams create the illusion of an old Mediterranean getaway in the middle of metropolitan Embarcadero Four.

But it's not the decor alone that procures Kudos from *Gourmet* and other culinary magazines. The food is beautifully presented, lovingly prepared, and consistently delicious. Starters might include fish soup, crispy crab cakes, or ravioli with prosciutto, mascarpone, and shallots. Main courses include grilled swordfish served on a bed of sweet white corn and braised leeks or grilled loin of lamb with white-bean/garlic flan. Save some room for dessert—some say the tiramisu with chocolate pine-nut bark is the best in town. When the weather is pleasant, you can eat under a canopy on the outdoor patio, or choose the seating in front of the open kitchen. Be sure to glance in the exhibition bakery near the entrance, where you might see chefs rolling fresh pasta.

✪ Tadich Grill. 240 California St. (between Battery and Front sts.). ☎ **415/391-1849.** Reservations not accepted. Main courses $12–$18. MC, V. Mon–Fri 11am–10pm, Sat 11:30am–10pm. Muni Metro: All Market Street trams. All Market Street buses. SEAFOOD.

This famous, venerated California institution arrived with the gold rush in 1849 and claims to be the very first to broil seafood over mesquite charcoal, back in the early 1920s.

The original mahogany bar extends the entire length of the restaurant while no-nonsense white linen–draped tables are topped with big plates of sourdough bread. Power-lunchers get one of the seven enclosed, private booths.

For a light meal you might try one of the delicious seafood salads, such as shrimp or prawn Louis. Hot dishes include baked avocado with shrimp diablo, baked casserole of stuffed turbot with crab and shrimp à la Newburg, and charcoal-broiled petrale sole with butter sauce, a local favorite. Almost everyone gets a side order of big, tasty french fries.

Yank Sing. 427 Battery St. (between Clay and Washington sts.). ☎ **415/781-1111.** Dim sum $2–$4.75 for 3 to 4 pieces. AE, DC, MC, V. Mon–Fri 11am–3pm. Cable Car: California. Bus: 1 or 42. CHINESE DIM SUM.

Loosely translated as "a delight of the heart," Yank Sing does dim sum like no other restaurant we've visited. Poor quality of ingredients has always been the shortcoming of all but the most expensive Chinese restaurants, but Yank Sing manages to be both affordable *and* excellent. Confident, experienced servers take the nervousness out of novices—they're good at guessing your gastric threshold. Most dim sum dishes are dumplings, filled with tasty concoctions of pork, beef, fish, or vegetables. Congees (porridges), spareribs, stuffed crab claws, scallion pancakes, shrimp balls, pork buns, and other palate-pleasers complete the menu. Like most good dim sum meals, at Yank Sing you get to choose the small dishes from a cart that's continually wheeled around the dining room. Tip: Sit by the kitchen and you're guaranteed to get it while it's hot. A second location is at 49 Stevenson St. (off First St.) (☎ 415/541-4949).

5 Japan Center & Environs

MODERATE

Yo Yo Tsumami Bistro. In the Miyako Hotel, 1611 Post St. (at Laguna St.). ☎ **415/922-7788.** Reservations not needed. Main courses $15–$21; continental breakfast buffet $7.50–$18. AE, DC, JCB, MC, V. Daily 6:30am–11am, 11:30am–2:30pm, and 5:30–10pm. Bus: 2, 3, 22, or 38. FRENCH/JAPANESE.

You'd be wise to venture out of downtown for a quiet dinner in Yo Yo's warm, eclectic dining room. Previously Elka, this restaurant changed hands in 1996 and is now run by ex-Elka employees, who have put a great deal of money and care into creating a quality dining experience. The room and the food combine contemporary and ancient, Asian and French. One of the best times to come is between 4 and 10pm for tsumami (Japanese tapas) where you can order à la carte or choose four dishes for $16 or six for $22. These scrumptious little creations are anything from fresh oysters to pork ribs, and all come with outstanding sauces. Main courses from the dinner menu will include fresh fish, duck, and chicken—all very well prepared. Only true chocolate lovers should embark on the chocolate pot au crème—it's like eating a giant portion of the inside of a truffle.

INEXPENSIVE

Sanppo. 1702 Post St. (at Laguna St.). ☎ **415/346-3486.** Reservations not accepted. Main courses $6–$15; combination dishes $10–$17. MC, V. Tues–Sat noon–10pm, Sun 3–10pm. Bus: 2, 3, 4, or 38. JAPANESE.

Simple and unpretentious though it is, Sanppo, across from the Japan Center, serves excellent, down-home Japanese food. You may be asked to share one of the few tables that surround a square counter in the small dining room. Lunches and dinners all include miso soup, rice, and pickled vegetables. At lunch you might have an order of fresh, thick-cut sashimi, teriyaki, tempura, beef donburi, or an order of gyoza (dumplings filled with savory meat and herbs) for $6 to $12. The same items are available at dinner for about $1 additional. Combination dishes, including tempura, sashimi, and gyoza, or tempura and teriyaki, are also available. Beer, wine, and sake are served.

6 Civic Center

EXPENSIVE

Act IV. In the Inn at the Opera, 333 Fulton St. (at Franklin St.). ☎ **415/553-8100.** Reservations recommended. Breakfast $5–$10; lunch courses $5–$12; main courses $19–$28. AE, MC,

V. Mon–Sat 7–10am and 11:30am–2pm; Mon–Thurs 5:30–9:30pm, Fri–Sat 5:30–10:30pm. Bus: 5. CALIFORNIA.

This small, intimate haven with its dark wood furnishings, Belgian tapestries, and elegant table settings is a popular venue for après-opera nasching. After a series of chef changes over the years, the management finally opted for a more traditional, substantial approach to its cuisine by hiring chef Kirke Byers, a long-time Californian with a penchant for sniffing out the finest local produce. Large portions of fresh, well-prepared meats and vegetables dominate each dish, such as the wonderful rack of lamb in a superb reduction sauce flavored with roasted garlic, carrots, turnips, and a potato gratin. The grilled Virginia striped bass with a tangy citrus vinaigrette and lemon aioli is another good choice. Perhaps the main reason people come here, though, is to listen to the live entertainment and for the chance encounter with the steady stream of celebrities who frequent the hotel.

○ Stars. 150 Redwood Alley (between McAllister and Golden Gate off Van Ness). ☎ **415/861-7827.** Reservations required. Main courses $23–$28. AE, MC, V. Mon–Fri 11:30am–2pm; Mon–Tues 6–9:30pm, Wed–Sun 5:30–9:30pm. Bus: 19, 31, or 38. CALIFORNIA.

San Francisco's celebrity hot spot nonpareil, Stars is the brainchild of superstar chef Jeremiah Tower. The large, loud, and vibrant restaurant—swathed in glimmering hardwoods, brass, and mirrors—features the longest bar in the city, which does little to guarantee you'll find a free stool when the place is hopping. Critics complain the quality of the food is slipping (as prices increase), but it obviously doesn't deter local celebrities like Robin Williams and Mayor Willie Brown from making regular appearances.

Though the menu changes daily, among the half-dozen main courses you might find a braised veal ragout with egg noodles, cipollini onions and wild mushrooms; medallion of pork loin with cabbage, leeks, and sauce hachee; or sea scallops with braised Belgian endive, lobster cream sauce, and tarragon. First courses exhibit the same approach. Crisp duck leg confit with white beans, mangos, and arugula; Belgian endive salad with white truffle oil, pistachio vinaigrette, and a toasted cheese sandwich are just two examples, along with an innovative minestrone of fish and shellfish chez Prunier. If you want to treat yourself extra well, order the house-cured sturgeon with mushrooms and deviled eggs or the foie gras with hazelnut toasts and watercress salad. Desserts are extraordinary, from the signature chocolate soufflé pastry layered with chocolate ganache and served with champagne sabayon, to the banana nut torte filled with praline and sliced bananas and frosted with white chocolate buttercream and a dark chocolate glaze, or any of the other offerings from tiramisu to Vermont maple cake.

MODERATE

○ Hayes Street Grill. 320 Hayes St. (near Franklin St.). ☎ **415/863-5545.** Reservations recommended. Main courses $13.50–$18.25. AE, DC, MC, V. Mon–Fri 11:30am–2pm and 5–8:30pm, Sat 6–10:30pm, Sun 5–8:30pm. Bus: 19, 31, or 38. SEAFOOD.

This small, no-nonsense seafood restaurant has built a solid reputation among San Francisco's picky epicureans for its impeccably fresh fish. Choices ranging from Hawaiian swordfish to Puget Sound salmon—cooked to perfection, naturally—are matched with your sauce of choice (Szechuan peanut, tomato salsa, herb shallot butter) and a side of their signature french fries. Fancier seafood specials are available too, such as bay scallops with chanterelle and shiitake mushrooms, as well as an impressive selection of garden-fresh salads and local grilled meats. Finish with the outstanding crème brûlée.

🌝 Family-Friendly Restaurants

Tommaso's *(see p. 128)*   Pizza comes with so many different toppings here that your kids will surely find one to suit their tastes. The chef stages a show of baking the pizzas in an oak-burning brick oven. Kids also go for the yummy pasta dishes.

Caffè Freddy's *(see p. 128)*   A longtime family favorite, this cafe will please not only the kids but their parents as well, especially with its low prices. But the food is good too—an array of gourmet pizzas, pastas, sandwiches, and unusual salads along with main dish specialties.

Mel's Diner *(see p. 121)*   This retro-style burger-slinging joint is not only neat to look at (it was the diner that starred in the movie *American Graffiti*), it also caters to kids. Youngsters get their own color-in menu (crayons are already on the table), and some meals are served in boxes shaped like classic American cars. Jukeboxes at each table will keep the whole family busy figuring out which oldie to select.

Millennium. In the Abigail Hotel, 246 McAllister St. (at Hyde St.). ☎ **415/487-9800.** Reservations recommended. Main courses $4–$8 lunch, $11–$16 dinner. MC, V. Tues–Fri 11:30am–2:30pm and 5pm–10pm; Sat–Sun 5pm–10pm. Bus: 5, 9, or 71. VEGAN.

Banking on the trend toward lighter, healthier cooking, chef Eric Tucker and his band of merry waiters have set out to prove that a meatless menu doesn't mean you have to sacrifice taste. Set in a narrow, handsome Parisian-style dining room with checkered tile flooring, French windows, and sponge-painted walls, the Millennium has had nothing but favorable reviews for its egg-, butter-, and dairy-free creations since the day it opened. Granted, it can be a hit-and-miss experience for nonvegans like ourselves, but we've also had some fantastic dishes, too (particularly the soups). Favorites include the root vegetable and wild mushroom terrine appetizer, as well as the sweet and spicy plantain torte served over a wonderful papaya and black bean salsa. For the main entrées, try the filo purse filled with a ragout of wild mushrooms, leeks, and butternut squash, or the warm Yukon Gold potato salad with sautéed portobello mushrooms. Even the wine and beer list has a good selection of organic labels.

Miss Pearl's Jam House. In the Phoenix Inn, 601 Eddy St. (at Larkin St.). ☎ **415/775-5267.** Reservations accepted. Main courses $8–$15. DC, MC, V. Wed–Thurs 6–10pm, Fri–Sat 6–11pm, Sun 11am–2:30pm and 5:30–9:30pm (bar open until 2am). Bus: 19, 31, or 38. CARIBBEAN.

Miss Pearl's pulls you off a dreary section of Polk Street and into a Caribbean party packed with young, funky locals, and eclectic guests of the adjoining Phoenix hotel. The atmosphere is casual and festive—the perfect place to gather with friends for dinner and reggae dancing. The Caribbean menu is what you'd expect: black-eyed-pea fritters or catfish fingers with Trinidadian pepper and cilantro pesto or sizzling catfish, jerk chicken, and Creole crawfish cakes—all in huge portions. On Sunday, come by for brunch or the soul food menu of barbecue ribs, chicken and dumplings, and biscuits with crawfish gravy. Before or after dinner, head to the bar where live music and dancing happens Thursday through Sunday.

✪ Zuni Café. 1658 Market St. (at Franklin St.). ☎ **415/552-2522.** Reservations recommended. Main courses $16–$22.50. AE, MC, V. Tues–Sat 7:30am–midnight, Sun 7:30am–11pm. Muni Metro: All Market St. trams. Bus: 6, 7, 71, or 75. MEDITERRANEAN.

Even factoring in the snotty wait staff, Zuni Café is still one of our favorite places in the city to have lunch. Its expanse of windows and prime Market Street location guarantee good people-watching—a favorite San Francisco pastime—and chef Judy Rodgers's Mediterranean-influenced menu is wonderfully diverse and satisfying. For the full effect, sit at the bustling, copper-topped bar and peruse the foot-long oyster menu (half a dozen or so varieties on hand at all times); you can also sit in the stylish, exposed-brick dining room or on the outdoor patio. Though the changing menu always includes meat, such as New York steak with Belgian endive gratin, and fish, either grilled or braised in the kitchen's brick oven, the proven winners are Rodgers's brick oven–roasted chicken for two with Tuscan-style bread salad, the polenta appetizer with mascarpone, and the hamburger on grilled rosemary focaccia bread (a strong contender for the city's best burger). Whatever you decide, be sure to order a side of the shoestring potatoes.

7 Pacific Heights/Cow Hollow

EXPENSIVE

Harris'. 2100 Van Ness Ave. (at Pacific Ave.). ☎ **415/673-1888.** Reservations recommended. Main courses $18–$30. AE, CB, DC, DISC, JCB, MC, V. Mon–Fri 6–11pm, Sat–Sun 5–11pm. Bus: 38 or 45. AMERICAN.

Every big city has a great steak restaurant, and in San Francisco, it's Harris'. Proprietor Ann Lee Harris knows steaks; she grew up on a cattle ranch and married the owner of the largest feedlot in California. In 1976, the couple opened the Harris Ranch Restaurant on Interstate 5 in central California, where they built a rock-solid reputation up and down the coast. The steaks, which can be seen hanging in a glass-windowed aging room, are cut thick—either New York-style or T-bone—and are served with a baked potato and seasonal vegetables.

Harris' also offers roast duckling, lamb chops, fresh fish, lobster, and venison, buffalo, and other types of game. Those who like brains rave about the restaurant's sautéed brains in brown butter.

Harris' wood-paneled dining room with curving banquettes is comfortably elegant.

☺ **La Folie.** 2316 Polk St. (between Green and Union sts.). ☎ **415/776-5577.** Reservations recommended. Main courses $22–$28; Five-course tasting menu $45. AE, DC, JCB, MC, V. Mon–Sat 5:30–10:30pm. Bus: 19, 41, 45, 47, 49, or 76. FRENCH.

For fantastic French food without attitude, La Folie is the place to feast. The minute you walk through the door, you'll know why this is many locals' favorite restaurant. The country-French decor is tasteful but not too serious, with whimsical chandeliers and a cloudy sky painted overhead. The staff is friendly, knowledgeable, and very accommodating; the food is outstanding. Unlike many renowned chefs, La Folie's Roland Passot is in the kitchen nightly, and it shows. Each of his California-influenced French creations is an architectural and culinary masterpiece. Best of all, they're served in a relaxed and comfortable environment. Start with an appetizer such as the roast quail and fois gras with salad, wild mushrooms, and roasted garlic—it's guaranteed to melt in your mouth. Main courses are not *petite* as in many French restaurants, and all are accompanied by flavorful and well-balanced sauces. Try the rôti of quail and squab stuffed with wild mushrooms and wrapped in crispy potato strings or the roast venison with vegetables, quince, and huckleberry sauce. Finish off with any of the delectable desserts.

MODERATE

Balboa Café. 3199 Fillmore St. (at Greenwich St.). ☎ **415/921-3944.** Reservations for 6 or more only. Main courses $5–$9 at lunch, $10–$14 at dinner, $7–$8 on weekend brunch. AE, DC, MC, V. Mon–Sun 11am–10:30pm; bar daily 11am–2am. Bus: 22. AMERICAN.

Back in the 1980s the Balboa Café was San Francisco's main "meet market," filled each week with the young and the restless. Though things bottomed out in the early 1990s, the wheel is turning once again for this trendy, stylish Cow Hollow hangout since the crew at the wildly popular PlumpJack Café took over (in fact, patrons put on hold at PlumpJack are usually sent here for a predinner cocktail). Though Balboa isn't nearly on the caliber as its around-the-corner cousin, you'll probably be forced to mingle with the Marina "pretty people" crowd at the bar until a table frees up. The limited menu offers some upscale options, such as braised lamb shank with roasted tomatoes, white beans, and zucchini, but it's the Balboa Burgers and Caesar salads that get the most requests.

Betelnut. 2030 Union St. (at Buchanan St.). ☎ **415/929-8855.** Reservations recommended. Main courses $9–$16. DC, MC, V. Sun–Thurs 11:30am–11pm, Fri–Sat 11:30am–midnight. Bus: 22, 41, or 45. CHINESE.

While San Francisco is teeming with Chinese restaurants, there are few that offer the posh, fashionable dining environment of this new restaurant on upscale Union Street. As the menu explains, the restaurant is themed after "Pejui Wu," a traditional Asian beer house offering local brews and savory dishes, but with the bamboo paneling, red Formica countertops, and low-hanging lamps, the place feels less like an authentic harbor restaurant and more like a set out of Madonna's movie *Shanghai Surprise*. Still, the atmosphere is pleasant, with dimly lit booths, ringside seating overlooking the bustling stir-fry chefs, sidewalk tables (weather permitting), and body-to-body flirting at the cramped but festive bar. Starters include sashimi and tasty salt and pepper whole gulf prawns; main courses offer wok-roasted clams with Thai basil and Singapore chili crab. While prices seem reasonable, it's the incidentals such as white rice ($1.50 per person) and tea ($3.50 per pot) that rack up the bill. Unfortunately, the wait staff is often so inattentive it ruins the entire experience. While the food is decent, it doesn't compare to many of the better Chinese restaurants in the city. In fact, the only reason to choose this restaurant over others is the atmosphere and their heavenly signature dessert: a mouth-watering tapioca pudding with sweet red adzuki beans.

Café Marimba. 2317 Chestnut St. (between Scott and Divisidero sts.). ☎ **415/776-1506.** Main courses $5–$13. AE, MC, V. Mon–Sun 11:30am–12am. Bus: 30. MEXICAN.

As much as we hate to plug the yuppified Marina District, we have to admit that we're completely addicted to Café Marimba's gilled Yucatan-spiced snapper and grilled chicken tacos. Add just the right amount of guacamole and pineapple salsa, and *acheewahwah!* that's good! The shrimp mojo de ajo is also a knockout (heck, even the chips and guac are the best in town). For parties of three or more, order the family style platter of grilled meats and vegetables and prepare to do battle. We're obviously not the only ones who fancy this fun, festive café, so expect a long wait during peak hours (our MO is to sneak seats at the bar and order there). But *hasta mañana* the margaritas—*muy mál.*

The Elite Café. 2049 Fillmore St. (between Pine and California sts.). ☎ **415/346-8668.** No reservations. Main courses $10.95–$21.95. AE, DC, DISC, MC, V. Mon–Sat 5–11pm, Sun 10am–3pm and 5–10pm. Bus: 41 or 45. CAJUN/CREOLE.

Olive's Gourmet Pizza, 3249 Scott St. ☎ 415/547-4488. *"I usually don't get too excited about pizza, but I still can't get over how good the pizza was at this tiny little place in the Marina District called Olive's. You have to try the vegetarian mushroom and eggplant combo, which comes on a wonderful, flaky cornmeal crust. Molto bene!"*

—Delynn Parker, Houston, Texas

If the shellfish in the window doesn't get you in the door, the festive atmosphere will. This place is always bustling with Pacific Heights's beautiful people who come for fresh oysters, blackened filet mignon with Cajun butter, redfish with crab and Creole cream sauce, or any of the other well-spiced Cajun dishes. The high-backed booths provide more intimate dining than the crowded tables and bar. Brunch is good, too, when all kinds of egg dishes—Benedict, sardou, and many more—are offered along with bagels and lox.

Flying Kamikazes. 3339 Steiner St. (at Chestnut St.). ☎ **415/567-4903.** Reservations for six or more. Main courses $4–$9. MC, V. Mon–Thurs, Sun 5:30–10:30pm; Fri–Sat 5–11pm. Bus: 30. JAPANESE/SUSHI.

Yeah, more sushi, but this time with a twist. What differentiates this Marina hot spot from the usual sushi spots around town are the unique combinations, the varied menu, and the young, hip atmosphere. Kamikazes's innovative rolls are a nice welcome to those bored with the traditional styles, though they may be too much ad-venture for some (don't worry, there's plenty of nonsea and nonraw items on the menu). Don't miss the rainbow "Three Amigos" roll or the "Rock and Roll" with cooked eel, avocado, and cucumber. The buckwheat noodle and julienne vegetable salad is also a treat. The service could be improved—you'll wait forever for your server to pour your Sapporo—but the staff is friendly and the atmosphere is fun, so nobody seems to mind.

✪ **Greens Restaurant, Fort Mason.** Building A, Fort Mason Center (enter Fort Mason opposite the Safeway at Buchanan and Marina sts.). ☎ **415/771-6222.** Reservations recom-mended 2 weeks in advance. Main courses $10–$13; fixed-priced dinner $38; brunch $7–$10. DISC, MC, V. Tues–Fri 11:30am–2pm, Sat 11:30am–2:30pm; Mon–Sat 8am–9pm and Sun 9am–2pm (bakery, Tues–Sat 9:30am–4:30pm, Sun 10am–3pm). Bus: 28 or 30. VEGETARIAN.

Knowledgeable locals swear by Greens, where executive chef Annie Somerville (author of *Fields of Greens*) cooks with the seasons, using produce from Green Gulch Farm and other local organic farms. Located in an old warehouse, with enormous windows overlooking the bridge and the bay, the restaurant is both a pioneer and a legend. A weeknight dinner might feature such appetizers as tomato, white-bean, and sorrel soup, or grilled asparagus with lemon, Parmesan cheese, and watercress and follow with such choices as spring vegetable risotto with asparagus, peas, shiitake and crimini mushrooms, and Parmesan cheese, or Sri Lankan curry made of new potatoes, cauliflower, carrots, peppers, and snap peas stewed with tomatoes, coconut milk, ginger, and Sri Lankan spices.

A special five-course dinner is served on Saturday. A recent example began with grilled asparagus, yellowfin potatoes, and peppers with blood-orange beurre blanc, followed by shiitake and crimini mushroom lasagna with leeks and mushroom port sauce. Desserts are equally adventuresome—try the chocolate pave with mint crème anglaise or the espresso ice cream with chocolate sauce. Lunch and brunch are some-what simpler, but equally as inventive. An extensive wine list is available.

Like the restaurant, the adjacent bakery is also operated by the Zen Center. It sells homemade breads, sandwiches, soups, salads, and pastries to take home.

North India Restaurant. 3131 Webster St. (at Lombard St.). ☎ **415/931-1556.** Reservations recommended. Main courses $14.50–$19.95; fixed-price dinner $9.95 5–7pm. AE, DC, MC, V. Mon–Fri 11:30am–2:30pm; daily 5–10pm. Bus: 41 or 45. INDIAN.

Unlike many Indian establishments that lack in atmosphere, chef Parvesh Sahi's full Indian menu is served in a plush, dimly lit dining room, providing the perfect ambience for an intimate evening out with some ethnic flair. As you settle into a maroon velvet chair and browse the menu, soft Indian music reminds you what part of the world your taste buds will venture to. Start by ordering a cup of the sweet and spicy chai tea, and the oversized, moist samosas (spiced potatoes and green peas served in a crisp pocket), then venture onward with any of the tandoori specials, such as the mixed seafood dish with sea bass, jumbo prawns, and scallops or a boti kebab leg of lamb. There are plenty of vegetarian dishes as well, ranging from aloo gobi (cauliflower and potatoes in curry sauce) to baingan aloo masala (eggplant, potatoes, tomatoes, ginger, garlic, green onions, and spices). All these tasty feasts are accompanied by bottomless pots of delicious mango chutney and cucumber-dill sauce. Anything you order here will be fresh, well prepared, and served by courteous waiters wearing vests adorned with Indian-style mirrors and gold embroidery. Although expensive for Indian food, it's worth the extra bucks if you want to be ensured good quality and atmosphere. Arrive between 5 and 7pm, and you can opt for the very affordable fixed-price dinner for $9.95.

Oritalia. 1915 Fillmore St. (between Pine and Bush sts.). ☎ **415/346-1333.** Pasta $9–$14; main courses $15–$18.50. AE, MC, V. Mon–Sat 5–11pm, Sun 5–10pm. Bus: 41 or 45. ASIAN/ ITALIAN.

If you can't decide between Italian and Asian food tonight, try both. Located on a busy section of Fillmore Street, Oritalia (derived from *Oriental* and *Italian*) has made its niche by blending the flavors of Italy, China, Korea, and Southeast Asia to create some truly unique dishes. Prince Edward mussels, for example, are mixed with Shao Xing wine and Chinese celery. Also popular are the Dungeness crab cakes with Tobiko caviar and a red pepper curry cream. Though full entrées are available, an assortment of the "Small Plates" makes for a more adventurous, family style dining experience. A charming, casual decor marked by papier-mâché paintings, hand-painted pendant lamps, painted gourds, and textured walls by Japanese artist Yoshi Hayashi are the perfect complement to the multicultural menu.

Osome. 1923 Fillmore St. (between Bush and Pine sts.). ☎ **415/346-2311.** Sushi $3–$7.50; main courses $8.95–$14.20. MC, V. Mon–Sat 5:30–11pm, Sun 5–10:30pm. JAPANESE.

What this neighborhood restaurant lacks in decor (there are few adornments and, frankly, the place looks half finished), it more than makes up for in fresh, well-presented Japanese cuisine. There are fewer than a dozen tables for large parties, but the best seats are definitely bar-side, where sushi chefs slice and roll maguro (tuna), unagi (eel), and close to 40 other savory rice-and-fish combinations. Many of our friends fill up before going out to sushi so they won't spend a fortune satisfying their hunger. There's no need to do that here because there's also a full, and reasonably priced, dinner menu with tempura, teriyaki, and sukiyaki. Start with the surprisingly sculptural spinach goma ae, a skyline of spinach towers bathing in a tangy sesame seed sauce. From there, let your taste buds be your guide. There's also a second location at 3145 Fillmore St. (☎ 415/931-8898).

⭐ **Pane e Vino.** 3011 Steiner St. (at Union St.). ☎ **415/346-2111.** Reservations recommended. Main courses $10–$18. MC, V. Mon–Sat 11:30am–2:30pm; daily 5–10pm. Bus: 41 or 45. ITALIAN.

Pane e Vino is one of San Francisco's top and most authentic Italian restaurants, as well as our personal favorite. The food is consistently excellent (careful not to fill up on the outstanding breads served upon seating), the prices reasonable, and the mostly Italian-accented staff always smooth and efficient under pressure (you'll see). The two small dining rooms, separated by an open kitchen that emanates heavenly aromas, offer only limited seating, so expect a wait even if you have reservations. A wide selection of appetizers is offered, including a fine carpaccio, vitello tonnato (sliced roasted veal and capers in a lemony tuna sauce), and the hugely popular chilled artichoke stuffed with bread and tomatoes and served with a vinaigrette. Our favorite, the antipasti of mixed grilled vegetables, always spurs a fork fight. A similar broad selection of pastas is available, including a flavorful pennette alla boscaiola with porcini mushrooms and pancetta in a tomato cream sauce. Other specialties are grilled fish and meat dishes, including a chicken breast marinated in lime juice and herbs. Top dessert picks are any of the Italian ice creams, the crème caramel, and (but of course) the creamy tiramisu.

⭐ **PlumpJack Café.** 3127 Fillmore St. (between Filbert and Greenwich sts.). ☎ **415/563-4755.** Reservations recommended. Main courses $14–$20. AE, MC, V. Mon–Fri 11:30am–2pm and 5:30–10:30pm, Sat 5:30–10:30pm. Bus: 41 or 45. CALIFORNIA/MEDITERRANEAN.

Wildly popular among San Francisco's style-setters, this small Cow Hollow restaurant has quickly become the "in" place to dine. This is partly due to the fact that it's run by one of the Getty clan (as in J. Paul), but mostly because chef Maria Helm's food is just plain good and the whimsical decor is a veritable work of art.

Though the menu changes weekly, you might find such appetizers as roasted portobello mushroom with vegetable stuffing, reggiano, and cippolini onions, or a salad of watercress and Belgian endive with kumquats, toasted pine nuts, shaved reggiano, and champagne vinaigrette. Main dishes range from pasta (such as the cavatappi with tiger prawns, green garlic, leeks, and roast tomato sauce) to roast local halibut with grilled asparagus and blood-orange chervil vinaigrette. Top it off with an apricot soufflé or the chocolate kahlua torte. The extraordinarily extensive California wine list—gleaned from the PlumpJack wine shop down the street—is sold at next to retail, with many wines available by the glass.

Prego. 2000 Union St. (at Buchanan St.). ☎ **415/563-3305.** Reservations accepted. Pasta and pizza $6–$13; main courses $11–$19. AE, CB, DC, MC, V. Mon–Sat 11:30am–midnight, Sun 10–midnight. Bus: 22, 41, or 45. ITALIAN.

A light and airy trattoria, frequented by an upscale clientele, Prego is a place to be seen or people-watch as you dine beyond the windows facing Union Street. Specialties include thin-crust, oak-fired pizzas, pasta, and grilled fish and meats. Spit-roasted, free-range chicken is prepared on a rotisserie and served with potatoes and vegetables. A good selection of wine is also available by the glass or bottle and there is a Sunday morning brunch, but unless you're partial to the view, breakfast can't be beat down the street at Doidge's (if you can get in, that is).

⭐ **Zinzino.** 2355 Chestnut St. (at Divisadero St.). ☎ **415/346-6623.** Reservations for 6 or more only. Main courses $4–$9 brunch, $7.50–$9.50 lunch and dinner. MC, V. Tues–Fri 5:30–10pm, Sat–Sun 10am–4pm, 5:30–10pm. Bus: 22 or 30. ITALIAN.

Usually we're under the impression that San Francisco needs another cute Italian cafe like it needs a tsunami headed its way. Well, it may not happen often, but we were wrong. Owner Ken Zankel and Spago-sired chef Andrea Rappaport have combined forces to create one of the city's top new Italian restaurants. Zinzino may look like a tiny trattoria from the outside, but you could fit a small nuclear sub in the space from the sun-drenched facade to the shaded back patio of this former Laundromat.

Italian movie posters, magazines, and furnishings evoke memories of past vacations, but we rarely recall the food in Italy being this good (and certainly not this cheap). Start off with the crispy calamari with a choice of herbed aioli or tomato sauces (second only to Scala's Earth and Turf), the roasted jumbo prawns wrapped in crisp pancetta and bathed in a tangy balsamic reduction sauce, or the peculiar-tasting shaved fennel and mint salad—or try them all. Rappaport is giving Zuni Café a run for its money with her version of roasted half chicken, the most tender bird we've ever tasted ("It's all the wood-fired oven," she admits); the accompanying goat cheese salad and potato frisee were also superb. The perfect light lunch for two is a half eggplant, half house-spiced Italian sausage pizza (a mere $4.50 per person), savored with the requisite glass of Chianti at the marble-topped wine bar. The huge focaccia sandwiches are also a big hit with the handful of locals who are privy to this San Francisco sleeper.

INEXPENSIVE

✪ **Doidge's.** 2217 Union St. (between Fillmore and Steiner sts.). ☎ **415/921-2149.** Reservations accepted and essential on weekends. Breakfast $5–$10; lunch $5–$8. MC, V. Mon–Fri 8am–1:45pm, Sat–Sun 8am–2:45pm. Bus: 41 or 45. AMERICAN.

Doidge's is sweet, small, and always packed, serving up one of the better breakfasts in San Francisco since 1971. Doidge's fame is based on eggs Benedict; eggs Florentine runs a close second, prepared with thinly sliced Motherlode ham. Invariably the menu includes a gourmet omelet packed with luscious combinations, and to delight the kid in you, hot chocolate comes in your very own teapot. The six seats at the original mahogany counter are still the most coveted by locals.

➌ **La Canasta.** 2219 Filbert St. (at Fillmore St.). ☎ **415/921-3003.** Main courses $2.80–$6.15. No credit cards. Mon–Sat 11am–10pm. Bus: 22, 41, or 45. MEXICAN.

Unless you forge to the Mission District, burritos don't get much better (or bigger) than those served here at this tiny takeout establishment where you can stuff yourself with a huge chicken burrito for a mere $4.80. There are no seats here, though, so you'll just have to find another place to devour your grub; fortunately, the Marina Green is a short walk away and offers a million-dollar view no restaurant can boast. There is another location at 3006 Buchanan St. (at Union Street) (☎ 415/474-2627).

Mel's Diner. 2165 Lombard St. (at Fillmore St.). ☎ **415/921-3039.** No reservations. Main courses $4–$5.50 breakfast, $6–$8 lunch, $8–$12 dinner. No credit cards. Sun–Thurs 6am–3am, Fri–Sat 24 hr (Lombard location only). Bus: 22, 43, or 30. AMERICAN.

Sure, it's contrived, touristy, and not even that good, but when you get that urge for a chocolate shake and banana cream pie at the stroke of midnight, no other place in the city comes through like Mel's Diner. Modeled after a classic 1950s diner right down to the nickel jukebox at each table, Mel's harks back to the halcyon days when cholesterol and fried foods didn't stroke your guilty conscience with every greasy, wonderful bite. Too bad the prices don't reflect the fifties; a burger with fries and a coke runs about $8, and they don't take credit. There's another Mel's at 3355 Geary St. (at Stanyan St.) (☎ 415/387-2244).

Sweet Heat. 3324 Steiner St. (between Lombard and Chestnut sts.). ☎ **415/474-9191.** No reservations accepted. All entrées under $6. MC, V. Daily 11am–midnight. MEXICAN.

If you're shopping on Chestnut Street and looking for a flavorful and light lunch, check out this casual place offering "healthy Mexican food to die for." Far from traditional Mexican food, Sweet Heat has capitalized on California's love affair with old-style food prepared in new ways—and the results are impressive. Prices are as low as $3.95 for a veggie burrito with grilled zucchini, eggplant, and roasted corn, or $4.25 for a tasty scallop burrito with green chile chutney. On a sunny day, the back patio is a great place to sun while you eat. The newest location, at 1725 Haight St. (☎ 415/387-8845), is equally popular and delicious.

World Wrapps. 2257 Chestnut St. (between Pierce and Scott sts.). ☎ **415/563-9727.** Burritos $3.95–$6.95. No credit cards. Daily 8am–11pm. Bus: 22, 28, 30, 43, or 76. INTERNATIONAL.

You'll know you've found World Wrapps when you come upon the trendy, health-conscious crowd standing in line on yuppified Chestnut Street. There are hardly any tables here and plenty of other eateries nearby, so what's the big deal? It's yet another version of San Franciscans' beloved burrito—only this time it's not Mexican-influenced, but rather a tortilla filled with your choice of cuisine from around the world (hence the name). Fresh ingredients, cheap prices, and the love affair Marina residents have with hanging out on this street make World Wrapps *the* place to grab a bite.

8 Haight-Ashbury

INEXPENSIVE

Cha Cha Cha. 1801 Haight St. (at Schrader St.). ☎ **415/386-5758.** Reservations not accepted. Tapas $4–$7; main courses $9–$13. No credit cards. Mon–Sun 11:30am–4pm; Sun–Thurs 5–11pm, Fri–Sat 5–11:30pm. Muni Metro: N line. Bus: 6, 7, 66, 71, or 73. CARIBBEAN.

This is one of our all-time favorite places to come for dinner, but it's not for every-body. Cha Cha Cha is not a meal, it's an *experience.* Put your name on the mile-long list, crowd into the minuscule bar, and drink sangria while you wait (and fight not to spill when you get bumped by all the young, attractive patrons who are also wait-ing). When you do finally get seated (it usually takes at least an hour), you'll dine in a loud (and we mean *loud*) dining room with Santeria altars, banana trees, and plastic tropical tablecloths. The best thing to do is order from the tapas menu and share the dishes family style. The fried calamari, fried new potatoes, Cajun shrimp, and mussels in saffron broth are all bursting with flavor and are accompanied by rich, luscious sauces—but whatever you choose, you can't go wrong. This is the kind of place where you take friends in a partying mood, let your hair down, and make an evening of it. If you want all the flavor without the festivities, come during lunch.

☺ Crepes on Cole. 100 Carl St. (at Cole St.). ☎ **415/664-1800.** Reservations not accepted. No prices over $6. No credit cards. Sun–Thurs 7am–11pm, Fri–Sat 7am–midnight. CREPES.

Every few years a new food trend becomes really hot in the city. Cajun, sushi, Thai—and when you thought restaurateurs had maximized them all, enter the crepe. These paper-thin, egg-based pancakes usually encase a glob of goodies and can be served as a main course or a dessert. If you are in the Cole Valley or Haight-Ashbury areas and are looking for a hearty, casual, and affordable meal, this is the place to try them. Build your own or order from choices such as the Florentine crepe made with cheddar cheese, onions, spinach, and cottage cheese, or the Mediterranean crepe with ched-dar, onion, eggplant, pesto, tomato, and roasted peppers. All options, including the less-celebrated omelets, come with a heaping pile of house potatoes. If you're adverse to anything remotely resembling an omelet, order one of the simple sandwiches, bagels, or an enormous Caesar salad. Nothing on the menu here is over $6.

Ⓢ **Zona Rosa.** 1797 Haight St. (at Shrader St.). ☎ **415/668-7717.** Burritos $3.45–$4.83. No credit cards. Daily 11am–10:30pm. Muni Metro: N line. Bus: 6, 7, 66, 71, or 73. MEXICAN.

This is a great place to stop and get a cheap (and healthful) bite. The most popular items here are the burritos, which are made to order and include your choice of beans (refried, whole pinto, or black), meats, or vegetarian ingredients. You can sit on a stool at the window and watch all the Haight Street freaks strolling by, relax at one of five colorful interior tables, or take it to go and head to Golden Gate Park (it's just two blocks away). Zona Rosa is one of the best burrito stores around.

9 Fisherman's Wharf
EXPENSIVE

Alioto's. Fisherman's Wharf (at Taylor St.). ☎ **415/673-0183.** Reservations recommended. Main courses $7–$14 at lunch; dinner $10–$50. AE, CB, DC, DISC, MC, V. Mon–Sun 11am–11pm. Cable car: Powell-Hyde. Bus: 30 or 42. SEAFOOD.

One of San Francisco's oldest restaurants, run by one of the city's most prominent families, the Aliotos, this Fisherman's Wharf landmark has a long-standing reputation for serving the Bay's best cioppino. The curbside crab stand, Oysteria Deli, and the new Steam Kettle Bar are great for a quick, inexpensive dose of San Francisco's finest; for more formal and fancy selections, continue up the carpeted stairs to the multilevel, harbor-view dining room. Don't mess around with the menu: It's the Dungeness crab you're after. Cracked, caked, stuffed, or stewed, its impossible to get your fill, so bring plenty of money—particularly if you intend to order from Alioto's prodigious (and pricey) wine list. If you happen to be insane and don't care for cracked crab, the griddle-fried sand dabs and rex sole served with tartar sauce are also quite good.

A. Sabella's. Fisherman's Wharf, 2766 Taylor St. (at Jefferson St.), 3rd floor. ☎ **415/771-6775.** Reservations accepted. Main courses $9–$41. AE, DC, MC, V. Daily 11am–3:30pm and 5–10:30pm. Cable Car: Powell-Mason line. ITALIAN/SEAFOOD.

The Sabella family has been serving seafood in San Francisco since the turn of the century and has operated A. Sabella's restaurant on the wharf continuously since 1920. Catering heavily to the tourist trade, the menu doesn't take any chances; traditional steak, seafood, and pasta dishes line the menu. Where A. Sabella's really shines, however, is in the shellfish department. Its 1,180-gallon saltwater tank allows for fresh crab, abalone, and lobster year-round, which means no restaurant in the city can touch A. Sabella's when it comes to feasting on fresh Dungeness crab out of season. A nice touch is the live piano music played nightly in the large, formal dining room overlooking the wharf.

MODERATE

Gaylord's. At Ghirardelli Square, 900 North Point St. ☎ **415/771-8822.** Reservations recommended. Main courses $12–$19; fixed-price meals $14–$18 lunch, $22–$28 dinner. AE, CB, DC, DISC, MC, V. Mon–Sat 11:45am–1:45pm, Sun noon–2:45pm; daily 5–10:45pm. Cable Car: Hyde St. line. Bus: 19, 42, 47, or 49. INDIAN.

With branches in London, New York, Beverly Hills, and New Delhi, this far-flung chain may be the most successful Indian restaurant in the world. Opened in 1976, San Francisco's Gaylord's has earned its reputation by serving accessible North Indian haute cuisine in stunning surroundings. The warm, candlelit interior is spiced with bay views from almost every seat. À la carte selections are available, but the fixed-price dinners are the most sensible choice, including soup; such main courses as tandoori chicken, lamb kebabs, or chicken tikka; Indian breads, saffron rice; dessert;

and tea or coffee. Lunch is a choice of fixed-price menus only. A second Gaylord's is located at One Embarcadero Center (☎ **415/397-7775**).

Cafe Pescatore. 2455 Mason St. (at North Point St.). ☎ **415/561-1111.** Reservations recommended. Main courses $3.95–$7.95 breakfast, $10–$16 lunch or dinner. AE, DC, DISC, MC, V. Mon–Thurs 11:30am–10pm, Fri 11:30am–11pm, Sat 5–11pm, Sun 5–10pm; Sat–Sun 7am–3pm brunch, 3–5pm cafe menu; Cable Car: Powell-Mason. Bus: 42, 15, or 39. ITALIAN.

Though San Francisco locals are a rarity at Cafe Pescatore, most agree that if they had to dine at Fisherman's Wharf, this cozy trattoria would be their first choice. Two walls of sliding glass doors offer pseudo-sidewalk seating when the weather's warm, although heavy vehicular traffic can detract from the alfresco experience. The general consensus is to order anything that's cooked in the open kitchen's wood-fired oven, such as the pizzas and roasts. A big hit with tourists is the calzone primavera— a pizza envelope sealed around artichokes, sweet yellow peppers, spinach, and goat cheese; the verde pizza (pesto-flavored prawns and spinach) and huge servings of roast chicken are also safe bets.

The Mandarin. At Ghirardelli Square, 900 North Point St. ☎ **415/673-8812.** Reservations accepted. Main courses $15–$38; fixed-price dinners $22, $25, $28, and $38. AE, CB, DC, MC, V. Daily 11:30am–11:30pm. Cable Car: Hyde St. line. Bus: 19, 30, 42, 47, or 49. CHINESE.

Created by Madame Cecilia Chiang in 1968, The Mandarin is meant to feel like a cultured, northern Chinese home; fine furnishings, silk-covered walls, and good-quality Asian art create one of most elegant Chinese restaurants in the city. Tables are spaced comfortably apart, and the better of two softly lit dining rooms offers matchless views of the bay.

True to its name, The Mandarin offers exceptional Beijing-style cookery. Take our advice and start with the sesame shrimp or minced squab appetizer, then follow through with the either the smoked tea duck (their version of Beijing duck, but smoked over burning tea leaves until crispy) or, if you have a party of four or more and call a day in advance, the Beggar's Chicken, which is encased in clay and cooked to slow perfection.

10 North Beach

EXPENSIVE

Bix. 56 Gold St. (between Sansome and Montgomery sts.). ☎ **415/433-6300.** Reservations recommended. Main courses $5–$12 lunch, $11–$25 dinner. AE, CB, DC, DISC, MC, V. Mon–Thurs 11:30am–11pm, Fri–Sat 11:30am–midnight, Sun 5–10pm. Bus: 15, 30, 41, or 45. CALIFORNIA.

If you feel like dressin' up and hittin' the town, this suave little back-alley bar and restaurant is a good place to start. Fashioned after a 1920s supper club, Bix is better known for its martinis than for its menu. Curving Honduran mahogany, massive silver columns, and art deco–style lighting set the stage for dancing to live music, though most locals settle for chatting with the friendly bartenders and nasching on appetizers. While the ultra-stylish setting tends to overshadow the food, Bix actually serves some pretty good grub. The lobster linguine with fresh prawns and mussels in a sun-dried tomato broth is the undisputed favorite, followed by the grilled filet mignon with mushrooms and chicken hash à la Bix. And for that special occasion, how can you say no to a round of $118 Beluga caviar on toast?

Caffè Sport. 574 Green St. (between Grant and Columbus aves.). ☎ **415/981-1251.** Reservations accepted only for parties of 4 or more. Main courses $14–$29. AE, DC, MC, V.

Dining Near North Beach

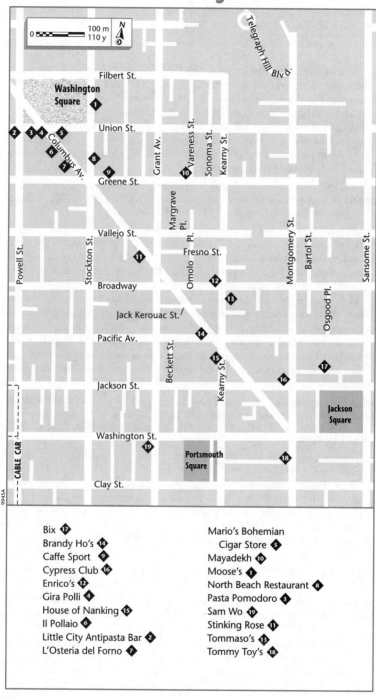

Bix **17**
Brandy Ho's **14**
Caffe Sport **9**
Cypress Club **16**
Enrico's **12**
Gira Polli **4**
House of Nanking **15**
Il Pollaio **6**
Little City Antipasta Bar **2**
L'Osteria del Forno **7**

Mario's Bohemian
    Cigar Store **5**
Mayadekh **10**
Moose's **1**
North Beach Restaurant **8**
Pasta Pomodoro **3**
Sam Wo **19**
Stinking Rose **11**
Tommaso's **13**
Tommy Toy's **18**

Tues–Thurs noon–2pm, Fri–Sat noon–2:30pm; Tues–Thurs seatings at 5, 6:30, 8:30, and 10pm, Fri–Sat at 6:30, 8:30, and 10pm. Bus: 15, 30, 41, or 45. ITALIAN.

People either love or hate this stodgy Sicilian eatery. Cluttered with hanging hams, fishnets, decorative plates, dolls, and mirrors, Caffè Sport is better known for its surly staff and eclectic ambience than for its food. Owner/chef/artiste Antonio Latona serves up healthy portions of attitude along with garlic-laden pasta dishes and is happy to report that this is Senator Dianne Feinstein's favorite North Beach hangout. Lunch is tame in comparison to dinner, when the Sport is mobbed and lively. Disregard the framed menu that sits on each table and accept the waiter's "suggestions." Whatever arrives—whether it be a dish of calamari, mussels, and shrimp in tomato-garlic sauce, or pasta in pesto sauce—it's bound to be *bene*. Bring a huge appetite, but above all, don't be late if you have a reservation.

Cypress Club. 500 Jackson St. (between Montgomery St. and Columbus Ave.). ☎ **415/296-8555.** Reservations recommended. Main courses $23–$28. AE, CB, DC, MC, V. Sun–Thurs 5:30–10pm, Fri–Sat 5:30–11pm. Bus: 15 or 41. AMERICAN.

Combine Aladdin's bedchamber, a handful of Far Side cartoons, and few hits of acid, and you still won't match the Daliesque decor of this pseudo supper club. It's not hard to find; just look for the tourists peering in the windows. Gilt banquettes, bulbous gilt columns, and udder-shaped light fixtures covered in billowing fabric create a lavish neo-Arabian atmosphere that, if you're in the neighborhood, is definitely worth a gander. Most of the regular clientele, dressed to blend, saunters around the bar. Those who wish to dine might start with foie gras, Dungeness crab rillette, or the sea scallops with curry, lemongrass, mango, and chervil. Main courses are equally extravagant, including the lobster with lemon emulsion and shaved black truffle; the maple-cured pork chop with pecan pancakes, collard greens, and grilled apple; or the wood-roasted chicken with wild mushrooms and rosemary soubise. Desserts are as creative as the decor.

Maykadeh. 470 Green St. (between Kearny St. and Grant Ave.). ☎ **415/362-8286.** Reservations recommended. Main courses $7.50–$16. MC, V. Mon–Fri 11:30am–2:30pm; Mon–Thurs 5–10:30pm, Fri 5–11pm, Sat noon–11pm, Sun noon–10:30pm. Bus: 15 or 41. PERSIAN/MIDDLE EASTERN.

If you're looking to add a little adventure to your evening dinner plans, this is the place. Surrounded by a sea of Italian bistros is one of San Francisco's best and most elegant Persian restaurants. The Middle East may no longer be the culinary capital of the world, but at Maykadeh you can still sample the exotic flavors that characterize Persian cuisine. Of the dozen or so appetizers offered on the menu, some of the best are the eggplant with mint garlic sauce, the stuffed grape leaves, and the lamb tongue with lime juice, sour cream, and saffron (c'mon, live a little). About eight mesquite-grilled items are offered, including filet of lamb marinated in lime, homemade yogurt, saffron, and onions. House specialties include half a dozen vegetarian dishes, such as the eggplant braised with saffron, fresh tomato, and dried lime.

Moose's. 1652 Stockton St. (between Filbert and Union sts.). ☎ **415/989-7800.** Reservations recommended. Main courses $8.50–$25. AE, CB, DC, MC, V. Mon–Thurs 11:30am–11pm, Fri–Sat 11:30am–midnight, Sun 10:30am–11pm. Bus: 15, 30, 41, or 45. CALIFORNIA.

You'll see the big blue neon Moose out front long before you pass through the doors, and once inside you'll notice you're in the largest dining room in North Beach. This is where Nob Hill socialites and local politicians come to dine and be seen. But Moose's is not just an image. In fact, the dining room itself is rather sparse and unintimate, but the food, well, that's a different story. Everything that comes out of Moose's kitchen is way above par. The appetizers are innovative, fresh, and well

Zax, 2330 Taylor St. ☎ 415/563-6266. *"We discovered a great place for California cuisine in North Beach, conveniently located at the terminus of the Powell-Mason cable car line. The interior is almost elegant yet unpretentious, an intimate and friendly atmosphere. All meals are prepared to order with ingredients hand-picked daily by the two owner-chefs, both graduates of the San Francisco Culinary Institute. The twice-baked goat cheese soufflé makes a rich yet light appetizer. The menu changes regularly, and is complemented by a superb selection of local wines. Highly recommended."*

—Jeff Zahn and Giselle Simons, New York, NY

balanced (try Mediterranean fish soup with rouille and croutons that's cooked in the wood-fired oven), and the main courses (especially the meats) are perfectly prepared. The menu changes every few months and might include a grilled veal chop with potato galette and a variety of pasta, chicken, and fish dishes. As we go to press, a new chef has just come on board. Cross your fingers that he maintains the quality expected from Moose's.

The bar, separated from the main dining room by a low, frosted-glass partition, remains busy long after the kitchen closes. Jazz featuring piano and bass is played there nightly.

MODERATE

Enrico's. 504 Broadway (at Kearny St.). ☎ **415/982-6223.** Reservations recommended. Main courses $8–$13 lunch, $13–$19 dinner. AE, DISC, MC, V. Mon–Sun noon–11pm; Fri–Sat noon–2am; bar daily noon–2am. Bus: 12, 15, 30, or 83. MEDITERRANEAN.

Though it's taking its sweet time, North Beach's bawdy stretch of Broadway is on the road to rehabilitation. Helping things along is the newly refurbished version of Enrico's, a glitzy sidewalk restaurant and supper club that was once *the* place to hang out before Broadway took its seedy downward spiral. Families may want to skip this one, but anyone with an appreciation for live jazz (played nightly), late-night nasching, and weirdo-watching from the outdoor patio would be quite content spending an alfresco evening under the heat lamps. Chewy brick-oven pizza, zesty tapas, and even a good ole pepper-encrusted top sirloin with garlic mashed potatoes are hot items on the menu. The best part? No cover charge and killer burgers are served until 2am.

Little City Antipasta Bar. 673 Union St. (at Powell St.). ☎ **415/434-2900.** Reservations accepted only for parties of 6 or more. Main courses $13–$15. AE, MC, V. Daily 11:30am–midnight (bar 11:30am–2am). Cable Car: Mason St. Bus: 15, 30, 41, or 45. MEDITERRANEAN/ITALIAN.

Like the name suggests, this stylish, brick-walled beauty of a restaurant specializes in antipasto dishes—dozens of them. During the day it's mostly vacant, but come nightfall the place quickly fills with fashion-conscious swingers, who like to stroll in late and nasch on the baked brie and roasted garlic (served with plenty of bread). The Manila clams, prawns borracho (marinated in tequila, chiles, garlic, and lime), and grilled baby artichokes with a tomato-tarragon aioli are also good bets. The best pasta is tortellini covered with a sauce of Gorgonzola, roasted red bell peppers, and toasted walnuts. Other dishes (which change daily) might include five grilled pork chops with spicy apple chutney, or salmon baked in parchment with a Burmese marinade of onion and oyster sauce, turmeric, and jalapeños. The sacripantina (rum-soaked sponge cake layered with zabaglione) is a must.

North Beach Restaurant. 1512 Stockton St. (between Union and Green sts.). ☎ **415/392-1587.** Reservations accepted only for parties of 3 or more. Main courses $12–$30; fixed-price dinner $35. AE, DC, MC, V. Daily 11:30am–11:30pm. Bus: 15, 30, 41, or 45. ITALIAN.

No restaurant epitomizes North Beach's Italian heritage more than this venerable "old school" bistro. Chef Bruno Orsi has been making his own pasta and prosciutto for years, serving them in a classic, Tuscan-style dining room complete with white cloths, tabletop candles in red holders, hanging meats, and the requisite braids of garlic suspended overhead. In addition to a choice of cooked-to-order dishes such as cioppino, eggplant parmigiana, and veal scaloppini marsala (highly recommended), full seven-course, fixed-price dinners are also available. À la carte choices include a selection of 22 house-made pasta dishes, while desserts range from an excellent zabaglione to a tray of cheese, walnuts, apples, and figs.

Stinking Rose. 325 Columbus Ave. (between Vallejo and Broadway). ☎ **415/781-7673.** Reservations accepted. Main courses $8–$18. AE, DC, JCB, MC, V. Sun–Thurs 11am–11pm, Fri–Sat 11am–midnight. Bus: 15, 30, 41, or 45. ITALIAN.

Garlic, of course, is the "flower" from which this restaurant gets its name. From soup to ice cream, the supposedly healthful herb is a star ingredient in most every dish. ("We season our garlic with food," exclaims the menu.) From a strictly gourmet point of view, the Stinking Rose is unremarkable. Pizzas, pastas, and meats smothered in simple, overpowering garlic sauces are tasty, but memorable only for their singular garlicky intensity. That said, this is a fun place; the restaurant's lively atmosphere and odoriferous aroma combine for good entertainment. Black and white floors, gray marble tables, and large windows overlooking the street help maintain the high energy. The best dishes here include garlic-steamed clams and mussels, garlic pizza, and 40-clove garlic chicken (served with garlic mashed potatoes).

Tommaso's. 1042 Kearny St. (at Broadway). ☎ **415/398-9696.** Reservations not accepted. Pasta and pizza $8–$17; main courses $10–$14. MC, V. Tues–Sat 5–10:30pm, Sun 4–9:30pm. Closed Dec 15–Jan 15. Bus: 15 or 41. ITALIAN.

From the street Tommaso's looks wholly unappealing; a drab, windowless brown facade sandwiched between sex shops. Then why are people always waiting in line to get in? Because everyone knows that Tommaso's bakes San Francisco's best pizza, and has for decades. The center of attention in the downstairs dining room is the chef, who continuously tosses huge hunks of garlic and mozzarella onto pizzas before sliding them into the oak-burning brick oven. Nineteen different toppings make the dish of choice, even though Italian classics such as veal marsala, chicken cacciatore, and a superb lasagna are also available (wonderful calzone, too). Half bottles of house wines are sold, as are homemade cannoli and good Italian coffee. If you can overlook the seedy surroundings, this fun, boisterous restaurant is great place to take the family.

INEXPENSIVE

Caffè Freddy's. 901 Columbus Ave. (corner of Lombard St.). ☎ **415/922-0151.** Reservations accepted. Main courses $2–$8 brunch; $4–$7 lunch; $5–$8 dinner. MC, V. Mon–Fri 10am–10pm, Sat 9am–10pm, Sun 9am–9pm. Bus: 15 or 41. ITALIAN.

Recognizable by the large, painted palms that frame the doorway, Caffè Freddy's attracts a young, hungry, and low-budgeted clientele that comes for the generous servings at generous prices. Pizzas, pastas, sandwiches, salads, and a large assortment of appetizers line the menu—try the antipasto plate of bruschetta, fresh melon, ham, sun-dried tomatoes, and pesto. Start with the warm cabbage salad with goat cheese, currants, walnuts, rosemary, and spinach, then move on to the restaurant's specialty: grilled polenta topped with a variety of meats, cheeses, and vegetables. It's not the best Italian food you'll ever eat, but it's good, cheap, and there's plenty of it.

Readers Recommend

Ristorante Ideale, 1315 Grant Ave. ☎ 415/391-4129. *"As the owner of a small cloth-ing store on Grant Avenue, I've eaten at just about everywhere in North Beach and I have to admit that Ristorante Ideale is arguably the best Italian restaurant in the area. Particu-larly good are the insalata Romana with arugula and pecorino cheese, and the fettucine verde with a butter/sage tomato sauce (the desserts and wine list are also excellent).*

Also a unique dining experience is **Café Macaroni** *(59 Columbus Ave., ☎ 415/956-9737). On the upper floor the ceiling is so low that everyone over five foot two has to duck when entering—and after molto vino, everyone must also make sure to stand up slowly. Architecture aside, the food is excellent, with antipasti and gnocchi leading the way. Desserts are very good as well."*

—Anthony Patella, owner, Wearever clothing boutique

Gira Polli. 659 Union St. (at Columbus Ave.). ☎ **415/434-4472.** Reservations recommended. Main courses $7.50–$12.50. AE, MC, V. Mon–Sun 4:30–9:30pm. Bus: 15, 30, 39, 41, or 45. ITALIAN.

I (Matthew) used to live three blocks from Gira Polli, and man-oh-man do I miss it. Whenever I'd rent a video, I'd drop by here for the Gira Polli Special: a foil-lined bag filled with half a wood-fired chicken (scrumptious), Palermo potatoes (the best in the city), a fresh garden salad, perfectly cooked vegetables, and a soft roll—all for under $10. Next, I'd nab a bottle of good, cheap wine from the liquor store next door, take my goodies home, disconnect the phone, and love life for a while. (Tip: On sunny days, there's no better place in North Beach for a picnic lunch than Washington Square, right across the street.)

Il Pollaio. 555 Columbus Ave. (between Green and Union sts.). ☎ **415/362-7727.** $5.50–$12.50. AE, MC, V. Mon–Sat 11:30am–9pm. Cable car: Powell-Mason line. Bus: 15, 30, 39, or 41. ITALIAN/ARGENTINEAN.

Simple, affordable, and consistently delicious is a winning combination at Il Pollaio. The dining room is casual, the menu simple, but the fresh-from-the-rotisserie chicken has lemon-tangy flavor and it's so moist it practically falls off the bone. Each meal is served with choice of salads, and if you're not in the mood for chicken, you can opt for Italian sausage, rabbit, or lamb.

L'Osteria del Forno. 519 Columbus Ave. (between Green and Union sts.). ☎ **415/982-1124.** Sandwiches $4.50–$8; pizzas $10–$13; main courses $2.50–$7.95. No credit cards. Mon–Wed 11am–10pm, Fri–Sat 11am–10:30pm, Sun noon–10pm. Bus: 15 or 41. ITALIAN.

L'Osteria del Forno may be only slightly larger than a walk-in closet, but it's one of the top three Italian restaurants in North Beach. Peer in the window facing Columbus Avenue, and you'll probably see two Italian women with their hair up, sweating from the heat of their brick-lined oven that cranks out the best focaccia (and focaccia sand-wiches) in the city. There's no pomp or circumstance involved: Locals come here strictly to eat. The menu features a variety of superb pizzas and fresh pastas, plus a few daily specials (pray for the roast pork braised in milk). Small baskets of warm focaccia bread keep you going till the entrées arrive, which should always be accom-panied by a glass of house red.

Mario's Bohemian Cigar Store. 566 Columbus Ave. ☎ **415/362-0536.** Sandwiches $5–$6. No credit cards. Daily 10am–11pm. Closed Dec 24–Jan 1. Bus: 15, 30, 41, or 45. ITALIAN.

Across the street from Washington Square is one of North Beach's most popular neighborhood hangouts: Mario's. The century-old bar—small, well worn, and perpetually busy—is best known for its focaccia sandwiches, including meatball or eggplant. Wash it all down with an excellent cappuccino or a house Campari as you watch the tourists stroll by. And no, they don't sell cigars.

⑤ Pasta Pomodoro. 655 Union St. (at Columbus Ave.). Main courses $3.95–$6.50. No checks or credit cards. ☎ **415/399-0300.** Mon–Fri 11am–11pm, Sat noon–midnight, Sun noon–11pm. ITALIAN.

If you're looking for a good, cheap meal in North Beach, this place across from Washington Square can't be beat. There's usually a 20-minute wait for a table, but after you're seated you'll be surprised at how promptly you're served. Every dish is fresh and sizable, and best of all, they're a third of what you'll pay elsewhere. Winners include the spaghetti frutti di mare, with calamari, mussels, scallops, tomato, garlic and wine, or cavatappi pollo with roast chicken, sun-dried tomatoes, cream, mushrooms, and Parmesan—both are under $7. Avoid the cappellini Pomodoro or ask for extra sauce—it tends to be dry. Their second location, at 2027 Chestnut St. (at Fillmore) (☎ 415/474-3400), is equally good, but cramped and noisy.

11 Chinatown

MODERATE

Brandy Ho's Hunan Food. 217 Columbus Ave. (at Pacific Ave.). ☎ 415/788-7527. Reservations accepted. Main courses $8–$13. AE, DC, DISC, MC, V. Sun–Thurs 11:30am–11pm, Fri–Sat 11:30am–midnight. Bus: 15 or 41. CHINESE.

Fancy black-and-white granite tabletops and a large, open kitchen give you the first clue that the food here is a cut above the usual Hunanese fare. Take our advice and start immediately with the fried dumplings (in the sweet-and-sour sauce) or cold chicken salad. Next, move on to the fish-ball soup with spinach, bamboo shoots, noodles, and other goodies. The best main course is Three Delicacies, a combination of scallops, shrimp, and chicken with onion, bell pepper, and bamboo shoots, seasoned with ginger, garlic, and wine, and served with black-bean sauce. Most dishes here are quite hot and spicy, but the kitchen will adjust the level to meet your specifications. There is a small selection of wines and beers, including plum wine and sake.

INEXPENSIVE

House of Nanking. 919 Kearny St. (at Columbus Ave.). ☎ 415/421-1429. Reservations not accepted. Main courses $4.95–$7.95. No credit cards. Mon–Fri 11am–10pm, Sat noon–10pm, Sun 4–10pm. Bus: 9, 12, 15, or 30. CHINESE.

To the unknowing passer-by, the shoebox-sized House of Nanking has "greasy dive" written all over it. To its legion of fans, however, the wait—sometimes up to an hour—is worth what's on the plate. Located on the edge of Chinatown just off Columbus Avenue, this inconspicuous little diner is one of San Francisco's worst-kept secrets. When the line is reasonable, we drop by for a plate of pot stickers (*still* the best we've ever tasted) and chef/owner Peter Fang's signature shrimp-and-green-onion pancake served with peanut sauce. Trust the waiter when he recommends a special, or simply point to what looks good on someone else's table. Seating is tight, so prepare to be bumped around a bit, and don't expect good service; it's all part of the Nanking experience.

Sam Wo. 813 Washington St. (by Grant Ave.). ☎ 415/982-0596. Reservations not accepted. Main courses $4–$5. No credit cards. Mon–Sat 11am–3am, Sun 12:30–9:30pm. Bus: 15, 30, 41, or 45. CHINESE.

Very handy for late-nighters, Sam's is a total dive that's well known and often packed. The restaurant's two pocket-size dining rooms are located on top of each other, on the second and third floors—take the stairs past the first-floor kitchen. You'll have to share a table, but this place is for mingling almost as much as for eating. The house specialty is jook (known as congee in its native Hong Kong)—a thick rice gruel flavored with fish, shrimp, chicken, beef, or pork; the best is Sampan, made with rice and seafood. Try sweet-and-sour pork rice, wonton soup with duck, or a roast-pork/rice-noodle roll. More traditional fried noodles and rice plates are available too. Chinese doughnuts sell for 50¢ each.

12 South of Market

EXPENSIVE

Boulevard. 1 Mission St. (at Embarcadero and Steuart St.). ☎ **415/543-6084.** Reservations recommended. Main courses $17.75–$22. AE, DC, MC, V. Mon–Fri 11:30am–2pm; daily 5:30–10:30pm. Bus: 15, 30, 32, 42, or 45. AMERICAN.

Master restaurant designer Pat Kuleto and Chef Nancy Oaks have teamed up to create one of San Francisco most exciting new restaurants. Art nouveau interior-vaulted brick ceilings, floral-design banquettes, and fluid, tulip-shaped lamps set a dramatic scene for Oaks's equally impressive dishes. Start with the delicate, soft egg ravioli with spinach, ricotta, and shaved white truffles, then embark on such wonderful concoctions as wood-oven roasted sea bass on a bed of sun-dried tomato and roasted garlic mashed potatoes (she makes a mean cured pork loin, too). Vegetarian items, such as roasted portobello mushrooms layered with mashed sweet potatoes, are also offered. Three levels of formality—bar, open kitchen, and main dining room—keep things from getting too snobby. Though steep prices prevent most from making Boulevard a regular gig, you'd be hard-pressed to find a better place for a special, fun-filled occasion.

Hawthorn Lane. 22 Hawthorn Lane (at Howard St. between Second and Third sts.). ☎ **415/777-9779.** Reservations recommended. Jacket appropriate but not required. Main courses $9.50–$13 lunch, $19.50–$24 dinner. CB, D, DC, JCB, MC, V. Mon–Fri 11:30am–2pm; Sun–Thurs 5:30–10pm. BART: Montgomery station. Muni Metro: F, J, K, L, M, or N. Bus: 12, 30, 45, or 76. CALIFORNIA.

Ever since Anne and David Gingrass left Postrio, the food there has never quite recovered. Thankfully they're heading the kitchen at Hawthorn Lane, their new SoMa restaurant strategically located a block away from the Museum of Modern Art. Anne and David are a culinary team who prepare their menu based on the best and freshest ingredients available. Menus change with the seasons and reflect the Asian and European influences that made them famous under Wolfgang Puck. Step through the doors and you'll immediately notice this restaurant was planned by seasoned professionals. The bar area is comfortable and inviting, with both cocktail tables and bar seating; continue on to the dining room, where earthquake reinforcement beams divide the room in a way that is not only functional, but is also decorative and creates the illusion that each section is a more intimate environment. And the decor is just right: not too fancy or pretentious, but well-lit and decorated with bright artwork, fresh floral arrangements, and a leaf motif throughout. But where the Gingrass's expertise really shines is in the food. The bread basket that arrives at your table is overflowing with fresh-baked goods of all tastes and types. Each dish arrives beautifully presented without being too contrived, but usually with a whimsical accent, such as a leaf-shaped pastry or a bird made of a carrot sliver. Dishes are remarkably well balanced, and accompaniments are often more exciting than the main course itself. If it's on the menu, don't pass up the black cod appetizer served with a miso glaze and spinach rolls. The light, flaky seafood tempura with a vegetable salad is another show-stopper, as is the main course of quail glazed with maple and perched on the most delightful potato gratin. Desserts are as good to look at as they are to eat.

Kyo-Ya. In the Sheraton Palace Hotel, 2 New Montgomery St. (at Market St.). ☎ **415/546-5090.** Reservations recommended. Sushi $4–$8; main courses $20–$35; fixed-price menus $45–$65. AE, CB, DC, JCB, MC, V. Tues–Fri 11:30am–2pm and Mon–Sat 6–10pm. All Market St. trams. All Market St. buses. JAPANESE/SUSHI.

This restaurant offers an authentic Japanese experience, from the decor down to the service and most assuredly the food. Specialties feature the freshest sushi and sashimi, as well as grilled and nabemono dishes (kettle dishes cooked at the table). To start, try any of the appetizers, and move on to the grilled butter fish with miso sauce. Complete dinners include kobachi, soup, rice, pickles, and dessert.

MODERATE

Bizou. 598 Fourth St. (at Brannan St.). ☎ **415/543-2222.** Reservations recommended. Main courses $10.50–$17.50. AE, MC, V. Mon–Fri 11:30am–2:30pm; Mon–Thurs 5:30–10pm, Fri–Sat 5:30–10:30pm. Bus: 15, 30, 32, 42, or 45. FRENCH/ITALIAN.

Around town almost everyone sings Bizou's praises and with good reason: The restaurant's golden yellow walls and terra-cotta ceiling are warmly lit by antique light fixtures and art deco wall sconces, and provide an atmosphere perfect for a first date or an evening out with Mom. The wait staff is friendly and professional, and all the ingredients are fresh and in creative combinations. Our only complaint is that literally every dish is so rich and powerfully flavorful (including the salads), it's a bit of a sensory overload. The menu's starters include an Italian flatbread with caramelized onions, fresh herbs, and Parmesan cheese, pizzas, grilled calamari with a citrus salsa and salsa verde, and batter-fried green beans with dipping sauce. The main courses may include a sautéed sea bass with olive couscous, fennel, bay leaf, and dried orange peel or grilled veal tenderloin with sautéed spinach, and garlic mashed potatoes bathing in a buttery mustard sauce. All main course portions are substantial here, so don't overindulge on appetizers. And save a little room for dessert—the meringue covered in chocolate and topped with coffee ice cream and candied almonds is quite a treat. Too bad there are no cots in a back room here—after your meal, you'll need a nap.

Cha Am. 701 Folsom St. (at Third St.). ☎ **415/546-9711.** Reservations recommended for 3 or more. Main courses $5.95–$6.95 lunch, $6.95–$14.95 dinner. AE, MC, V, DC. Mon–Sat 11am–10pm, Sat–Sun 5–10pm, happy hour Mon–Fri 3–7pm. Bus: 9 or 15. THAI.

Cha Am is one of those sleeper restaurants you'd never find unless someone told you about it. Hidden behind the Moscone Center, this wonderful little Thai restaurant does a brisk lunch business when large conventions are in town (how conventioneers know about this place, we have no idea). A good opener is the Cha Am prawn appetizer: stuffed, grilled prawns layered with a spicy tamarind sauce. Other favorites are the mu yang (marinated sweet and sour pork chops) and pla sam rod (a whole striped bass that's deboned and deep fried until crispy, then topped with a spicy sweet-and-sour sauce)—a steal at $10.95. Service by the mostly Thai staff is efficient and friendly (be sure to ask them about the daily specials), and prices are surprisingly reasonable.

Fly Trap. 606 Folsom St. (at Second St.). ☎ **415/243-0580.** Reservations recommended. Main courses $9.50–$16.75. AE, DC, MC, V. Mon–Thurs 11:30am–10pm, Fri 11:30am–10:30pm, Sat 5:30–10:30pm. Bus: 12, 15, or 76. AMERICAN.

If all these chic, new SoMa restaurants have you craving for the good ole days of thick steaks and buttered calf brains, head to the Fly Trap, one of the few restaurants left serving "old San Francisco" dishes. Don't let the unappealing moniker fool you: The

Fly Trap boasts one of the most handsome dining rooms in the city (the full "fly" story is printed on the back of the menu).

Arrive early for a predinner cocktail at the glimmering, custom-tailored bar, then start things off with the crab cake appetizer (their best seller) or sweetbreads with pancetta. The poached celery Victor and white salad are the house specialties, as is the Hangtown fry, chicken coq au vin, and the side order of creamed spinach. Seafood, pasta, grilled meats, and a half-dozen daily specials give diners plenty of options. Avoid the midweek lunch-hour scene if you prefer a quiet meal.

✪ **Fringale Restaurant.** 570 Fourth St. (between Brannan and Bryant sts.). ☎ **415/ 543-0573.** Reservations recommended. Main courses $9–$18; lunch $4–$12. AE, MC, V. Mon–Fri 11:30am–2:30pm; Mon–Sat 5:30–10:30pm. Bus: 30 or 45. FRENCH.

One of San Francisco's top restaurants, Fringale—French colloquial for "sudden urge to eat"—has enjoyed a week-long waiting list since the day chef/co-owner Gerald Hirigoyen first opened this small SoMa bistro. Sponged, eggshell-blue walls and other muted sand and earth tones provide a serene dining environment, which is all but shattered when 15-table room inevitably fills with Hirigoyen's fans. For starters, try the potato and goat cheese galette with black olives or the sheep's milk cheese and prosciutto tureen with figs and greens. Among the dozen or so main courses you might find a filet of tuna basquaise, pork tenderloin confit with onion and apple marmalade, or macaroni gratin with mushrooms. Desserts are worth savoring, too, particularly the hazelnut and roasted almond mousse cake or the signature crème brûlée with vanilla bean. The mostly French waiters provide uncharacteristically charming service, and prices are surprisingly reasonable.

✪ **Lulu.** 816 Folsom St. (at Fourth St.). ☎ **415/495-5775.** Reservations recommended. Main courses $7–$13 lunch, $9–$17 dinner. AE, MC, V. Mon–Fri 7am–11pm, Sat–Sun 9am–10:30pm. Bus: 15, 30, 32, 42, or 45. CONTINENTAL.

It's hard not to love LuLu, even through there's always a long wait (reserve a table in advance or starve!) and it's one of the noisier rooms in town. The energy of the enormous, converted warehouse dining room is the thing: the expansive view of the sunken seating and open kitchen; the pizzas sliding in and out of the wood-fired oven; and the chefs communicating via headsets. It makes dining out an event. The main room seats 170, but even as you sit amidst a sea of stylish diners, the room somehow feels warm and convivial. And then there's the food, which is consistently delicious. Locals return again and again for the roasted mussels piled high on an iron skillet; the chopped salad with lemon, anchovies, and tomatoes; the pork loin with fennel, garlic, and olive oil; and any of the other wonderful dishes. Everything is served "family style" and is meant to be shared. Save room for dessert; opt for the gooey chocolate cake that oozes with chocolate to be scooped up with the side of melting ice cream. The adjoining cafe serves breakfast, and much of the menu remains at lunch, with the addition of gourmet sandwiches.

INEXPENSIVE

Hamburger Mary's. 1582 Folsom St. (at Twelfth St.). ☎ **415/626-5767.** Reservations recommended. Breakfast $5–$9; main courses $6–$9. AE, MC, V. Tues–Thurs 11am–1am, Fri 11:30am–2am, Sat 10am–2am, Sun 10am–1am. Bus: 9, 12, 42, or 47. AMERICAN.

San Francisco's most . . . *alternative* burger joint, Hamburger Mary's is popular with the late-night SoMa dance club crowd. The restaurant's kitsch decor includes thrift-shop floral wallpaper, family photos, garage-sale prints, stained glass, religious drawings, and Oriental screens. You'll get to know the bar well—it's where you'll stand with the tattooed masses while you wait for a table. Don't despair: They mix a good drink, and people-watching is what you're here for anyway. Sandwiches, salads, and vegetarian dishes provide an alternative to their famous greasy burgers, served on healthful nine-grain bread (like it makes a difference). Tip: Go with the home fries over the french fries. In the morning Hamburger Mary's doubles as a breakfast joint, a good stop for a three-egg omelet or French toast.

Manora's. 1600 Folsom St. (at 12th St.). ☎ **415/861-6224.** Main courses $5.95–$10. Mon–Fri 11:30am–2:30pm and 5–10pm, Sat 5–10:30pm, Sun 5–10pm. MC, V. THAI.

Manora's cranks out some of the best Thai in town and is well worth a jaunt to its SoMa location. But this is no relaxed dining affair. It's perpetually packed (unless you come early), and you'll be seated sardine-like at one of the cramped but well-appointed tables. During the dinner rush, the noise level can make conversation almost impossible among larger parties, but the food is so darn good, you'll probably prefer to turn your head toward your plate and stuff your face. Start with a Thai iced tea or coffee and one of the tangy soups or the chicken satay, which comes with a decadent peanut sauce. Follow up with any of the wonderful dinner dishes—which should be shared—and a side of rice. There are enless options, including a vast array of vegetarian plates. Every remarkably flavorful dish arrives seemingly seconds after you order it, which is great if you're hungry, a bummer if you were planning a long, leisurely dinner. Come before seven or after nine if you don't want a loud, rushed meal.

South Park Café. 108 South Park Ave. (between Brannan and Bryant sts.). ☎ **415/495-7275.** Reservations recommended. Main courses $10–$15. AE, MC, V. Mon–Fri 7:30am–10pm, Sat 6–10pm. FRENCH.

Whenever we get the urge to dump everything and fly to Paris (which is about every day), we drive across town to the South Park Café—it's not quite the same thing as a bistro on Boulevard Montparnasse, but it's close. Usually we're content with an espresso and pastry; a splurge involves the saffron mussels or blood sausage served with sautéed apples. For the ultimate romantic intention, bring a blanket and dine *sur l'herbe* at the adorable park across the street. Beware of the midweek lunch rush, though.

13 Mission District

EXPENSIVE

Flying Saucer. 1000 Guerrero St. (at 22nd St.). ☎ **415/641-9955.** Reservations recommended. Main courses $15–$24. No credit cards. Tues–Sun 5:30–9:30pm. FRENCH.

Outrageously yet artfully presented food is the hallmark of this Mission District fixture. Peering into the glass-walled kitchen, diners can catch the kitchen staff leaning over plates, carefully standing a jumbo prawn on its head atop a baked column of potato polenta. Fish, beef, and fowl dishes are competently grilled, baked, or flamed before being surrounded by a flurry of sauces and garnishes. While the pricey food is certainly intense and flavorful, the overwhelming sensation at this bistro is visual. The party extends from the plate to the decor, where plastic flying saucers mingle with colorful murals and creative lighting. The menu changes frequently, and there are almost always specials. If you ask your waiter to bring you the chef's most flamboyant-*looking* offering, chances are you won't be disappointed. Reservations are essential, as is a blind eye to the sometimes infuriatingly snotty service.

MODERATE

Val 21. 995 Valencia St. (at 21st St.). ☎ **415/821-6622.** Reservations recommended. Main courses $8–$18. MC, V. Mon–Fri 5:30–10pm, Sat–Sun 10am–2pm and 5:30–10pm. Muni Metro: J line to 16th St. Station. CALIFORNIA.

Hip, eclectic decor, perpetually friendly service, and hefty portions of multiethnic fare have made Val 21 one of the Mission District's most popular restaurants. The menu changes frequently, although you might find such dishes as artichoke empanada, southwestern blackened chicken, or grilled salmon in a red curry sauce (plenty of vegetarian plates, too). Sometimes the menu gets a little too creative, sending mixed messages to your mouth, but the overall dining experience makes it worth the trip.

INEXPENSIVE

Universal Café. 2814 19th St. (at Bryant St.). ☎ **415/821-4608.** Reservations recommended for dinner. Main courses $2–$7 at breakfast, $4–$8 at lunch, $7–$16 at dinner. AE, DISC, MC, V. Tues–Fri 7:30am–2:30pm and 6–10pm, Fri 9am–11:30pm, Sat–Sun 11:30am–10pm. Bus: 27. AMERICAN/FRENCH.

We stumbled onto the Universal Café last year completely by accident, coming home from a play in SoMa's semi-industrial sector. It was love at first sight (as well as bite). Not only does it look good—suave and stylish with thick floor-to-ceiling windows and a profusion of sculptured metal and marble—it also attracts a nightly gaggle of locals who come for the delicious focaccia sandwiches, inventive thin-crust pizzas, and gourmet salads. Granted, it's on the way to nowhere, but if you're near the Mission and have a few minutes to spare, it's well worth the detour.

14 Around Town

EXPENSIVE

Alain Rondelli. 126 Clement St. (between Second and Third aves.). ☎ **415/387-0408.** Reservations necessary Fri and Sat. Main courses $16–$19, tasting menu from $45. MC, V. Tues–Sun 5:30–10:30pm. Bus: 2 or 38. FRENCH.

French chef Rondelli does more than simply serve exquisite and innovative French food; he dishes up a gastronomic experience you're likely to dream about for years to come. You may order à la carte, but you'd be better off ordering from the 6-, 9-, 12-, or 20-course tasting menus (for the entire table only)—and to complete the experience, wine can be ordered by the half glass. One spoonful of the calamare—a "salad" of calamari, jalapeño, and mint floating in a heavenly tomato water, and topped off with fresh carrot juice—and you'll be inclined to jump out of your chair and scream "*c'est magnifique!*" The house-made foie gras stuffed with black mission figs and served over warm brioche will melt you back into your seat, until you are again tempted to raise your fork for the crispy-skin salmon with quinoa pilaf and bell pepper, followed by the "Agneau" lamb, pot au Feu, oregano, lemon, and horseradish. Take a breather with poire and Roquefort (pear and Roquefort with champagne vinegar and black pepper gastric) before embarking on one of the sumptuous desserts. The grandest conjuration of all is that after such a didactic and tantalizing feast, you'll feel light as a feather, entirely satiated but not overly full, and you'll float out the front doors onto Clement street as relaxed as if you'd just had a massage. If you're debating between dining here and La Folie, bear in mind that Rondelli's portions are smaller and the atmosphere is far more formal.

The Big Four. In the Huntington Hotel, 1075 California St. (between Mason and Taylor sts.). ☎ **415/474-5400.** Reservations recommended. Breakfast from $9; main courses $14–$26.50. AE, DC, MC, V. Mon–Fri 7–10am; Sat–Sun 7–11am; Mon–Fri 11:30am–3pm; daily 5:30–10:30pm. Cable Car: California St. (direct stop). Bus: 1. CALIFORNIA/FRENCH.

Shining brass, historic California photographs, forest-green leather banquettes, and ram's horn sconces establish the clubby atmosphere at this Nob Hill restaurant that's known for its wild game specialties. At dinner, you might find venison chili with black beans, cheddar, and onion crisps to start, as well as a rib-eye of Wyoming ranch buffalo in a zinfandel-laced rosemary sauce to follow. Even Australian ostrich saddle and Louisiana alligator medallions have been rumored to be on the menu. If game doesn't interest you, there are plenty of other down-to-earth dishes, including grilled halibut over vine-ripened tomatoes and spinach with black-olive vinaigrette, or the angel-hair pasta with Monterey prawns, eggplant, garlic, basil, and shaved Romano. If you can't do dinner here, at least drop by for a nightcap to see what the big four railroad tycoons considered high fashion back then.

Charles Nob Hill. 1250 Jones St. (at Clay St.). ☎ **415/771-5400.** Main courses $16–$26. AE, DC, MC, V. Daily 5:30–10pm. Cable car: California and Powell-Hyde lines. Bus: 1, 12, 27, or 83. FRENCH.

We never knew beef could actually melt in your mouth until Aqua owner Charles Condy bought historic restaurant "Le Club" and introduced us to Aqua's executive chef Michael Mina's culinary magic (it really did melt!). The menu lists the "classically inspired light French fare," which is served in two divided dining rooms with velvet banquettes, fresh floral arrangements, and the loud buzz of the older socialite crowd. Start with a bowl of the soup of the day. When we dined here it was a spinach and roasted garlic soup with cumin-scented rock shrimp and crumbled bacon that was surprisingly beautiful, electric green, and overflowing with flavor. Scallop and black truffle pot pie is another must-try. And for the main course, you might choose the Poele (melt-in-your-mouth) of beef tenderloin with wild mushroom and potato torte, balsamic glazed onions, and foie gras, or a delicate seared red snapper with chive and preserved lemon juice, artichoke, and chanterelle ragout. Although the room itself is romantic, the atmosphere and noise level are too convivial for real intimacy. But it sure is fun to watch everyone else. Wrap up the evening with the outstanding pear and Roquefort tart. Lunch hours were in the works when this book went to press, so call for details. And no matter what, don't drive here unless you valet it; you may spend over an hour looking for parking.

✪ **Ritz-Carlton Dining Room.** 600 Stockton St. (at California St.). ☎ **415/296-7465.** Reservations recommended. Fixed-price menu $37–$57. AE, DC, DISC, MC, V. Mon–Sat 6am–10pm. Cable car: Powell-Hyde and Powell-Mason lines (direct stop). CALIFORNIA/FRENCH.

Never a hotel to do anything second best, when the Ritz-Carlton opened in 1991, it acquired one of the finest chefs in the country, Gary Danko, to help establish its dining room as one of the premier restaurants in San Francisco. And it worked.

The setting, as you would imagine, is regal and sumptuous: Crystal chandeliers, rich tapestries, elegant table settings, and live harp music reek of formality. The wait staff, trained to perfection by maître d' extraordinaire Nick Peyton, is equally impeccable. The star of this princely production, however, is Danko, winner of the 1995 James Beard Award—the Academy Award of the food world—for best chef in California. His penchant for seasonal Northern California produce combined with classic French techniques has drawn nothing but four-star reviews. Standout dishes include his pan-roasted squab stuffed with foie gras, leeks, and garlic confit, the warm grilled-quail salad with apricot-ginger chutney, and his legendary raspberry soufflé with fresh raspberry sauce. The menu, which changes monthly, offers a choice of three-, four-, or five-course dinners, the latter including wine paired with each course by Master Sommelier Emmanuel Kemiji for an additional $29. The dining room also features the country's only "rolling" cheese cart, laden with at least two dozen individually ripened cheeses.

MODERATE

Cliff House. 1090 Point Lobos (at Merrie Way). ☎ **415/386-3330.** Two dining areas: upstairs and main room. Reservations recommended for upstairs and brunch only. Main courses $4–$10 upstairs breakfast; $6–$10 upstairs lunch, $7.50–$18 main lunch; $10–$19 main and upstairs dinner. AE, DC, MC, V. Upstairs: Mon–Fri 8am–3:30pm and 5–10pm, Sat–Sun 8am–4pm and 5–10pm. Main room: Mon–Sat 11am–10:30pm, Sun 9am–2pm and 3:30–10:30pm. Bus: 38 or 18. CONTINENTAL.

Back in the old days the Cliff House was *the* place to go for a romantic night on the town. Nowadays, this aging San Francisco landmark caters mostly to tourists who arrive by the busloads to gander at the Sutro Bath remains next door. Three restaurants in the main, two-story building give diners a choice of how much they wish to spend. Phineas T. Barnacle is the least expensive; sandwiches, salads, soups and such are served hof brau–style across from the elaborate saloon-style bar, after which you can seat yourself at the window-side tables overlooking the shore or beside the fireplace if you're chilled. A step up from the P.T.B. (literally) is Upstairs at the Cliff House, a slightly more formal setting that's best known for its breakfast omelets, and the main room, known as the Seafood and Beverage Co., the fanciest of the lot. Refurbished back to its glory days near the turn of the century, it offers superb ocean views, particularly at sunset, when the fog lets up; unfortunately, the food is a distant second to the scenery. The best MO is to arrive before dusk, request a window seat, order a few appetizers and cocktails, and enjoy the view.

Fog City Diner. 1300 Battery St. (at Lombard St.). ☎ **415/982-2000.** Reservations accepted. Main courses $11–$17. CB, DC, DISC, MC, V. Sun–Thurs 11:30am–11pm, Fri–Sat 11:30am–midnight. Bus: 42. AMERICAN.

Made famous by a Visa commercial, the restaurant looks like a genuine American metallic diner—but only from the outside. Inside, dark polished woods, inspired lighting, and a well-stocked raw bar tell you this is no hash-slinger.

   Dressed-up dinner dishes include gourmet chili dogs, salads, sandwiches, burgers, pork chops, and pot roast. Fancier fish and meat meals include grilled catches of the day and thick-cut steaks. Lighter eaters can make a meal out of the long list of "small plates" that include sautéed mushrooms with garlic custard and seasoned walnuts; or quesadilla with chile peppers and almonds. The place is cute and the food is fine, but if your heart is set on coming here, do so at lunch—you'll be better off elsewhere if you want a special dinner.

✪ 42 Degrees. 235 16th St. (at Illinois St., 1 block off Third St.). ☎ **415/777-5558.** Main courses $12.50–$18. Reservations recommended. Mon–Fri 11:30am–3pm; Wed–Sat 7–midnight. Bus: 22. MEDITERRANEAN.

Tucked behind the Esprit Outlet in the industrial area is the oh-so-chic jazz supper club 42 Degrees. A three-piece jazz trio sets the mood in the warehouselike, but velvet-soft, two-story dining room. Sleek cocktailers hang out at the dark bar area, which specializes in scotches, cognacs, and a selection of small vintners' wines. The dining mezzanine has a men's smoking club feel with a great view of the Bay Bridge, and the downstairs is all 1940s sophistication, from the red velvet curtains that frame 22-foot windows right down to the wait staff and clientele. There's also a dining patio that's a perfect spot for a sunny luncheon. Dishes are Mediterranean-influenced and the menu changes weekly, but usually includes house favorites such as hearts of romaine salad with Caesar dressing, marrow bones with toast, Atlantic salmon, and Niman-Schell meats. It's easier to book a table at lunch, but the time to come is for dinner when the chi chi vibe is full-force.

Hyde Street Bistro. 1521 Hyde St. (between Pacific and Jackson sts.). ☎ **415/441-7778.** Reservations recommended. Main courses $12–$16. MC, V. Daily 5:30–10:30pm. Cable Car: Powell-Mason and Powell-Hyde lines. CALIFORNIA/AUSTRIAN.

Small, intimate, and very European in style, the Hyde Street Bistro has been a neighborhood favorite for years. Ebullient chef/owner Albert Rainer combines his Austrian background with a California twist to create some truly captivating dishes such as strudel filled with a mélange of vegetables, and a roasted Sonoma chicken with a potato pancake and double blanched garlic. Of the many pasta dishes, Chef Rainer recommends ravioli with wild mushroom sauce, or penne with sausage, peppers, tomato, and eggplant. Save room for dessert; Ranier's brother Klaus works wonders with pastries. Parking in this neighborhood is ludicrous, so either splurge on valet or wear walking shoes.

Gordon Biersch Brewery Restaurant. 2 Harrison St. (on the Embarcadero). ☎ **415/243-8246.** Reservations recommended. Main courses $8–$16. AE, MC, V. Sun–Mon 11am–9:30pm, Tues–Sat 11am–10pm. (Bar stays open later.) Bus: 32. CALIFORNIA.

Popular with the young Republican crowd (loose ties and tight skirts predominate), this modern, two-tiered brewery and restaurant eschews the traditional brewpub fare—no spicy chicken wings on *this* menu—in an attempt to attract a more upscale clientele. And it works: It's been four months since our last visit, and we still can't get over how wonderful the smoked lamb shank (bathed in a superb andouille stew) tasted. The baby back ribs with garlic fries is their best seller, followed by the lemon roasted chicken with garlic mashed potatoes. Start with the delicate and crunchy calamari fritti appetizer or, if you're garlic hounds like us, the tangy Caesar salad. Couples bent on a quiet, romantic dinner can skip this one; when the lower-level bar fills up, you practically have to shout to be heard. But food and beer lovers will be quite content.

Il Fornio. Levi Plaza, 1265 Battery St. (bounded by Sansome, Battery, Union, and Greenwich sts.). ☎ **415/986-0100.** Main courses $7.50–$18. Mon–Thurs 7am–11pm, Fri–Sat 11:30am–midnight, Sun 9am–11pm. AE, DC, MC, V. Bus: 12, 32, or 42. ITALIAN.

While we can't say Il Fornio would be our choice if we could only eat at one spot for the rest of our lives, it's one of our favorite standbys, producing consistently good Italian fare at decent prices. Located in Levi Plaza a few minutes away from Pier 39, this trattoria has great atmosphere: It bustles, it's big, and though a little cramped the decor is not overwhelming, but smart Italian. By day it is buzzing with Financial District types and socialites, by night, with couples and gathering friends.

Stacks of fresh-baked Italian cookies behind glass greet you when you first walk through the door. If you don't have a reservation and can't wait to eat, pull up a stool at the marble-topped bar, where the view of the open kitchen and dining room is unobstructed. Better yet, on a sunny day, grab a patio table that looks onto Levi Plaza's fountain. The divided dining room, with high ceilings and enormous, Italian-style paintings, is also warm and convivial. The first of many delights is the basket of fresh-baked breads and breadsticks that arrive at your table accompanied by a dipping dish of olive oil. Complement them with any of the delicious salads or the daily soup (especially if it's carrot), then forge onward to any of the pastas, pizzas, or main courses. Our favorite is the rotisserie duck in balsamic vinegar, which

Il Fornio somehow serves without all the fat you'd expect from duck and all the crispy skin you wish for. Desserts are decadent and wonderful. Try the tiramisu and a glass of rose grappa—a perfect way to end the meal. Breakfasts here are a treat as well.

Kabuto Sushi. 5116 Geary Blvd. (at 15th Ave.). ☎ **415/752-5652.** Sushi $3–$8; main courses $12–$20. AE, MC, V. Tues–Sat 5:30–11pm. Bus: 2, 28, or 38. JAPANESE/SUSHI.

For a town overflowing with seafood and pretentious taste buds, you'd think it'd be easier to find great sushi. But the truth is, finding an outstanding sushi restaurant in San Francisco is more challenging than spotting a parking space in Nob Hill. Still, chop-sticking these fish-and-rice delicacies is one of the most joyous and adventurous ways to dine, and Kabuto is one of the best (and most expensive) places to do it. Chef Sachio Kojima, who presides over the small, ever-crowded sushi bar, constructs each dish with smooth, lightning-fast movements known only to master chefs. Last time we were here, we were lucky enough to sit next to some businessmen visiting from Japan who were ordering things we'd never seen before. We followed their lead and had perhaps the best sushi dinner to date. If you're big on wasabi, ask for the stronger stuff Kojima serves on request.

Khan Toke Thai House. 5937 Geary Blvd. ☎ **415/668-6654.** Reservations recommended. Main courses $6–$11; fixed-price dinner $16.95. MC, V. Daily 5–11pm. Bus: 38. THAI.

Khan Toke Thai is so traditional you're asked to remove your shoes before being seated. Popular for special occasions, this Richmond Distinct fixture is easily the prettiest Thai restaurant in the city; lavishly carved teak interiors evoke the ambience of a Thai temple.

To start, order the tom yam gong lemongrass shrimp with mushroom, tomato, and cilantro soup. Follow with such well-flavored dishes as ground pork with fresh ginger, green onion, peanuts, and lemon juice; prawns with hot chiles, mint leaves, lime juice, lemongrass, and onions; or the chicken with cashew nuts, crispy chiles, and onions. For a real treat, have the deep-fried pompano topped with sautéed ginger, onions, peppers, pickled garlic, and yellow bean sauce; or deep-fried red snapper with "three-flavors" sauce and hot basil leaves. A complete dinner including appetizer, soup, salad, two main courses, dessert, and coffee is a great value.

Cafe Riggio. 4112 Geary Blvd. (at 5th Ave.). ☎ **415/221-2114.** Reservations for 8 or more only. Main courses $7.50–$14.95. MC, V. Mon–Thurs 5–10pm, Fri–Sat 5–11pm, Sun 4:30–10pm. Bus: 38. ITALIAN.

Packed nightly with Richmond District regulars, John Riggio's friendly, unpretentious little cafe has been going strong since it opened some 17 years back. The reason for its longevity is no big secret: consistently good, but not great, Italian food that costs less than a trip to the market (so why bother eating at home?). For example, a dinner plate of tortellini filled with veal and prosciutto and smothered with plenty of garlic, Parmesan cheese, basil, and pine nuts is a mere $8.75. A good selection of nightly seafood specials is also offered, as is the best tiramisu we have ever tasted (the recipe is a family secret). No reservations are accepted for parties smaller than seven, so expect a wait.

INEXPENSIVE

Hard Rock Café. 1699 Van Ness Ave. (at Sacramento St.). ☎ **415/885-1699.** Reservations sometimes accepted (depending on season). Main courses $5.50–$14. AE, MC, V. Sun–Thurs 11:30am–11pm, Fri–Sat 11:30am–midnight. Cable Car: California. Bus: 1. AMERICAN.

Like its affiliated restaurants around the world, this loud, nostalgia-laden place offers big portions of decent food at moderate prices, and plenty of blaring music to an almost exclusively tourist clientele. The real draw, of course, is the merchandise shop, which often has as long a line as the restaurant.

The cafe is decorated with gold records, historic front pages, and the usual "Save the Planet" clutter. The menu offers burgers, baby back ribs, grilled fish, chicken, salads, and sandwiches. Although it's nothing unique to San Francisco, the Hard Rock is a fine place to bring the kids and grab a bite.

✪ **Hong Kong Flower Lounge.** 5322 Geary Blvd. (between 17th and 18th aves.). ☎ **415/ 668-8998.** Most main dishes $5.95–$10.95; dim sum dishes $1.20–$3.20. Mon–Fri 11am– 2:30pm, Sat–Sun 10am–2:30pm; daily 5–9:30pm. Bus: 1, 2, or 38. CHINESE/DIM SUM.

You know you're at a good Chinese restaurant when most people waiting for a table are Chinese. And if you come for dim sum, be prepared to stand in line because you're not the only one who's heard this is the best in town. The Hong Kong Flower Lounge has been one of our very favorite restaurants for years now. It's not the pink and green decor or the live fish swimming in the tank, or even the beautiful marble bathrooms; it's simply that every little dish that comes our way is so darn good. Don't pass up taro cake, salt-fried shrimp, shark-fin soup, and shrimp or beef crepes.

Marcello's Pizza. 420 Castro St. (at Market St.). ☎ **415/863-3900.** Pizza slices $1.89–$2.80; pies $8.12–$18.52. No credit cards. Sun–Thurs 11am–1am, Fri–Sat 11am–2am. Muni Metro: L, M, or N line to Castro St. Station. PIZZA.

Marcello's isn't a fancy place, just a traditional pizza joint with a couple of tables and tasty pizza by the slice and a few other basic dishes. Weekend nights, there's a line out the door of drunk and/or stoned Castro Street partiers with the late-night munchies.

Straits Café. 3300 Geary Blvd. (at Parker St.). ☎ **415/668-1783.** Reservations recommended. Main courses $4.95–$10.95. AE, MC, V. Sun–Thurs 11:30am–10pm, Fri–Sat 11:30am–11pm. Bus: 2, 3, 4, or 38. SINGAPOREAN.

Straits Café is what we like to call "adventure dining," because you never know quite what you're going to get. Burlap palm trees, pastel-painted trompe l'oeil houses, faux balconies, and clotheslines strung across the walls evoke a surreal image of a Singaporean village at this Richmond District restaurant; the cuisine, however, is the real thing. Among chef Chris Yao's spicy Malaysian/Indian/Chinese offerings there's murtabak (stuffed Indian bread), chili crab, basil chicken, nonya daging rendang (beef simmered in lime leaves), ikan pangang (fish stuffed with a chili paste), and hottest of all, sambal udang (prawns sautéed in a chili shallot sambal sauce). For dessert try the sago pudding or the bo bo cha cha (taro root and sweet potato in sweetened coconut milk). The best fun can be had at the banana leaf lunches and brunch when you dine off banana leaf platters with your fingers.

Swan Oyster Depot. 1517 Polk St. (between California and Sacramento sts.). ☎ **415/ 673-1101.** Reservations not accepted. Seafood cocktails $5–$8, clams and oysters on the half shell $6–$7.50 per half dozen. No credit cards. Mon–Sat 8am–5:30pm. Bus: 27. SEAFOOD.

Almost 85 years old and looking even older, Swan Oyster Depot is classic San Francisco. Opened in 1912, this tiny hole in the wall with the city's friendliest servers is little more than a narrow fish market that decided to slap down some stools. There are only 20 or so seats jammed cheek by jowl along a long marble bar. Most patrons come for a quick cup of chowder or a plate of half-shelled oysters that arrive chilling on crushed ice. The menu is limited to fresh crab, shrimp, oyster, and clam cocktails, Maine lobster, and Boston-style clam chowder. Fish is only available raw or smoked and to go. Beer and wine are available.

Tommy's Joynt. 1109 Geary St. (at Van Ness Ave.). ☎ **415/775-4216.** Reservations not accepted. Main courses $4–$7. No credit cards. Bar, daily 10am–2am. Bus: 2, 3, 4, or 38. AMERICAN.

With its colorful mural exterior, it's hard to miss Tommy's Joynt, a late-night favorite for those in search of a cheap and hearty meal. Tommy's is one big collage, the interior crammed with suspended hockey sticks, bamboo poles with attached stuffed birds, a mounted buffalo head, an ancient piano, rusty firearms, fading prints, a beer-guzzling lion, and Santa Claus masks. The cafeteria-style buffet offers a cornucopia of rib-clinging à la carte dishes such as buffalo stew, corned beef, meatballs, and mashed potatoes. There's also a slew of seating and almost 100 varieties of beer.

Woodward's Garden. 1700 Mission St. (at Duboce Ave.). ☎ **415/621-7122.** Reservations required. Main courses $14–$17. MC, V. Four dinner seatings Wed–Sun 6, 6:30, 8, 8:30pm. Bus: 14, 26, or 49. AMERICAN.

If you find yourself parking along a dank industrial street where no decent restaurant would dare to set up shop, you're in the right place. Woodward's Garden, named after a turn-of-the-century amusement center in the same location, is the kind of gem many San Franciscans don't even know about. And good thing: There are only nine tables in the entire place. Foodies will mention Woodward's as if everyone should know about it, but its location (under a freeway on-ramp in SoMa) and disguised exterior of simple curtains and a minuscule sign keep this upscale restaurant well under wraps. Still, its simple decor and intimate (okay, tiny) environment make for sincerely romantic dining. And with so few tables, both the kitchen (formerly of Postrio and Greens) and the wait staff are attentive enough to make you feel they opened their doors just for you. Don't traipse down here without reservations, or a car for that matter.

15 Gay-Friendly Restaurants

While you will see gay and lesbian singles and couples at almost every restaurant in San Francisco, the following spots cater particularly to the gay set, but being gay is certainly not a requirement for enjoying them. Most are located in the Castro and all can be classified as inexpensive.

Café Flore. 2298 Market St. (at Noe St.). ☎ **415/621-8579.** Reservations not accepted. American breakfast $5.95; main courses $4.50–$7.50. No credit cards. Daily 7:30am–midnight. Muni Metro: F. Bus: 8. CALIFORNIA.

Sheathed with glass on three sides, and overlooking Market Street, Noe Street, and a verdant patio in back, Café Flore attracts young, bright, and articulate members of the gay (mostly male) community. Local wits refer to it as a place where body piercing is encouraged but not mandatory, although this kind of exhibitionism tends to be more prevalent in the evening rather than during the daytime.

Many of the menu items are composed of mostly organic ingredients, and include a succulent version of roasted (sometimes free-range) chicken, soups, pastas, and steaks. Café latte costs $2 a cup. Plan on hearing a lot of noise and possibly seeing a handsome young man sending not particularly furtive glances your way.

Caffè Lutia Pietia. 558 Castro St. (between 18th and 19th sts.). ☎ **415/621-2566.** Reservations recommended for brunch. Main courses $9–$15. AE, DISC, MC, V. Mon 11am–3pm, Tues–Fri 11am–3pm and 5:30–10:30pm, Sat–Sun 9am–3pm and 5:30–10:30pm. ITALIAN.

Much to the relief of residents tired of the burger and pizza joints strewn throughout the Castro, this new venue opened its doors in March 1995, offering a more warm and sophisticated dining environment complete with rich yellow, brush-painted walls adorned with local artwork. The room stretches all the way back to the outdoor dining patio (yes, there are heat lamps) and a lush Japanese garden. The fare is contemporary American with Italian and Mediterranean influences. Lunch offers soups, salads, sandwiches (with a choice of garlic fries or a green salad) such as the grilled eggplant with roasted red pepper and smoked mozzarella on pane integrale; or main lunch courses that may include seared tiger prawns with mixed greens, blanched vegetables, and a lemon caper vinaigrette. Dinner features such dishes as braised chicken with cranberries, squash, and soft polenta. Desserts follow city folks' favorites: crème brulée and tiramisu. Counter diners can watch chefs at work in the partially open kitchen. If you come for Saturday or Sunday brunch, reserve in advance or be prepared to wait in line for a yeast-raised waffle with strawberries, poached eggs with soft polenta, smoked salmon and shrimp cream, or any of the other breakfast treats.

Mad Magda's Russian Tearoom & Café. 579 Hayes St. (between Octavia and Laguna sts.). ☎ **415/864-7654.** Reservations not accepted. Soups, salads, sandwiches 75¢–$6.95. No credit cards. Mon–Tues 8am–9pm, Wed–Fri 8am–midnight, Sat 9am–midnight, Sun 9am–7pm. Bus: 21. SOUPS/SALADS/SANDWICHES.

Set within a late 19th-century Victorian house, this small and mysterious cafe located in Hayes Valley (between the Civic Center and the Western Addition) is a charmingly fun place for a light meal if you're meandering the Hayes Valley shops—and everything costs under $8. Its guardian spirit is that of Magda, a long-dead relative of the owners who is said to share an ongoing relationship with the staff here. In her honor, the floor is decorated with numerological and tarot symbols, walls painted in an imitation of cloud-covered skies, and imperial Russian decorations that include a large and extraordinary rendering, in wood and fabric, of the onion domes in Moscow. Munch on a Catherine the Great (tuna with Swiss cheese) or The Czar (with chicken salad) sandwich or a Russian blintz (served only on weekends), and cough up a spare $13 for a 15-minute session with one of the in-house tarot and tea-leaf readers who will divine your future—if you dare to ask.

✪ **"No Name".** 2223 Market St. (between Sanchez and Noe sts.). ☎ **415/431-0692.** Reservations recommended. $12.95–$16.95. MC. V. Mon–Fri 11:30am–2:30pm, Sun 10am–2pm; Sun–Thurs 5:30–10pm, Fri–Sat 5:30–11pm. Muni metro: F, L, K, or M. Bus: 8, 22, 24, or 37. CALIFORNIA.

It seems this new Castro area restaurant is already so popular, there's no big hurry to give it a name. Run by the owners of the infamous Cypress Club, the decor here is substantially less opulent than its counterpart, but the energy level is definitely more lively. Surrounded by hardwood floors, candles, streamlined modern light fixtures and loud music, festive gays and straights come here to cocktail on the heavy-handed specialty drinks and dine on grilled ahi tuna with pickled veggies and Canton noodles, or the ever popular roasted chicken with garlic mashed potatoes. This is currently *the* dining and schmoozing spot in the area.

Patio Café. 531 Castro St. (at 18th St.). ☎ **415/621-4640.** Reservations not accepted. Main courses $9.50–$12.50. AE, MC, V. Sun–Thurs 8am–10:30pm, Fri–Sat 8am–11pm. Bus: 24 or 33. AMERICAN.

Since the early 1970s, this Castro Street bar and restaurant has served as the rendezvous point for uncounted numbers of trysts, peccadilloes, and love affairs of all kinds that have blossomed within the premises. Originally established as The Baker's Café, it retains the original ovens that contributed to its early reputation, which are today purely decorative. Ringed with trellises and verdant plants, and set in the back yard of a cluster of shops, the patio features a glass roof (whose entertainment value derives from the heft and brawn of the staff, who climb skyward to manually crank it open during clement weather). Menu items include virtually any drink you can think of, and such dishes as Caesar salads, Chinese chicken salad (laced with fresh ginger), prime rib, roasted chicken, and grilled salmon with Cajun hollandaise sauce. The most popular drinks include a Melon Margarita ($3.75) and a Patio Mai-Tai ($4.75).

Without Reservation. 460 Castro St. (at Market St.). ☎ **415/861-9510.** Reservations not accepted. Main courses $5–$10. DC, MC, V. Sun–Thurs 7:30am–2:30am, Fri–Sat 7:30am–3am. Bus: 8, 18, 24, or 35. AMERICAN.

Outfitted with wood-sheathed walls, high wainscoting, hanging lamps, and a white ceiling, this establishment is called the grande dame of Castro Street greasy spoons. Noted for a deliberate lack of culinary glamour, the menu focuses mainly on club sandwiches (some of the best and biggest in town), omelets (including a version named after Popeye, which includes spinach), patty melts, salads, and steaks.

With no more than 16 tables and a commodious countertop, it was originally established in the 1930s as Andy's Doughnut Shoppe. Around 1967 (thanks to the slogan "without reservation," which was scrawled across its windows in lipstick by a disgruntled drag queen), the place was dubbed with a name which has remained ardently in place ever since. Virtually all of the wait staff, which includes an amused but politically correct corps of women, is openly gay. Each contributes to the hijinks and shenanigans, which sometimes dominate the ambience here. Foremost among these is the awarding of prenumbered signs (1 to 10) based on the attractiveness of whatever Castro Street passerby happens to become visible through the plate-glass window. Breakfast is served daily until 4pm, and lunch is available virtually any time, so no matter what your schedule, you can usually rustle up something to eat without reservation.

7

What to See & Do in San Francisco

San Francisco's parks, museums, tours, and landmarks are favorite haunts for travelers the world over and offer an array of activities to suit every visitor. But it's not any particular activity or place that makes the city the most popular tourist destination in the world. It's San Francisco itself—its charm, its atmosphere, its perfect blend of big metropolis with small-town hospitality. No matter what you do while you're here—whether you spend all your time in central areas like Union Square or North Beach or explore the intricacies of outer neighborhoods—you're bound to collect a treasure of vacation memories that can only be found in this culturally rich, strikingly beautiful City by the Bay.

1 The Top Attractions

Alcatraz Island. Pier 41, near Fisherman's Wharf. ☎ **415/705-1045.** Admission (includes ferry trip and audio tour) $10 adults, $8.25 seniors 62 and older, $4.75 children 5–11. Winter daily 9:30am–2:45pm; summer daily 9:15am–4:15pm. Advance purchase advised. Ferries depart every half hour, at 15 and 45 minutes after the hour. Arrive at least 20 minutes before sailing time.

Visible from Fisherman's Wharf, Alcatraz Island (aka "The Rock") has seen a checkered history. It was discovered in 1775 by Juan Manuel Ayala, who named it after the many pelicans that nested on the island. From the 1850s to 1933, when the army vacated the island, it served as a military post protecting the Bay shoreline. In 1934, the buildings of the military outpost were converted into a maximum-security prison. Given the sheer cliffs, treacherous tides and currents, and frigid temperatures of the waters, it was believed to be a totally escape-proof prison. Among the famous gangsters who were penned in cell blocks A through D were Al Capone, Robert Stroud, the so-called Birdman of Alcatraz (because he was an expert in ornithological diseases), Machine Gun Kelly, and Alvin Karpis. It cost a fortune to keep them imprisoned here because all supplies, including water, had to be shipped in. In 1963, after an apparent escape in which no bodies were recovered, the government closed the prison, and in 1972 it became part of the Golden Gate National Recreation Area. The wildlife that was driven away during the military and prison years has begun to return—the black-crested night heron and other sea birds are nesting here again—and a new trail has been built that passes through the island's nature areas. Tours, including an audio tour of the prison block and a slide show, are given by the park's rangers, who entertain their guests with interesting anecdotes.

It's a popular excursion and space is limited, so purchase tickets as far in advance as possible. The tour is operated by **Red and White Fleet** (☎ **415/546-2700** or 800/ 229-2784 in California) and can be charged to a credit card (AE, MC, V; $2 per ticket service charge on phone orders). Tickets may also be purchased in advance from the Red and White Fleet ticket office on Pier 41.

Wear comfortable shoes and take a heavy sweater or windbreaker because even when the sun's out, it's cold. The National Parks Service also notes that there are a lot of steps to climb on the tour.

For those who want to get a closer look at Alcatraz without going ashore, two boat-tour operators offer short circumnavigations of the island. (See "Organized Tours," below, for complete information.)

Cable Cars

Although they may not be San Francisco's most practical means of transportation, cable cars are certainly the best loved. Designated official historic landmarks by the National Parks Service in 1964, they clank up and down the city's steep hills like mobile museum pieces, tirelessly hauling thousands of tourists each day to nowhere in particular.

San Francisco's cable cars were invented in 1869 by London-born engineer Andrew Hallidie, who got the idea by way of serendipity. As the story goes, Hallidie was watching a team of overworked horses haul a heavily laden carriage up a steep San Francisco slope. As he watched, one horse slipped and the car rolled back, dragging the other tired beasts with it. At that moment Hallidie resolved that he would invent a mechanical contraption to replace such horses, and just four years later, in 1873, the first cable car made its maiden run from the top of Clay Street. Promptly ridiculed as "Hallidie's Folly," the cars were slow to gain acceptance. One early onlooker voiced the general opinion by exclaiming, "I don't believe it—the damned thing works!"

Even today, many visitors have difficulty believing that these vehicles, which have no engines, actually work. The cars, each weighing about six tons, are hauled along by a steel cable, enclosed under the street in a center rail. You can't see the cable unless you peer straight down into the crack, but you'll hear its characteristic clickity-clanking sound whenever you're nearby. The cars move when the gripper (*not* the driver) pulls back a lever that closes a pincerlike "grip" on the cable. The speed of the car therefore is determined by the speed of the cable, which is a constant $9^{1}/_{2}$ miles per hour—never more, never less.

The two types of cable cars in use hold, respectively, a maximum of 90 and 100 passengers and the limits are rigidly enforced. The best views are had from the outer running boards, where you have to hold on tightly when taking curves. Everyone, it seems, prefers to ride on the running boards.

Often imitated but never duplicated, similar versions of Hallidie's cable cars have been used throughout the world, but all have been replaced by more efficient means of transportation. San Francisco planned to do so, too, but the proposal was met with so much opposition that the cable cars' perpetuation was actually written into the city charter in 1955. This mandate cannot be revoked without the approval of a majority of the city's voters—a distant and doubtful prospect.

San Francisco's three existing lines comprise the world's only surviving system of cable cars. For more information on riding them, see "Getting Around" in Chapter 4, "Getting to Know San Francisco."

Major San Francisco Sights

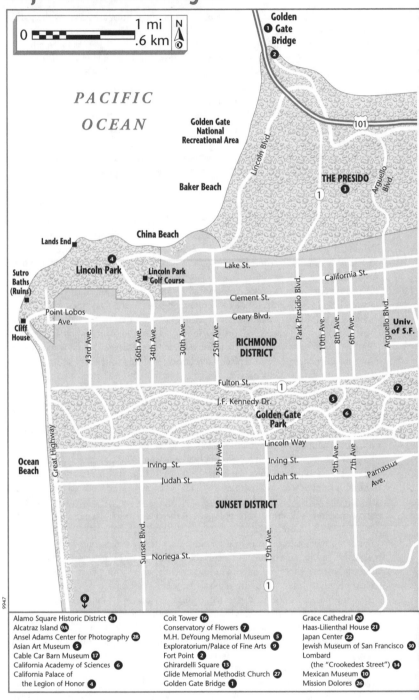

PACIFIC
OCEAN

Golden Gate
National
Recreational Area

Baker Beach

China Beach

Lands End

Sutro
Baths
(Ruins)

Cliff
House

Point Lobos
Ave.

Lincoln Park

Lincoln Park
Golf Course

Lake St.

Clement St.

Geary Blvd.

Fulton St.

J.F. Kennedy Dr.

Golden Gate
Park

Lincoln Way

Irving St.

Judah St.

Irving St.

Judah St.

Ocean
Beach

Great Highway

Sunset Blvd.

Noriega St.

SUNSET DISTRICT

RICHMOND
DISTRICT

California St.

THE PRESIDO

Lincoln Blvd.

Arguello Blvd.

Park Presidio Blvd.

10th Ave.

8th Ave.

6th Ave.

Arguello Blvd.

Univ.
of S.F.

Parnassus
Ave.

9th Ave.

7th Ave.

19th Ave.

25th Ave.

25th Ave.

43rd Ave.

36th Ave.

34th Ave.

30th Ave.

25th Ave.

Golden
Gate
Bridge

101

1

1

1

1

1 mi
0
.6 km

N

9947

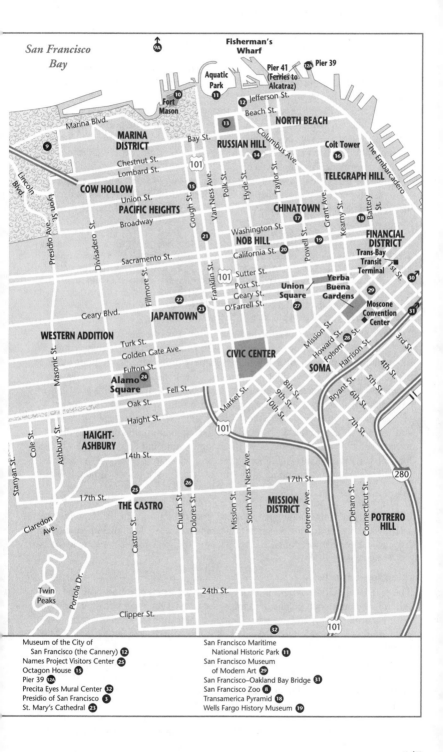

San Francisco Bay

Fisherman's Wharf

Pier 41 (Ferries to Alcatraz)

Pier 39

Aquatic Park

Fort Mason

Jefferson St.

Beach St.

NORTH BEACH

MARINA DISTRICT

Bay St.

RUSSIAN HILL

Coit Tower

Chestnut St.

Lombard St.

TELEGRAPH HILL

COW HOLLOW

Columbus Ave.

The Embarcadero

PACIFIC HEIGHTS

Union St.

Marina Blvd.

Lincoln Blvd

Presidio Ave.

Lyon St.

Broadway

Divisadero St.

CHINATOWN

Battery St.

Washington St.

Grant Ave.

Kearny St.

NOB HILL

FINANCIAL DISTRICT

Sacramento St.

California St.

Powell St.

Trans-Bay Transit Terminal

1st St.

Franklin St.

Sutter St.

Post St.

Union Square

Yerba Buena Gardens

Fillmore St.

Geary St.

O'Farrell St.

Moscone Convention Center

Geary Blvd.

JAPANTOWN

St. Mary's Cathedral

Hyde St.

Polk St.

Van Ness Ave.

Gough St.

Taylor St.

WESTERN ADDITION

Turk St.

Golden Gate Ave.

Fulton St.

CIVIC CENTER

Mission St.

Howard St.

Folsom St.

SOMA

Harrison St.

3rd St.

Masonic Ave.

Alamo Square

Fell St.

Bryant St.

4th St.

Oak St.

Haight St.

Market St.

8th St.

9th St.

10th St.

5th St.

6th St.

7th St.

HAIGHT-ASHBURY

14th St.

Stanyan St.

Cole St.

Ashbury St.

17th St.

26

MISSION DISTRICT

17th St.

South Van Ness Ave.

Potrero Ave.

280

POTRERO HILL

THE CASTRO

Castro St.

Church St.

Dolores St.

Mission St.

Deharo St.

Connecticut St.

Claredon Ave.

Twin Peaks

Portola Dr.

24th St.

Clipper St.

32

101

Museum of the City of San Francisco (the Cannery) 12	San Francisco Maritime National Historic Park 11
Names Project Visitors Center 25	San Francisco Museum of Modern Art 29
Octagon House 15	San Francisco–Oakland Bay Bridge 31
Pier 39 12A	San Francisco Zoo 8
Precita Eyes Mural Center 32	Transamerica Pyramid 18
Presidio of San Francisco 3	Wells Fargo History Museum 19
St. Mary's Cathedral 23	

Coit Tower. Atop Telegraph Hill. ☎ **415/362-0808.** Admission (to the top of the tower) $3 adults, $2 seniors and students, $1 children 6–12. Daily 10am–6pm. Bus: 39 ("Coit").

In a city known for its great views and vantage points, Coit Tower is tops. Located atop Telegraph Hill, just east of North Beach, the round, stone tower offers panoramic views of the city and the Bay.

Completed in 1933, the tower is the legacy of Lillie Hitchcock Coit, a wealthy eccentric who left San Francisco a $125,000 bequest "for the purpose of adding beauty to the city I have always loved" and also as a memorial to its volunteer firemen. She had been saved from a fire as a child and thereafter held the city's firefighters in particularly high esteem.

Inside the base of the tower are the impressive murals titled *Life in California, 1934,* which were completed under the WPA during the New Deal. They were completed by more than 25 artists, many of whom had studied under Mexican muralist Diego Rivera.

The Exploratorium. 3601 Lyon St., in the Palace of Fine Arts (at Marina Blvd.). ☎ **415/ 563-7337** or 415/561-0360 for recorded information. Admission $9 adults, $7 senior citizens, $5 children 6–17, $2.50 children 3–5, free for children under 3; free for everyone first Wed of each month. Summer (Memorial Day–Labor Day) and holidays, Mon–Tues and Thurs–Sun 10am–6pm, Wed 10am–9:30pm; the rest of the year Tues and Thurs–Sun 10am–5pm, Wed 10am–9:30pm. Closed Mon after Labor Day–Memorial Day (except holidays), Thanksgiving Day, and Christmas Day. Bus: 30 from Stockton St. to the Marina stop.

Scientific American magazine rates the Exploratorium as "the best science museum in the world," pretty heady stuff for this exciting hands-on science fair that contains more than 650 permanent exhibits that explore everything from giant bubble blowing to Einstein's Theory of Relativity. It's like a mad scientist's penny arcade, an educational funhouse and an experimental laboratory all rolled into one. Touch a tornado, shape a glowing electrical current, fingerpaint via computer, or take a sensory journey in total darkness in the Tactile Dome—you could spend all day here and still not see everything. Every exhibit at the Exploratorium is designed to be interactive, educational, safe, and, most importantly, fun. And don't think this is just for kids; parents inevitably end up being the most reluctant to leave. On the way out, be sure to stop in the wonderful gift store, which is chock-full of affordable brain candy.

The museum is located in San Francisco's Marina District at the beautiful Palace of Fine Arts, the only building left standing from the Panama-Pacific Exposition of 1915, which celebrated the opening of the Panama Canal. The adjoining park and lagoon—the perfect place for an afternoon picnic—is home to ducks, swans, seagulls, and grouchy geese, so bring bread.

Golden Gate Bridge

The year 1996 marks the 60th birthday of what is possibly the most beautiful, and certainly the most photographed, bridge in the world. Often half veiled by the city's trademark rolling fog, San Francisco's Golden Gate spans tidal currents, ocean waves, and battering winds to connect the City by the Bay with the Redwood Empire to the north.

With its gracefully swung single span, spidery bracing cables, and sky-zooming twin towers, the bridge looks more like a work of abstract art than the practical engineering feat that it is, among the greatest of this century. Construction began in May 1937 and was completed at the then-colossal cost of $35 million. Contrary to pessimistic predictions, the bridge neither collapsed in a gale or earthquake nor proved to be a white elephant. A symbol of hope when the country was afflicted with widespread joblessness, the Golden Gate single-handedly changed the Bay Area's economic life, encouraging the development of areas north of San Francisco.

The mile-long steel link, which reaches a height of 746 feet above the water, is an awesome bridge to cross. Traffic usually moves quickly, so crossing by car won't give you too much time to see the sights. If you drive ($3 toll, payable southbound) from the city, park in the lot at the foot of the bridge on the city side and make the crossing by foot. Back in your car, continue to Marin's Vista Point, at the bridge's northern end. Look back and you'll be rewarded with one of the greatest views of San Francisco.

Millions of pedestrians walk or bike across the bridge each year, gazing up at the tall red towers, out at the vistas of San Francisco and Marin County, and down into the stacks of ocean-going liners. You can walk out onto the span from either end, but be prepared: It's usually windy and cold, and the bridge vibrates. Still, walking even a short way is one of the best ways to experience the immense scale of the structure.

Bridge-bound Golden Gate Transit buses (☎ **415/332-6600**) depart every 30 to 60 minutes during the day for Marin County, starting from the Transbay Terminal at Mission and First streets and making convenient stops at Market and Seventh streets, at the Civic Center, and along Van Ness Avenue and Lombard Street.

Golden Gate National Recreation Area

San Francisco's Golden Gate National Recreation Area makes New York's Central Park look like a putting green. The largest urban park in the *world*, the GGNRA covers three counties along 28 miles of stunning, condo-free shoreline. Run by the National Parks Service, the Recreation Area wraps around the northern and western edge of the city, and just about all of it is open to the public with no access fees. The Muni bus system provides transportation to the more popular sites, including Aquatic Park, the Cliff House, Fort Mason, and Ocean Beach. For more information, contact the **National Park Service** (☎ **415/556-0560**). For more detailed information on particular sites, see the "Staying Active" section at the end of this chapter and "Easy Excursions from San Francisco" in Chapter 11.

Here is a brief rundown of the salient features of the park's peninsula section, starting at the northern section and moving westward around the coastline:

Aquatic Park, adjacent to the Hyde Street Pier, has a small swimming beach, although it's not that appealing (and darn cold). Far more entertaining is a visit to the ship-shaped museum across the lawn that's part of the San Francisco Maritime National Historical Park (see below for more information).

Fort Mason Center occupies an area from Bay Street to the shoreline and consists of several buildings and piers that were used during World War II. Today they are occupied by a variety of museums, theaters, and organizations as well as by **Greens** vegetarian restaurant, which affords views of the Golden Gate Bridge (see Chapter 6, "Dining," for more information). For information about Fort Mason events, call **415/441-5705.** The park headquarters is also at Fort Mason.

Farther west along the Bay at the northern end of Laguna Street is **Marina Green,** a favorite locals spot for kite-flying, jogging, and walking along the Promenade. The **St. Francis Yacht Club** is also located here.

From here begins the 3½-mile paved **Golden Gate Promenade,** San Francisco's best and most scenic biking, jogging, and walking path, which runs along the shore past **Crissy Field** (be sure to stop and watch the gonzo windsurfers) and ends at Fort Point under the Golden Gate Bridge.

Fort Point (☎ **415/556-1373**) was built in 1853 to protect the narrow entrance to the harbor. It was designed to house 500 soldiers manning 126 muzzle-loading

Golden Gate National Recreation Area

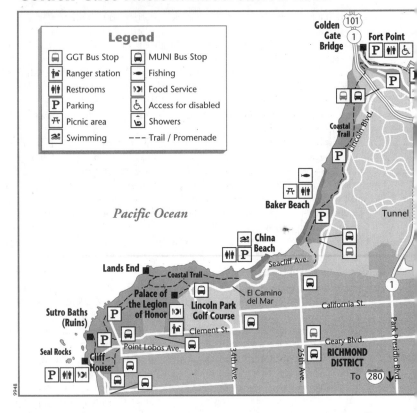

cannons. By 1900, the fort's soldiers and obsolete guns had been removed, but the formidable brick edifice still remains. Guided tours and cannon demonstrations are given at the site Wednesday through Sunday from 10am to 5pm.

Lincoln Boulevard sweeps around the western edge of the Bay to **Baker Beach,** where the waves roll ashore—a fine spot for sunbathing, walking, or fishing. Hikers can follow the Coastal Trail from Fort Point along this part of the coastline all the way to Land's End.

A short distance from Baker, **China Beach** is a small cove where swimming is permitted. Changing rooms, showers, a sundeck, and rest rooms are available.

A little farther around the coast appears **Lands End** looking out to Pyramid Rock. A lower and an upper trail provides a hiking opportunity amid windswept cypress and pine on the cliffs above the Pacific.

Still farther along the coast lies **Point Lobos,** the **Sutro Baths,** and the **Cliff House.** The latter has been serving refreshments to visitors since 1863 and providing views of Seal Rocks, home to a colony of sea lions and many marine birds. There's an information center here (open daily from 10am to 4:30pm; ☎ **415/556-8642**) as well as the incredible **Musée Mecanique,** an authentic old-fashioned arcade with 150 coin-operated amusement machines. Only traces of the Sutro Baths remain today to the northeast of the Cliff House. This swimming facility was a major summer attraction that could accommodate up to 24,000 people before it burned down in 1966.

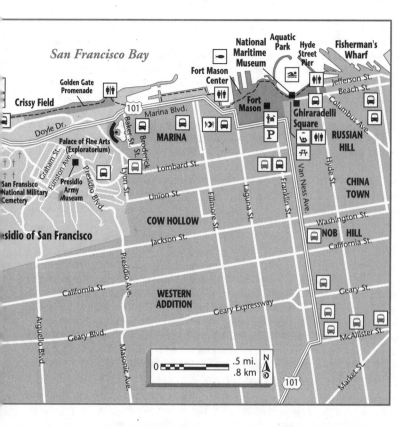

A little farther inland at the western end of California Street is **Lincoln Park,** which contains a golf course and the Palace of the Legion of Honor.

At the southern end of Ocean beach, 4 miles down the coast, is another area of the park around Fort Funston where there's an easy loop trail across the cliffs (ranger station ☎ **415/239-2366**). Here, too, you can watch the hang gliders taking advantage of the high cliffs and strong winds.

Farther south along route 280, Sweeney Ridge, which can only be reached by car, affords sweeping views of the coastline from the many trails that crisscross this 1,000 acres of land. It was from here that the expedition led by Don Gaspar de Portolá first saw San Francisco Bay in 1769. It's located in Pacifica and can be reached via Sneath Lane off Route 35 (Skyline Boulevard) in San Bruno.

The GGNRA also extends into Marin County, where it encompasses the **Marin Headlands, Muir Woods National Monument, Muir Beach** and **Stinson Beach,** and the **Olema Valley** behind the **Point Reyes National Seashore.** See Chapter 11 for information on these areas.

Golden Gate Park

Everybody loves Golden Gate Park: people, dogs, birds, frogs, turtles, bison, and flowers. Literally everything feels unified here in San Francisco's enormous arboreal front yard. But this great city landmark wasn't always a favorite place to convene. It was conceived in the 1860s and 1870s but took its current shape in the 1880s and 1890s thanks to the skill and effort of John McClaren, a Scot who arrived in 1887 and began the landscaping of the park. Totaling 1,017 acres, the park is a narrow strip that stretches from the Pacific Coast inland. No one had thought about the challenge the sand dunes and wind would present to any landscape artist. McClaren, a clever lad, developed a new strain of grass called "sea bent," which he had planted to hold the sandy soil along the Firth of Forth, and he used this to anchor the soil here too. He also built the two windmills that stand on the western edge of the park to pump water for irrigation. Every year the ocean eroded the western fringe of the park, and he solved this problem too. It took him 40 years to build a natural wall, putting out bundles of sticks which were then covered with sand by the tides. Under his brilliant eye, the park took shape over the next 10 years.

For information on the park, head first to the **McClaren Lodge and Park Headquarters** (open Monday through Friday). There are several special gardens in the park, notably the Rhododendron Dell, the Rose Garden, the Strybing Arboretum and at the western edge of the park a springtime array of thousands of tulips and daffodils around the Dutch windmill.

In addition to the highlights below, the park contains several recreational facilities: tennis courts, baseball, soccer and polo fields, golf course, riding stables, flycasting pools, and boat rentals at the Strawberry Hill boathouse. It is also the home of three major museums: the **M. H. de Young Memorial Museum,** the **Asian Art Museum,** and the **California Academy of Sciences** (see separate listings below). If you plan to visit all the park's attractions, consider buying the Culture Pass, which enables you to visit the three museums, the Japanese Tea Garden, and the Conservatory of Flowers for $10. Passes are available at each site and at the Visitor Information Center. For further information call **415/391-2000** Enter the park at Kezar Drive, an extension of Fell Street. Bus: 16AX, BX, 5, 6, 7, 66, 71.

CONSERVATORY OF FLOWERS (1878)   Built for the 1894 Midwinter Exposition, this striking assemblage of glass architecture contains a rotating display of plants and shrubs at all times of the year. The orchids in particular are spectacular. It's modeled on the famous glass house at Kew Gardens in London.

JAPANESE TEA GARDEN (1894)   McClaren hired the Hagiwara family to care for this garden developed for the 1894 Midwinter Exposition. It's a quiet place with cherry trees, shrubs, and bonsai crisscrossed by winding paths and high-arched bridges crossing over pools of water. Focal points and places for contemplation include the massive bronze Buddha that was cast in Japan in 1790 and donated by the Gump family, the Shinto wooden pagoda, and the Wishing Bridge, which reflected in the water looks as if it completes a circle. The garden is open daily from 9am to 6pm; the tea house (which invented the fortune cookie) serves from 10:30am to 5pm.

STRYBING ARBORETUM & BOTANICAL GARDENS   Six thousand plant species grow here; among them some very ancient plants in a special "primitive garden," rare species, and a grove of California redwoods. Docent tours are available during operating hours, which are Monday through Friday 8am to 4pm and Saturday and Sunday from 10am to 5pm.

STRAWBERRY HILL/STOW LAKE   Rent a paddle boat, rowboat, or motor boat here and cruise around the circular lake as painters create still-lifes and joggers pass along the grassy shoreline. Ducks waddle around waiting to be fed and turtles bathe on rocks and logs. Strawberry Hill, the 430-foot-high artificial island that lies at the center of Stow Lake, is a perfect picnic spot and boasts a bird's-eye view of San Francisco and the bay.

Golden Gate Park

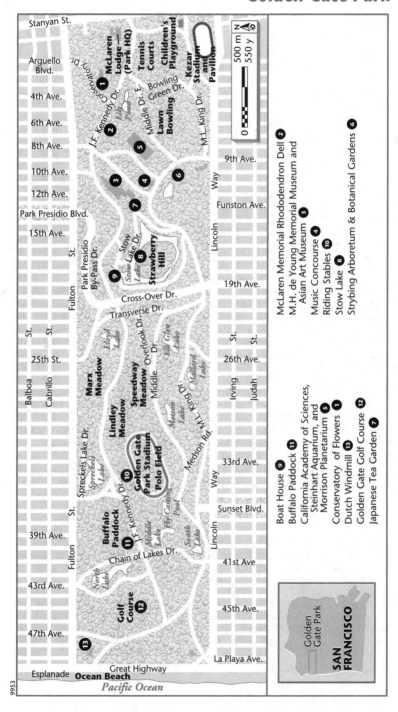

Stanyan St.

Arguello Blvd.

4th Ave.

6th Ave.

8th Ave.

10th Ave.

12th Ave.

Park Presidio Blvd.

15th Ave.

McLaren Lodge — (Park HQ) **1**

Tennis Courts

Children's Playground

Kezar Stadium and Pavilion

J.F. Kennedy Dr.

Conservatory Dr.

Liby. Plaza

Middle Dr. E.

Bowling Green Dr.

Lawn Bowling

M.L. King Dr.

500 m
550 y

0

2

5

3 **4** **6**

7

9th Ave.

Funston Ave.

Way

Lincoln

Park Presidio By-Pass Dr.

Park Presidio St.

Fulton St.

Stow Lake Dr.

Stow Lake Dr.

Stow Lake

8 Strawberry Hill

9

Cross-Over Dr.

Transverse Dr.

19th Ave.

25th St.

Balboa St.   Cabrillo St.

Marx Meadow

Lindley Meadow

Speedway Meadow

Lloyd Lake

Overlook Dr.

Middle Dr.

Elk Glen Dr.

M.L. King Dr.

Elk Glen Lake

Mallard Lake

Metson Lake

26th Ave.

Irving   Judah

St.   St.

33rd Ave.

Golden Gate Park Stadium / Polo Field

10

J.F. Kennedy Dr.

Medson Rd.

Sunset Blvd.

Lincoln Way

Spreckels Lake Dr.

Spreckels Lake

Buffalo Paddock

11

Middle Lake

South Lake

Fly Casting Pool

Chain of Lakes Dr.

39th Ave.

41st Ave

North Lake

Golf Course **12**

43rd Ave.

45th Ave.

13

47th Ave.

Fulton St.

Esplanade   **Ocean Beach**

Great Highway

La Playa Ave.

Pacific Ocean

9953

McLaren Memorial Rhododendron Dell **2**

M.H. de Young Memorial Museum and Asian Art Museum **3**

Music Concourse **4**

Riding Stables **10**

Stow Lake **8**

Strybing Arboretum & Botanical Gardens **6**

Boat House **9**

Buffalo Paddock **11**

California Academy of Sciences, Steinhart Aquarium, and Morrison Planetarium **5**

Conservatory of Flowers **1**

Dutch Windmill **13**

Golden Gate Golf Course **12**

Japanese Tea Garden **7**

Golden Gate Park

SAN FRANCISCO

153

The Presidio

In October 1994, the Presidio was transferred from the U.S. Army to the National Park Service and became one of a handful of urban national parks that combines historical, architectural, and natural elements into one giant arboreal expanse. The 1,480-acre area incorporates a variety of terrain—coastal scrub, dunes, and prairie grasslands that shelter many rare plants and more than 150 species of birds, some of which nest here.

This military outpost has a 220-year history, stretching from its founding in September 1776 by the Spanish under José Joaquin Moraga to its closure in 1995. From 1822 to 1835 the property was in Mexican hands.

During the war with Mexico, American forces occupied the fort, and in 1848, when California became part of the Union, it was formally transferred to the United States. When San Francisco suddenly became an important urban area during the gold rush, the U.S. government installed battalions of soldiers, built Fort Point to protect the entry to the harbor, and expanded the post during the Civil War and later during the Indian Wars of the 1870s and 1880s. By the 1890s it was no longer a frontier post but a major base for American expansion into the Pacific. During the war with Spain in 1898, thousands of troops camped in tent cities awaiting shipment to the Philippines, and the sick and wounded were treated at the Army General Hospital. By 1905, 12 coastal defense batteries were built along the headlands. In 1914, troops under the command of Gen. John Pershing left here to pursue Pancho Villa and his men. The Presidio expanded during the 1920s when Crissy Army Airfield (the first airfield on the West Coast) was established, but the major action was seen during World War II after the attack on Pearl Harbor. Soldiers dug foxholes along nearby beaches, and the Presidio became the headquarters for the Western Defense Command. Some 1.6 million men shipped out from nearby Fort Mason to fight in the Pacific and many returned to the hospital, whose capacity peaked one year at 72,000 patients. In the 1950s, the Presidio served as the headquarters for the Sixth U.S. Army and a missile defense post, but its role has slowly been reduced. In 1972, it was included in new legislation establishing the Golden Gate National Recreation Area; in 1989, the Pentagon decided to close the post and transfer it to the National Park Service.

Today, the area features more than 510 historic buildings, a scenic golf course, a national cemetery, and a variety of terrain and natural habitats. The National Park Service offers a variety of walking and biking tours around the Presidio; reservations are suggested. The **Presidio Museum,** located at the corner of Lincoln Boulevard and Funston Avenue (open 10am to 4pm Wednesday through Sunday), tells its story in dioramas, exhibitions, and photographs.

The **Visitor Information Center** is in Building 102 on the west side of Montgomery Street on the main parade ground (open daily from 10am to 5pm; ☎ **415/556-4323**). Take the 82X, 28, or 76 bus.

San Francisco Museum of Modern Art (MOMA). 151 Third St. (2 blocks south of Market St., across from Yerba Buena Gardens). ☎ **415/357-4000.** Admission $7 adults, $3.50 seniors and students 14–18, free for children 13 and under; half price for everyone Thurs 6–9pm, and free for everyone the first Tues of each month. Tues–Sun 11am–6pm (until 9pm Thursday). Closed Mon and holidays. Muni Metro: J, K, L, M to Montgomery Station. Bus: 15, 30, or 45.

Swiss architect Mario Botta, in association with Hellmuth, Obata, and Kassabaum, designed the $62 million museum, which opened in SoMa in January 1995. The building is the most welcomed new development in years and has made SoMa one of the more popular areas to visit for tourists and residents alike. The museum's collection consists of more than 15,000 works, including close to 5,000 paintings and

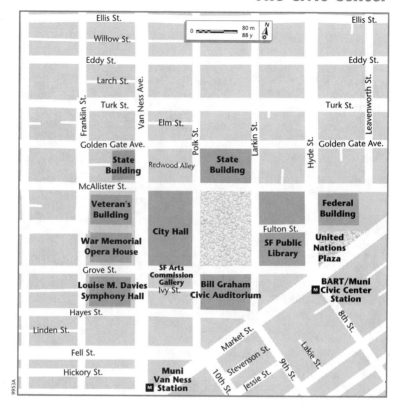

sculptures by artists such as Henri Matisse, Jackson Pollock, and Willem de Kooning. Other artists represented include Diego Rivera, Georgia O'Keeffe, Paul Klee, the Fauvists, and exceptional holdings of Richard Diebenkorn. MOMA was also one of the first to recognize photography as a major art form; its extensive collection includes more than 9,000 photographs by such notables as Ansel Adams, Alfred Steiglitz, Edward Weston, and Henri Cartier-Bresson. Docent-led tours are offered daily. Times are posted at the museum's admission desk. Phone for current details of upcoming special events.

The Caffè Museo, located on the right of the museum entrance sets a new precedent for museum food with flavorful and fresh soups, sandwiches, and salads that are as respectable as those served in many local restaurants.

No matter what, don't miss the MuseumStore, which carries a wonderful array of architectural gifts, books, and trinkets. It's one of the best stores in town.

Note: Beginning on January 1, 1997, the museum will be open on Mondays but closed on Wednesdays.

2 More Attractions

ARCHITECTURAL HIGHLIGHTS

Alamo Square Historic District

San Francisco's collection of Victorian houses, known as "Painted Ladies," is one of the city's most famous assets. Most of the 14,000 extant structures date from the

Yerba Buena Gardens

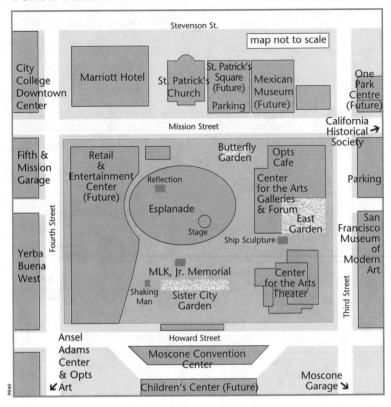

second half of the 19th century and are private residences. Spread throughout the city, many have been beautifully restored and ornately painted. The small area bordered by Divisadero Street on the west, Golden Gate Avenue on the north, Webster Street on the east, and Fell Street on the south—about 10 blocks west of the Civic Center—has one of the city's greatest concentrations of these Painted Ladies. One of the most famous views of San Francisco—seen on postcards and posters all around the city—depicts sharp-edged Financial District skyscrapers behind a row of Victorians. This fantastic juxtaposition can be seen from Alamo Square, in the center of this historic district, at Fulton and Steiner streets.

City Hall & Civic Center

Built in 1881 to a design by Brown and Bakewell, it is part of this "City Beautiful" complex done in the beaux arts style. The dome rises to a height of 308 feet on the exterior and is ornamented with occuli and topped by a lantern. The interior rotunda soars 112 feet and is finished in oak, marble, and limestone with a monumental marble staircase leading to the second floor, but you won't be able to see it; City Hall is currently closed for a complete renovation and isn't expected to reopen for a few years.

Yerba Buena Gardens

Between Mission and Howard streets, at Third Street, the Yerba Buena Center, which opened in 1993 adjacent to the Moscone Convention Center, is the city's new cultural facility similar to New York's Lincoln Center. It stands on top of the northern extension of the underground Moscone Convention center. The **Center for the Arts** presents music, theater, dance, and visual arts. It consists of two buildings, a 755-seat theater designed by James Stewart Polshek, and the **Galleries and Arts Forum** designed by Fumihiko Maki, which features three galleries and a space designed specially for dance. The complex also includes a five-acre garden featuring several artworks. The most dramatic outdoor art piece is an emotional mixed-media memorial to Martin Luther King. Created by sculptor Houston Conwill, poet Estella Majozo, and architect Joseph de Pace, it features 12 glass panels, each inscribed with quotations from King, sheltered behind a 50-foot-high waterfall. Future plans call for a Children's Center on top of the Moscone Convention Center and a cinema complex next to the gardens, both to open in late 1996. The **California Historical Society** opened at 678 Mission in late 1995; the Mexican Museum will relocate in the area in 1998. For recorded information and tickets, call **415/978-ARTS.**

Take the Muni Metro to Powell or Montgomery, or the 30, 45, or 9X bus.

OTHER ARCHITECTURAL HIGHLIGHTS

San Francisco is a center of many architecturally striking sights. This section concentrates on a few highlights.

Around Union Square and the Financial District, you can see the **Circle Gallery** at 140 Maiden Lane. It's the only building in the city designed by Frank Lloyd Wright (in 1948) and was the prototype for the seashell-shaped circular gallery space of the Guggenheim, even though it was meant to serve as a retail space for V. C. Morris, a purveyor of glass and crystal. Note the arresting exterior, a solid wall with a circular entryway to the left. Maiden Lane is just off Union Square between Geary and Post.

The **Hallidie Building,** at 130–150 Sutter St., which was designed by Willis Polk in 1917, is an ideal example of glass-curtain building. The vast glass facade is miraculously suspended between the two cast-iron cornices. The fire escapes that course down each side of the building complete the proscenium-like theatrical effect.

The **Medical Dental Building,** at 450 Sutter St., is a steel-frame structure beautifully clad in terra-cotta. It was designed by Miller and Pflueger in 1929. The entrance and the window frames are elaborately ornamented with Mayan relief work; the lobby ceiling is similarly decorated with additional gilding. Note the ornate elevators, too.

Two prominent pieces of San Francisco's skyline are in the Financial District. The **TransAmerica Pyramid,** at 600 Montgomery St. between Clay and Washington streets, is one of the tallest structures in San Francisco. This corporate headquarters was completed in 1972, stands 48 stories tall, and is capped by a 212-foot spire. The former **Bank Of America World Headquarters,** at 555 California St., was designed by Wurster, Bernardi, and Emmons in conjunction with Skidmore Owings and Merrill. This carnelian marble–covered building dates from 1969. Its 52 stories are topped by a panoramic restaurant and bar, the Carnelian Room (see Chapter 10, "San Francisco After Dark," for complete information). The focal point of the building's formal plaza is an abstract black granite sculpture, known locally as the "Banker's Heart," which was designed by Japanese architect Masayuki Nagare.

At the foot of Market Street, you will find the **Ferry Building.** Built between 1895 and 1903, it served as the city's major transportation hub before the Golden Gate and Bay bridges were built, and some 170 ferries docked here daily unloading Bay Area commuters until the 1930s. The tower that soars above the building was inspired by the Campanile of Venice and the Cathedral Tower in Seville. Plans are afoot to restore the building to its former glory, opening up the soaring galleries to the sky again. If you stop by the Ferry Building, you might also want to go to **Rincon Center,** at 99 Mission St. to see the WPA murals painted by the Russian artist Refregier in the post office that is located here.

Several important buildings can be found on or near Nob Hill. **The Flood Mansion,** at 1000 California St. at Mason Street, was built between 1885 and 1886 for James Clair Flood, who, thanks to the Comstock Lode, rose from being a bartender to being one of the city's wealthiest men. He established the Nevada bank that later merged with Wells Fargo. The house cost $1.5 million; the fence alone cost $30,000. It was designed by Augustus Laver and modified by Willis Polk after the earthquake to accommodate the Pacific Union Club.

Built in 1913 for the sugar magnate Adolph Spreckels by George Applegarth, the **Spreckels Mansion,** at 2080 Washington St., is currently home to romance novelist Danielle Steele (don't even *try* to get in to see her!). The extraordinary building has rounded-arch French doors on the first and second floors and curved balconies on the second floor. Inside, the original featured an indoor pool in the basement, Adamesque fireplaces, and a circular Pompeian room with fountain.

Finally, one of San Francisco's most ingenious architectural accomplishments is the **San Francisco–Oakland Bay Bridge.** Although it's visually less appealing than the nearby Golden Gate, the Bay Bridge is in many ways more spectacular. The silvery giant that links San Francisco with Oakland is 8^1/$_4$ miles long and is one of the world's longest steel bridges. It opened in 1936, six months before the Golden Gate. Each of its two decks contains five automobile lanes. The Bay Bridge is not a single bridge at all but a superbly dovetailed series of spans joined in midbay, at Yerba Buena Island, by one of the world's largest (in diameter) tunnels. To the west of Yerba Buena, the bridge is really two separate suspension bridges, joined at a central anchorage. East of the island is a 1,400-foot cantilever span, followed by a succession of truss bridges. And it looks even more complex than it sounds. You can drive across the bridge (the toll is $1, paid westbound), or you can catch a bus at the Transbay Terminal (Mission at First Street) and ride to downtown Oakland.

CHURCHES & RELIGIOUS BUILDINGS

Some of San Francisco's churches and religious buildings are worth a special look. West of Union Square, you can see **Glide Memorial United Methodist Church,** at 330 Ellis St. There would be nothing special about this plain Tenderloin-area church if it weren't for its exhilarating pastor Cecil Williams. Williams's enthusiastic and uplifting preaching and singing with homeless and poor people of the neighborhood has attracted nationwide fame. In 1994, during the pastor's 30th anniversary celebration, singers Angela Bofill and Bobby McFerrin joined with comedian Robin Williams, author Maya Angelou, and talk-show queen Oprah Winfrey to honor him publicly. Reverend Williams's nondogmatic, fun Sunday services attract a diverse audience that crosses all socioeconomic boundaries. Services are held at 9 and 11am each Sunday. The closest Muni Metro stop is Powell, or you can take the no. 37 bus.

Grace Cathedral, located on Nob Hill on California Street, between Taylor and Jones streets, was begun in 1928 on the site of the Crocker mansion, but it was not completed until 1964. Although the cathedral, which was designed by architect Lewis P. Hobart, looks like it is made of stone, it is in fact constructed of reinforced concrete, beaten to achieve a stonelike effect. Among the more interesting features of the building are its stained-glass windows, particularly those by the French Loire studios, depicting such modern figures as Thurgood Marshall, Robert Frost, and Albert Einstein; the replicas of Ghiberti's bronze Doors of Paradise at the east end;

the series of religious frescoes completed in the 1940s by Polish artist John de Rosen; and the 44-bell carillon.

Mission Dolores. 16th St. (at Dolores St.). ☎ **415/621-8203.** Admission $2 adults, $1 children 5–12. May–Oct daily 9am–4:30pm; Nov–Apr daily 9am–4pm; Good Fri 10am–noon. Closed Thanksgiving Day and Christmas Day. Muni Metro: J line to the corner of Church and 16th sts. Bus: 22.

San Francisco's oldest standing structure, the **Mission San Francisco de Assisi** (aka Mission Delores) has withstood the test of time, as well as two major earthquakes, relatively intact. In 1776, at the behest of Franciscan Missionary Junípero Serra, Father Francisco Palou came to the Bay Area to found the sixth in a series of missions that dotted the California coastline. From these humble beginnings grew what was to become the city of San Francisco. The mission's small, simple chapel, built solidly by Native Americans who were converted to Christianity, is a curious mixture of native construction methods and Spanish-colonial style. A statue of Father Serra stands in the mission garden, although the portrait looks somewhat more contemplative, and less energetic, than he must have been in real life.

MUSEUMS

Ansel Adams Center for Photography. 250 Fourth St. ☎ **415/495-7000.** Admission $4 adults, $3 students, $2 seniors and children 12–17. Tues–Sun 11am–5pm; until 8pm the first Thurs of each month. Muni Metro: Powell. Bus: 30, 45, or 9X.

This popular SoMa museum features five separate galleries for changing exhibitions of contemporary and historical photography. One area is dedicated solely to displaying the works and exploring the legacy of Ansel Adams.

Asian Art Museum. In Golden Gate Park, near 10th Ave. and Fulton St. ☎ **415/668-7855** (recording); 415/752-2635 for the hearing impaired. Admission (including the M. H. De Young Memorial Museum and California Palace of the Legion of Honor) $6 adults, $4 seniors 65 and over, $3 youth 12–17, free for children 11 and under (fees may be higher for special exhibitions); reduced admission for everyone the first Wednesday (all day) of each month. Wed–Sun 10am–4:45pm. Bus: 5, 44, or 71.

Adjacent to the M. H. De Young Museum and the Japanese Tea Garden, this exhibition space, opened in 1966, can only display about 1,800 pieces from the museum's vast collection of 12,000. About half of the works on exhibit are in the ground-floor Chinese and Korean galleries and include world-class sculptures, paintings, bronzes, ceramics, jades, and decorative objects spanning 6,000 years of history. There is also a wide range of exhibits from more than 40 Asian countries—Pakistan, India, Tibet, Japan, Southeast Asia—including the world's oldest-known "dated" Chinese Buddha. The museum's free daily guided tours are highly informative and sincerely recommended. Call for times.

California Academy of Sciences. On the Music Concourse of Golden Gate Park. ☎ **415/ 221-5100** or 415/750-7145 for recorded information. Admission (aquarium and science exhibits) $7 adults, $4 students 12–17 and seniors 65 and over, $1.50 children 6–11, free for children under 6; free for everyone the first Wed of every month. Planetarium shows $2.50 adults, $1.25 children under 18 and seniors 65 and over. Labor Day–July 4 daily 10am–5pm; July 4–Labor Day daily 10am–7pm; first Wed of every month 10am–9pm. Muni Metro: N line to Golden Gate Park. Bus: 5, 71, or 44.

Clustered around the Music Concourse in Golden Gate Park are three outstanding world-class museums and exhibitions that are guaranteed to entertain every member of the family. The **Steinhart Aquarium,** for example, is the most diverse aquarium in the world, housing some 14,000 specimens, including amphibians, reptiles, marine mammals, penguins, and much more, in 189 displays. A huge hit with the youngsters is the California tide pool and a "hands-on" area where children can touch starfish and sea urchins. The living coral reef is the largest display of its kind in the country and the only one in the West. In the Fish Roundabout, visitors are surrounded by fast-swimming schools of fish kept in a 100,000-gallon tank. Seals and dolphins are fed every two hours, beginning at 10:30am; the penguins are fed at 11:30am and 4pm.

The **Morrison Planetarium** presents sky shows as well as laser light shows. Its sky shows offer guided tours through the universe projected onto a 65-foot domed ceiling. Approximately four major exhibits, with titles such as *Star Death: The Birth of Black Holes* and *The Universe Unveiled,* are presented each year. Related cosmos exhibits are located in the adjacent **Earth and Space Hall.** Sky shows are featured at 2pm on weekdays and hourly every weekend and holiday (☎ **415/750-7141** for more information). Laserium laser light shows are also presented in the Planetarium Thursday through Sunday nights (☎ **415/750-7138** for more information).

The **Natural History Museum** includes several halls displaying classic dioramas of fauna in their habitats. The **Wattis Hall of Human Cultures** traces the evolution of different human cultures and how they adapted to their natural environment; the "Wild California" exhibition in **Meyer Hall** includes a 14,000-gallon aquarium and seabird rookery, life-size battling elephant seals, and two larger-than-life views of microscopic life forms; in **McBean-Peterson Hall** visitors can walk through an exhibit tracing the course of $3^1/_2$ billion years of evolution from the earliest life forms to the present day; in the **Hohfeld Earth and Space Hall** visitors can experience a simulation of two of San Francisco's biggest earthquakes, determine what their weight would be on other planets, see a real moon rock, and learn about the rotation of the planet at a replica of Foucault's Pendulum (the real one is in Paris).

Cable Car Barn Museum. Washington and Mason sts. ☎ **415/474-1887.** Free admission. Apr–Oct daily 10am–6pm; Nov–Mar daily 10am–5pm. Cable Car: Both Powell St. lines stop by the museum.

If you've ever wondered how cable cars work, this nifty museum will explain (and demonstrate!) it all to you. Yes, this is a museum, but the Cable Car Barn is no stuffed shirt. It's the living powerhouse, repair shop, and storage place of the cable car system and is in full operation. Built for the Ferries and Cliff House Railway in 1887, the building underwent an $18 million reconstruction to restore its original gaslight-era look, install an amazing spectators' gallery, and add a museum of San Francisco transit history.

The exposed machinery, which pulls the cables under San Francisco's streets, looks like a Rube Goldberg invention. Stand in the mezzanine gallery and become mesmerized by the massive groaning and vibrating winches as they thread the cable that hauls the cars through a huge figure eight and back into the system via slack-absorbing tension wheels. For a better view, move to the lower-level viewing room where you can see the massive pulleys and gears operating underground.

Also on display here is one of the first grip cars developed by Andrew S. Hallidie, operated for the first time on Clay Street on August 2, 1873. Other displays include an antique grip car and trailer that operated on Pacific Avenue until 1929, and dozens of exact-scale models of cars used on the various city lines. There's also a shop where you can buy a variety of cable car gifts.

✪ **California Palace of the Legion of Honor.** In Lincoln Park (at 4th Ave. and Clement St.). ☎ **415/750-3600** or 415/863-3330 for recorded information. Admission (including the Asian Art Museum and M. H. De Young Memorial Museum) $6 adults, $4 seniors 65 and over, $3 youths 12–17, free for children 11 and under (fees may be higher for special exhibitions); free the second Wednesday of each month. Open Tues–Sun 10am–4:45pm; Open first Sat. of the month until 8:45pm. Bus: 38 or 18.

Designed as a memorial to California's World War I casualties, the neoclassical structure is an exact replica of the Legion of Honor Palace in Paris, right down to the inscription "Honneur et Patrie" above the portal.

The Legion of Honor reopened in late 1995 after a two-year, $34.6 million renovation and seismic upgrading that was stalled by the discovery of almost 300 turn-of-the-century coffins. The exterior's grassy expanses, cliff-side paths, and incredible view of the Golden Gate make this an absolute must-visit attraction before you even get in the door. But the inside is equally impressive. The museum collection covers 4,000 years of art and includes paintings, sculpture, and decorative arts from Europe, as well as international tapestries, prints, and drawings. The chronological display of more than 800 years of European art includes one of the world's finest collections of Rodin sculpture.

M. H. De Young Memorial Museum. In Golden Gate Park (near 10th Ave. and Fulton St.). ☎ **415/750-3600** or 415/863-3330 for recorded information. Admission (including the Asian Art Museum and California Palace of the Legion of Honor) $6 adults, $4 seniors over 65, $3 youths 12–17, free for children 11 and under (fees may be higher for special exhibitions); reduced admission for everyone the first Wed of each month. Wed–Sun 10am–4:45pm (first Wed of the month until 8:45pm). Bus: 44.

One of the city's oldest museums, it's best known for its American art dating from colonial times to the 20th century, and includes paintings, sculptures, furniture, and decorative arts by Paul Revere, Winslow Homer, John Singer Sargent, and Georgia O'Keeffe. Special note should be taken of the American landscapes, as well as the fun trompe l'oeil and still-life works from the turn of the century.

Named after the late 19th-century publisher of the *San Francisco Chronicle*, the museum also possesses an important textile collection, with primary emphasis on rugs from central Asia and the Near East. Other collections on view include decorative art from Africa, Oceania, and the Americas. Major traveling exhibitions are equally eclectic, including everything from ancient rugs to great Dutch paintings. Call the museum to find out what's on. Tours are offered daily; call for times.

The museum's **Café de Young** is exceptional, serving daily specials that might include Peruvian stew, Chinese chicken salad, and Italian vegetables in tomato-basil sauce. In summer, visitors can dine in the garden, among bronze statuary. The cafe is open Wednesday through Sunday from 10am to 4pm.

Haas-Lilienthal House. 2007 Franklin St. (at Washington St.). ☎ **415/441-3004.** Admission $5 adults, $3 children 6–12, $3 seniors. Wed noon–3:15pm, Sun 11am–4:15pm (hours vary in July, call ahead). Cable car: California St. line.

Of the city's many gingerbread Victorians, this handsome Queen Anne house is one of the most flamboyant. The 1886 structure features all the architectural frills of the period, including dormer windows, flying cupolas, ornate trim, and wistful turrets. The elaborately styled house is now a museum; its rooms are fully furnished with period pieces. The house is maintained by the Foundation for San Francisco's Architectural Heritage, which offers tours two days a week. A new Costume Exhibit has been added, which features such themes as ragtime-era costumes, artifacts, and accessories.

The Jewish Museum San Francisco. 121 Steuart St. (between Mission and Howard sts.). ☎ **415/543-8880.** Admission $3 adult, $1.50 students and seniors; free the first Monday of each month. Mon–Wed noon–6pm, Thurs noon–8pm, Sun 11am–6pm. Closed Fri–Sat.

The Jewish Museum San Francisco was inaugurated in 1984 to educate the community about Jewish history, traditions, and values. The museum hosts a variety of shows that concentrate on the themes of immigration, assimilation, and identity of the Jewish community in the United States and around the world. They are illustrated by paintings, sculptures, and photographs, as well as educational programs involving nonsectarian schools and summer camps.

Mexican Museum. Bldg. D, Fort Mason, Marina Blvd. (at Laguna St.). ☎ **415/441-0404.** Admission $3 adults; $2 children. Free first Wed of the month. Wed–Sun noon–5pm. Bus: 76 to 28.

The first museum in the nation dedicated to the work of Mexican and other Latino artists, the Mexican Museum maintains a impressive collection of art covering pre-Hispanic, colonial, folk, Mexican fine art, and Chicano/Mexican American art. Revolving art shows range from the art of New Mexican women to such subjects as Mexican surrealism. Note: The museum is expected to be relocated to the Yerba Buena Center area in 1998.

Octagon House. 2645 Gough St. (at Union St.). ☎ **415/441-7512.** Free admission (donation suggested). Open only on the second Sun and second and fourth Thurs of each month noon–3pm. Closed Jan and holidays. Bus: 41 or 45.

This unusual, eight-sided, cupola-topped house dates from 1861 and is maintained by the National Society of Colonial Dames of America. The architectural features are extraordinary, and from the second floor it is possible to look up into the cupola, which is illuminated at night. Now a small museum, you'll find furniture, silverware, and American pewter from the colonial and federal periods. There are also some historic documents, including signatures of 54 of the 56 signers of the Declaration of Independence. Even if you're not able to visit during opening hours, this strange structure is worth a look.

San Francisco Maritime National Historical Park. At the foot of Polk St. (near Fisherman's Wharf). ☎ **415/556-3002.** Museum free; ships $3 adults, $1 children 11–17, free for children under 11 and seniors over 62. Museum daily 10am–5pm; ships on Hyde St. Pier May 16–Sept 15 daily 10am–6pm, Sept 16–May 15 daily 9:30am–5pm. Closed Thanksgiving Day, Christmas Day, and New Year's Day. Cable Car: Hyde St. line to the last stop. Bus: 19, 30, 32, 42, or 47.

Shaped like an art deco ship, the Maritime Museum is filled with sailing, whaling, and fishing lore. Remarkably good exhibits include intricate model craft, scrimshaw, and a collection of shipwreck photographs and historic marine scenes, including an 1851 snapshot of hundreds of abandoned ships, deserted en masse by crews dashing off to participate in the gold rush. The museum's walls are lined with beautifully carved, brightly painted wooden figureheads from old windjammers.

Two blocks east, at the park's Hyde Street Pier, are several historic ships, now moored and open to the public.

The *Balclutha,* one of the last surviving square-riggers and the handsomest vessel in San Francisco Bay, was built in Glasgow, Scotland, in 1886 and used to carry grain from California at a near-record speed of 300 miles a day. The ship is now completely restored. Visitors are invited to spin the wheel, squint at the compass, and imagine they're weathering a mighty storm. Kids can climb into the bunking quarters, visit the "slop chest" (galley to you, matey), and read the sea chanteys (clean ones only) that decorate the walls.

The 1890 *Eureka* still carries a cargo of nostalgia for San Franciscans. It was the last of 50 paddle-wheel ferries that regularly plied the bay; it made its final trip in 1957. Restored to its original splendor at the height of the ferryboat era, the side-wheeler is loaded with deck cargo, including antique cars and trucks.

The black-hulled, three-masted *C. A. Thayer,* built in 1895, was crafted for the lumber trade and carried logs felled in the Pacific Northwest to the carpentry shops of California.

Other historic ships docked here include the tiny two-masted *Alma,* one of the last scow schooners to bring hay to the horses of San Francisco; the *Hercules,* a huge 1907 oceangoing steam tug; and the *Eppleton Hall,* a side-wheel tugboat built in England in 1914 to operate on London's River Thames.

At the pier's small-boat shop, visitors can follow the restoration progress of historic boats from the museum's collection. It's located behind the maritime bookstore on your right as you approach the ships.

Wells Fargo History Museum. 420 Montgomery St. (at California St.). ☎ **415/396-2619.** Free admission. Mon–Fri 9am–5pm. Closed bank holidays. Muni Metro: Montgomery St. Bus: Any to Market St.

Wells Fargo, one of California's largest banks, got its start in the Wild West. Its history museum, at the bank's head office, houses hundreds of genuine relics from the company's whip and six-shooter days, including pistols, photographs, early banking articles, posters, and mining equipment.

Center for the Arts at Yerba Buena Gardens. 701 Mission St. ☎ **415/978-2700.** Admission $4 adult, $2 seniors and students; free every first Thurs of the month from 6–8pm. Tues–Sun 11am–6pm. Muni Metro: Powell or Montgomery. Bus: 30, 45, or 9X.

Cutting-edge computer art and multimedia shows are on view in the high-tech galleries. The initial exhibition, "The Art of Star Wars," featured the special effects created by George Lucas for the film.

OTHER ATTRACTIONS

The Names Project AIDS Memorial Quilt Visitors Center. 2362-A Market St. ☎ **415/ 863-1966.** Thurs–Tues noon–5pm, Wed noon–10pm. Muni Metro: J, K, L, M line to Castro St. Station; F line to Church and Market sts.

The Names Project began in 1987 as a memorial for people who have died from AIDS. The idea was to direct grief into positive action and help the world understand the devastating impact of AIDS. Sewing machines and fabric were acquired, and the public was invited to make coffin-sized panels for a giant memorial quilt. More than 31,000 individual panels now commemorate the lives of those who have died of complications related to AIDS. Each has been uniquely designed and sewn by the victims' friends, lovers, and family members.

The AIDS Memorial Quilt, which would cover 12 football fields if laid out end to end, was first displayed on the Capitol Mall in Washington, D.C., during a 1987 national march on Washington for lesbian and gay rights. Although sections of the quilt are often on tour throughout the world, portions of the largest community art project in the world are on display here. A sewing machine and fabrics are also available here, free, for your use.

Lombard Street. Between Hyde and Leavenworth sts.

Known as the "crookedest street in the world," the whimsically winding block of Lombard Street draws thousands of visitors each year (much to the chagrin of neighborhood residents, most of whom would prefer to block off the street to tourists). The angle of the street is so steep that the road has to snake back and forth to make a descent possible. The brick-lined street zigzags around the residences' bright flower gardens that explode with color during warmer months. This short stretch of Lombard Street is one way, downhill, and fun to drive. Take the curves slowly and in low gear, and expect a wait during the weekend. Save your film for the bottom, where, if you're lucky, you can find a parking space and take a few snapshots of the silly spectacle. You can also walk the block, either up or down, via staircases (without curves) on either side of the street.

NEIGHBORHOODS

To really get to know San Francisco, break out of the downtown and Fisherman's wharf areas to explore the ethnically and culturally diverse neighborhoods. Walk the streets, browse the shops, grab a bite at a local restaurant—you'll find that San Francisco's beauty and charm is around every corner, not just at the popular tourist destinations.

The Castro

Castro Street, between Market and 18th, is the center of the city's gay community anchored by the bookstore **A Different Light** and the many shops, restaurants, bars, and other institutions that cater to the community. Among the landmarks are **Harvey Milk Plaza, the Names Project quilt,** and the **Castro Theatre,** a 1930s movie palace with a Wurlitzer. The gay community began to move here in the late 1960s and early 1970s from the earlier gay neighborhood called Polk Gulch, which still has a number of gay-oriented bars and stores. Castro is one of the most lively streets in the city, and the perfect place to shop for gifts and revel in how free-spirited this town is.

Chinatown

California Street to Broadway and Kearny Street to Stockton Street mark the boundaries of today's Chinatown.

The first Chinese came to San Francisco in the early 1800s to work as servants. By 1851, there were 25,000 Chinese working in California, most of whom had settled in San Francisco's Chinatown. Fleeing famine and the Opium Wars, they had come seeking the promise of good fortune in the "Gold Mountain" of California, hoping to return with that prosperity to their families back in China. For the vast majority the reality of life in California did not live up to the promise. First employed as workers in the gold mines during the gold rush, they were later used to build the railroads, working as little more than slaves and facing constant prejudice. Yet the community, segregated in the Chinatown ghetto, thrived. Growing prejudice led to the Chinese Exclusion Act of 1882, which halted all Chinese immigration for 10 years and limited it severely thereafter; the Chinese Exclusion Act was not repealed until 1943. The Chinese were also denied the opportunity to buy homes outside of the Chinatown ghetto until the 1950s.

Today San Francisco has the second largest community of Chinese in the United States (about 33% of the city's population is Chinese). More than 80,000 people live in Chinatown, but the majority of Chinese have moved out into newer areas like the Richmond and Sunset districts.

The gateway at Grant and Bush marks the entry to Chinatown. The **Chinese Historical Society of America,** at 650 Commercial St. (☎ **415/391-1188**), has a small but interesting collection relating to the Chinese in San Francisco. The heart of Chinatown is at Portsmouth Square where the Chinese practice tai chi in the morning and relax later in the day playing board games or just sitting quietly.

On Waverly Place, a street where the Chinese celebratory colors of red, yellow, and green are much in evidence, you'll find three temples, **Jeng Sen** at 146, **Tien Hou** at 125, and **Norras** at 109.

A block north of Grant, Stockton from 1000 to 1200 is the main shopping street of the community lined with grocers, fishmongers, tea sellers, herbalists, noodle

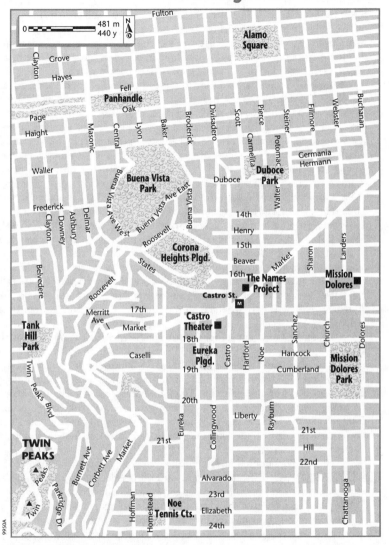

parlors, and restaurants. Here, too, is the **Kon Chow Temple** at 855 above the Chinatown post office. Explore at your leisure.

Fisherman's Wharf & Vicinity

Few cities in America are as adept at wholesaling their historical sites as San Francisco, which has converted Fisherman's Wharf into one of the most popular tourist destinations in the world. Unless you come really early in the morning, you won't find any traces of the traditional waterfront life that once existed here; the only fishing going on around here is for tourists' dollars.

Originally called Meigg's Wharf, this bustling strip of waterfront got its present moniker from generations of fishers who used to base their boats here. Today, the bay has become so polluted with toxins that bright yellow placards warn against eating fish from these waters. A small fleet of fewer than 30 boats still operates from here, but basically Fisherman's Wharf has been converted into one long shopping mall stretching from Ghirardelli Square at the west end to Pier 39 at the east. Some people love it, others can't get far enough away from it, but most agree that Fisherman's Wharf, for better or for worse, has to be seen at least once in your life.

Ghirardelli Square, at 900 North Point, between Polk and Larkin streets (☎ 415/775-5500), dates from 1864 when it served as a factory making Civil War uniforms, but it's best known as the former chocolate-and-spice factory of Domingo Ghirardelli. The factory has been converted into a 10-level mall containing 50-plus stores and 20 dining establishments. Scheduled street performers play regularly in the West Plaza. The stores generally stay open until 8 or 9pm in the summer and 6 or 7pm in the winter. Incidentally, the Ghirardelli Chocolate Company still makes chocolate, but it's located in a lower-rent district in the East Bay.

The Cannery, at 2801 Leavenworth St. (☎ 415/771-3112) was built in 1894 as a fruit-canning plant and converted in the 1960s into a mall containing 50-plus shops and several restaurants and galleries, including **Jacks Cannery Bar** (☎ 415/931-6400), which features 110 beers on tap (the most anywhere in the country). Vendors' stalls and sidewalk cafes are set up in the courtyard amid a grove of century-old olive trees, and on summer weekends street performers are out in force entertaining tourists. The **Museum of the City of San Francisco** (☎ 415/928-0289), which traces the city's development with displays and artifacts, is on the third floor. The museum is free and is open Wednesday through Sunday from 10am to 4pm.

Pier 39, on the waterfront at Embarcadero and Beach Street (☎ 415/981-8030; shops are open daily from 10:30am to 8:30pm), is a $4^{1}/_{2}$-acre, multilevel waterfront complex a few blocks east of Fisherman's Wharf. Constructed on an abandoned cargo pier, it is, ostensibly, a re-creation of a turn-of-the-century street scene, but don't expect a slice of old-time maritime life. This is the busiest mall of the lot and, according to the *London Observer,* the third most visited attraction in the *world* behind Disney World and Disneyland—with more than 100 stores, 10 bay-view restaurants, a two-tiered Venetian carousel, and a new big-screen Cinemax Theater showing the "Secret of San Francisco."

The latest major addition to Fisherman's Wharf is Underwater World, a $38 million, 707,000 gallon marine attraction filled with sharks, stingrays, and more, all witnessed via a moving footpath that transports visitors through clear acrylic tunnels.

Accommodating a total of 350 boats, two marinas flank the pier and house the Blue and Gold bay sightseeing fleet. In recent years some 600 California sea lions have taken up residence on the adjacent floating docks. Until they abandon their new playground, which seems more and more unlikely, these playful, noisy creatures (some nights you can hear them all the way from Washington Square) create one of the best free attractions on the Wharf. Ongoing docent-led programs are offered at Pier 39 on weekends from 11am to 5pm that teach visitors about the range, habitat, and adaptability of the California sea lion.

Japantown/Japan Center

Today more than 12,000 citizens of Japanese descent live in San Francisco, or Soko, as it is often called by the Japanese who first emigrated here. Initially, they settled in Chinatown and also South of Market along Stevenson and Jessie streets from Fourth to Seventh. After the earthquake in 1906, SoMa became a light industrial and warehouse area and the largest Japanese concentration took root in the Western Addition between Van Ness Avenue and Fillmore Street, the site of today's Japantown. By 1940 it covered 30 blocks.

In 1913 the Alien Land Law was passed, depriving Japanese Americans of the right to buy land. From 1924 to 1952 Japanese immigration was banned by the United States. During World War II, the U.S. government froze Japanese bank accounts, interned community leaders, and removed 112,000 Japanese Americans—two-thirds of them citizens—to camps in California, Utah, and Idaho. Japantown was emptied of Japanese, and their place was taken by war workers. Upon their release in 1945, the Japanese found their old neighborhood occupied. Most of them resettled in the Richmond and Sunset districts; some did return to Japantown but it had shrunk to a mere six or so blocks. Among the community's notable sights are the **Buddhist Church of San Francisco** at 1881 Pine St. at Octavia; the **Konko Church of San Francisco** at 1909 Bush at Laguna; the **Soto Zen Mission Sokoji** at 1691 Laguna St. at Sutter; **Nihonmachi Mall,** 1700 block of Buchanan Street between Sutter and Post, which contains two steel fountains by Ruth Asawa; and the Japan Center.

Japan Center is an Asian-oriented shopping mall occupying three square blocks bounded by Post, Geary, Laguna, and Fillmore streets. At its center stands the five-tiered Peace Pagoda, designed by world-famous Japanese architect Yoshiro Taniguchi "to convey the friendship and goodwill of the Japanese to the people of the United States." Surrounding the pagoda, in a network of arcades, squares, and bridges, are dozens of shops and showrooms featuring everything from TVs and tansu chests to pearls, bonsai (dwarf trees), and kimonos. When it opened in 1968, the complex seemed as modern as a jumbo jet. Today, the concrete structure seems less impressive, but it still holds some interesting surprises. The **Kabuki Hot Spring,** at 1750 Geary Blvd. (☎ **415/922-6002**), is the center's most famous tenant, an authentic traditional Japanese bathhouse with deep ceramic communal tubs, as well as private baths. The other delight is the **Ikenobo Ikebana Society,** in the Kintetsu Building, 1737 Post St. (☎ **415/567-1011**), which stocks everything you need to practice the art of flower arranging and also displays fine examples in its windows. The Japan Center also houses numerous restaurants, teahouses, shops, and the luxurious 14-story **Miyako Hotel** (see Chapter 5, "Accommodations," for complete information).

There is often live entertainment on summer weekends, including Japanese music and dance performances, tea ceremonies, flower-arranging demonstrations, martial-arts presentations, and other cultural events. The Japan Center is open Monday through Friday from 10am to 10pm, Saturday and Sunday from 9am to 10pm. It can be reached by the no. 2, 3, or 4 bus (exit on Buchanan and Sutter streets); or 22 or 38 (exit on the northeast corner of Geary Boulevard and Fillmore Street).

The Mission District

Once inhabited almost entirely by Irish immigrants, the Mission District is now the center of the city's Latino community, an oblong area stretching roughly from 14th to 30th streets between Potrero Avenue in the east and Dolores on the west. In the outer areas many of the city's finest Victorians still stand, though many seem strangely out of place in the mostly lower-income neighborhoods. The heart of the community lies along 24th Street between Van Ness and Potrero, where dozens of excellent ethnic restaurants, bakeries, bars, and specialty stores attract people from all over the city. Walking through the Mission District at night isn't a good idea, but it's usually quite safe during the day and highly recommended.

For an even better insight into the community, go to the **Precita Eyes Mural Arts Center** at 348 Precita Ave., at Folsom Street (☎ **415/285-2287**) and take one of the hour-long tours conducted on Saturday, which cost $4 for adults, $3 for seniors, $1 for under 18s. You'll see 70 murals in an eight-block walk. Every year they also hold a Mural Awareness Week (usually the second week in May) when tours are given

Playland at the Beach

Mention the word *Playland* to any longtime San Franciscan and their eyes light up. Prompt them to talk about the place and they'll launch into a wealth of stories about fun and wild times at the city's bygone and beloved amusement park, whose origins are embedded in local history as far back as the 1800s.

The city was in its beginnings: the mid-1800s, miles of sand dunes, horses and carriages, gold miners, and adventurers who had traveled to the western end of the country and settled along the Pacific shore. While most of the city's residents lived downtown (the desolate and undeveloped beach area was a long carriage ride away), a shantytown of squatters popped up along Ocean Beach and was dubbed after a favorite resident named Mooney "Mooneysville-by-the-Sea."

In the late 1800s, thousands started journeying to the furthest end of the city to visit the Cliff House, Seal Rock Resort, Ocean Beach Pavilion, and the Sutro Baths, which were perched on the hill just north of Mooneysville. In response to the overflow of visitors who ventured down to Ocean Beach and the shantytown, Mooneysville residents built a row of carnival stands that became equally, if not more, popular with beachgoers than the impressive neighboring establishments. By the early 1900s, the squatters' carnival grew into a burgeoning amusement center.

In 1914, as the park continued to evolve, a design team formed between two creative concessionaires, John Friedle and Arthur Looff. These two were ultimately responsible for turning the campy amusement center into four square blocks of classic amusement park entertainment. By 1921, Ocean Beach hosted the "grandest amusement park on the Pacific coast" (not yet deemed Playland-at-the-Beach) and drew crowds of up to 65,000 on weekends with rides like the Dodge 'Em bumper cars, a Ferris wheel, a merry-go-round, the Fun House, the Bob Sled Dipper (the "highest, fastest, and most sensational" roller coaster on earth), the Chutes (a boat ride with an incredible view and a splash of a finish), and the Big Dipper, which opened in 1922 and was considered Looff's ultimate creation.

Ocean Beach became *the* place to go. Elite and laymen alike swarmed here to picnic, play, hear jazz, ride the rides, eat at the dozens of restaurants, dance, and be seen in the scene. The place was the pulsing heart of San Francisco folly.

During The Great Depression, the amusement park went through some changes. One of San Francisco's wealthy developers, George K. Whitney, with his brother Leo, protected Playland from the failing economy by buying up each of the

daily. Other signs of cultural life include a number of progressive theaters—Eureka, Theater Rhinoceros, and Theater Artaud, to name only a few.

At 16th and Dolores is the **Mission San Francisco de Assisi** (better known as **Mission Delores**), which is the city's oldest surviving building (see the separate listing above) and the district's namesake.

Nob Hill

When the cable car was invented in 1873, this hill became the exclusive residential area of the city. The Big Four and the Comstock Bonanza kings built their mansions here, but they were all destroyed by the earthquake and fire in 1906. The only two surviving buildings were the Flood Mansion, which serves today as the Pacific Union Club, and the Fairmont, which was under construction when the earthquake struck. Today the burned-out sites of former mansions are occupied by the city's luxury hotels—the Mark Hopkins, the Stanford Court, the Fairmont, and the Huntington—

concessions. By 1942, the Whitneys owned everything from Sutro Baths to Fulton Street. The Whitney brothers rebuilt all of Playland in the late 1940s and early 1950s, but by the 1960s its popularity had deteriorated. After George Whitney died in 1971, Playland was snatched up by real estate developer Jeremy Ets-Hokin, who planned to build "a small, beautiful, urban community at the edge of a great city."

While there are hundreds of memorable mementos, locals' most vivid memory of Playland is usually the Fun House. The last attraction open to the public, the Fun House welcomed visitors through the early 1970s, offering residents good old-fashioned fun. No Fun House guest can forget approaching the entrance and being greeted by the hideous, yet lovable, hostess Laughing Sal. A mechanical woman created by the Philadelphia Toboggan Company, Sal cackled incessantly at guests from a Fun House window, frightening children with her loud laugh, missing front tooth, and enormous bobbing figure (her replica is housed at the Musée Mechanique).

Eager to escape Sal, visitors were coaxed through the Fun House entrance with a rolling "fun barrel," staggering staircase, and surprising blasts of air from the floor-boards. Once inside, fun-seekers cavorted amidst "the world's longest indoor wooden slide," a "fun wheel," a dizzying mirror maze, wooden rocking horses, and wobbly moving bridges.

Although deteriorating in its later years, Playland remained a grand and colorful peek back in time to San Francisco's history and the excitement of a great city in the making. Sadly, Playland was demolished in 1972, attended by locals and visitors alike up until its very last day in operation (even Herb Caen wandered the place during its last hours and reminisced about its wonder in his column the following day). There are thousands who fondly remember it and there's a club honoring it and its keepsakes. But there's only one remaining memory of this wonderful place that not only brought joy to generations of San Franciscans, but also played an essential role developing the city as a fun-loving town: an art piece made in 1995 by local artist Ray Beldner.

If San Francisco history and Playland are interesting to you, check out Ray's sculpture garden at the corners of Cabrillo and La Playa by Ocean Beach. Here you'll find five playful commemorations of Playland, as well as photos and a brief history of the area.

as well as spectacular Grace Cathedral, which stands on the Crocker mansion site. It's worth a visit to Nob Hill if only to stroll around Huntington Park, attend a Sunday service at the Cathedral, or ooh and aah your way around the Fairmont's spectacular lobby.

North Beach

In the late 1800s, an enormous influx of Italian immigrants into North Beach firmly established this aromatic area as San Francisco's "Little Italy." Today, dozens of Italian restaurants and coffee houses continue to flourish in what is still the center of the city's Italian community. Walk down Columbus Avenue any given morning and you're bound to be bombarded with the wonderful aromas of roasting coffee and savory pasta sauces. Though there are some interesting shops and bookstores in the area, it's the dozens of eclectic little cafes, delis, bakeries, and coffee shops that give North Beach its Italian-Bohemian character.

Seeing the City by Seaplane

For those of you seeking a little thrill and adventure during your vacation, consider booking a flight with **San Francisco Seaplane Tours,** the Bay Area's only seaplane tour company. For more than 50 years this locally owned outfit has provided its customers an opportunity to see the city from a bird's-eye view, flying directly over San Francisco at an altitude of about 1500 feet. Sights along the 30- and 45-minute guided excursions include the Golden Gate and Bay Bridges, Alcatraz, the Pacific coastline, Tiburon, and Sausalito. Half the fun, however, is taking off and landing on the water (which is surprisingly smooth).

Trips depart from Pier 39 and Sausalito, with prices ranging from $74 to $89 per adult for the 30-minute Golden Gate Tour. For $104 per person you can take the horribly romantic Champagne Sunset Flight, which includes a bottle of bubbly and a cozy backseat for two. Family discounts and children's rates are available, and cameras are welcome (on calm days, the pilot will even roll the window down). For more information or reservations call **415/332-4843.**

For a proper perspective of North Beach, follow the detailed walking tour in Chapter 8, "City Strolls," or sign up for a guided **Javawalk** with coffee-nut Elaine Sosa (see "Walking Tours" in this chapter).

South of Market (SoMa)

From Market Street to Townsend and the Embarcadero to Division Street, SoMa has become the city's newest cultural and multimedia center. The process started when alternative clubs began opening in the old warehouses in the area nearly a decade ago, followed by a wave of entrepreneurs seeking to start new businesses in what was once an extremely low-rent district compared to the neighboring Financial District. Today, gentrification and high rents are well underway, spurned by a building boom that started with the Moscone Convention Center and continues today with the new **Center for the Arts at Yerba Buena Gardens** and the **San Francisco Museum of Modern Art,** all of which continue to be supplemented by other institutions, businesses, and museums that are moving into the area daily.

PARKS, GARDENS & ZOOS

In addition to Golden Gate Park and the Golden Gate National Recreation Area discussed in "The Top Attractions" section above, San Francisco boasts more than 2,000 additional acres of parkland, most of which is perfect for picnicking or throwing around a Frisbee.

Smaller city parks include: **Buena Vista Park** (Haight Street between Baker and Central streets), which affords fine views of the Golden Gate and is also a favored lounging ground for gay lovers; **Ina Coolbrith Park** (Taylor Street between Vallejo and Green streets), offering views of the Bay Bridge and Alcatraz; and **Sigmund Stern Grove** (at 19th Avenue and Sloat Boulevard) in the Sunset District, which is the site of the famous free summer music festival.

One of our personal favorites is **Lincoln Park,** a 270-acre green on the northwestern side of the city at Clement Street and 34th Avenue. The **California Palace of the Legion of Honor** is here (see "Museums," above), as is a scenic 18-hole municipal golf course (see "Staying Active," below). But the best things about this park are the 200-foot cliffs that overlook the Golden Gate Bridge and San Francisco Bay. To get to the park, take bus no. 38 from Union Square to 33rd and Geary streets, then walk a few blocks to the park.

San Francisco Zoo & Children's Zoo. Sloat Blvd. and 45th Ave. ☎ **415/753-7080.** Main Zoo $7 adults, $3.50 seniors and youths 12–15, $1.50 for children 3–11, and free for children 2 and under if accompanied by an adult; (children's zoo) $1, free for children under 3. Main zoo daily 10am–5pm; Children's zoo daily 11am–4pm. Muni Metro: L line from downtown Market St. to the end of the line.

Located between the Pacific Ocean and Lake Merced, in the southwest corner of the city, the San Francisco Zoo is among America's highest-rated animal parks. Begun in 1889 with a grizzly bear named Monarch donated by the *San Francisco Examiner,* the zoo now sprawls over 65 acres and is growing. It attracts up to a million visitors each year. Most of the 1,000-plus inhabitants are contained in landscaped enclosures guarded by concealed moats. The innovative Primate Discovery Center is particularly noteworthy for its many rare and endangered species. Expansive outdoor atriums, sprawling meadows, and a midnight world for exotic nocturnal primates house such species as the owl-faced macaque, ruffed-tailed lemur, black-and-white colobus monkeys, patas monkeys, and emperor tamarins, pint-size primates distinguished by their long, majestic mustaches.

Other highlights include Koala Crossing, which is linked to the new Australian WalkAbout exhibit that opened in 1995, housing kangaroos, emus, and walleroos; Gorilla World, one of the world's largest exhibits of these gentle giants; and Penguin Island, home to a large breeding colony of Magellanic penguins. The new Feline Conservation Center is a wooded sanctuary and breeding facility for the zoo's endangered snow leopards, Persian leopards, and other jungle cats. Musk Ox Meadow is a 2¹/₂-acre habitat for a herd of rare white-fronted musk oxen brought from Alaska. The Otter River exhibit features waterfalls, logs, and boulders for the North American otters to climb on. And the Lion House is home to rare Sumatran and Siberian tigers, Prince Charles (a rare white Bengal tiger), and the African lions (you can watch them being fed at 2pm Tuesday through Sunday).

The Children's Zoo, adjacent to the main park, allows both kids and adults to get close to animals. The barnyard is alive with strokable domestic animals such as sheep, goats, ponies, and a llama. Also of interest is the Insect Zoo, which showcases a multitude of insect species, including the hissing cockroach and walking sticks.

A free, informal walking tour of the zoo is available on weekends at 11am. The *Zebra Zephyr* train tour takes visitors on a 20-minute "safari" daily (in winter, only on weekends). The tour is $2.50 for adults, $1.50 for children 15 and under and seniors.

3 Especially for Kids

The following San Francisco attractions have major appeal to kids of all ages:

- Alcatraz Island *(p. 144)*
- Cable cars *(p. 145)*
- Cable Car Museum *(p. 160)*
- California Academy of Sciences, including Steinhart Aquarium *(p. 159)*
- The Exploratorium *(p. 148)*
- Golden Gate Bridge *(p.148)*
- Golden Gate Park (including the Children's Playground, Bison Paddock, and Japanese Tea Garden) *(p. 151)*
- Marine World Africa USA *(p. 249)*

- National Maritime Museum and the historic ships anchored at Hyde Pier *(p. 162)*
- The San Francisco Zoo *(p. 171)*

In addition to the sights listed above, the following attractions are of particular interest to kids.

FAVORITES AT FISHERMAN'S WHARF

The following sights are all clustered on or near Fisherman's Wharf. To reach this area by cable car, take the Mason line to the last stop and walk to the wharf; by bus, take no. 30, 32, or 42. If you're arriving by car, park on adjacent streets or on the wharf between Taylor and Jones streets.

The Haunted Gold Mine. 113 Jefferson St. ☎ **415/202-0400.** Admission $5.95 adults, $4.95 seniors, $2.95 children 6–12, free for children under 6. Summer, Sun–Thurs 9am–11pm, Fri–Sat 9am–midnight; winter, Sun–Thurs 9am–10pm, Fri–Sat 9am–11pm.

Under the same ownership as the Wax Museum, the Haunted Gold Mine is a fun house complete with mazes, a hall of mirrors, spatial-disorientation tricks, wind tunnels, and animated ghouls. Even very young children will probably not find it too scary and it's good old-fashioned carnival fun.

U.S.S. Pampanito. Pier 45, Fisherman's Wharf. ☎ **415/441-5819.** Admission $5 adults; $3 for seniors, students, and children 6–11; free for children under 6; $15 for a family. May–Oct daily 9am–9pm; Nov–Apr daily 9am–6pm.

This popular battle-scarred World War II fleet submarine saw plenty of action in the Pacific. It has been completely restored, and visitors are free to crawl around inside. An audio tour is available.

Ripley's Believe It or Not! Museum. 175 Jefferson St. ☎ **415/771-6188.** Admission $8 adults, $6.75 teens 13–17 and seniors over 60, $5 children 5–12, free for children under 5. June 15–Labor Day Sun–Thurs 9am–11pm and Fri–Sat 9am–midnight; the rest of the year Sun–Thurs 10am–10pm, Fri–Sat 10am–midnight.

This museum has been drawing curious spectators through its doors for 30 years. Inside, you will experience the extraordinary world of improbabilities: a one-third scale match-stick cable car, a shrunken human torso once owned by Ernest Hemingway, a dinosaur made from car bumpers, a walk through a kaleidoscope tunnel, and video displays and illusions. Robert LeRoy Ripley's infamous arsenal may lead you to ponder whether truth is in fact stranger than fiction.

Wax Museum. 145 Jefferson St. ☎ **415/202-0400.** Admission $9.95 adults, $7.95 for teens 13–17, $6.95 seniors over 60, $4.95 children 6–12, free for children under 6. Summer, Sun–Thurs 9am–11pm, Fri–Sat 9am–midnight; the rest of the year, Sun–Thurs 9am–10pm, Fri–Sat 9am–midnight.

Conceived and executed in the Madame Tussaud mold, San Francisco's wax museum features more than 250 lifelike figures of the rich and famous. The "museum" donates the lion's share of its space to images of modern superstars like singer Michael Jackson and political figures like former president George Bush. Tableaux include "Royalty," "Great Humanitarians," "Wickedest Ladies," "World Religions," and "Feared Leaders," the last including Fidel Castro, Nikita Krushchev, Benito Mussolini, and Adolf Hitler. The Chamber of Horrors, which features Dracula, Frankenstein, and a werewolf, along with bloody victims hanging from meat hooks, is the stuff tourist traps are made of. It may also scare younger children.

Fisherman's Wharf & Vicinity

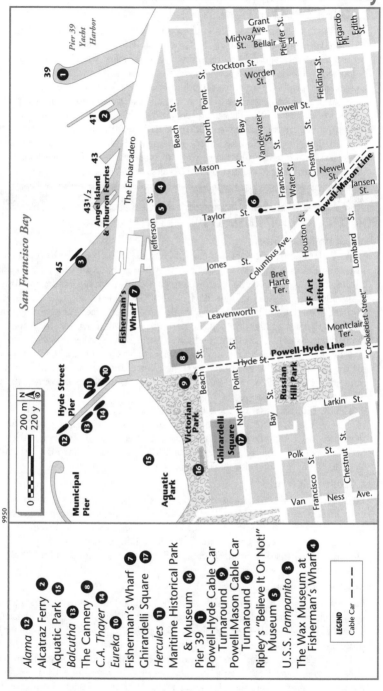

Pier 39 Yacht Harbor

San Francisco Bay

39 ❶

41 ❷

43 ❸ Angel Island & Tiburon Ferries

43½

45

The Embarcadero

Grant Ave.
Midway St.
Bellair
Pfeiffer St.
Edgardo Pl.
Edith St.

Stockton St.
Worden St.
Powell St.

Beach St.
North Point St.
Bay St.
Vandewater St.
Chestnut St.
Newell St.
Fielding St.

Mason St.
Francisco St.
Water St.
Jansen St.

Powell-Mason Line

❹ ❺ ❻

Jefferson St.
Taylor St.
Jones St.
Columbus Ave.
Houston St.
Lombard St.

Bret Harte Ter.

Leavenworth St.

SF Art Institute

Montclair Ter.

"Crookedest Street"

Powell-Hyde Line

Hyde St.

❼ Fisherman's Wharf

❽
❾ Beach St.
Point St.
North St.
Russian Hill Park

Hyde Street Pier

❶❶
❶⓪
❶③ ❶④
❶②

Larkin St.

Bay St.
Chestnut St.

Victorian Park

❶⑥
Ghirardelli Square ❶⑦

Polk St.

❶⑤

Aquatic Park

Municipal Pier

Francisco St.
Van Ness Ave.

N
200 m
220 y
0

9950

LEGEND
Cable Car – – –

Alama ❶②
Alcatraz Ferry ❷
Aquatic Park ❶⑤
Balcutha ❶③
The Cannery ❽
C.A. Thayer ❶④
Eureka ❶⓪
Fisherman's Wharf ❼
Ghirardelli Square ❶⑦
Hercules ❶❶
Maritime Historical Park & Museum ❶⑥
Pier 39 ❶
Powell-Hyde Cable Car Turnaround ❾
Powell-Mason Cable Car Turnaround ❻
Ripley's "Believe It Or Not!" Museum ❺
U.S.S. *Pampanito* ❸
The Wax Museum at Fisherman's Wharf ❹

173

CHILDREN'S PLAYGROUNDS

One of the most enormous and fun playgrounds for kids is in Golden Gate Park. In addition, there are several others. The **Cow Hollow Playground,** on Baker Street, between Greenwich and Filbert streets, is surrounded by apartment buildings on three of four sides. This landscaped playground features a bilevel play area fitted with well-conceived, colorful play structures including a tunnel, slides, swings, and a miniature cable car. **Huntington Park,** on Taylor Street, between Sacramento and California streets, sits atop Nob Hill. This tiny play area contains several small play structures that are particularly well suited to children under five. **Julius Kahn Playground,** on West Pacific Avenue, at Spruce Street, is a popular playground situated inside San Francisco's great Presidio park. Larger play structures and forested surroundings make this ground attractive to children and adults alike.

4 Special-Interest Sightseeing

FOR LITERARY ENTHUSIASTS

Dashiell Hammett Sites

Dashiell Hammett, a native of Baltimore, moved to San Francisco in 1921 to marry Josephine Dolan, a nurse whom he had met while being treated for tuberculosis. Because of his poor health, he was forced to give up his work as a private eye for the Pinkerton Detective Agency (originally located at 870 Market St. in the **Flood Building**) and started writing ad copy for a jeweler on Market Street during the day and "whodunit" novels at night. Except for *The Thin Man* and *The Glass Key,* Hammett wrote almost all of his short stories and novels, including *The Maltese Falcon, The Big Knockover,* and *The Dain Curse,* in San Francisco. Several of them were written at his residence at **620 Eddy St.** (in the Civic Center area) where he lived from the summer of 1921 to 1926. He also lived at **891 Post St.** and **1155 Leavenworth St.,** where he began *The Glass Key.*

The **St. Francis Hotel** is believed to be the model for the St. Mark in the Maltese Falcon. The most famous Hammett landmark, marked by a plaque, is at **9 Burritt St.,** where Miles Archer was killed by Brigid O'Shaugnessy. **John's Grill,** at 63 Ellis St., still retains the atmosphere of the period when Sam Spade dined here regularly (see Chapter 6, "Dining," for more information).

Ina Coolbrith's House

From her house at **1067 Broadway** (Russian Hill), Ina Coolbrith reigned over the city's literary scene. Here, Mark Twain, Bret Harte, and many other famous figures came to court her. She became the state's first Poet Laureate and was the only woman granted honorary membership of the Bohemian Club, the haunt of a raffish group of writers and artists that included Ambrose Bierce, George Sterling, John Muir, and Bret Harte.

Jack London Landmarks

Jack London was born at **605 Third St.** in the neighborhood south of Market Street (a small plaque marks the location). His family moved shortly thereafter to Oakland, where he worked to help support them. **Jack London Square** is named in honor of this period of his life, but it is a hokey tourist site with little authenticity. The only real landmark is **Heinold's First and Last Chance Saloon,** where London drank and also, it is said, purchased his first boat, the *Razzle Dazzle,* which he used for oyster pirating. In East Oakland there is a series of London homes: **1914 Foothill Boulevard** is where he wrote his first book, *The Son of the Wolf;* and **575 Blair** is where he wrote *Call of the Wild* and began *The Sea Wolf.*

If you still haven't gotten your fill of Jack, about 8 miles north of Sonoma (a mile west of Glen Ellen) the 800-acre Jack London State Park, which includes a museum built by Jack's wife, Charmian, for the purpose of housing the considerable collection of objects and memorabilia from the author's life. The Londons cottage is also here, along with the ruins of the mansion and their graves.

Armistead Maupin Associations

Macondray Lane on Russian Hill is thought to be the inspiration for Maupin's Barbary Lane in his *Tales of the City*. **Number 60–62 Alta St.** on Telegraph Hill, commonly referred to as the "Duck House" because of the paintings under the eaves, is where Maupin lived after arriving from Raleigh, North Carolina, in 1971.

For Rapid Transit Lovers

One of the world's best commuter systems, **Bay Area Rapid Transit (BART)** runs along 71 miles of rail, linking eight San Francisco stations with Daly City to the south and 25 stations in the East Bay. Under the bay, BART runs through one of the longest underwater transit tubes in the world. This link opened in September 1974, two years behind schedule and six months after the general manager resigned under fire. The train cars are 70 feet long and are designed to represent the last word in public transport luxury. Twenty years later they no longer seem futuristic, but they're still attractively modern, with carpeted floors, tinted picture windows, automatic air conditioning, and recessed lighting. The trains can hit a top speed of 80 miles per hour; a computerized control system monitors and adjusts their speed.

The people who run BART think so highly of their trains and stations that they sell a $3 "Excursion Ticket," which allows you, in effect, to "sightsee" the BART system. Tour the entire system as much as you like for up to three hours as long as you exit from the same station you entered (if you get out anywhere along the line, the fare gate will instantly compute the normal fare). For more information call **415/ 992-BART (2278).**

5 Self-Guided & Organized Tours

The 49-Mile Scenic Drive

The self-guided, 49-mile drive is one easy way to orient yourself and to grasp the beauty of San Francisco and its extraordinary location. Beginning in the city, it follows a rough circle around the bay and passes virtually all the best-known sights from Chinatown to the Golden Gate Bridge, Ocean Beach, Seal Rocks, Golden Gate Park, and Twin Peaks. Originally designed for the benefit of visitors to San Francisco's 1939 and 1940 Golden Gate International Exposition, the route is marked with blue-and-white seagull signs. Although it makes an excellent half-day tour, this mini excursion can easily take longer if you decide, for example, to stop to walk across the Golden Gate Bridge or to have tea in Golden Gate Park's Japanese Tea Garden.

The San Francisco Visitor Information Center, at Powell and Market streets (see "Tourist Information" in Chapter 4), distributes free route maps. Since a few of the Scenic Drive marker signs are missing, the map will come in handy. Try to avoid the downtown area during the weekday rush hours from 7 to 9am and 4 to 6pm.

Boat Tours

One of the best ways to look at San Francisco is from a boat bobbing on the bay. There are several cruises to choose from, many of which start from Fisherman's Wharf. There are two major companies.

Red and White Fleet, at Pier 41, Fisherman's Wharf (☎ **415/546-2700** or 800/ 229-2784 in California), is the city's largest boat tour operator, offering more than half a dozen itineraries on the bay. The fleet's primary ships are two-toned, double-and triple-deckers, capable of holding 150 to 500 passengers. You can't miss the observation tower ticket booths, at Pier 43½, located next to the Franciscan Restaurant.

The Golden Gate Bay Cruise is a 45-minute cruise by the Golden Gate Bridge, Angel Island, and Alcatraz Island. Tours cost $16 for adults, $12 for juniors 12 to 18 and seniors 62 and older, and $8 for children 5 to 11. Tour prices include audio narration in six languages: English, French, German, Japanese, Mandarin, and Spanish. They depart from Pier 41 and Pier 43½ several times daily. The Blue and Gold Fleet acquired this company in 1996 so details may vary. Call for departure schedules.

Blue and Gold Fleet, at Pier 39, Fisherman's Wharf (☎ **415/705-5444**), tours the bay year-round in a sleek, 400-passenger sightseeing boat, complete with food and beverage facilities. The fully narrated, 1¼-hour cruise passes beneath the Golden Gate and Bay bridges, and comes within yards of Alcatraz Island. Frequent daily departures from Pier 39's West Marina begin at 10am during summer and 11am in winter. Tickets cost $15 for adults, $8 for juniors 5 to 17, and seniors over 62; children under 5 sail free.

Bus Tours

Gray Line, with offices in the Transbay Terminal, First and Mission streets, Pier 39, or Union Square (☎ **415/558-9400** or 800/826-0202), is San Francisco's largest bus tour operator. They offer several itineraries on a daily basis. There is a free pickup and return service between centrally located hotels and departure locations. Reservations are required for most tours, which are available in several foreign languages including French, German, Spanish, Italian, Japanese, and Korean.

Three Babes and a Bus (☎ **415/552-2582**) is perhaps the world's hippest scheduled tour operator. This unique company runs regular nightclub trips for out-of-towners and locals who want to experience the city's night scene. The Babes' ever-changing 3½-hour itinerary waltzes into four different clubs per night, cutting in front of every line with priority entry. The party continues en route, when the Babes entertain. Their bus departs on weekends only, at locations throughout the city. Phone for complete information and reservations. The tour costs $30, including club entrances, and departs Friday and Saturday nights only, from 9:30pm to 1:30am.

Walking Tours

Javawalk is a two-hour walking tour by self-described "coffeehouse lizard" Elaine Sosa. As the name suggests, it's loosely a coffee walking tour through North Beach, but there's a lot more going on than drinking cups of brew. Javawalk also serves up a good share of historical and architectural trivia, offering something for everyone. The best part of the tour, however, may be the camaraderie that develops among the tour-goers. Sosa keeps the tour interactive and fun, and it's obvious that she knows a profusion of tales and trivia about the history of coffee and its North Beach roots. It's a guaranteed good time, particularly if you're addicted to caffeine. Javawalk is offered Tuesday through Saturday at 10am. The price is $20 per person, kids 12 and under at half price. For information and reservations ☎ **415/673-WALK (9255).**

Cruisin' the Castro (☎ **415/550-8110**) is an informative historical tour of San Francisco's most famous gay quarter and will give you a totally new insight into the contribution of the gay community to the political maturity, growth, and beauty of San Francisco. Tours are personally conducted by Trevor Hailey, who was involved in the development of the Castro in the 1970s. She knew Harvey Milk, the first

openly gay politician elected to office in the United
rise from shopkeeper to city supervisor and visit
marches, rallies, and protests begin. In addition
visitors center, Castro Theatre, and side streets
torians, as well as the plethora of community
shops, bookstores, restaurants, jewelers—wh
Tours are conducted Tuesday through Saturday, n.
at Harvey Milk Plaza, atop the Castro Street Muni station.
at the Lutia Pietia garden restaurant. Reservations are required. The .
costs $30 for adults, $25 for seniors 62 and older and for children 16 ana .

The **Haight Ashbury Walking Tour** (☎ 415/221-8442) is for you if Woodsto.
2 made you nostalgic for the 1960s or if you want to tour the hippie haunts with
Rachel Heller and revisit in two short hours the Grateful Dead's crash pad, Janis
Joplin's house, and other reminders of the Summer of Love. Tours begin at 9:30am
Tuesday and Saturday. The cost is $15 per person. Reservations are required.

San Francisco's Chinatown is always fascinating, but for many visitors with limited time it's hard to know where to search out the "nontouristy" shops, restaurants,
and historical spots in this microcosm of Chinese culture. **Wok Wiz Chinatown
Walking Tours,** with offices at 750 Kearny St., Suite 800 (☎ 415/355-9657),
founded by author, TV personality, cooking instructor, and restaurant critic Shirley
Fong-Torres is the answer. Wok Wiz tours take you into nooks and crannies not
usually seen by tourists. Most of her guides are Chinese, speak fluent Cantonese or
Mandarin, and are intimately acquainted with all of Chinatown's alleys and small
enterprises.

Tours are conducted daily from 10am to 1:30pm, include a Chinese lunch, and
begin in the lobby of the Chinatown Holiday Inn at 750 Kearny St. (between
Washington and Clay streets). It's an easy walk, fun and fascinating, and you're
bound to make new friends. Groups are generally held to a maximum of 12, and reservations are essential. Prices (including lunch) are $35 for adults, $33 for seniors 60
and older, $25 for children under 12. Shirley Fong-Torres also operates a gastronomic
tour that starts with a Chinese breakfast in a noodle house, moves to a wok shop, and
then makes further stops at a vegetarian restaurant, rice noodle factory, and a super-
market before taking a break for a sumptuous luncheon. It's offered every Saturday
for $50 (including lunch).

6 Staying Active

Half the fun in San Francisco takes place outdoors. If you're not in the mood to
trek it, there are plenty of other things to do that will allow you to enjoy the
surroundings.

BALLOONING

More than a dozen hot-air ballooning companies will take you up for a silent flight
over the nearby Wine Country. These are two solid choices.

Adventures Aloft. P.O. Box 2500, Vintage 1870, Yountville, CA 94599. ☎ **707/944-4408**
or 800/367-6272. Flights daily 6–8am. Fee $165 per person.

The Napa Valley's oldest hot-air balloon company is staffed with full-time professional pilots. Groups are small, and the flight will last about an hour. The cost of
$165 per person includes a preflight continental breakfast, a postadventure cham-
pagne brunch, and a framed "first-flight" certificate.

n Adventures. P.O. Box 795, Calistoga, CA 94515. ☎ **707/942-6546.**
–7am. Fee $125–$175 per person.

our balloon flight costs $125 per person and includes a photo and flight
. If you'd like to be picked up from your hotel and also receive a champagne
afterward you'll pay $175 per person. Call for other ride packages.

CHES

or beach information call **415/556-8371.** Most days it's too chilly to hang out at
the beach. But when the fog evaporates and the wind dies down, one of the best ways
to spend the day is oceanside in the city. On any truly hot day, thousands flock to
worship the sun, build sand castles, and throw the ball around. Without a wetsuit,
swimming is a fiercely cold endeavor and there are only two beaches that are considered safe for swimming: **Aquatic Park** is adjacent to the Hyde Park Pier, and
China Beach is a small cove on the western edge of the South Bay. But dip at your
own risk—there are never lifeguards on duty.

Also on the South Bay, **Baker Beach** is ideal for picnicking, sunning, walking, or
fishing against the backdrop of the Golden Gate.

Ocean Beach, at the end of Golden Gate Park, on the westernmost side of the city,
is San Francisco's largest beach—4 miles long. Just offshore, at the northern end of
the beach in front of Cliff House, are the jagged Seal Rocks inhabited by various shore
birds and a large colony of barking sea lions (bring binoculars for a close-up view).
To the left, Kelly's Cove is one of the more challenging surf spots in town. Ocean
Beach is ideal for strolling or sunning, but don't swim here—tides are tricky, and each
year bathers drown in the rough surf.

Stop by Ocean beach bus terminal at the corner of Cabrillo and La Playa to
learn about San Francisco's playful history in local artist Ray Beldner's whimsically
historical sculpture garden. Then hike up the hill to explore the Cliff House and the
ruins of Sutro Baths. These baths, able to accommodate 24,000 bathers, were lost to
fire in 1966.

BICYCLING

Two city-designated bike routes are maintained by the Parks and Recreations department. One winds 7 $1/2$ miles through Golden Gate Park to Lake Merced; the other
traverses the city, starting in the south, and follows a route over the Golden Gate
Bridge. These routes are not dedicated to bicyclists, and caution must be exercised.
Helmets are recommended. A bike map is available from the San Francisco Visitor
Information Center, at Powell and Mason streets (see "Tourist Information" in Chapter 4), and from bicycle shops all around town.

Ocean Beach has a public walk and bikeway that stretches along five waterfront
blocks of the Great Highway between Noriega and Santiago streets. It's an easy ride
from Cliff House or Golden Gate Park.

Park Cyclery, at 1749 Waller St. (☎ **415/752-8383**), is one of two shops in the
Haight Street/Stanyan Street area that rent bikes. Located next to Golden Gate Park,
the cyclery rents mountain bikes exclusively, along with helmets, locks, and accessories. The charge is $5 per hour, $25 per day, and it's open Thursday through
Tuesday from 10am to 6pm.

BOATING

At the **Golden Gate Park Boat House** (☎ 415/752-0347) on Stow Lake, the park's
largest body of water, you can rent a rowboat or pedal boat by the hour and steer over
to Strawberry Hill, a large, round island in the middle of the lake, for lunch. There's

usually a line on weekends. The boat house is open daily from June to September, from 9am to 4pm; the rest of the year, on Tuesday through Sunday, 9am to 4pm.

Cass Marina, 1702 Bridgeway, in Sausalito (☎ **415/332-6789** or 800/472-4595) rents sailboats measuring 22 to 101 feet. Sail under the Golden Gate Bridge on your own or with a licensed skipper. In addition, large sailing yachts leave from San Francisco and Sausalito on a regularly scheduled basis. Call for schedules, prices, and availability of sailboats or check them out on the web at **http://www.sonic.net/cass/.** The marina is open daily, from 9am to sunset.

CITY STAIR-CLIMBING

Many U.S. health clubs now have stair-climbing machines and step classes, but in San Francisco, you need only to go outside. The following city stair climbs will provide you not only with a good workout, but with great sightseeing too.

Filbert Street Steps, between Sansome Street and Telegraph Hill, are a particular challenge. Scaling the sheer eastern face of Telegraph Hill, this 377-step climb wends its way through verdant flower gardens and charming 19th-century cottages. Napier Lane, a narrow wooden plank walkway, leads to Montgomery Street. Turn right, and follow the path to the end of the cul-de-sac where another stairway continues to Telegraph's panoramic summit.

The **Lyon Street Steps,** between Green Street and Broadway, were built in 1916. This historic stairway street contains four steep sets of stairs totaling 288 steps in all. Begin at Green Street and climb all the way up, past manicured hedges and flower gardens, to an iron gate that opens into the Presidio. A block east, on Baker Street, another set of 369 steps descends to Green Street.

CROQUET

The **San Francisco Croquet Club** (☎ **415/776-4104**) offers public lessons from 11am to 2pm on the first Saturday of each month (or anytime by reservation for parties of four or more). The game is taught according to international six-wicket rules at the croquet lawns in Stern Grove, at 19th Avenue and Wawona Street. Players over 60 years of age can play free from 1 to 4pm on the first and third Wednesdays of each month.

FISHING

New Easy Rider Sport Fishing, at 225 University Ave. in Berkeley (☎ 415/285-2000), makes daily salmon runs from Fisherman's Wharf from June to October. Fishing equipment is available; the cost of $49 per person includes bait. Reservations are required. Departures are daily at 6am, returning at 2pm; there's a second daily departure at 3pm, returning at dusk.

GOLF

San Francisco has a few beautiful golf courses. Unfortunately, the most lavish, including the course at the Presidio, are not open to the public. But if you're in town and are itching to put on your golf shoes and swing some clubs, there are two decent municipal golf courses.

Golden Gate Park Course. 47th Avenue and Fulton St. ☎ **415/751-8987.** Greens fees $10 per person Mon–Fri, $13 Sat–Sun. Daily 6am–dusk.

This small nine-hole course covers 1,357 yards and is par 27. All holes are par 3, tightly set, and well trapped with small greens. The course is a little weathered in spots, but it's a casual, fun, and inexpensive place to tee off local-style.

Work It Out

While San Francisco has plenty to offer in the way of outdoor exercise and activities, there are plenty of indoor places to relieve stress, work up a sweat, or treat your body to a little TLC.

The **San Francisco Bay Club,** located at 150 Greenwich St., at Battery St. (☎ **415/433-2200**), is one of the most exclusive and extensive gyms-turned-spas in the Bay Area. Celebrities such as Tom Cruise, Cindy Crawford, and Hugh Grant have flexed a few muscles here when on location and regular members include the city's old and new elite. The club takes up almost a full block and offers three floors filled with health equipment, including two pools (one's heated); tennis, squash, racquetball and basketball courts; aerobics and yoga; free weights, cardiovascular, and Nautilus equipment; a sundeck; sauna, steam, and whirlpool; and a cafe. Although walk-in guests are not permitted, sign up for any of the luxurious spa treatments you're extended full work-out privileges for the day. Services include massage, facials, manicures, and pedicures.

A more spiritual workout can be found at **The Mindful Body,** a center for movement, body, and personal inner work. It is located at 2876 California St., between Broderick and Divisadero (☎ **415/931-2639** for class schedules). After an intense yoga or stretch class, guided meditation, or massage, you'll be a new person.

Adventurers can hone their skills at **Mission Cliffs Rock Climbing Center** at 2295 Harrison, at 19th St. (☎ **415/550-0515**). For $12 (plus $6 if you need rental equipment) you can climb 14,000 feet of terrain and 2,000 square feet of boulders. Lessons, which cost extra and include children's and outdoor programs, can be arranged. Once you're worn out, relax in the sauna.

If getting your heart rate up seems like a chore, take a less painful approach at the **Metronome,** which offers Ballroom, swing, Latin, night club, and salsa dance classes for individuals and groups. Call for information on class times, package deals, and weekend dance parties (☎ **415/252-9000**).

Lincoln Park Golf Course. 34th Avenue and Clement St. ☎ **415/221-9911.** Greens fees $23 per person Mon–Fri, $27 Sat–Sun. Daily 6:30am–dusk.

San Francisco's prettiest municipal course has terrific views and fairways lined with Monterey cypress trees. Its 18 holes encompass 5,081 yards, for a par 68, and the 17th hole has a glistening ocean view. This is the oldest course in the city and one of the oldest in the West.

HANDBALL

The city's best handball courts are in **Golden Gate Park,** opposite Seventh Avenue, south of Middle Drive East. Courts are available free, on a first-come, first-served basis.

RUNNING

The **Bay to Breakers Foot Race** is an annual 7¹/₂-kilometer run from downtown to Ocean Beach. Around 80,000 entrants gather—many dressed in wacky, innovative, and sometimes X-rated costumes for what's considered one of San Francisco's favored trademark events. The event is sponsored by the *San Francisco Examiner* and is held the Third Sunday of May. Call **415/777-7770** for details.

The **San Francisco Marathon,** held annually in the middle of July. For further information, contact USA Track and Field (☎ **415/391-2123**).

SKATING (CONVENTIONAL & IN-LINE)

Although people skate in Golden Gate Park all week long, Sunday is best, when John F. Kennedy Drive, between Kezar Drive and Transverse Road, is closed to automobiles. A smooth "skate pad" is located on your right, just past the Conservatory. **Skates on Haight,** at 1818 Haight St. (☎ **415/752-8376**), is the best place to rent either in-line or conventional skates, and is located only one block from the park. Protective wrist guards and knee pads are included free. The cost is $7 per hour for in-line Rollerblades, $6 per hour for "conventionals." Major credit card and ID deposit are required. The shop is open Monday and Wednesday to Friday from 11:30am to 6:30pm, and Saturday and Sunday from 10am to 6pm.

TENNIS

More than 100 courts throughout the city are maintained by the **San Francisco Recreation and Parks Department** (☎ **415/753-7001**). All are available free, on a first-come, first-served basis. The exception are the 21 courts in Golden Gate Park; a $4 to $6 fee is charged for their use, and courts must be reserved in advance for weekend play. Call the number above on Wednesday from 7 to 9pm, or on Thursday and Friday from 9am to 5pm.

WALKING & HIKING

The **Golden Gate National Recreation Area** offers plenty of opportunities for walking and hiking. One pleasant walk, or bike ride, for that matter, is along the Golden Gate Promenade, from Aquatic Park to the Golden Gate Bridge. The 3$\frac{1}{2}$-mile paved trail leads along the northern edge of the Presidio, out to Fort Point. You can also hike along the Coastal Trail all the way from near Fort Point to the Cliff House. The park service maintains several other trails in the city. For more information or to pick up a map of the Golden Gate National Recreation Area, stop by the park service headquarters at Fort Mason at the north end of Laguna Street (☎ **415/556-0560**).

Though most drive to this spectacular vantage point, a more rejuvenating way to experience **Twin Peaks** is to walk up from the back roads of U.C. Medical Center (off Parnassus) or from either of the two roads that lead to the top (off Woodside or Clarendon avenues). Early morning is the best time to trek, when the city is quiet, the air is crisp, and the sightseers haven't crowded the parking lot. Keep an eye out for cars, since there's no real hiking trail and be sure to walk beyond the lot and up to the highest vantage point.

7 Spectator Sports

The Bay Area's sports scene includes several major professional franchises, including football, baseball, and basketball. Check the local newspapers' sports sections for daily listings of local events.

Baseball is represented by the **San Francisco Giants,** who play at 3Com/Candlestick Park, Giants Drive and Gilman Avenue (☎ **415/467-8000**). From April through October, the National League Giants play their home games at Candlestick Park, off U.S. 101 about 8 miles south of downtown. Tickets are usually available up until game time, but seats can be dreadfully far from the action. Tickets may be obtained through BASS Ticketmaster (☎ **510/762-2277**). Special express bus service is available from Market Street on game days; call Muni (☎ **415/673-6864**) for pickup points and schedule information. Bring a coat, as this 60,000-seat stadium is known for chilly winds.

The Bay Area's other team is the **Oakland Athletics,** who play at the Oakland Coliseum Complex, at the Hegenberger Road exit from I-880, in Oakland (☎ **510/**

430-8020). The 1989 world-champion A's play across the Bay. The stadium holds close to 50,000 spectators and is serviced by BART's Coliseum station. Tickets are available from the Coliseum Box Office or by phone through BASS Ticketmaster (☎ **510/762-2277**).

Basketball is represented by the **Golden State Warriors,** who play at the Oakland Coliseum Complex, at the Hegenberger Road exit from I-880, in Oakland (☎ **510/638-6300**). The NBA Warriors play basketball in the 15,025-seat Oakland Coliseum Arena. The season runs from November through April, and most games are played at 7:30pm. Tickets are available at the arena, and by phone through BASS Ticketmaster (☎ **510/762-2277**).

The Bay Area once again has two professional **football** teams. The **San Francisco 49ers,** play at 3Com/Candlestick Park, Giants Drive and Gilman Avenue (☎ **415/ 468-2249**). Games are played on Sunday from August through December; kickoff is usually at 1pm. Tickets sell out early in the season, but are available at higher prices through ticket agents beforehand and from scalpers at the gate. Ask your hotel concierge or visit City Box Office, 141 Kearny St. (☎ 415/392-4400). Special express bus service is available from Market Street on game days; call Muni (☎ 415/ 673-6864) for pickup points and schedule information.

Also back in the Bay Area are the 49ers' arch enemy, the **Oakland Raiders.** Home games play at the Oakland Alameda County Coliseum, off the 880 Freeway (Nimitz) (☎ **800/949-2626** for ticket information).

The **University of California Golden Bears** play in Memorial Stadium at 61 Harmon Gym, University of California, Berkeley (☎ **510/642-5150** or 800/ GO-BEARS), on the university campus across the bay. Tickets are usually available at game time. Phone for schedules and information.

Fans can see **horse racing** at **Golden Gate Fields,** located on Gilman Street, off I-80, in Albany, 10 miles northeast of San Francisco (☎ **510/559-7300**). Scenic thoroughbred races are held here from January to March and from April to the end of June. The park is located on the seashore. Call for admission prices and post times.

The nearest autumn racing is at **Bay Meadows,** 2600 S. Delaware St., off U.S. 101, in San Mateo (☎ **415/574-7223**). This thoroughbred and quarter-horse track, on the peninsula about 20 miles south of downtown San Francisco, hosts races four or five days each week from September through January. Call for admission and post times.

City Strolls

8

The Bay City is a stroller's paradise to the same extent that Los Angeles is a motorist's metropolis. The tours listed here will give you some insights, both historical and modern, into two neighborhoods unique to San Francisco.

WALKING TOUR 1
Chinatown

Start: Grant Avenue and Bush Street.
Finish: Grant and Columbus avenues.
Time: 1½ hours, not counting food stops.
Best Times: Daily from 11am to 9pm, when the streets are in full swing.
Worst Times: Very early or very late, when shops are closed and the quarter is not at its most cluttered.

The first Chinese immigrants reached San Francisco during the gold rush of 1849. They called the collection of huts around the bay somewhat optimistically Gum San Dai Foo, "Great City of the Golden Hill." The Chinese were not concentrated here entirely by choice—they were segregated by anti-Asian prejudice. Chinatown was a cramped, hideously overcrowded ghetto. The opium trade and child prostitution flourished here, as did disease, poverty, and hunger.

Conditions worsened until the Great Earthquake and subsequent fire wiped out the area in 1906. After it was rebuilt, Chinatown became the renowned commercial and culinary quarter that it is today. The seven-block-long, three-block-wide district is now one of the largest Chinese settlements outside Asia, and growing.

Start at the corner of Grant Avenue and Bush Street. You'll know you're at the right place when you spot the:

1. **Chinatown Arch,** a two-story, green-tiled, dragon-topped gate. This pretty Chinese portal is the main entrance to San Francisco's Chinatown. Erected in 1969, it was a gift from the Republic of China (Taiwan).

   Walk uphill, under the arch, and you are strolling on:

2. **Grant Avenue,** the eight-block-long main stem of Chinatown. This primary thoroughfare is a multiethnic parade every day of the

year. The shops are crammed with goods ranging from ordinary utility wares to exotic treasures and, of course, mountains of "souvenirs." Some of it is pure junk, not even of Chinese origin.

Walk two blocks up Grant Avenue, just past the corner of California Street. On your right you'll see:

3. **Old St. Mary's Church** (☎ **415/986-4388**). Built largely with Chinese labor, Old St. Mary's was the city's first cathedral, dedicated on Christmas Day 1854. A survivor of the 1906 earthquake, the balconied church was constructed from brick brought around Cape Horn and a granite cornerstone quarried in China. Its Gothic lines look oddly out of place amid the surrounding Asian-style structures. Actively serving its parish, the church is open to visitors most days. You can attend services here, too, or go to one of the free concerts, held on Tuesday at 12:30pm.

Turn right on California Street and walk half a block to:

4. **St. Mary's Square,** the heart of Chinatown's raucous red-light district before the 1906 earthquake, the square is now a placid, flower-filled park. Its centerpiece is the:

5. **Statue of Dr. Sun Yat-sen,** founder of the Chinese Republic. Sculpted by Benjamino Bufano, the statue's most outstanding feature is its stainless-steel cloak. A second monument in the square honors the Chinese American victims of the two world wars.

Return to Grant Avenue and turn right. Almost immediately you'll see the:

6. **Canton Bazaar,** 616 Grant Ave. (☎ **415/362-5750**). Among a variety of handicrafts you'll find an excellent selection of rattan and carved furniture, cloisonné enamelware, rose Canton chinaware, glassware, carved jade, embroidery, jewelry, and antiques from mainland China.

Half a block ahead, on the corner of Sacramento Street, is the:

7. **Bank of America,** 701 Grant Ave. This pretty building, an imitation of Chinese architecture, has gold dragons ornamenting its front doors and entwining its columns. Some 60 dragon medallions line its facade.

Turn right on Sacramento Street. Half a block down is the:

8. **Chinese Chamber of Commerce,** 730 Sacramento St. (☎ **415/982-3000**), where the famous dragon resides when it's not parading around the streets during the New Year celebration. You can also stop in for specialized information on Chinatown's shops and services, and the city's Chinese community in general. The office is open Monday through Friday from 9am to 5pm.

Return to Grant Avenue and continue to:

9. **Chinatown Kite Shop,** 717 Grant Ave. (☎ **415/989-5182**). This shop's astonishing assortment of flying objects includes attractive fish kites, windsock kites in nylon or cotton, hand-painted Chinese paper kites, wood-and-paper biplanes, and pentagonal kites—all of which make great souvenirs or decorations. Computer-designed stunt kites have two control lines to manipulate loops and dives.

⬤ **TAKE A BREAK**   Opened in 1924, Eastern Bakery, 720 Grant Ave., between Clay and Sacramento streets (☎ **415/392-4497**) is the oldest Chinese American bakery in San Francisco. Stop for some fermented soybean cakes, almond cookies, mooncakes, and other Oriental sweets that will probably take some getting used to.

Turn right down Commercial Street, and walk two blocks to the:

Walking Tour, Chinatown

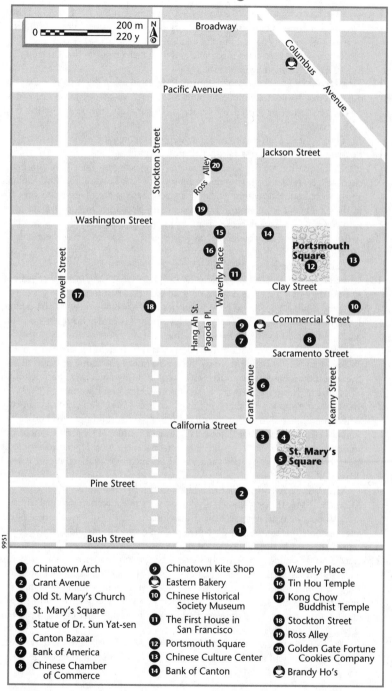

0 ——— 200 m / 220 y

N

Broadway

Columbus Avenue

Pacific Avenue

Stockton Street

Jackson Street

Ross Alley ❷⓿

❶⓽

Washington Street

❶⓹

❶⓸

❶⓺

Waverly Place

Portsmouth Square

❶⓷

❶❶

❶⓶

Powell Street

Clay Street

❶⓻

❶⓼

❶⓪

Hang Ah St.

Pagoda Pl.

Commercial Street

⓽

⓻

⓼

Sacramento Street

Grant Avenue

⓺

California Street

❸ ❹

St. Mary's Square

⓹

Kearny Street

Pine Street

❷

❶

Bush Street

9951

- ❶ Chinatown Arch
- ❷ Grant Avenue
- ❸ Old St. Mary's Church
- ❹ St. Mary's Square
- ⓹ Statue of Dr. Sun Yat-sen
- ⓺ Canton Bazaar
- ⓻ Bank of America
- ⓼ Chinese Chamber of Commerce
- ⓽ Chinatown Kite Shop
- ◉ Eastern Bakery
- ❶⓪ Chinese Historical Society Museum
- ❶❶ The First House in San Francisco
- ❶⓶ Portsmouth Square
- ❶⓷ Chinese Culture Center
- ❶⓸ Bank of Canton
- ❶⓹ Waverly Place
- ❶⓺ Tin Hou Temple
- ❶⓻ Kong Chow Buddhist Temple
- ❶⓼ Stockton Street
- ❶⓽ Ross Alley
- ❷⓪ Golden Gate Fortune Cookies Company
- ◉ Brandy Ho's

185

10. **Chinese Historical Society Museum,** 650 Commercial St. (☎ **415/391-1188**). This pocket-size museum traces the history of Chinese immigrants in California by means of gold rush relics, photos, and artifacts.

    Return to Grant Avenue, turn right, and walk half a block to the corner of Clay Street. At this corner once stood the:

11. **First House in San Francisco.** Constructed in 1836 when the fledgling town was called Yerba Buena, the house was built by a merchant named Jacob Leese, next to the tent then occupied by Captain Richardson, the settlement's first harbormaster.

    Turn right down Clay Street. A few steps down on your left is:

12. **Portsmouth Square,** a quiet little park atop a parking garage. This was the birthplace of Yerba Buena, the central plaza around which grew the city of San Francisco. It was also a favorite contemplation spot for Jack London, Rudyard Kipling, and Robert Louis Stevenson. Today this grassy slope is not the most restful park in the city, but it is interesting as the gathering place for Chinatown's old men, who perform tai chi, gamble over games of mah-jongg and Chinese cards, and chat with each other. The wooden pagoda-style structures were placed here only in 1990.

    Cross the footbridge over Kearny Street into the:

13. **Chinese Culture Center,** 750 Kearny St. (☎ **415/986-1822**), inside the Financial District Holiday Inn. Pass display cases of Chinese art into a gallery presenting changing exhibits on Chinese history and culture. Depending on what's on exhibit, it can be very interesting. It's open Tuesday through Saturday from 10am to 4pm and Sunday noon to 4pm; admission is free.

    Return to the park, walk to the far end, and turn right on the path, toward Washington Street. Before you exit the green, notice the statue of Robert Louis Stevenson that stands on your left in the park's northwest corner. Turn left onto Washington Street, back toward Grant Avenue. Here you'll see the:

14. **Bank of Canton,** 743 Washington St., which boasts the oldest (1909) Asian-style edifice in Chinatown. This three-tiered temple-style building once housed the China Telephone Exchange, known as "China-5" until 1945; operators spoke five dialects, and were famous for their phenomenal memories. Operators reputedly knew every subscriber by name and would often correct a caller: "No, that's not Mrs. Wu's number; you're calling Mr. Chang."

    Cross Grant Avenue, walk half a block, and turn left onto:

15. **Waverly Place,** the best known of Chinatown's side streets. This small street is popular because of its especially colorful architecture. Most of the balconied buildings that line this thoroughfare are private family associations and temples, few of which are open to the public. An exception is the:

16. **Tin Hou Temple,** 125 Waverly Place. Accessible via a narrow stairway, this incense-laden sanctuary is decorated in traditional black, red, and gold lacquered woods. Chinese Buddhists don't attend scheduled services—they enter temples to pray, meditate, and send offerings to their ancestors. You are welcome to visit, but do so unobtrusively. It's customary to drop a dollar in the offering box, or to buy a bundle of stick incense.

    Back on the street, continue for just a few steps and turn right on Clay Street. Walk one block and turn left onto Stockton Street. On the right-hand side, above the post office, you'll find the:

17. **Kong Chow Buddhist Temple,** 855 Stockton St., fourth floor. This is the oldest and prettiest of Chinatown's many temples. Feel free to take a look, but have respect for those who have come to pray. Exit the temple and backtrack up:

18. Stockton Street. This stretch of Stockton is the center of the Chinese food-market district, an unusual conglomeration of glazed ducks, bamboo shoots, sharks' fins, gingerroots, fish, and chickens.

Walk one block and turn right onto Washington Street. After half a block, turn left onto the small:

19. Ross Alley, a passage connecting Washington and Jackson streets. Along the left-hand side of this alley are a number of Chinese sweatshops, hiding behind boarded-up screen doors—an eerie reminder of the bad old days.

Toward the end of the block is the:

20. Golden Gate Fortune Cookies Company, 56 Ross Alley (☎ **415/781-3956**). It's a tiny place where only one woman sits at the end of a conveyer belt and folds messages into the warm cookies. The manager will try to sell you a big bag of cookies. X-rated fortunes are their specialty.

Turn right at the end of Ross Alley, walk half a block, then turn left and you're back on Grant Avenue. Chinatown terminates at Columbus Avenue, where it fades into strip joints and the beginning of North Beach. Turn around and explore Chinatown on your own, or turn left, up Columbus Avenue, and take a tour of North Beach, San Francisco's Italian quarter (see below).

☕ **TAKE A BREAK**   You can turn right on Columbus and walk half a block to **Brandy Ho's Hunan Food,** 217 Columbus Ave. (☎ **415/788-7527**). This down-to-earth place with great food is one of our favorite restaurants in Chinatown. (See Chapter 6, " Dining," for complete information.)

WALKING TOUR 2
North Beach

Start: At the foot of Columbus Avenue, where it meets Washington Street.
Finish: Coit Tower.
Time: 1¹/₂ hours, not including cafe stops.
Best Times: 11am to dusk, when shops, restaurants and cafes are open and well lit.
Worst Times: After dark, when the neighborhood is hopping, but many stores are closed and it's hard to get a good look at things.

Along with Chinatown, North Beach is one of the city's oldest neighborhoods. Originally the city's Latin Quarter, Italian immigrants moved "uphill" in the early 1870s, crossing Broadway from the Jackson Square area and settling in. They quickly set up restaurants, cafes, bakeries and other businesses familiar to them from their homeland. The "beat generation" helped put North Beach on the map, with the likes of Jack Kerouac and Allen Ginsberg holding court in the area's cafes during the 1950s. Although most of the original beat poets are gone, their spirit lives on in North Beach, which is still a haven for bohemian artists and writers. The neighborhood, thankfully, still retains the Italian village feel, where residents from all walks of life enjoy taking time for conversation over pastry and a frothy cappuccino.

With your back to the TransAmerica Pyramid, start walking up:

1. Columbus Avenue. This busy thoroughfare is the unofficial divider between Chinatown and North Beach. Among the cobblers and watchmakers are an assortment of restaurants, cafes, and shops that cater to every whim.

The copper-green building on your left, at the corner of Kearny Street, is the:

2. **Sentinel Building,** a 1906 flatiron beauty that was restored by Francis Ford Coppola in the mid-1970s and is now home to his film production company, American Zoetrope Studios. This is one of the few pre–1906 earthquake buildings in the city center.

   Walk up about half a block and peer into the windows of:

3. **Tosca Café,** 242 Columbus Ave. (☎ **415/986-9651**), one of the city's oldest cafes, dating from 1919. The stately espresso machines at either end of the long bar are the oldest in San Francisco. Waiters in short white waistcoats are happy to fix you a "coffeeless cappuccino," a concoction of steamed milk, brandy and chocolate which is sure to please most any palate.

   Around the corner from Tosca in tiny Saroyan Place is:

4. **Spec's Adler Museum Café,** 12 Saroyan Place (☎ **415/421-4112**), one of the city's funkiest bars. It's crammed with memorabilia and characters as colorful as the owner, Specs Simmons, who is often seen holding court. The tiny bar's small street is named for William Saroyan, who penned *The Time of Your Life*, which describes a 1930s dive akin to this bar.

   Directly across Columbus Avenue you'll find:

5. **Vesuvio,** 255 Columbus Ave. (☎ **415/362-3370**), a legendary North Beach watering hole. The building itself dates from 1913, and is an excellent example of pressed-tin architecture. Inside, the ghost of Jack Kerouac lingers, and old black-and-whites of many of the beat poets grace the cluttered walls. The gas-fired chandelier hanging over the bar, nearly 100 years old, is a beauty. At Vesuvio, you can belly up to the bar day and night; hours are from 6am to 2am.

   Next door and across the aptly named Jack Kerouac Alley, pop into:

6. **City Lights Bookstore,** 261 Columbus Ave. (☎ **415/362-8193**), a literary mecca. Owned by Larry Ferlinghetti, one of the first beat poets to arrive in San Francisco, this well-stocked bookshop prides itself on its collection of art, poetry, and political paperbacks. It was Ferlinghetti who published Allen Ginsberg's epic and controversial poem *Howl* in 1956, causing a public outcry and resulting in a much-ballyhooed obscenity trial. The law was on the side of the beats, a decision which paved the way for the publication of the likes of D. H. Lawrence's *Lady Chatterly's Lover*. City Lights still publishes about a dozen avant-garde works every year.

   Continue up Columbus and turn right on:

7. **Grant Avenue,** the city's oldest thoroughfare, a chameleon of a street that changes its color, texture, and character three times in its barely 1¹/₂-mile length. At its origin at Market Street, it's a chic downtown shopping street. Crossing Bush Street, it's Chinatown's main venue. Above Broadway, it turns into North Beach's bohemian drag, teeming with one-of-a-kind shops, offbeat bars, and some of the neighborhood's best-loved coffeehouses.

   On the right is:

8. **The Saloon,** 1232 Grant Ave. (☎ **415/989-7666**), whose swinging doors have been greeting patrons since 1861. Not much seems to have changed since that time, and those looking for a comfortable chair in which to sip their cocktail will have to go elsewhere. The music, though, is top-notch, and a serious blues jam is on tap every Sunday afternoon from 4 to 8pm.

☕ **TAKE A BREAK** At the corner of Grant and Vallejo is the venerable **Caffe Trieste,** 601 Vallejo St. (☎ **415/392-6739**), founded by Gianni Giotta in 1956 and still run by family members. The quintessential San Francisco coffeehouse, Trieste features opera on the jukebox and the real thing, performed by the Giottas,

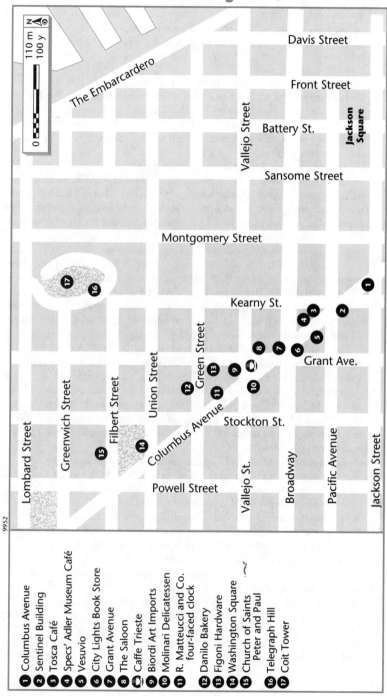

Walking Tour, North Beach

Davis Street

Front Street

The Embarcardero

Vallejo Street

Battery St.

Jackson Square

Sansome Street

Montgomery Street

Kearny St.

Green Street

Union Street

Grant Ave.

Stockton St.

Columbus Avenue

Filbert Street

Greenwich Street

Lombard Street

Powell Street

Vallejo St.

Broadway

Pacific Avenue

Jackson Street

110 m
100 y
0

9952

1 Columbus Avenue
2 Sentinel Building
3 Tosca Café
4 Specs' Adler Museum Café
5 Vesuvio
6 City Lights Book Store
7 Grant Avenue
8 The Saloon
9 Caffe Trieste
10 Biordi Art Imports
11 Molinari Delicatessen
12 R. Matteucci and Co. four-faced clock
13 Danilo Bakery
14 Figoni Hardware
15 Washington Square
16 Church of Saints Peter and Paul
17 Telegraph Hill
18 Coit Tower

on Saturday afternoons. Any day of the week is a good one to stop in for a cappuccino or espresso, since the beans are roasted right next door. The cafe also offers tasty sandwiches and antipasto salads, and the palm-sized pastries, delivered fresh every morning, are often available well into the afternoon.

Heading back down Grant to Columbus, turn right and stop in at:

9. **Biordi Art Imports,** 412 Columbus Ave. (☎ 415/392-8096), possibly the loveliest shop in all of North Beach. The shopkeepers have been importing hand-painted Majolica pottery from the hill towns of central Italy for more than 50 years. Some of the colorful patterns date from the 14th century. Biordi will also ship your purchases.

Across Columbus Avenue at the corner of Vallejo is:

10. **Molinari Delicatessen,** 373 Columbus Ave. (☎ **415/421-2337**), which has been selling its pungent, air-dried salamis for nearly 100 years. They still make their own ravioli and tortellini in the back of the shop, but it's the mouthwatering selection of cold salads, cheeses and marinades up front that captures the attention of most folks. The Italian subs are big enough for two hearty appetites.

Continue north on Columbus half a block and stop at:

11. **R. Matteucci and Co. four-faced clock,** halfway between Vallejo and Green streets and directly in front of the R. Matteucci jewelry store at 450 Columbus Ave. (☎ **415/781-1063**). The ornate clock, which dates from 1908, is the only four-faced clock in working order in San Francisco. It's a spring-wound clock manufactured by Seth Thomas, and the proprietor of the jewelry store, Matteo Ciuffreda, dutifully winds it every Saturday morning.

Turn right at Green Street and proceed halfway up the block to:

12. **Danilo Bakery,** 516 Green St. (☎ **415/989-1806**), which has been owned by the DiPiramo family for the past 25 years. The elder DiPiramo starts the baking downstairs in the wee hours of the morning, and the loaves of bread and breadsticks are all rolled by hand the old-fashioned way. They are well known for their "tortes," round, doughy loaves with a hodgepodge of ingredients, among them an intriguing chocolate and rice combination. As if that weren't enough, Danilo's biscotti may be the best in town.

At the corner of Green and Grant, head left up the block and stop in at:

13. **Figoni Hardware,** 1352 Grant Ave. (☎ **415/392-4765**), a hardware store and then some, the likes of which is rarely seen today. The shop has been providing everything from screws to salad bowls since 1907, and there is still a Figoni selling the wares. Melvin Figoni has been working in the store since 1924, when he came to work for his Uncle Louis. He always keeps everything—from the oiled wood floors to the floor-to-ceiling displays—in tip-top shape.

Make a left at Union Street and head downhill to:

14. **Washington Square,** a pentagonal park with plenty of grass, benches, and elbow room. This is North Beach's heart and soul and a window on the multiculturalism of the neighborhood. Old Italian men sit on the benches and swap stories while the Chinese practice tai chi and younger folks soak up the sun. The statue of Ben Franklin in the center of the park marks the spot of a time capsule, which was planted in 1979 and is to be opened a century later. Those doing the honors will find it includes some Levi's, perhaps a bit faded, but it is hoped the right size.

Looming over the park is the:

15. **Church of Saints Peter and Paul,** often referred to as the "Church of the Fisherman" in honor of the neighborhood's many men of the sea. Once catering to the Italian community exclusively, the church now offers mass in Italian, English, and

---

Travel Tip

Even San Francisco locals who feel they've "been there and done that" in North Beach always learn something new when taking the **Javawalk,** Elaine Sosa's coffee-inspired walking tour of the city's caffeine district. The two-hour tour, starting at 10am Tuesday through Saturday, covers the city's coffee history and coffeehouse culture along with a bit of San Francisco history, trivia, and other tales of the city. For information and reservations, call **415/673-WALK** (9255).

Cantonese. Although many folks believe that Joe DiMaggio and Marilyn Monroe tied the knot here, the baseball legend married a different actress in this church, his first wife, Dorothy Arnold. Joe and Marilyn said their vows at City Hall, but did snap a few publicity photos on the church steps afterward for good measure.

Head back to Union Street and meander uphill through the center of North Beach's residential area. Turn left on Montgomery Street and climb the steps to:

16. Telegraph Hill, a region of narrow alleys and small frame houses perched on alpine inclines. This charming, quiet area, offering panoramic views in all directions, was once solidly Italian. Rents were low, which helped to attract a diverse crowd, including many artists and writers. Just as they spruced up the neighborhood, a more upwardly mobile crowd found the sunny weather and inspiring vistas too hard to resist. Prices have skyrocketed, leaving Telegraph Hill to a few well-heeled and lucky souls.

At the top of the hill, you'll see:

17. Coit Tower, which stands sentinel over North Beach. In a city known for its awe-inspiring views and vantage points, Coit Tower has one of the best. Completed in 1933, the tower is the legacy of Lillie Hitchcock Coit, a wealthy socialite and staunch supporter of the city's firemen. She bequeathed $100,000 to the city "for the purpose of adding beauty to the city I have always loved." The result is a memorial to the city's firefighters, and many who gaze up at the tower find it resembles a large fire hose nozzle, which was not the architect's intent. Inside the tower's base are a series of colorful murals titled *Life in California, 1934.* Commissioned by the Public Works of Art Project under FDR's New Deal, the frescoed paintings, which have been recently restored, are a social realist's vision of America in the midst of the Great Depression. Many of the artists drew their inspiration from the Mexican painter Diego Rivera and his politically charged murals.

9 Shopping

Like its population, San Francisco's shopping is worldly and intimate. Every persuasion, style, era, and fetish is represented here, not in a big, tacky shopping mall, but rather in hundreds of quaint and dramatically different boutiques scattered throughout the city. Whether its Chanel or Chinese herbal medicine you're looking for, San Francisco's got it. Just pick a shopping neighborhood and break out your credit cards—you're sure to end up with at least a few take-home treasures.

1 The Shopping Scene

MAJOR SHOPPING AREAS

San Francisco has many shopping areas, but the following are where most of the action is:

Union Square and Environs San Francisco's most congested and popular shopping mecca is centered around Union Square and enclosed by Bush, Taylor, Market, and Montgomery streets. Most of the big department stores and many high-end specialty shops are in this area. Be sure to venture to Grant Avenue, Post and Sutter streets, and Maiden Lane.

Chinatown When you pass under the gate to Chinatown on Grant Avenue, say good-bye to the world of fashion and hello to a swarm of cheap tourist shops selling everything from linen and jade to plastic toys and $2 slippers. But that's not all Chinatown has to offer. The real gems here are tucked on side streets or are small, one-person shops selling Chinese herbs, original art, and jewelry. Grant Avenue is the area's main thoroughfare, and side streets between Bush Street and Columbus Avenue are full of restaurants, markets, and eclectic shops. Walking is best, since traffic through this area is slow at best and parking next to impossible. Most of the stores in Chinatown are open daily from 10am to 10pm. Serviced by bus lines 9X, 15, 30, 41, and 45.

Union Street Union Street, from Fillmore to Van Ness, caters to the upper middle class crowd. It's a great place to stroll, window shop the plethora of boutiques, cafes, and restaurants, and watch the beautiful people parade by. Serviced by bus lines 22, 41, 42, and 45.

Chestnut Street Parallel to and a few blocks north of Union Street, Chestnut is a younger Union Street, with endless shopping and dining choices, and the ever-tanned, superfit population of postgraduate singles who hang around cafes and scope each other out. Serviced by bus lines 22, 28, 30, 41, 42, 43, and 76.

Fillmore Street   Some of the best shopping in town is packed into five blocks of Fillmore Street in Pacific Heights. From Jackson to Sutter streets, Fillmore is the perfect place to grab a bite and peruse the high-priced boutiques, craft shops, and incredible houseware stores. Don't miss Zinc Details and Fillamento. Serviced by bus lines 1, 2, 3, 4, 12, 22, and 24.

Haight Street   Green hair, spiked hair, no hair, or mohair—even the hippies look conservative next to Haight Street's dramatic fashion freaks. The shopping in the six blocks of upper Haight Street, between Central Avenue and Stanyan Street, reflects its clientele and offers everything from incense and European and American street styles to furniture and antique clothing. Bus lines 7, 66, 71, and 73 run the length of Haight Street. The Muni metro N line stops at Waller Street and at Cole Street.

SoMa   Though this area isn't suitable for strolling, you'll find almost all the discount shopping in warehouse spaces South of Market. You can pick up a discount shopping guide at most major hotels. Many bus lines pass through this area.

Hayes Valley   It may not be the prettiest area in town (with some of the shadier housing projects a few blocks away), but while most neighborhoods cater to more conservative or trendy shoppers, lower Hayes Street, between Octavia and Gough, celebrates anything vintage, artistic, or downright funky. Though still in its developmental stage, its definitely the most interesting new shopping area in town, with furniture and glass stores, thrift shops, trendy shoe stores, and men's and women's clothiers. There are also lots of great antique shops south on Octavia and on nearby Market Street. Bus lines include 16AX, 16BX, and 21.

Fisherman's Wharf and Environs   The tourist-oriented malls run along Jefferson Street and include hundreds of shops, restaurants, and attractions. Ghirardelli Square, Pier 39, the Cannery, and the Anchorage are all outlined under "Shopping Centers and Complexes," below.

HOURS, TAXES & SHIPPING

Store hours are generally Monday through Saturday from 10am to 6pm and on Sunday from noon to 5pm. Most department stores stay open later, as do shops around Fisherman's Wharf, the most heavily visited area.

Sales tax in San Francisco is 8.5%, which is added on at the register for all goods and services purchased. If you live out of state and buy an expensive item, you may want to consider having the store ship it home for you. You will escape paying the sales tax, but will have to pay for its transport.

Most of the city's shops can wrap your purchase and ship it anywhere in the world via United Parcel Service (UPS). If they can't, you can send it yourself, either through UPS (☎ **415/952-5200**) or through the U.S. mail (see "Fast Facts: San Francisco" in Chapter 4).

2 Shopping A to Z

ANTIQUES

Jackson Square, a historic district just north of the Financial District's Embarcadero Center, is the place to go for the top names in fine furniture and fine art. There are also a lot of Asian art dealers here. More than a dozen dealers on the two blocks between Columbus and Sansome streets specialize in European furnishings from the 17th to the 19th centuries. Most shops here are open Monday through Friday from 9am to 5pm, and on Saturday from 11am to 4pm.

Fumiki Fine Asian Arts. 2001 Union St. (at Buchanan St.). ☎ **415/922-0573.**

Specializing in fine Asian art and antiques, including Japanese baskets and Chinese artifacts and embroidery, the shop has one of the largest collections of antique Japanese Imari and Korean and Japanese tansus in the country. Open Monday through Saturday from 10am to 6pm and on Sunday from noon to 5pm.

ART

The **San Francisco Gallery Guide,** a comprehensive, bimonthly publication listing the city's current shows, is available free by mail. Send a self-addressed stamped envelope to San Francisco Bay Area Gallery Guide, 1369 Fulton St., San Francisco, CA 94117 (☎ **415/921-1600**), or pick one up at the San Francisco Visitor Information Center. Most of the city's major art galleries are clustered downtown in the Union Square area.

Atelier Dore. 771 Bush St. (between Mason and Powell sts.). ☎ **415/391-2423.**

Atelier Dore features American and European paintings from the 19th and 20th centuries, including some WPA art. Open Tuesday through Saturday from 11am to 5pm.

Eleonore Austerer. 540 Sutter St. (between Powell and Mason sts.). ☎ **415/986-2244.**

Limited-edition graphics by modern masters like Braque, Matisse, Miró, Picasso, Calder, Chagall, and Hockney as well as original works by European and American contemporary artists can be found at Eleonore Austerer. The gallery, located in a beautiful old building near Union Square, is open Monday through Saturday from 10am to 6pm.

Fraenkel Gallery. 49 Geary St., 4th floor (between Grant Ave. and Kearny St.). ☎ **415/981-2661.**

This photography gallery features works by contemporary American and European artists. Excellent shows change frequently. Open Tuesday through Friday from 10:30am to 5:30pm and on Saturday from 11am to 5pm.

Harcourts Modern & Contemporary Art. 706 Mission St., 2nd floor (between Mission and Third sts.). ☎ **415/227-0400.**

This international contemporary gallery exhibits paintings, sculpture, and graphics by modern masters as well as established contemporary artists. Open Tuesday through Saturday from 10am to 5:30pm.

Images of the North. 1782 Union St. (at Octavia St.). ☎ **415/673-1273.**

The highlight here is one of the most extensive collections of Canadian and Alaskan Inuit art in the United States. There's also a fine collection of Native American masks and jewelry. Open Monday through Saturday from 11am to 5:30pm and on Sunday from noon to 4pm.

Maxwell Galleries. 559 Sutter St. (between Powell and Mason sts.). ☎ **415/421-5193.**

The specialties at Maxwell Galleries are 19th- and 20th-century European and American sculpture and paintings, including works by Raphael and Butler. Open Monday through Friday from 9:30am to 5:15pm and on Saturday from 11am to 5pm.

Meyerovich Gallery. 251 Post St., 4th floor (at Stockton St.). ☎ **415/421-7171.**

Works by modern and contemporary masters here include Chagall, Haring, Hockney, Lichtenstein, Matisse, Miró, Motherwell, Picasso, Rosenquist, and Warhol, as well as sculpture by Bruskin and Chadwick. Open Monday through Friday from 10am to 5:30pm and on Saturday from 11am to 5pm.

BOOKS

The Booksmith. 1644 Haight St. (between Clayton and Cole sts.). ☎ **415/863-8688.**

Haight Street's best selection of new books is housed in this large, well-maintained shop. It carries all the top titles, along with works from smaller presses, and more than 1,000 different magazines. Open Monday through Saturday from 10am to 9pm and on Sunday from 10am to 6pm.

Charlotte's Web. 2278 Union St. (between Steiner and Fillmore sts.). ☎ **415/441-4700.**

A first-rate children's bookstore, Charlotte's Web is notable for its particularly knowledgeable owner, who sells everything from cloth books for babies to histories and poetry for young adults. Nonliterary items include music cassettes, videos, posters, and cards. Open Tuesday through Saturday from 10am to 6pm, and Sunday from 10am to 5pm.

City Lights Book Store. 261 Columbus Ave. (at Broadway). ☎ **415/362-8193.**

Brooding literary types browse this famous bookstore owned by Lawrence Ferlinghetti, the renowned beat generation poet. The three-level bookshop prides itself on a comprehensive collection of art, poetry, and political paperbacks, as well as more mainstream books. Open daily from 10am to 11:45pm.

A Clean, Well-Lighted Place for Books. 601 Van Ness Ave. (between Turk St. and Golden Gate Ave.). ☎ **415/441-6670.**

Voted best bookstore by the *San Francisco Bay Guardian,* this independent has good new fiction and nonfiction sections and also specializes in music, art, mystery, and cookbooks. The store is very well known for its schedule of author readings and events. For a calendar of events, call the store or check their web site at **http://www.bookstore.com/.** Open Sunday through Thursday from 10am to 11pm, and Friday and Saturday from 10am to midnight. Additional branches are in Marin County at 2417 Larkspur Landing Circle, Larkspur (☎ **415/461-0171**) and in Cupertino at 21269 Steven's Creek Blvd. (☎ **408/255-7600**).

Eastwind Books & Arts. 1435A Stockton St. (at Columbus Ave.). ☎ **415/772-5877.**

The emphasis here is on Chinese books, stationery, and stamps. Another branch at 633 Vallejo St. (☎ **415/772-5899**) carries Asian-American and English books covering health, history, cooking, martial arts, medicine, art, and culture. Both locations are open Monday through Saturday from 10am to 6pm and Sunday from noon to 5pm.

Green Apple Books. 506 Clement St. (at 6th Ave.). ☎ **415/387-2272.**

The local favorite for used books, Green Apple is crammed with titles—more than 60,000 new and 100,000 used books. Their extended sections in psychology, cooking, art, history, collection of modern first editions, and rare graphic comics is only superseded by the staff's superlative service. Open Sunday through Thursday from 9:30am to 11pm and Friday through Saturday from 9:30am to midnight.

Markus Books. 1712 Fillmore St. (at Post St.). ☎ **415/346-4222.**

Markus has the Bay Area's best selection of books relating to African American and African culture. In addition to a good collection of children's books, you'll find strong sections for fiction, history, politics, art, and biography. Open Monday through Saturday from 10am to 7pm, and Sunday from noon to 5pm.

McDonald's Bookshop. 48 Turk St. (at Market St.). ☎ **415/673-2235.**

San Francisco's biggest used-book shop claims to stock more than a million volumes, including out-of-print, esoteric, and hard-to-find books in all categories and languages. As a birthday novelty, they'll find a copy of *Life* magazine from the month and year in which you were born. Open Monday, Tuesday, and Thursday from 10am to 6pm; and Wednesday, Friday, and Saturday from 10:30am to 6:30pm.

CHINA, SILVER & GLASS

The Enchanted Crystal. 1895 Union St. (at Laguna St.). ☎ **415/885-1335.**

This shop has an extensive collection of fine crystal, art glass, jewelry, and one-of-a-kind decorative art, including one of the largest crystal balls in the world (from Madagascar). Open Monday through Saturday from 10am to 6pm, and on Sunday from noon to 5pm.

Gump's. 135 Post St. (between Kearny St. and Grant Ave.). ☎ **415/982-1616.**

San Francisco's favored house-and-home store is located between Grant Avenue and Stockton Street. Founded almost a century ago, Gump's offers gifts and treasures ranging from Asian antiquities to contemporary art glass and exquisite jade and pearl jewelry. Many items are made specifically for the store. Gump's also has one of the most revered window displays each holiday season. Open Monday through Wednesday 10am to 6pm, Thursday from 10am to 7pm, Friday and Saturday from 10am to 6pm.

CRAFTS

The Canton Bazaar. 616 Grant Ave. (between Sacramento and California sts.). ☎ **415/362-5750.**

Amid a wide variety of handicrafts you'll find an excellent selection of rosewood and carved furniture, cloisonné enamelware, rose Canton chinaware, porcelain ware, carved jade, embroideries, jewelry, and antiques from mainland China. Open daily from 10am to 10pm.

The New Unique Company. 838 Grant Ave. (between Clay and Washington sts.). ☎ **415/981-2036.**

Primarily a calligraphy and watercolor supplies store, the shop also has a good assortment of books relating to these topics. In addition, there is a wide selection of carved stones for use as seals on letters and documents. The store will carve seals to order should you want a special design or group of initials. Open daily from 10am to 10pm.

Silkroute International. 3119 Fillmore St. (at Filbert St.). ☎ **415/563-4936.**

Owned and operated by an Afghan who offers fascinating wares, old and new, from his native country, the shop sells oriental and tribal rugs, kilims, dhurries, textiles, jewelry, clothing, pillows, arts, and antiques. Open Monday through Friday from 11am to 7pm, on Saturday from 11am to 6pm, and on Sunday from 1 to 5pm.

DEPARTMENT STORES

Macy's. Corner of Stockton and O'Farrell sts., Union Square. ☎ **415/397-3333.**

One of the largest stores in San Francisco, Macy's had occupied two distinct buildings until it recently acquired the Market Street Emporium, adding it to its list of shopping facilities. When this book went to press, Macy's takeover was still underway, and the new facilities not yet completed. Meantime, the seven-story Macy's West continues to feature contemporary fashions for women and juniors, including jewelry, fragrances, cosmetics, and accessories. The top floors contain home furnishings, while the Cellar sells kitchenware and gourmet foods. Across the street, Macy's East has five floors of men's and children's fashions. Open Monday through Saturday from 10am to 8pm, and on Sunday from 11am to 7pm.

Neiman-Marcus. 150 Stockton St., Union Square. ☎ **415/362-3900.**

Some call this unit of the Texas-based chain "Needless Mark-up." But if you've got the cash, the men's and women's clothes, precious gems, and conservative formal wear here are some of the most glamorous in town. The Rotunda Restaurant, on the top floor, is a beautiful, relaxing place for lunch and afternoon tea. Open Monday, Thursday, and Friday from 10am to 8pm; Tuesday, Wednesday, and Saturday from 10am to 7pm, and on Sunday from noon to 6pm.

Nordstrom. 865 Market St. (in the San Francisco Shopping Centre). ☎ **415/243-8500.**

Renowned for its personalized service, this is the largest member of the Seattle-based fashion department store chain. Nordstrom occupies the top five floors of the San Francisco Shopping Centre (see "Shopping Centers and Complexes," below) and is that mall's primary anchor. Equally devoted to women's and men's fashions, the store has one of the best shoe selections in the city, and thousands of suits in stock. The Nordstrom Café, on the fourth floor, has a panoramic view and is an ideal place for an inexpensive lunch or light snack. The fifth floor is occupied by Nordstrom Spa, the perfect place to relax after a hectic day of bargain-hunting. Open Monday through Saturday from 9:30am to 9pm, and on Sunday from 10am to 7pm.

DISCOUNT SHOPPING

There are many factory outlet stores in San Francisco, selling overstocked and discontinued fashions at bargain prices. All of the following shops are located south of Market Street, in the city's warehouse district (SoMa).

Esprit Outlet Store. 499 Illinois St. (at 16th St.). ☎ **415/957-2550.**

All the Esprit collections and Susie Tompkins merchandise are available here at 30% or more off regular prices. In addition to clothes, the store sells accessories, shoes, and assorted other items. Open Monday through Friday from 10am to 8pm, Saturday from 10am to 7pm, and Sunday from 11am to 5pm.

Glasser Designs. 32 Otis St. (near Mission St. and Van Ness Ave.). ☎ **415/552-3188.**

The beautiful soft leather handbags, totes, and business bags sold here are all handmade in San Francisco. Open Monday through Friday from 9am to 5:30pm, on Saturday from noon to 5pm.

N.E. Wear. 96 Townsend St. (at Second St.). ☎ **415/357-1002.**

For the coziest outdoor sportswear in thick, durable fabrics, there's no better bargain in town than this young design company's outlet store. Casual wear ranges from sweats to skirts, jackets, and vests. And while a fleece pullover may run you about $30 here, you'd pay up to $75 for it elsewhere—and the sale rack always has unbeatable deals. Open Monday through Saturday from 10am to 6pm and Sunday from noon to 5pm.

New West. 426 Brannan St. (between Third and Fourth sts.). ☎ **415/882-4929.**

This SoMa boutique offers top designer fashions from shoes to suits at rock-bottom prices. There are no cheap knockoffs here, just good men's and women's clothes and accessories. New West also has its own stylish clothing line. Open Monday through Saturday from 10am to 5pm and Sunday from noon to 5pm.

The North Face. 1325 Howard St. (between Ninth and Tenth sts.). ☎ **415/626-6444.**

Well known for its sporting, camping, and hiking equipment, this off-price outlet carries a limited but high-quality selection of skiwear, boots, sweaters, and goods such as tents, packs, and sleeping bags. The North Face makes heavy use of Gore-Tex, down, and other durable, lightweight materials. Open Monday through Saturday from 10am to 6pm and Sunday from 11am to 5pm.

FASHIONS

Eddie Bauer. 250 Post St. (between Stockton St. and Grant Ave.). ☎ **415/986-7600.**

One of the first to use goose down in outdoor clothing, Eddie Bauer is known for its high-quality mail-order goods. There's an especially good fishing department. Open Monday through Friday from 10am to 8pm, Saturday from 10am to 7pm, and on Sunday from noon to 5pm.

Grand. 1435 Grant Ave. (between Green and Union sts.). ☎ **415/951-0131.**

Invited to an underground club and forgot your funky rave attire? Grand's North Beach shop features the latest in fashion-forward street wear by local designers. Garb comes both baggy and tight; the style is club, and the price is right. Open from noon to 7pm daily.

Gucci America. 200 Stockton St. (between Geary and Post sts.). ☎ **415/392-2808.**

Donning Gucci's golden Gs is not a cheap endeavor. But if you've got the cash, you'll find all the latest lines of shoes, leather goods, scarves, and pricey accessories, such as a $7,000 handmade crocodile bag. Open Monday through Saturday from 10am to 6pm, and on Sunday from noon to 5pm.

One by Two. 418 Hayes St. (at Gough St.). ☎ **415/252-1460.**

Hayes Valley features fashion comparable to New York's SoHo, though disappointing in comparison because there are so few shops. Still, if you're interested in the latest chic and wild trendy wear, browse local designer Al Abayan's boutique featuring urban sportswear with a modern twist. His style is young, clean, and colorful in thick, expensive fabrics. "In" wear doesn't come cheaply here, but you can bet you won't see everyone wearing your outfit in your hometown. Open Monday through Saturday from 11am to 7pm and Sunday from noon to 5pm.

Three Bags Full. 2181 Union St. (at Fillmore). ☎ **415/567-5753.**

Snuggling up in a cozy sweater can be a fashionable event if you do your shopping at this pricey boutique, which carries the gamut in handmade and one-of-a-kind playful and extravagant knitwear. Open Monday through Friday from 11am to 6pm, Saturday from 11am to 5:30pm, and on Sunday from noon to 5pm. Other city locations are 500 Sutter St. and 3314 Sacramento St.

Wearever. 1420 Grant Ave. (between Union and Green sts.). ☎ **415/392-1248.**

Labels such as Double RL by Ralph Lauren, Mossimo, Calvin Klein underwear, Miss Sixty, French Connection, and many others are featured at this small fashion boutique for both men and women. Also offered are silver rings made from antique American coins.

MEN'S FASHIONS

All American Boy. 463 Castro St. (between Market and 18th sts.). ☎ **415/861-0444.**

Long known for setting the mainstream style for gay men, All American Boy is the quintessential Castro clothing shop. Open Monday through Saturday from 10am to 9pm, and Sunday from 11am to 7pm.

Brooks Brothers. 201 Post St. (at Grant Ave.). ☎ **415/397-4500.**

In San Francisco, this bulwark of tradition is located one block east of Union Square. Brooks Brothers introduced the button-down collar and single-handedly changed the standard of the well-dressed businessman. The multilevel shop also sells traditional casual wear, including sportswear, sweaters, and shirts. Open Monday through Saturday from 9:30am to 6:30pm, and on Sunday from noon to 5pm.

Cable Car Clothiers. 246 Sutter St. (between Grant Ave. and Kearny St.). ☎ **415/397-4740.**

Dapper men head to this beautiful landmark building for traditional attire, such as three-button suits with natural shoulders, Aquascutum coats, McGeorge sweaters, and Countess Mara neckwear. Open Monday through Saturday from 9:30am to 5:30pm.

Citizen Clothing. 536 Castro St. (between 18th and 19th sts.). ☎ **415/558-9429.**

The Castro has some of America's best men's casual clothing stores, and this is one of them. Stylish (but not faddish) pants, tops, and accessories are sold here. Open Monday through Saturday from 10am to 8pm and Sunday from 11am to 7pm.

MAC. 5 Claude Lane (off Sutter St. between Grant Ave. and Kearny St.). ☎ **415/837-0615.**

The more classic than corporate man shops here for imported tailored suits in new and intriguing fabrics. Lines include London's Katherine Hamnette, Belgium's SO, Italy's Alberto Biani, New York's John Bartlett, and San Francisco's Lat Naylor. Open Monday through Saturday from 11am to 7pm and Sunday from noon to 5pm. Their women's' store is located at 1543 Grant Ave. (between Filbert and Union sts.) (☎ **415/837-1604**).

Under Cover. 535 Castro St. (between 18th and 19th sts.). ☎ **415/864-0505.**

This Castro shop sells the latest trends in "club couture"—tight, stretchy, Lycra-blend shirts and pants, swimwear, underwear, and more. Open Monday through Friday from 11am to 8pm, Saturday from 10am to 8pm, and Sunday from 11am to 7pm.

WOMEN'S FASHIONS

Bella Donna. 539 Hayes St. (between Laguna and Octavia sts.). ☎ **415/861-7182.**

Another blessing to the small but growing Hayes Valley alternative shopping mecca is this expensive, but quality, boutique offering luxurious women's clothing, such as hand-knit sweaters, silky slip dresses, and fashionable knit hats. There's also a wonderful (albeit expensive) collection of vases and other household trinkets, as well as a small selection of remainder fabrics. Upstairs the wedding and bridal section focuses on the vintage look. Open daily from 11am to 7pm and Sunday from 11am to 5pm.

The Chanel Boutique. 155 Maiden Lane (between Stockton St. and Grant Ave.). ☎ **415/981-1550.**

Ever fashionable and expensive, Chanel is appropriately located on Maiden Lane, the quaint downtown side street where the most exclusive stores and spas cluster. You'll find what you'd expect from Chanel: clothing, accessories, scents, cosmetics, and jewelry. Open Monday through Friday from 10am to 6:30pm, Saturday from 10am to 6pm, and on Sunday from 10am to 5pm.

Métier. 50 Maiden Lane (at Grant Ave. and Kearny St.). ☎ **415/989-5395.**

Classic and sophisticated creations for women include European ready-to-wear lines and designers Peter Cohen, Harriet Selwyn, Alberto Biani, Victor Victoria, and local Lat Naylor, as well as a distinguished collection of Antique-style, high-end jewelry. Open Monday through Saturday from 10:30am to 6:30pm and Sunday from noon to 5pm.

Solo Fashion. 1599 Haight St. (at Clayton St.). ☎ **415/621-0342.**

While strolling upper Haight, stop in here for a good selection of upbeat, contemporary, English-style street wear, along with a collection of dresses designed exclusively for this shop. Open daily from 11am to 7pm.

CHILDREN'S FASHIONS

Kids Only. 1608 Haight St. (at Clayton St.). ☎ **415/552-5445.**

Your baby doesn't have to miss out on the sixties entirely—you will find adorable tie-dyed children's outfits here, as well as more ordinary and conservative children's clothes, Nature's Wear brands that are made from all-natural, dye-free cloths, and books and toys. Open Monday through Saturday from 10am to 6pm, and Sunday from 11am to 5pm.

Minis. 2042 Union St. (between Webster and Buchanan sts.). ☎ **415/567-9537.**

Christina Profili, a San Francisco native who used to design for Banana Republic, opened this children's clothing store selling her own creations. Every piece, from shirts to pants and dresses, is made from cotton or organic cotton. Every outfit perfectly coordinates with everything else in the store. Minis also offers educational and creative toys and storybooks with matching dolls. Open daily 10:30am to 6:30pm.

FOOD

Bepples Pie Shop & Restaurant. 1934 Union St. (at Laguna St.). ☎ **415/931-6225.**

One of the most celebrated shops on Union Street is this naschery selling soups, muffins, breads, and pies. Open Sunday through Thursday from 8am to midnight and Friday 8am to 2am; and Saturday 9am to 2am.

Golden Gate Fortune Cookies Co. 56 Ross Alley (between Washington and Jackson sts.). ☎ **415/781-3956.**

This tiny, touristy factory sells fortune cookies hot off the press. You can purchase them in small bags or in bulk, and if your order is large enough, you may even be able to negotiate your own message. Even if you're not buying, stop in to see how these sugary treats are made. Open Daily from 10am to 7pm.

Joseph Schmidt Confections. 3489 16th St. (at Sanchez St.). ☎ **415/861-8682.**

Chocolate takes the shape of exquisite sculptural masterpieces—such as long-stemmed tulips and heart-shaped boxes—that are so beautiful, you'll be hesitant to bite the head off your adorable chocolate panda bear. But once you do, you'll know why this is the most popular chocolatier in town. Prices are also remarkably reasonable. Open from Monday through Saturday from 10am to 6:30pm.

Pure T. 2238 Polk St. (between Vallejo and Green sts.). ☎ **415/441-7878.**

If you're asked to bring dessert to a dinner party or are simply aching for a treat, it'd be a sin to miss out on what we consider the best ice cream shop in the city. The freshly made, all natural ice creams here redefine "gourmet." They're light and delicate to the taste and flavored with, you guessed it, pure tea. Treat your tongue to a scoop of black currant or Thai tea and you'll be hooked. Open Wednesday through Monday from 11:30am to 10pm.

Ten Ren Tea Company. 949 Grant Ave. (between Washington and Jackson sts.). ☎ **415/362-0656.**

At the Ten Ren Tea Company, you will be offered a steaming cup of roselle tea, made of black tea and hibiscus. In addition to a selection of almost 50 traditional and herbal teas, the company stocks related paraphernalia, such as pots, cups, and infusers. If you can't make up your mind, take home a mail-order form. Open daily from 9am to 9pm.

GIFTS

Art of China. 839–843 Grant Ave. (between Clay and Washington sts.). ☎ **415/981-1602.**

Amid a wide variety of collectibles, this shop features exquisite, hand-carved Chinese figurines. You'll also find a lovely assortment of ivory beads, bracelets, necklaces, and earrings. Pink-quartz dogs, jade figurines, porcelain vases, cachepots, and blue-and-white barrels suitable for use as table bases are just some of the many collectibles on offer. Open daily from 10am to 6pm.

Babushka. 333 Jefferson St. (at Leavenworth St.). ☎ **415/673-6740.**

Located near Fisherman's Wharf, adjacent to the Anchorage Shopping Center, Babushka sells only Russian products, most of which are wooden or papier-mâché nesting dolls. Open daily from 9am to 10pm.

Cost Plus Imports. 2552 Taylor St. (between North Point and Bay sts.). ☎ **415/928-6200.**

At the Fisherman's Wharf cable-car turntable, Cost Plus is a vast warehouse crammed to the rafters with Chinese baskets, Indian camel bells, Malaysian batik scarves, and innumerable other items from Algeria to Zanzibar. More than 20,000 items from 40 nations are purchased directly from their country of origin and packed into this well-priced warehouse. They also have a decent wine shop. Open daily from 9am to 9pm.

Distractions. 1552 Haight St. (between Ashbury and Clayton sts.). ☎ **415/252-8751.**

This is the best of the Haight St. shops selling pseudo-sixties memorabilia. You'll find retro hippie clothes, pipes, toys, and stickers are liberally intermixed with tie-dyed Grateful Dead paraphernalia and lots of cool stuff to look at. Open Monday through Saturday from 11am to 6:45pm, and Sunday from 11am to 6pm.

The Dolls & Bears of Charlton Court. 1957 Union St. (between Laguna and Buchanan sts.). ☎ **415/775-3740.**

A pint-sized shop cluttered with collectable dolls in all sizes, this store is actually located in a tiny alleyway off Union Street. Call for hours, which vary.

Flax. 1699 Market St. (at Valencia and Gough sts.). ☎ **415/552-2355.**

If you're the type of person who goes into an art store for a special pencil and comes out $300 later, don't go near this shop. Flax has everything you can think of in art and design supplies, along with an amazing collection of locals' arts and crafts, blank bound books, children's art supplies, frames, calendars, you name it. There's a gift for every type of person here, especially you. Open Monday through Saturday from 9:30am to 6pm.

Good Vibrations. 1210 Valencia St. (at 23rd St.). ☎ **415/974-8980** or mail order at 800/BUY-VIBE.

A laypersons' sex toy, book, and video emporium, Good Vibrations is specifically designed (but not exclusively) for women. Unlike most sex shops, it's not a back-alley business, but rather a straight-forward shop with healthy and open attitudes about human sexuality. They also have a vibrator museum. Open daily from 11am to 7pm.

Off Your Dot. 2241 Market St. (between Sanchez and Noe sts.). ☎ **415/252-5642.**

Wonderfully attractive and artistic handmade gifts cover almost every inch of this Castro district store. There's everything from wall art to candles, picture frames, lamps, and glasswork here and most of it is locally made, and prices are the best in town.

Oggetti. 1846 Union St. (between Laguna and Octavia sts.). ☎ **415/346-0631.**

This fascinating Florentine shop specializes in objects adorned with marbleized paper (a decorative technique invented in the 17th century by Mace Ruette, the royal bookbinder to Louis XIII). If it can be marbleized, Oggetti has got it—from covered frames, jewelry boxes, pencils, and pencil boxes to blank notebooks. About 95% of Oggetti's items are imported from Italy and are exclusive to the store. Open Monday through Saturday from 10am to 6pm, and on Sunday from 11am to 6pm.

PlaNetweavers Treasures Store. 1573 Haight St. (between Ashbury and Clayton sts.). ☎ **415/864-4415.**

There truly are real treasures here: a huge selection of unusual arts and collectibles including wind chimes, natural body products, jewelry, and crafts from around the world. Best of all, the store is committed to working with socially conscious vendors, so you get an extra karma bonus when you shop here. Open daily from 11am to 7pm.

Smile. 500 Sutter St. (between Powell and Mason sts.). ☎ **415/362-3436.**

Need a little humor in your life? Smile specializes in whimsical art guaranteed to make you grin. Open Monday through Saturday from 9:30am to 5:30pm.

Quantity Postcards. 1441 Grant St. (at Green St.). ☎ **415/986-8866.**

You'll find the perfect postcard for literally everyone you know here, as well as some depictions of old San Francisco, movie stars, and Day-Glo posters featuring concert-poster artist Frank Kozik. Prices range from 15¢ to 75¢ per card, and even if you don't need any cards, you'll enjoy browsing the eclectic collection of mailables.

HOUSEWARES

Fillamento. 2185 Fillmore St. (at Sacramento St.). ☎ **415/931-2224.**

Fillamento's three floors are always packed with shoppers searching for the most classic, artistic, and refined housewares. Whether you're looking to set a good table or revamp your bedroom, you'll find it all here. Open Monday through Friday from 11am to 7pm, Saturday and Sunday from 10am to 6pm.

Victorian Interiors. 575 Hayes St. (at Laguna St.). ☎ **415/431-7191.**

Draped with an array of period floral wallpapers, this little store is the perfect place to shop for any Victorian fanatic. Along with traditional Victorian houseware such as wallpapers, moldings, drapery cornices and rods, tiles, fabrics, and carpets, you'll find a great collection of old pipes and knickknacks. Open Tuesday through Saturday from 11am to 6pm and Sunday noon to 5pm.

The Wok Shop. 718 Grant Ave. (at Clay St.). ☎ **415/989-3797.**

This shop has every conceivable implement for Chinese cooking, including woks, brushes, cleavers, circular chopping blocks, dishes, oyster knives, bamboo steamers, strainers—you name it. The shop also sells a wide range of kitchen utensils, baskets, handmade linens from China, and aprons. Open Sunday through Friday from 10am to 6pm, Saturday from 10am to 10pm.

Z Gallerie. 2071 Union St. (between Buchanan and Webster sts.). ☎ **415/346-9000.**

This California-based chain sells a good selection of affordable framed poster art, trendy gifts, and furniture that's a little more hip but along the same line as Pottery Barn. Other stores are located in the San Francisco Shopping Centre (see "Shopping Centers and Complexes," below) and at 1465 Haight St. (☎ **415/863-7466**). Open Monday through Thursday from 10am to 7pm, Friday and Saturday from 10am to 10pm, Sunday from 11am to 7pm. Hours at other locations vary.

Zinc Details. 1905 Fillmore St. (between Bush and Pine sts.). ☎ **415/776-2100.**

One of our favorite stores in the city, Zinc Details has received accolades from everyone from *Elle Decor Japan* to *Metropolitan Home* for its amazing collection of locally hand-crafted glass vases, pendant lights, ceramics, and furniture. Each piece is a true work of art created specifically for the store (except vintage items) and these pieces are in such high demand that their wholesale accounts include Barney's New York and The Guggenheim Museum Store. Open from 11am to 7pm daily.

JEWELRY

Jerusalem Shoppe. 313 Noe St. (at Market St.). ☎ **415/626-7906.**

Known for its extensive collection of silver and gold gemstone jewelry by more than 300 local and international artists, this shop also displays other unique treasures, from clothing and accessories to imported antique Indian quilts. Open Monday through Saturday from 10am to 8:30pm and Sunday from 10am to 7pm.

The Magical Trinket. 524 Hayes St. (between Laguna and Octavia sts.). ☎ **415/626-0764.**

Do-it-yourself jewelry makers beware. This store, brimming with beads, baubles, and bangles, will inspire you to make your own knickknacks and kick yourself for the prices you've been paying for costume jewelry in retail stores. If you're overwhelmed by all the bead options, colors, shapes, and styles, owner Eve Blake calmly explains how to create your wearable masterpiece and offers more extensive classes for those who are really bead-dazzled. Open Tuesday through Saturday from 11am to 7pm, Sunday from noon to 5pm.

Old & New Estates. 2181A Union St. (at Fillmore St.). ☎ **415/346-7525.**

Buy yourself a bauble, treat yourself to a trinket at this shop featuring top-of-the-line antique jewelry: pendants, diamond rings, necklaces, bracelets, and natural pearls. For a special gift, check out the collection of platinum wedding and engagement rings and vintage watches. Open Thursday through Tuesday from noon to 6pm.

Pearl Empire. 127 Geary St. (between Stockton St. and Grant Ave.). ☎ **415/362-0606.**

The Pearl Empire has been importing jewelry from all over the world since 1957. They are specialists in unusual pearls and jade, and offer restringing on the premises. Open Monday through Saturday from 9:30am to 5:30pm.

Tiffany & Co. 350 Post St. (at Stockton St.). ☎ **415/781-7000.**

Even if you don't have lots of cash to buy an exquisite bauble that comes in Tiffany's famous light blue box, enjoy this renowned store as Audrey Hepburn did at the New

York store in *Breakfast at Tiffany's*. The designer collection features Paloma Picasso, Jean Schlumberger, and Elsa Peretti in both silver and 18-karat gold, and there's an extensive gift collection in sterling, china, and crystal. Open Monday through Saturday from 10am to 6pm.

Union Street Goldsmith. 1909 Union St. (at Laguna St.). ☎ **415/776-8048.**

A showcase for Bay Area goldsmiths, this exquisite shop sells custom-designed jewelry in all karats. Many pieces emphasize colored stones in their settings. Open Monday through Saturday from 11am to 5:45pm, and on Sunday from noon to 4:45pm.

LEATHER

Mark Cross. 170 Post St. (between Grant Ave. and Kearney St.). ☎ **415/391-7770.**

For more than 150 years this store has been known for the quality and beauty of its workmanship. All leather goods are hand constructed and classically styled of calfskin, pigskin, ostrich, alligator, and lizard. The store will emboss your purchase with gold initials, free of charge. Open Monday through Saturday from 10am to 6pm, Sunday from noon to 5pm.

North Beach Leather. 1365 Columbus Ave. (at Beach St.). ☎ **415/441-3208.**

Primarily selling leather jackets and dresses, this shop has up-to-the-minute fashions at high prices. Other leather items from casual to elegant are sold. A second shop is located on Union Square at 190 Geary St. (☎ **415/362-8300**). Open Monday through Saturday from 10am to 7pm and Sunday from noon to 6pm.

Overland Sheepskin Co. 21 Grant Ave. (between Geary and O'Farrell sts.). ☎ **415/296-9180.**

Inside this pretty, southwestern-style shop, just off Market Street, are beautiful sheepskin hats, jackets, booties, and bears. They stock some of the nicest sheepskin styles we've ever seen. Open daily from 8am to 8pm.

MARKETS/PRODUCE

Farmers Market. Embarcadero, in front of the Ferry Building. ☎ **510/528-6987.**

Every Saturday from May to November Northern California fruit, vegetable, bread, and dairy vendors join local restaurateurs in selling fresh, delicious edibles. There's no better way to enjoy a bright San Francisco morning than strolling this gourmet street market and snacking your way through breakfast. You can also pick up locally made vinegars and oils—they make wonderful gifts.

RECORDS & CDS

Groove Merchant Records. 776 Haight St. (at Pierce and Steiner sts.). ☎ **415/252-5766.**

Collectors of rare vinyl jazz, soul, funk and Latin must check out Groove Merchant, whose own record label was in the forefront of the Bay Area acid jazz movement and continues to reissue old and rare groove and contemporary artists. Open Tuesday through Sunday from noon to 7pm.

Recycled Records. 1377 Haight St. (between Central and Masonic). ☎ **415/626-4075.**

Easily one of the best used-record stores in the city, this loud shop in the Haight has a good selection of promotional CDs and cases of used "classic" rock LPs. Sheet music, tour programs, and old *TV Guides* are sold. Open Monday through Saturday from 10am to 10pm, Sunday from 10am to 8pm.

Rough Trade Records. 695 Third St. (at Townsend). ☎ **415/543-7091.**

Both mainstream and alternative (both new and used) CDs, tapes, and vinyl are sold in this well-stocked shop. Some local bands and hard-to-find international titles are available. Open Monday through Saturday from 11am to 6pm, and on Sunday from noon to 6pm.

Streetlight Records. 3979 24th St. (between Noe and Sanchez sts.). ☎ **415/282-3550.**

Overstuffed with used music in all three formats, this place is best known for its records and excellent CD collection. Rock music is cheap here, and a money-back guarantee guards against defects. Their second location is at 2350 Market St. (between Castro and Noe sts.) (☎ **415/282-8000**). Open Monday through Saturday from 10am to 10pm, and on Sunday from 11am to 8pm.

SHOES

Birkenstock Natural Footwear. 1815 Polk St. (between Washington and Jackson sts.). ☎ **415/776-5225.**

This relaxed store is known for its California-style, form-fitting sandals. Other orthopedically correct shoes are also available, including Finn Comforts and traditional Danish clogs by Dansko. Open daily from 10:30am to 6pm.

Kenneth Cole. 865 Market St. (in the San Francisco Shopping Centre). ☎ **415/227-4536.**

High-fashion footwear for men and women is sold at this trendy shop. There is also an innovative collection of handbags and small leather goods and accessories. A second shop is located at 2078 Union St., at Webster Street (☎ **415/346-2161**). Open Monday through Saturday from 9:30am to 8pm, and on Sunday from 11am to 6pm.

Taming of the Shoe. 1736 Haight St. (at Cole St.). ☎ **415/221-4453.**

For both men and women, this contemporary shoe and boot shop is filled with the hippest names from America and Europe. It also sells many original styles under its own name, and vintage footwear from the 1950s, 1960s, and 1970s. Open Monday through Saturday from 11am to 7pm, and on Sunday from noon to 6pm.

SHOPPING CENTERS & COMPLEXES

The Anchorage. 2800 Leavenworth St. (at Beach and Jefferson sts. on Fisherman's Wharf). ☎ **415/775-6000.**

This touristy waterfront mall has close to 55 stores that offer everything from music boxes to home furnishings; street performers entertain during opening hours. **The Incredible Christmas Store** (☎ **415/928-5700**) sells holiday items year-round. Open in summer daily from 10am to 9pm; the rest of the year, daily from 10am to 6pm.

The Cannery. 2801 Leavenworth St. (at Jefferson St.). ☎ **415/771-3112.**

Once a Del Monte fruit-canning plant, this complex is now occupied by a score or two of shops, restaurants, and nightspots, are thankfully only a few chain stores. Shops include **Gourmet Market** (☎ **415/673-0400**), selling international foods, coffees, and teas; **The Print Store** (☎ **415/771-3576**), offering a well-chosen selection of fine-art prints and local original art; and the **Basic Brown Bear Factory** (☎ **415/931-6670**), where you can stuff your own teddy bear. Vendors' stalls and sidewalk cafes are also set up in the courtyard, amid a grove of olive trees. On summer weekends street performers entertain. **The Museum of the City of San Francisco** (☎ **415/928-0289**) is on the third floor.

Cobb's Comedy Club (see Chapter 10, "San Francisco After Dark") is also here, along with several restaurants. The Cannery is open daily from 10am to 6pm; there are extended hours during the summer and on holidays.

Crocker Galleria. 50 Post St. (at Kearny St.). ☎ **415/393-1505.**

Modeled after Milan's Galleria Vittorio Emanuele, this glass-domed, three-level pavilion, about three blocks east of Union Square, features about 40 high-end shops. Fashions include **Stephane Kelian** designs, **Nicole Miller, Gianni Versace,** and **Polo/Ralph Lauren.** Open Monday through Friday from 10am to 6pm, and on Saturday from 10am to 5pm.

Ghirardelli Square. 900 North Point (between North Point and Beach sts.). ☎ **415/775-5500.**

This former chocolate factory is one of the city's largest malls and most popular landmarks. It dates from 1864 when it served as a factory making Civil War uniforms, but it's best known as the former chocolate-and-spice factory of Domingo Ghirardelli. The whole complex is crowned by a clock tower that is an exact replica of the one at France's Château de Blois. Inside the tower, on the mall's plaza level, is the Ghirardelli soda fountain, where small amounts of chocolate are still made and are available for purchase, along with other candy and ice cream. A free map and guide to the mall is available from the information booth, located in the center courtyard.

Many chain stores are located here, including the women's clothier **Ann Taylor** (☎ 415/775-2872) and **The Sharper Image** (☎ 415/776-1443) for unique, upscale electronics and designs.

The complex is open daily from 10am to 6pm. Main plaza shops are open Sunday through Thursday from 10am to 6pm, Friday and Saturday from 10am to 9pm, and on Sunday from 11am to 6pm; extended hours during the summer. Restaurant hours vary. (Incidentally, the Ghirardelli Chocolate Company still makes chocolate, but it's located in a lower-rent district in the East Bay.)

Pier 39. Embarcadero and Beach St. (on the waterfront). ☎ **415/981-8030.**

The automated information voice mail boasts Pier 39 is the "third most visited attraction in the country" and in almost the same breath reminds callers not to forget to bring along their Visa card. To residents, that pretty much wraps up Pier 39—an expensive tourist trap where out-of-towners go to waste money on worthless souvenirs and greasy fast food. For vacationers, though, Pier 39 does have some redeeming qualities—fresh crab (when in season), playful sea lions, phenomenal views, and plenty of fun for the kids. If you want to get to know the real San Francisco, skip the cheesy T-shirt shops and limit your time here to one afternoon.

Some of the most interesting stores include **Puppets on the Pier** (☎ 415/781-4435), a store that sells, you guessed it, puppets; **Kite Flight** (☎ 415/956-3181), where you can buy a fanciful creation to fly in the breezes off the bay; **Left Hand World** (☎ 415/433-3547), where southpaws can stock up on scissors, pot holders, watches, and corkscrews, all made for "lefties"; and the **House of Magic** (☎ 415/346-2218), where tricksters can find rubber chickens, fake blood and scars, and unusual masks.

Open weekdays from 10:30am to 8:30pm; weekends 10am to 8:30pm; store and restaurant hours vary; extended hours during the summer.

San Francisco Shopping Centre. 865 Market St. (at Fifth St.). ☎ **415/495-5656.**

Opened in 1988, this $140 million complex is one of the few vertical malls in the United States. Its most stunning features are the four-story spiral escalators that circle their way up to **Nordstrom** (see "Department Stores," above) and the nine-story atrium covered by a retractable skylight. More than 90 specialty shops include **Adrienne Vittadini, Ann Taylor, Bebe, Mondi, Benetton, Footlocker, J. Crew,** and **Victoria's Secret.** Open Monday through Saturday from 9:30am to 8pm and on Sunday from 11am to 6pm; holiday hours may vary.

SPORTS ATTIRE

City Fitness. 155 Greenwich St. (at Battery St.). ☎ **415/421-7442.**

If you're like us, you go crazy with options when looking for a new pair of running or aerobic shoes. Thankfully, Mimi, the ultra-fit owner of this fitness wear and fitness-inspired street wear shop knows her stuff—and she's also got great taste in women's lingerie and casual-but-sexy street clothes. The overstocked sales rack always offers 50% off exercise attire. Open Monday through Friday from 11am to 7pm, Saturday from 11am to 5pm, and Sunday from noon to 4pm.

TOYS

The Chinatown Kite Shop. 717 Grant Ave. (between Clay and Sacramento sts.). ☎ **415/989-5182.**

This shop's astonishing assortment of flying objects includes attractive fish kites, wind socks in nylon or cotton, hand-painted Chinese paper kites, wood-and-paper biplanes, pentagonal kites, and do-it-yourself kite kits, all of which make great souvenirs or decorations. Computer-designed stunt kites have two or four control lines to manipulate loops and dives. Open daily from 10am to 9pm.

F.A.O. Schwarz. 48 Stockton St. (at O'Farrell St.). ☎ **415/394-8700.**

The world's greatest toy store for both children and adults is filled with every imaginable plaything, from hand-carved, custom-painted carousel rocking horses, dolls, and stuffed animals, to gas-powered cars, train sets, and hobby supplies. At the entrance is a singing 22-foot clock tower with 1,000 different moving parts. Open Monday through Friday 10am to 6pm and on Sunday from 11am to 6pm.

TRAVEL GOODS

On the Road Again. Embarcadero and Beach St. (in Pier 39). ☎ **415/434-0106.**

In addition to lightweight luggage, this smart shop sells toiletry kits, travel bottles, travel-size items, and a good selection of other related goods. Open daily from 10am to 8:30pm; hours vary seasonally.

Thomas Bros. Maps & Books. 550 Jackson St. (at Columbus Ave.). ☎ **415/981-7520** or 800/969-3072.

The best map shop in the city, Thomas Bros. sells street, topographic, and hiking maps depicting San Francisco, California, and the world. A selection of travel-related books is also sold. Open Monday through Friday from 9:30am to 5:30pm.

VINTAGE CLOTHING

Aardvark's. 1501 Haight St. (at Ashbury St.). ☎ **415/621-3141.**

One of San Francisco's largest second-hand clothing dealers, Aardvark's has seemingly endless racks of shirts, pants, dresses, skirts, and hats from the last 30 years. Open daily from 11am to 7pm.

Buffalo Exchange. 1555 Haight St. (between Clayton and Ashbury sts.). ☎ **415/431-7733.**

This large storefront on upper Haight Street is crammed with racks of antique and new fashions from the 1960s, 1970s, and 1990s. It stocks everything from suits and dresses to neckties, hats, handbags, and jewelry. Buffalo Exchange anticipates some of the hottest new street fashions. Open Monday through Saturday from 11am to 7pm, Sunday from noon to 6pm. A second shop is located at 1800 Polk St. (at Washington Street) (☎ **415/346-5741**).

La Rosa. 1711 Haight St. (at Cole). ☎ **415/668-3744.**

On a street packed with vintage clothing shops, this is one of the more upscale options, featuring a selection of high-quality, dry-cleaned second-hand goods. Formal suits and dresses are its specialty, but you'll also find sport coats, slacks, and shoes. You may also want to visit its more moderately priced sister store, **Held Over,** on Haight near Ashbury. Open Monday through Saturday from 11am to 7pm, and Sunday from noon to 6pm.

Wasteland. 1660 Haight St. (at Belvedere St.). ☎ **415/863-3150.**

The enormous art-filled exterior fronts a large collection of vintage and contemporary clothes for men and women. Leathers, natural fibers, and dark colors predominate. Grandma's furniture is also for sale. Open daily from 11am to 7pm.

WINES

Wine Club San Francisco. 953 Harrison St. (between Fifth and Sixth sts.). ☎ **415/512-9086.**

The Wine Club is a discount warehouse that offers bargain prices on more than 1,200 domestic and foreign wines. Bottles cost from $3.99 to $1,100. Open Monday through Saturday from 9am to 7pm, and Sunday 11am to 6pm.

San Francisco After Dark

For a city with fewer than a million inhabitants, San Francisco's overall artistic enterprise is nothing short of phenomenal. The city's opera is justifiably world renowned, the ballet is well respected, and the theaters are high in both quantity and quality. Dozens of piano bars and top-notch lounges are augmented by one of the best dance-club cultures this side of New York, and skyscraper lounges offer some of the most dazzling city views in the world. In short, there's always *something* going on in The City, so get off your fanny and get out there.

For up-to-date nightlife information, turn to the *San Francisco Weekly* and the *San Francisco Bay Guardian,* both of which contain comprehensive current listings. They are available free at bars and restaurants, and from street-corner boxes all around the city. *Where,* a free tourist monthly, also has information on programs and performance times; it's available in most of the city's finer hotels. The Sunday edition of the *San Francisco Examiner and Chronicle* also features a "Datebook" section, printed on pink paper, with information and listings on the week's upcoming events.

TICKETS

Tix Bay Area (☎ 415/433-7827) sells half-price tickets to theater, dance, and music performances on the day of the show only; tickets for Sunday and Monday events, if available, are sold on Saturday. They also sell advance, full-price tickets for most performance halls, sporting events, concerts, and clubs. A service charge, ranging from $1 to $3, is levied on each ticket. Only cash or traveler's checks are accepted for half-price tickets; Visa and MasterCard are accepted for full-price tickets. Tix is located on Stockton Street, between Post and Geary streets on the east side of Union Square (opposite Maiden Lane). It's open Tuesday through Thursday from 11am to 6pm, Friday and Saturday from 11am to 7pm.

Tickets to most theater and dance events can also be obtained through **City Box Office,** 153 Kearny St., Suite 402 (☎ 415/392-4400). Visa, MasterCard, and American Express are accepted.

BASS Ticketmaster (☎ 510/762-2277) sells computer-generated tickets to concerts, sporting events, plays, and special events. Downtown BASS Ticketmaster ticketing offices include Tix Bay Area (see above) and at **Warehouse** stores throughout the city. The most convenient location is at 30 Powell St.

1 The Performing Arts

Special concerts and performances are staged in San Francisco year-round. **San Francisco Performances,** 500 Sutter St., Suite 710 (☎ **415/398-6449**), has been bringing acclaimed artists to the Bay Area for more than 15 years. Shows run the gamut from classical chamber music to dance and jazz. Performances are in several venues, including the city's Performing Arts Center and the Center for the Performing Arts at Yerba Buena Center. The season lasts from late September through May. Tickets cost $12 to $55, and are available through City Box Office (☎ **415/392-4400**). There is also a 6pm Thursday after-work concert series at the **EC Cabaret,** 3 Embarcadero Center, in fall and winter, $6 admission at the door (☎ **415/ 398-6449** for information).

CLASSICAL MUSIC

In addition to two world-class groups, described below, visitors might also be interested in the **San Francisco Contemporary Music Players** (☎ **415/252-6235**), whose concerts are held at the Center for the Arts at Yerba Buena Gardens; they play modern chamber works by international artists. Tickets, available by phone (☎ **415/ 978-ARTS**), cost $14 for adults, $10 for seniors, and $6 for students. Another commendable group is the **Women's Philharmonic** (☎ **415/543-2297**). For more than 15 years, this critically acclaimed orchestra has been playing works by historical and contemporary women composers. Most performances are held at the Center for the Arts at Yerba Buena Gardens. Phone for dates, programs, and ticket prices.

Philharmonia Baroque Orchestra. Performing in the Herbst Theatre, 401 Van Ness Ave. ☎ **415/392-4400** (box office). Tickets $23–$33.

Acclaimed by *The New York Times* as "the country's leading early music orchestra," Philharmonia Baroque performs in San Francisco and all around the Bay Area. The season lasts from September to April. The company's administrative offices can be reached at ☎ **415/391-5252.**

San Francisco Symphony. Performing at Davies Symphony Hall, 201 Van Ness Ave. (at Grove St.). ☎ **415/864-6000** (box office). Tickets $10–$68.

Founded in 1911, the internationally respected San Francisco Symphony has long been an important part of this city's cultural life under such legendary conductors as Pierre Monteux and Seiji Ozawa. In 1995, Michael Tilson Thomas took over from Herbert Blomstedt and has already led the orchestra to new heights and crafted an exciting repertoire of classical and modern music. The season runs from September to May. Summer symphony activities include a Composer Festival and a Summer Pops series.

OPERA

In addition to San Francisco's major opera company, you might also check out the amusing **Pocket Opera,** 333 Kearny St., Suite 703 (☎ **415/989-1855**). From mid-January through mid-June, this comic company stages farcical performances in English of well-known operas accompanied by a chamber orchestra. The staging is intimate and informal, without lavish costumes and sets. The cast ranges from three to 16 players, and is supported by a similar-size orchestra. The rich repertoire includes such works as *Don Giovanni* and *The Barber of Seville.* Performances are on Saturday or Sunday. Call for complete information and show times. Tickets cost $18 to $22.

Major Concert Halls & Auditoriums
Center for the Arts, Yerba Buena Gardens, Third Street (between Mission and Howard sts.), ☎ **415/978-ARTS (2787)**. **Cow Palace,** 2600 Geneva Ave. (at Santos Street), Daly City, ☎ **415/469-6065**. **Louise M. Davies Symphony Hall,** 201 Van Ness Ave. (at Grove Street), ☎ **415/864-6000**. **Great American Music Hall (GAMH),** 859 O'Farrell St. (between Polk and Larkin streets), ☎ **415/885-0750**. **Herbst Theatre,** 401 Van Ness Ave., ☎ **415/621-6600** (415/392-4400 for the box office). **War Memorial Opera House,** 301 Van Ness Ave. (at Grove Street), ☎ **415/864-3330**.

San Francisco Opera. Performing at the Civic Auditorium and Orpheum Theater (the Opera House is currently closed for renovation). ☎ **415/864-3330** (box office). Tickets $25–$140.

The San Francisco Opera was the United States's first municipal opera, and is one of the city's cultural icons. Brilliantly balanced casts may feature celebrated stars like Frederica Von Stade and Placido Domingo, along with promising newcomers and the regular members, in productions that range from traditional to avant-garde. All productions have English supertitles. The opera season starts in September and lasts just 14 weeks. Performances are held most evenings, except Monday, with matinees on Sundays. Tickets go on sale as early as August, and the best seats quickly sell out. Unless Pavarotti or Domingo is in town, some less-coveted seats are usually available until curtain time.

THEATER

After 11 successful years, **Climate,** 252 Ninth St., at Folsom Street (☎ **415/978-2345**), is still showcasing avant-garde and experimental works in a casual and intimate atmosphere. **Eureka Theatre Company,** 330 Townsend, Suite 210, at Fourth Street (☎ **415/243-9899**), produces contemporary and classical plays. The season runs from September to June, and performances are usually presented Wednesday through Sunday. Tickets cost $13 to $25, with discounts for students and seniors. **Theatre Rhinoceros,** 2926 16th St. (☎ **415/861-5079**), founded in 1977, was America's first (and still the foremost) theater ensemble devoted solely to works addressing gay and lesbian issues. The company presents five main stage shows and a dozen studio productions of new and classic works each year. The theater is located one block east of the 16th Street/Mission BART station.

American Conservatory Theater (A.C.T.). Performing at the Geary Theater, 415 Geary St. (at Mason St.). ☎ **415/749-2228**. Tickets $13–$45.

American Conservatory Theater (A.C.T.) made its debut in 1967 and quickly established itself as the city's premier resident theater group. The troupe is so venerated that A.C.T. has been compared to the superb British National Theatre, the Berliner Ensemble, and the Comédie Française. The A.C.T. season runs from October through June and features both classical and experimental works.

After six years on the road, A.C.T. has finally returned to its home, the fabulous Geary Theater (1910), a national historic landmark. The theater sustained severe damage in the 1989 earthquake and was closed for renovations, but has been fully refurbished and modernized to such an extent that it is now regarded as one of America's finest performance spaces.

Lorraine Hansberry Theatre. Performing at 620 Sutter St. ☎ **415/474-8800.**

San Francisco's top African American theater group performs in a 300-seat theater off the lobby of the Sheehan Hotel, near Mason Street. Special adaptations from literature are performed along with contemporary dramas, classics, and world premieres. Phone for dates, programs, and ticket prices.

The Magic Theatre. Performing at Building D, Fort Mason Center, Marina Blvd. (at Buchanan St.). ☎ **415/441-8822.** Tickets $15–$24. Discounts for students and seniors.

The highly acclaimed Magic Theatre continues to be a major West Coast company dedicated to presenting the works of new playwrights; over the years it has nurtured the talents of such luminaries as Sam Shepard and Jon Robin Baitz. Shepard's Pulitzer prize–winning play *Buried Child* premiered here. More recent productions have included works by Athol Fugard, Claire Chafee, and Nilo Cruz. The season usually runs from September to July; performances are offered Wednesday through Sunday.

DANCE

In addition to the local companies, top traveling troupes like the Joffrey Ballet and the American Ballet Theatre make regular appearances. Primary modern dance spaces include the **Theatre Artaud,** 450 Florida St., at 17th Street (☎ 415/621-7797); the **Cowell Theater,** at Fort Mason Center, Marina Boulevard, at Buchanan Street (☎ 415/441-3400); **Dancer's Group/Footwork,** 3221 22nd St., at Mission Street (☎ 415/824-5044); and the **New Performance Gallery,** 3153 17th St., at Shotwell in the Mission District (☎ 415/863-9834). Check the local papers for schedules or contact the theater box offices directly.

San Francisco Ballet. ☎ **415/865-2000** or 415/703-9400. Tickets and information. Tickets $10–$75.

Founded in 1933, the San Francisco Ballet is the oldest professional ballet company in the United States and regarded as one of the country's finest, performing an eclectic repertoire of full-length, neoclassical, and contemporary ballets. Even *The New York Times* proclaimed, "The San Francisco Ballet under Helgi Tomasson's leadership is one of the spectacular success stories of the arts in America." The 1996/1997 Repertory Season opens with 16 performances of San Francisco Ballet's Family Holiday Festival presented at the Palace of Fine Arts through December 1996. From February through June, several programs will be held at the Palace of Fine Arts and the Center for the Arts at Yerba Buena Gardens, and Zellerbach Hall in Berkeley. All performances are accompanied by the San Francisco Ballet Orchestra.

2 The Club & Music Scene

The greatest legacy from the 1960s is the city's continued tradition of live entertainment and music, which explains the great variety of clubs and music scenes available in a city of this size. The hippest dance places are located South of Market Street (SoMa), in former warehouses, while most popular cafe culture is still centered in North Beach.

CABARET & COMEDY

Bay Area Theatresports (BATS). Bayfront Theater at the Fort Mason Center, Bldg. B, 3rd Floor. ☎ **415/824-8220.** Tickets $8.

Combining improvisation with competition, Bay Area Theatresports (BATS) oper-ates an improvisational tournament, in which four-actor teams compete against each other, taking on improvisational challenges from the audience. Judges then flash scorecards good-naturedly, or honk a horn for scenes that just aren't working. Shows are staged on Mondays only. Phone for reservations.

Beach Blanket Babylon. At Club Fugazi, 678 Green St. (between Powell St. and Columbus Ave.). ☎ **415/421-4222.** Tickets $18–$45.

Now a San Francisco tradition, Beach Blanket Babylon evolved from Steve Silver's Rent-a-Freak service—a group of party-givers extraordinaire who hired themselves out as a "cast of characters" to entertain, complete with fabulous costumes and sets, props, and gags. After their act caught on, it was moved into the Savoy-Tivoli, a North Beach bar. By 1974, the audience had grown too large for the facility, and Beach Blanket has been at the 400-seat Club Fugazi ever since.

The show is a comedic musical send-up that is best known for its outrageous costumes and oversize headdresses. It's been playing almost 21 years now, and still almost every performance sells out. The show is updated often enough that locals still attend. Those under 21 are welcome at Sunday matinees at 3pm when no alcohol is served; photo ID is required for evening performances. It's wise to write for tickets at least three weeks in advance, or obtain them through Tix (see above). *Note:* When you purchase tickets, they will be within a specific section depending upon price; however, seating is still first-come/first-seated within that section. Per-formances are given on Wednesday and Thursday at 8pm, on Friday and Saturday at 7 and 10pm, and on Sunday at 3 and 7pm.

Cobb's Comedy Club. 2801 Leavenworth St. (at Hyde St.). ☎ **415/928-4320.** Cover $5 Mon, $8–$15 Tues–Sun (plus a two-beverage minimum nightly).

Located in the Cannery at Fisherman's Wharf, Cobb's features such national head-liners as George Wallace, Emo Philips, and Jake Johannsen. There is comedy every night, including a 14-comedian All-Pro Monday showcase (a three-hour marathon). Cobb's is open to those 18 and over, and occasionally to kids aged 16 and 17 if they are accompanied by a parent or legal guardian (call ahead first). Shows are Monday at 8pm, Tuesday through Thursday and Sunday at 9pm, and Friday and Saturday at 9 and 11pm.

Finocchio's. 506 Broadway (at Kearny St.). ☎ **415/982-9388.** Cover $12–15 (no drink minimum).

For more than 50 years this family-run cabaret club has showcased the best female impersonators in a funny, *kitschy* show. Three different revues are presented nightly (usually Thursday through Saturday at 8:30, 10, and 11:30pm), and a single cover is good for the entire evening. Drinks begin at $2.75. Parking available next door at the Flying Dutchman.

Punch Line. 444 Battery St., plaza level (between Washington and Clay sts.). ☎ **415/ 397-4337** or 415/397-7573 for recorded information. Cover $5 Sun, $6–$15 Mon–Sat (plus a two-drink minimum nightly).

Adjacent to the Embarcadero One office building, this is the largest comedy night-club in the city. Three-person shows with top national and local talent are featured Tuesday through Saturday. Showcase night is Sunday, when 15 to 20 rising stars take the mike. There's an all-star showcase or a special event on Monday nights. Buy tick-ets in advance (if you don't want to wait in line) from BASS outlets (☎ **510/ 762-2277**). Shows are Sunday through Thursday at 9pm, on Friday at 9 and 11pm, and on Saturday at 9 and 11pm. Drinks range from $2.75 to $12.

ROCK & BLUES CLUBS

In addition to the following listings, see "Dance Clubs," below, for (usually) live, danceable rock.

The Fillmore. 1805 Geary Blvd. (at Fillmore St.). ☎ **415/346-6000.** Tickets $16–$30.

Reopened after years of neglect, The Fillmore, made famous by promoter Bill Graham in the 1960s, is once again attracting big names. Check the local listings in magazines, or call the theater for information on upcoming events.

Grant & Green. 1371 Grant Ave. (at Green St.). ☎ **415/693-9565.** Cover $3 Fri–Sat.

The atmosphere at this North Beach dive rockery is not that special, but the local bands are pretty good. Look for daytime shows on the weekends.

The Saloon. 1232 Grant Ave. (at Vallejo St.). ☎ **415/989-7666.** Cover $3–$5 Fri–Sat.

An authentic gold rush survivor, this North Beach dive is the oldest extant bar in the city. Popular with both bikers and daytime pinstripers, there's live blues nightly. Drinks run $3 to $5.

Slim's. 333 11th St. (at Folsom St.). ☎ **415/522-0333.** Cover $10–$20 (plus a two-drink minimum).

New Orleans–style Slim's is co-owned by musician Boz Scaggs, who sometimes takes the stage under the name "Presidio Slim." This glitzy restaurant/bar seats 300, serves California cuisine, and specializes in excellent American music—home-grown rock, jazz, blues, and alternative music—almost nightly. Drink prices range from $2.25 to $7, with plates of food costing from $3 to $8.50.

JAZZ & LATIN CLUBS

Cesar's Latin Palace. 3140 Mission St. (at Army St.). ☎ **415/648-6611.** Cover $5–$8.

Live Latin bands perform to a very mixed crowd—ethnically, economically, and generationally. There's plenty of dancing and drinking in this high-energy club. Drinks cost from $1 to $5.

Jazz at Pearl's. 256 Columbus Ave. (at Broadway). ☎ **415/291-8255.** No cover, but there is a two-drink minimum.

This is one of the best venues for jazz in the city. Ribs and chicken are served with the sounds, too. The live jams last until 2am nightly. Drink prices range from $4 to $7.50, with plates of food costing $4 to $8.95.

Mason Street Wine Bar. 342 Mason St. (at Geary St.). ☎ **415/391-3454.** No cover, except for special performances.

Originally built as a bank, this building was later converted into a contemporary wine bar with dramatic wall art. It attracts a mixed crowd of office workers, locals, and tourists with nightly live jazz. Small cabaret tables with black club chairs face a small stage; the old bank safe is used as a private room and a wine storage area. More than 100 different wines are served from the half-moon–shaped bar. Glasses of wine begin at $4 each.

Rasselas. 2801 California St. (at Divisadero St.). ☎ **415/567-5010.** Cover free–$5.

Large, casual, and comfortable with couches and small tables, this is a favorite spot for hearing local jazz and R&B combos. The adjacent restaurant serves Ethiopian cuisine under an elegant Bedouin tent. Plates of food cost from $3 to $10.75, with drinks priced from $2 to $6.

CLUBS

Note that the club scene is always changing, often outdating recommendations before the ink can dry on a page. Most of the venues below are promoted as different clubs on various nights of the week, each with its own look, sound, and style. Discount passes and club announcements are often available at hip clothing stores and other shops along upper Haight Street.

Three Babes and a Bus (☎ 415/552-2582) runs regular nightclub trips on Friday and Saturday nights to the city's busiest clubs. See "Self-Guided and Organized Tours" in Chapter 7 for complete information.

Albion. 3139 16th St. (between Valencia and Guerrero sts.). ☎ **415/552-8558.** Cover $5.

This Mission District club is a gritty, leather, in-crowd place packed with artistic slummers and various SoMa hipsters. Drinks cost $1.75 to $12.

Caribbean Zone. 55 Natoma St. (between 1st and 2nd sts.). ☎ **415/541-9465.** Cover $3–$5.50.

Not just another restaurant bar, Caribbean Zone is a visual Disneyland, jam-packed with a cluttered, tropical decor that includes a full-size airplane fuselage. It's been around a little too long, but tourists seem to love it.

Club DV8. 540 Howard St. (between 1st and 2nd sts.). ☎ **415/777-1419** or 415/957-1730 for recorded information. Cover $5 Thurs, $10 Fri–Sat, $5 Sun (usually free before 10pm).

This SoMa club has been attracting the black-garb crowd longer than almost any other establishment. There are two DJs spinning music on separate dance floors, each perpetually packed with a lively 20-something crowd. The decor is an interesting mix of trompe l'oeil, pop art, candelabra, mirrors, and some extraordinary Daliesque props. Several quieter VIP lounges provide relief from the pounding.

Club 1015. 1015 Folsom St. (at 6th St.). ☎ **415/431-0700.** Cover $10–$15.

Get decked out and plan for a late-nighter if you're headed to this enormous party warehouse. Three levels and dance floors offer a variety of dancing venues, complete with a 20-something gyrating mass who live for the DJs' pounding house, disco, and acid jazz music. Each night is a different club that attracts its own crowd that ranges from yuppie to hip-hop. Currently, **Dakota** (☎ 415/431-1200) is held on Fridays from 10pm to 7am, featuring four different sounds: 1970s, progressive house, funk, and rare groove. Saturday is **Release,** a combo of 1970s funk and disco, deep house, and acid jazz (☎ 415/431-1200 for schedules). Drinks cost $2.75 to $8.

Nickie's Bar-be-cue. 468 Haight St. (between Fillmore and Webster sts.). ☎ **415/621-6508.** $2 cover.

Don't show up here for dinner. The only hot thing you'll find here is the small, crowded dance floor. But don't let that stop you from checking it out. Nickie's is a sure thing. Every time we go here, the old-school disco hits are in full-force, casually dressed happy dancers lose all inhibitions, and the crowd is mixed with all types of friendly San Franciscans. This place is perpetually hot, so dress accordingly. And you can always cool down with a pint from the wine-and-beer bar. Keep in mind, lower Haight is on the periphery of some shady housing projects, so don't make your rental car look tempting, and stay alert as you walk through the area.

181 Eddy. 181 Eddy St. (at Taylor St.). ☎ **415/673-8181.** Cover $5–$7.

Twenty-something and looking to gyrate the night away in a dark retro club crammed with glamorous hotties? Since this place is located on probably the absolute shadiest street in San Francisco, we thought that its popularity would die down once the limos stopped double-parking out front, but we were dead wrong. It may be true that the core hip crowd long abandoned this scene for newer and less-known parties, but that doesn't mean the place isn't jumping. With a combination of great ambience, decent food, and throw-down funk and acid jazz, 181 has made a niche for itself. Early evening there's live entertainment and later a DJ spinning slamming old-school. All night the pool room is packed with both players and voy-eurs who recline along terraced banquettes, smoke cigarettes, and look cool. In the front room, if you're not dancing, head to the bar or you're liable to get swept away in the sweaty groove. A decent dinner is served here too, and there's parking next door for $5. Dress code says no tennis shoes, torn Levi's, or baseball caps.

Oz. 335 Powell St., in the St. Francis Hotel, 32nd Floor (between Post and Geary sts.). ☎ **415/774-0116.** Cover $8 Sun–Thurs, $15 Fri–Sat.

Euro-chic DJs mix contemporary American dance music with the latest European sounds. Reached via glass elevator, Oz has a marble dance floor and good lighting, including mirrored columns with Tivoli lights that bounce to the beat. The interior attempts to mimic a forest glade, complete with birch trees, ferns, and rockery, but in actuality it looks more like the Flintstones on acid. The Oz's best draw are the large windows offering fantastic views of the city. Drinks cost from $5.50 to $9.

Paradise Lounge. 1501 Folsom St. (at 11th St.). ☎ **415/861-6906.** Cover $3–$15.

Labyrinthine Paradise features three dance floors simultaneously vibrating to differ-ent beats. Smaller, auxiliary spaces include a pool room with a half dozen tables. Poetry readings are also given. Drinks cost from $3.50.

Sound Factory. 525 Harrison St. (at 1st St.). ☎ **415/543-1300.** Cover $10 (free before 10pm).

Herb Caen, who dubbed this the "mother of all discos," would never be found shak-ing it all night at this disco theme park. The maze of rooms and nonstop barrage of house, funk, lounge vibes, and club classics attracts swarms of young urbanites look-ing to rave it up until sometimes as late as 6am. Management tries to eliminate the riffraff by enforcing a dress code (no sneakers, hooded sweatshirts, or sports caps).

330 Ritch. 330 Ritch (between Third and Fourth sts. off Townsend). ☎ **415/541-9574.** Cover $3–$10.

If you can find the place, you must be cool. It's located on a two-block alley in SoMa, and even locals have a hard time remembering how to get there. But once you do, expect happy hour cocktails (specials on a few select mixed drinks and draft brews), pool tables, and a hip, young crowd at play. Weekends, the place really livens up when bands take center stage on Fridays, and the Latin lovers salsa all night to the spicy beat.

3 The Bar Scene

Finding your idea of a comfortable bar has a lot to do with picking a neighborhood filled with your kind of people and investigating that area. There are hundreds of bars throughout San Francisco, and although many are obscurely located and can't be clas-sified by their neighborhood, the following is a general description of what you'll find and where.

- Chestnut and Union Street bars attract a postcollegiate crowd.
- Mission District haunts are frequented by young alternatives.

- Upper Haight caters to eclectic neighborhood cocktailers.
- Lower-Haight is skate/snowboarder grungy.
- Downtown pubs mix tourists with theater-goers and thirsty business people.
- North Beach serves all types.
- Castro caters to gay locals and tourists.
- South of Market (SoMa) offers an eclectic mix.

The following is a list of a few of San Francisco's more interesting bars.

Albion. 3139 16th St. (between Valencia and Guerrero sts.). ☎ **415/552-8558.**

This Mission District club is a grit-and-leather in-crowd place packed with artistic types and various SoMa hipsters. Live music plays Sunday between 5 and 8pm and ranges from ragtime and blues to jazz and swing. Drinks cost $1.75 to $6.

Chalkers Billiards Club. 101 Spear St. (at Mission St.). ☎ **415/512-0450.**

Poolhall meets mens' smoking club at this enormous, classy billiards joint. Food and drinks are delivered to the 31 cherry-wood tables that you can rent by the hour. Happy hour on weekdays from 5–7pm offers more beer for your buck. Otherwise drinks cost from $2.50 to $6 each.

Edinburgh Castle. 950 Geary St. (between Polk and Larkin sts.). ☎ **415/885-4074.**

Since 1958 this legendary Scottish pub has been known for unusual British ales on tap and the best selection of single-malt scotches in the city. The huge pub, located near Polk Street, is decorated with Royal Air Force mementos, horse brasses, steel helmets, and an authentic Ballantine caber used in the annual Scottish games. You might want to avoid Saturday nights, when live bagpipers supplement the jukebox. Fish and chips and other traditional foods are available until 11pm. Drinks cost $3 to $5.

The Great Entertainer. 975 Bryant (at 8th St.). ☎ **415/861-8833.**

This is a glorified pool hall with 42 pool tables, plus five private billiard suites, snooker, shuffleboard, darts, table tennis, and a video arcade. Drinks, pizza, and other dishes accompany the games. Drinks cost from $2.50 to $5.50, with plates of food going for $2 to $18.

Harry Denton's. 161 Steuart St. (between Mission and Howard sts.). ☎ **415/882-1333.** Cover charge after 9pm: $3 Wed; $5 Thurs; $10 Fri–Sat (free other times).

Early evening it's filled with working "suits" and secretaries on the prowl. But weekend nights reflect the restaurant owner, Harry Denton, who, although now sober, is known for getting himself and his guests intoxicated and dancing on tables and being the all-around wildest party host in town. When the stately restaurant with mahogany bar, red velvet furnishings, and chandeliers clears away dining utensils and turns up the music, a glitzy crowd pulls up to the valet with their boogie shoes on. In the front lounge R&B or jazz performers usually play loud enough to drown out the disco and pop dancing in the back room. But that's where all the action is, so head back there and join the 30- and 40-something yuppie masses flailing to 1970s disco hits. Eat dinner at neighboring Boulevard first—the food here is not memorable. Drinks range from $3 to $9.

Johnny Love's. 1500 Broadway. ☎ **415/931-6053.** Cover Fri–Sat $9, $5 Wed–Thurs. Free before 9pm.

Named after the friendly owner-cum-house bartender who woos flocks of women with a canned line, boyish grin, and a kiss, Johnny Love's is the city's quintessential singles spot and one of the best bars in town to dance to live music. The crowd here is definitely out for a good time, so the scene is festive (while most bar atmospheres around town are too posed to really get down). This place is mainly a bar and restaurant, so be prepared to bump elbows with your neighbors on the small dance floor. Love's serves food, too, but there are better dining options within a few blocks. Your money is best spent on drinks, which cost $3 to $5.75.

Julie's Supper Club. 1123 Folsom St. (at 7th St.). ☎ **415/861-0707.** Cover starts at 9pm, $5 Fri–Sat (unless a full meal is ordered).

Julie's is a long-time standby for cocktailing and late-dining. Divided into two rooms, the vibe is very 1950s cartoon, with a space-aged Jetsons appeal. Good-looking singles prowl, cocktails in hand, as live music plays by the front door. The food is hit-and-miss, but the atmosphere is definitely a casual and playful winner with a little interesting history; this building is one location where the Symbionese Liberation Army held Patty Hearst hostage back in the 1970s. Plates of food range from $7.50 to $15, with drinks costing from $4 to $8.

Li Po Cocktail Lounge. 916 Grant Ave. (between Washington and Jackson sts.). ☎ **415/982-0072.**

A divey Chinese bar, Li Po is made special by a clutter of dusty Asian furnishings and mementos that include an unbelievably huge rice paper lantern hanging from the ceiling, and a glittery golden shrine to Buddha behind the bar. Drinks cost from $3.50.

Perry's. 1944 Union St. (at Laguna St.). ☎ **415/922-9022.**

If you read *Tales of the City,* you already know that this bar and restaurant has a colorful history as a pick-up place for Pacific Heights and Marina singles. Though the times are not as wild, locals still come to casually check out the happenings at the dark mahogany bar. A separate dining room offers breakfast, lunch, dinner, and brunch at candlelit tables. It's a good place for hamburgers, simple fish dishes, and pasta. Drinks run $3 to $7; plates of food range from $4.25 to $17.50.

Persian Aub Zam Zam. 1633 Haight St. (at Clayton St.). ☎ **415/861-2545.**

Step through the forbidding metal doors and you'll feel as if you're in *Casablanca.* And although it's full of character, regulars come here for the acerbic owner/bartender, Bruno, who kicks almost everyone else out. Order a Finlandia vodka martini and you'll be allowed to stay. Sit at the bar; the tables are "closed." Drinks cost from $3.50.

Pied Piper Bar. In the Sheraton Palace Hotel, 2 New Montgomery (at Market St.). ☎ **415/392-8600.**

The huge Pied Piper mural by Edwardian illustrator Maxfield Parrish steals the show at this historic mahogany bar, where high stakes were once won and lost on the roll of the dice. Drinks cost from $3.80.

The Savoy-Tivoli. 1434 Grant Ave. (at Green and Union sts.). ☎ **415/362-7023.**

Euro-trash (and wannabees) crowd the few pool tables and indoor and patio seating to smoke cigarettes and look cool at this popular, trendy bar. It's mostly tourists and newcomers who frequent here because posing gets tiring after a while, and there are far cooler bars in town. But a sidewalk-facing table in the heart of North Beach allows for great people-watching and the high-profile clientele does create an entertaining atmosphere. Take heed of the waitresses, who have been known to over-charge for drinks, which are *supposed* to range from $3.50 to $6.

BREWPUBS

Gordon-Biersch Brewery. 2 Harrison St. (on the Embarcadero). ☎ **415/243-8246.**

Gordon-Biersch Brewery is San Francisco's largest brew-restaurant, serving decent food and tasty brew. There are always several beers to choose from, ranging from light to dark. Plates of food cost from $3.50 to $17.50, with drinks ranging from $2.50 to $7.75. (See the review in Chapter 6, "Dining," for more information.)

San Francisco Brewing Company. 155 Columbus Ave. (at Pacific St.). ☎ **415/434-3344.**

Surprisingly low-key for an ale house, this cozy brewpub serves its brew along with burgers, fries, and the like. The bar is one of the city's few remaining old saloons, aglow with stained-glass windows, tile floors, skylit ceiling beveled glass, a mahogany bar, and a massive overhead fan running the full length of the bar—a bizarre contraption crafted from brass and palm fronds. The handmade copper brew kettle is visible from the street. There's music most evenings. Darts, chess, backgammon, cards, and dice are all available. Plates of food cost from $3.25 to $8, with drinks ranging from $2.50 to $4. The happy hour special, a buck a beer, runs daily from 4 to 6pm and midnight to 1am.

20 Tank Brewery. 316 11th St. (at Folsom St.). ☎ **415/255-9455.**

Right in the heart of SoMa's popular strip, this huge, come-as-you-are bar is known for serving good beer at fair prices. Pizzas, sandwiches, chilis, and assorted appetizers are also available. Plates of food cost from $1.95 to $12.95, with drinks ranging from $1 to $4.50. Live jazz is performed two nights a week. Other nights you can amuse yourself with darts, shuffleboard, and dice.

CAFES

If Europe hadn't already invented the cafe, San Francisco would have. City folks love to sit at a scenic site and sip strong coffee—and for every good cup of java brewed here, there's an equally robust and charming coffee house. See Chapter 6, "Dining," for additional listings.

Café Picaro. 3120 16th St. (between Valencia and Guerrero sts.). ☎ **415/431-4089.**

Café Picaro is an enormous, colorful, and affordable Mission District cafe that serves up espresso drinks and Spanish food. At night, tables fill up with the area's young, artistic types. Plates of food cost from $2 to $17.50, with drinks ranging from $2.75 to $18.

Caffè Greco. 423 Columbus Ave. (between Green and Vallejo sts.). ☎ **415/397-6261.**

Doing the North Beach thing is little more than hanging out in a sophisticated but relaxed atmosphere over a well-made cappuccino. You can do it here, and grab a bite, too. The affordable cafe fare includes beer, wine, a good selection of coffees, focaccia sandwiches, and desserts (try the gelato or house-made tiramisu).

Caffè Trieste. 601 Vallejo St. (at Grant Ave.). ☎ **415/392-6739.**

One of San Francisco's most beloved cafes is very down-home Italian, with only espresso drinks, pastries, and indoor and outdoor seating. Opera is always on the jukebox, unless its Saturday afternoon, when the family and their friends break out in operatic arias from 2 to 5pm. Drinks cost $1.95 to $3.75, except during performances when they're $3.50.

Spec's Adler Museum Café. 12 Saroyan Place (off Columbus Ave.). ☎ **415/421-4112.**

Specs's incognito locale on Saroyan Place, a tiny alley at 250 Columbus Ave., makes it less of a walk-in bar and more of a lively locals' hangout. Its funky decor—maritime flags that hang from the ceiling, exposed brick walls lined with posters, photos, and various oddities—gives it character that intrigues every visitor. A "museum," displayed under glass, contains memorabilia and items brought back by seamen who drop in between sails, and the clientele is funky enough to keep you preoccupied while you drink a beer. Beer and wine cost $2.50 to $3.50; mixed drinks $3 to $5.

Vesuvio. 255 Columbus Ave. (at Broadway). ☎ **415/362-3370.**

Situated across Jack Kerouac Alley from the famed City Lights Bookstore, this renowned literary beatnik hangout is not merely riding its historic coattails. The atmosphere is way cool, as are the people who frequent it. Bring a chess board, borrow a game there, or write in a notebook, but whatever you do, look brooding and intense. Popular with neighborhood writers, artists, songsters, and wannabes, Vesuvio is crowded with self-proclaimed philosophers, and everyone else ranging from longshoremen and cab drivers to business people. The convivial space is two stories of cocktail tables, complemented by a changing exhibition of local art and an ongoing slide show. In addition to drinks, Vesuvio features an espresso machine. Drinks cost from $2.50. No credit cards are accepted.

COCKTAILS WITH A VIEW

The Carnelian Room. 555 California St., in the Bank of America Building (between Kearny and Montgomery sts.). ☎ **415/433-7500.**

On the 52nd floor of the Bank of America building, the Carnelian Room offers uninterrupted views of the city. From a window-front table you feel as if you can reach out, pluck up the TransAmerica Pyramid, and stir your martini with it. In addition to cocktails, sunset dinners are served nightly, for about $45 per person. Jackets and ties are required for men. Drinks are $5 to $7. *Note:* The restaurant has the most extensive wine list in the city—1,275 selections to be exact.

Cityscape. Atop Hilton Tower I, 333 O'Farrell St. (at Mason St.), 46th Floor. ☎ **415/776-0215.**

When you sit under the glass roof and sip a drink here, it's as if you're sitting out under the stars and enjoying views of the bay. There's nightly dancing to a DJ's picks from 8pm. The rich gold and blue carpeting, mirrored columns, and floor-to-ceiling draperies are both elegant and romantic. Drinks average $6.

Crown Room. In the Fairmont Hotel, 950 Mason St., 24th Floor. ☎ **415/772-5131.**

Of all the bars listed here, the Crown Room is definitely the plushest. Reached by an external glass elevator, the panoramic view from the top will encourage you to linger. In addition to drinks, dinner buffets are served for $31. Drinks cost $4 to $6.

Equinox. In the Hyatt Regency Hotel, 5 Embarcadero Center. ☎ **415/788-1234.**

The sales "hook" of the Hyatt's rooftop Equinox is a revolving floor that gives each table a 360° panoramic view of the city every 45 minutes. In addition to cocktails, lunch and dinner are served daily. Drinks run $4 to $6.

Harry Denton's Starlight Room. Atop the Sir Francis Drake Hotel, 450 Powell St., 21st Floor. ☎ **415/395-8595.**

Come dressed to the nines or in casual attire to this old-fashioned cocktail lounge-cum-nightclub where tourists and locals sip cocktails at sunset and boogie down to live swing and big-band tunes after dark. The room is classic 1930s San Francisco, with red-velvet banquettes, chandeliers, and fabulous views. But what really attracts flocks of all ages is a night of Harry Denton–style fun, which usually includes plenty of drinking and unrestrained dancing. The full bar stocks a decent collection of single-malt scotches and champagnes, and you can snack from the pricey Starlight appetizer menu. Like Harry's SoMa dance club, early evening is more relaxed, but come the weekend, this place gets loose. Drinks run $4 to $26.

Top of the Mark. In the Mark Hopkins Intercontinental, 1 Nob Hill (California and Mason sts.). ☎ **415/392-3434.**

This is one of the most famous cocktail lounges in the world. During World War II, it was considered de rigueur for Pacific-bound servicemen to toast their good-bye to the States here. The spectacular glass-walled room features an unparalleled view. Live entertainment is offered Wednesday through Saturday nights, but there is a $4 cover charge these nights, too. Sunday brunch, served from 10am to 2pm, costs about $32. Drinks cost $6 to $8.

PIANO BARS

San Francisco is lucky to have several lively piano bars. As in other cities, these specialized lounges are perfectly suited to the grand hotels in which they are usually located.

The Lower Bar. In the Mark Hopkins Intercontinental, 1 Nob Hill (California and Mason sts.). ☎ **415/392-3434.**

Drinks are served nightly in a delightfully intimate, skylit room with hand-painted murals. It's located just off the lobby. Drinks run $5 to $8.

The Piazza Lounge. In the Parc Fifty-Five Hotel, 55 Cyril Magnin St. (Market and North Fifth sts.). ☎ **415/392-8000.**

Sink into a handsome velvet chair, gaze out into the three-story atrium, and relax to a mix of old and new melodies played on an ebony grand piano. Drinks cost $5 to $6.

The Redwood Room. In the Clift Hotel, 495 Geary St. ☎ **415/775-4700.**

A true art deco beauty, this ground-floor lounge is one of San Francisco's most comfortable and nostalgic piano bars. Its gorgeous redwood interior was completely built from a single 2,000-year-old tree. It's further enhanced by the large, brilliantly colored Gustav Klimt murals. Drinks go for $6 to $7.

4 Gay and Lesbian Bars & Clubs

As with straight establishments, gay and lesbian bars and clubs target varied clienteles. Whether you're into leather or Lycra, business or bondage, there's gay nightlife here just for you.

Check the free weeklies, the ***San Francisco Bay Guardian*** and ***San Francisco Weekly,*** for listings of events and happenings. The ***Bay Area Reporter*** is a gay paper with comprehensive listings, including a weekly community calendar. All the above papers are free, and are distributed weekly on Wednesday or Thursday. They can be found stacked at the corner of 18th and Castro streets, and 9th and Harrison streets, as well as in bars, book shops, and stores around town. There are also a number of gay and lesbian guides to San Francisco. See the Gay and Lesbian section in Chapter 2, "Planning a Trip to San Francisco," for further details.

Listed below are some of the city's more established, mainstream gay hangouts.

Alta Plaza. 2301 Fillmore St. (at Clay St.). ☎ **415/922-1444.** No cover.

Pacific Heights's wealthy gays flock to this classy Fillmore establishment, with both bar and restaurant. Cocktail hour, from 4 to 7pm nightly, offers $2.50 well and call drinks and is especially festive on Friday and Saturday. Later in the evening, the restaurant fills with yuppie diners who come for the Northern California cuisine with Pacific Rim and Italian influences or to hang at the bar area and check out the hotties.

Badlands. 4121 18th St. (at Castro St.). ☎ **415/626-9320.** No cover.

This popular hangout is decorated with license plates from practically everywhere, even southern states perceived to be homophobic. Neon throws a stream of multi-colored light on Levi's-clad patrons, some in sizes too small. Drinks run from $1.75 to $4.50.

Castro Station. 456 Castro St. (between 17th and 18th sts.). ☎ **415/626-7220.** No cover.

A well-known gay hangout in the Castro District, this bar is popular with the leather and Levi's crowd, as well as trendy boys from around the country who come here looking for action. Drinks range from $1.75 to $4, except for during "Beer Bust," when it's $6 for all the suds you can drink.

The Cinch Saloon. 1723 Polk St. (near Washington St.). ☎ **415/776-4162.** No cover.

Among the popular attributes of this cruisy neighborhood bar are the outdoor patio, Sunday barbecue or buffet, and progressive music and videos. Forty-niner fans also gather here for televised games. Decorated in a southwestern theme ("down home in Arizona"), the bar attracts a mixed crowd of gays, lesbians (now that there are almost no exclusively lesbian bars left in San Francisco), and gay-friendly straight folk. There are "beer busts" or theme drink-nights weekly. The nominal charge for barbecues and buffets is donated entirely to various AIDS organizations. Drinks cost from $2 to $8.

Detour. 2348 Market St. (near Castro St.). ☎ **415/861-6053.** No cover.

Right in the heart of gay San Francisco, this bar attracts a young, often hot crowd of boys, with its low lighting and throbbing house music. Chain-link fences seem to hold in the action, while a live DJ spins a web of popular hits. Special events, including the Saturday go-go dancers, keep this place jumping. Drinks range in price from $2 to $6.

The Eagle. 398 12th St. (at Harrison St.). ☎ **415/626-0880.**

One of the city's most traditional leather bars, the Eagle boasts a heated outdoor patio and a popular Sunday afternoon beer fest. Drinks cost from $2.75 to $7.50. There's an $8 donation at the beer bust on Sunday, which goes to benefit local AIDS and other organizations.

The End Up. 401 6th St. (at Harrison St.). ☎ **415/543-7700.** Cover varies.

It's a different nightclub every night of the week, but regardless of who's throwing the party, the place is always jumping with the DJ's blasting tunes. There are two pool tables, a flaming fireplace, outdoor patio, and a mob of gyrating souls on the dance floor. Some nights are straight, so call for gay nights.

Giraffe Lounge. 1131 Polk St. (near Sutter St.). ☎ **415/474-1702.** No cover.

Favored by a younger, action-seeking crowd, this video bar, with its 12 ceiling-mounted monitors, is a good place for cruising or shooting pool. It's a friendly neighborhood hang-out during the week and livens up on weekend. Drinks cost from $2.50 to $5.

Kimo's. 1351 Polk St. (at Pine St.). ☎ **415/885-4535.** No cover.

This neighborhood bar located in the seedier gay section of town is a friendly oasis, decorated with plants, pictures, and "gay banners." The bar provides a relaxing venue for chatting, drinking, and quiet cruising, and things occasionally liven up when drag shows preside. Drinks are $2.50 to $4.

Lonestar. 1354 Harrison St. (between 9th and 10th sts.). ☎ **415/863-9999.** No cover.

Expect dykes and a heavier, furrier motorcycle crowd (both men and women) most every night. The Sunday afternoon beer bust on the patio is especially popular.

Metro. 3600 16th St. (at Market St.). ☎ **415/703-9750.** No cover.

With modern art on the walls and much use of terra-cotta, the Metro provides the gay community with high-energy dance music and the best view of the Castro District from its large balcony. The bar seems to attract people of all ages who enjoy the friendly bartenders and the highly charged, cruising atmosphere. Drinks range from $1.75 to $5. There's also a Chinese restaurant on the premises if you get hungry.

The Mint. 1942 Market St. (at Laguna St.). ☎ **415/626-4726.** No cover.

Come out of the closet *and* the shower and into The Mint, where every night you can sing show tunes at this gay and lesbian karaoke bar. Along with song, you'll encounter a mixed 20- to 40-something crowd who like to combine cocktails with do-it-yourself cabaret.

Nightshift. 469 Castro St. (between 17th and 18th sts.). ☎ **415/626-5876.** No cover.

Deep in the heart of the Castro District, young men and their pursuers show up here, enjoying the low lighting, the cruising atmosphere, and even the occasional exhibition of a local artist's work. The age group ranges from the early 20s to the 50s, and it's a convivial place with sometimes exciting shows. For would-be Jeff Strykers, "The Battle of the Bulge" (a jockey underwear contest) takes place on the second Sunday of the month. Drinks cost from $1 to $5.

Phoenix. 484 Castro St. (at 18th St.). ☎ **415/552-6827.** Cover $1 on Friday and Saturday between 10pm and 1am.

By night, this is an industrial-looking dance club frequented by Latin lovers, with an occasional off-duty police officer stopping in to wet his whistle. However, during the day, it's almost a neighborhood Archie's Bar. Drinks range in price from $1.50 to $5.50. There's disco dancing.

Rawhide II. 280 Seventh St. (at Folsom St.). ☎ **415/621-1197.** Weekend cover charge includes two free drinks.

Gay or straight, this is one of the city's top country-western dance bars, patronized by both men and women. Free dance lessons are offered Monday through Friday from 7:30 to 9:30pm. Drinks range from $2.50 to $5.

The Stud. 399 Ninth St. (at Harrison St.). ☎ **415/863-6623.** Cover $2–$6 weekends.

The Stud has been around for 30 years, is one of the most successful gay establishments in town, and is mellow enough for straights as well as gays. The interior has an antique shop look and a miniature train circling over the bar and dance floor. Music here is a balanced mix of old and new, retro-disco for boys on Wednesdays and women's nights on Thursdays and Saturdays. Drink prices range from $1.25 to $5.75.

The Swallow. 1750 Polk St. (between Clay and Washington sts.). ☎ **415/775-4152.** No cover.

Some consider this classy piano bar for the middle-age and up crowd the best gay bar on Polk.

Twin Peaks Tavern. 401 Castro St. (at 17th and Market sts.). ☎ **415/864-9470.** No cover.

Right at the intersection of Castro, 17th, and Market streets is one of the Castro's most famous gay hangouts, which caters to an older crowd and is considered the first gay bar in America. Because of its relatively small size and desirable location, the place becomes fairly crowded and convivial by 8pm, earlier than many neighboring bars. Drinks run from $2 to $5.

5 Film

The **San Francisco International Film Festival,** held in March of each year, is one of America's oldest film festivals. Tickets are relatively inexpensive. Entries include new films by beginning and established directors. For a schedule or information, call **415/931-FILM.** Tickets can be charged by phone through BASS Ticketmaster (☎ **510/835-3849**).

Even if you're not here in time for the festival, don't despair. The classic, independent, and mainstream cinemas in San Francisco are every bit as good as the city's other cultural offerings.

REPERTORY CINEMAS

Castro. 429 Castro St. (near Market St.). ☎ **415/621-6120.**

One of the largest and funkiest theaters in the city, the Castro is known for its screenings of classics and for its Würlitzer organ, which is played before each show. There's a different feature here almost nightly, and more often than not it's a double feature. Bargain matinees are usually offered on Wednesday, Saturday, Sunday, and holidays. Phone for schedules, prices, and show times.

Red Vic. 1727 Haight St. (between Cole and Shrader sts.). ☎ **415/668-3994.**

The worker-owned Red Vic movie collective recently moved from the Victorian building that gave it its name. The theater specializes in independent releases and contemporary cultish hits. Prices are $5.50 for adults, $3 for seniors 65 and over, kids 12 and under. Phone for schedules and show times.

Roxie. 3117 16th St. (at Valencia St.). ☎ **415/863-1087.**

The Roxie consistently screens the best new alternative films anywhere. The low-budget contemporary features shown here are largely devoid of Hollywood candy coating; many are West Coast premieres. Films change weekly, sometimes sooner. Phone for schedules, prices, and show times.

Easy Excursions from San Francisco

11

The Bay City is, without question, captivating, but don't let it ensnare you to the point of ignoring its environs. They contain a multitude of natural spectacles like Mount Tamalpais and Muir Woods; scenic communities like Tiburon and Sausalito; and cities like gritty Oakland and its youth-oriented next-door neighbor, Berkeley. A little farther north stretch the valleys of Napa, Sonoma, and Alexander, the finest wine region in the nation.

From San Francisco you can reach any of these points in a few hours or less by car or public transport.

Tower Tours, 77 Jefferson St. (☎ **415/434-8687**), operates regularly scheduled tours by micro bus to San Francisco's neighboring towns and countryside. Half- and full-day trips visit Muir Woods, Sausalito, Napa, and Sonoma. Other excursions trek to Yosemite as well as to the Monterey Peninsula. Phone for price and departure information.

1 Oakland

10 miles E of San Francisco

Though it's less than a dozen miles from San Francisco, the city of Oakland is worlds apart from its sister city across the bay. Originally little more than a cluster of ranches and farms, Oakland's size and stature exploded practically overnight as the last mile of transcontinental railroad track was laid down. Major shipping ports soon followed, and to this day Oakland has retained its hold as one of the busiest industrial ports on the West Coast.

The price for all this economic success, however, is Oakland's lowbrow reputation for being a predominantly working-class city, forever in the shadow of San Francisco's chic spotlight. But with all its shortcomings and bad press, Oakland still manages to offer a few pleasant surprises up its sleeve for the handful of tourists who venture this way. Rent a sailboat on Lake Merritt, stroll along the waterfront, explore the fantastic Oakland Museum: They're all great reasons to hop the bay and spend a fog-free day exploring one of California's largest and most ethnically diversified cities.

ESSENTIALS

Bay Area Rapid Transit (BART) makes the trip from San Francisco to Oakland through one of the longest underwater transit tunnels in

The Bay Area

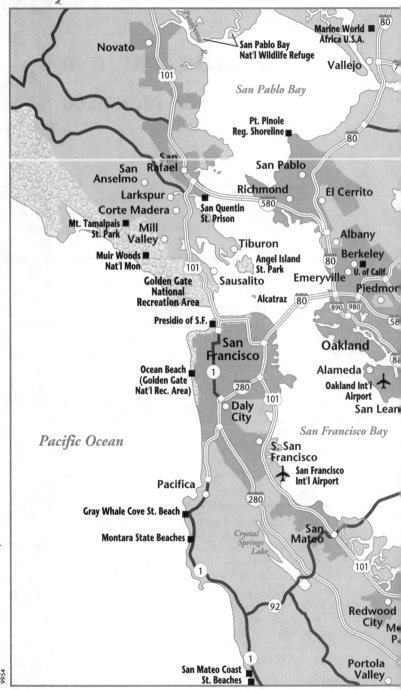

Novato

San Pablo Bay
Nat'l Wildlife Refuge

Marine World
Africa U.S.A.

Vallejo

San Pablo Bay

Pt. Pinole
Reg. Shoreline

San Pablo

Richmond

El Cerrito

San
Anselmo

San
Rafael

Larkspur

Corte Madera

San Quentin
St. Prison

Albany

Mt. Tamalpais
St. Park

Mill
Valley

Tiburon

Berkeley

Muir Woods
Nat'l Mon

Angel Island
St. Park

U. of Calif.

Golden Gate
National
Recreation Area

Sausalito

Emeryville

Piedmor

Alcatraz

Presidio of S.F.

San
Francisco

Oakland

Ocean Beach
(Golden Gate
Nat'l Rec. Area)

Alameda

Oakland Int'l
Airport

San Lean

Daly
City

Pacific Ocean

San Francisco Bay

S. San
Francisco

San Francisco
Int'l Airport

Pacifica

Gray Whale Cove St. Beach

Montara State Beaches

*Crystal
Springs
Lake*

San
Mateo

Redwood
City

92

San Mateo Coast
St. Beaches

Portola
Valley

9954

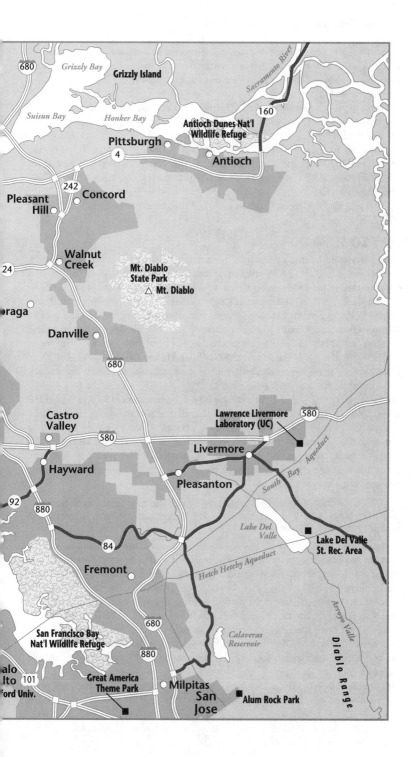

the world. Fares range from 80¢ to $3, depending on your station of origin; children four and under ride free. BART trains operate Monday through Saturday, from 6am to midnight, and on Sunday from 9am to midnight. Exit at the 12th Street station for downtown Oakland.

By car from San Francisco, take I-80 across the San Francisco-Oakland Bay Bridge and follow the signs to downtown Oakland. Exit at Grand Avenue South for the Lake Merritt area.

Downtown Oakland is bordered by Grand Avenue on the north, I-980 on the west, Inner Harbor on the south, and Lake Merritt on the east. Between these landmarks are three BART stations (12th Street, 19th Street, and Lake Merritt), City Hall, the Oakland Museum, Jack London Square, and several other sights.

For a recorded update on Oakland's arts and entertainment happenings, call **510/835-2787.**

WHAT TO SEE & DO

Lake Merritt is Oakland's primary tourist attraction along with Jack London Square (see below). Three and a half miles in circumference, the tidal lagoon was bridged and dammed in the 1860s and is now a wildlife refuge that is home to flocks of migrating ducks, herons, and geese. It's surrounded on three sides by the 122-acre **Lakeside Park,** a popular place to picnic, feed the ducks, and escape the fog. The *Merritt Queen,* a miniature Mississippi sternwheeler, plies the lake on Saturdays and Sundays from 11am to 3pm; each trip is half an hour and only costs $1.75 for adults and 75¢ for kids and seniors. At the **Sailboat House** (☎ 510/444-3807), in Lakeside Park along the north shore, you can rent sailboats, rowboats, pedal boats, and canoes for $6 to $12 per hour.

Another site worth visiting is Oakland's **Paramount Theatre** (☎ 510/893-2300), an outstanding example of art deco architecture and decor. Built in 1931 and authentically restored in 1973, it now functions as the city's main performing arts center. Guided tours of the 3,000-seat theater are given the first and third Saturdays of each month, excluding holidays. No reservations are necessary; just show up at 10am at the box office entrance on 21st Street at Broadway. Cameras are allowed, and admission is $1.

Jack London Square. Broadway and Embarcadero. Take I-880 to Broadway, turn south, and go to the end. BART: 12th St. station; then walk south along Broadway (about ¹/₂ mile) or take bus no. 51a to the foot of Broadway.

If you take pleasure from strolling sailboat-filled wharves or are a die-hard fan of Jack London, you might actually enjoy a visit to **Jack London Square.** Oakland's only patent tourist area, this low-key version of San Francisco's Fisherman's Wharf shamelessly plays up the fact that Jack London spent most of his youth along this waterfront. The square fronts the harbor, housing a tourist-tacky complex of boutiques and eateries that are about as far away from the "call of the wild" as you can get. Most are open from Monday through Saturday from 10am to 9pm (some restaurants stay open later). In the center of the square is a small reconstructed Yukon cabin in which Jack London lived while prospecting in the Klondike during the gold rush of 1897.

In the middle of Jack London Square you'll find a more authentic memorial, **Heinold's First and Last Chance Saloon**—a funky, friendly little bar and historic landmark that's actually worth a visit. This is where London did some of his writing and most of his drinking; the corner table he used has remained exactly as it was nearly a century ago. Also in the square are the mast and nameplate from the **U.S.S.**

Oakland, a ship that saw extensive action in the Pacific during World War II, and a wonderful museum filled with interesting London memorabilia.

Children's Fairyland. Lakeside Park, Grand Ave. and Bellevue Dr. ☎ **510/452-2259.** Admission $3 adults, $2.50 children 12 and under. Summer: Sat–Sun 10am–5:30pm, Mon–Fri 10am–4:30pm; Spring and Fall: Wed–Sun 10am–4:30pm; Winter: Fri–Sun and holidays 10am–4:30pm. From I-580 south, exit at Grand Ave.; Children's Fairyland is at the far end of the park, on your left at Bellevue Ave. BART: Exit at 19th St. and walk north along Broadway; turn right on Grand Ave. to the park.

Located on the north shore of Lake Merritt is one of the most imaginative children's parks in the United States, enough so to inspire Walt Disney to construct Disneyland. Kids can peer into old Geppetto's workshop, watch the Mad Hatter eternally pouring tea for Alice, see Noah's Ark overloaded with animal passengers, and view Beatrix Potter's village of storybook characters. Fairy tales also come alive during puppet show performances at 11am, 2pm, and 4pm.

Oakland Museum of California. 1000 Oak St. ☎ **510/238-3401.** Admission $5 adults, $3 students and seniors, free for children 6 and under; free for everyone Sun 4–7pm. Wed–Sat 10am–5pm, Sun noon–7pm. Closed Thanksgiving Day, Christmas Day, New Year's Day, and July 4. From I-880 north, take the Oak St. exit; the museum is 5 blocks east at Oak and 10th sts. Alternatively, take I-580 to I-980 and exit at the Jackson St. ramp. BART: Lake Merritt station (1 block south of the museum).

Located two blocks south of the lake, the Oakland Museum of California includes just about everything you'd want to know about the state, its people, history, culture, geology, art, environment, and ecology. Inside a low-swept, modern building set down among sweeping gardens and terraces, it's actually three museums in one: exhibitions of works by California artists from Bierstadt to Diebenkorn; collections of artifacts from California's history, from Pomo Indian basketry to Country Joe McDonald's guitar; and re-creations of California habitats from the coast to the White Mountains. The museum holds major shows of California artists, like the recent exhibit of the work of ceramic sculptor Peter Voulkos, or shows dedicated to major California movements, such as arts and crafts from 1890 to 1930. The museum also frequently shows photography from its huge collections.

There are 45-minute guided tours leaving the gallery information desks on request or by appointment. There is a fine cafe, a gallery (☎ **510/834-2296**) selling works by California artists, and a book and gift shop. The cafe is open Wednesday through Saturday from 10am to 4pm, and on Sunday from noon to 5pm.

WHERE TO DINE
EXPENSIVE

Oliveto Café & Restaurant. 5655 College Ave. (off the northeastern end of Broadway at Keith St., across from the Rockbridge BART station). ☎ **510/547-5356.** Reservations accepted. Main courses $17–$23. AE, DISC, MC, V. Mon–Fri 11:30am–2pm, 5:30–9:30pm, Sat 5:30–9:30pm, Sun 9:30am–2pm, 5:30–9:30pm. ITALIAN

Paul Bertolli, chef at the world-renowned Chez Panisse restaurant for the past 10 years, has jumped ship and opened one of the top Italian restaurants in the Bay Area and certainly the best in Oakland. During the week it's a madhouse at lunch, when BART commuters pile in for the wood-fired pizzas and tapas served at the lower corner cafe. The main dining room upstairs—suavely bedecked with neoindustrial decor and partial open kitchen—is slightly more civil, packed nightly with fans of Bertolli's house-made pastas, sausages, and prosciutto. Start with a warm pigeon salad with Picholine olive vinaigrette, followed by the agnolotti of veal—small, stuffed crescent-shaped pasta so fresh you can actually taste the flour. An assortment of pricey grills, braises, and roasts anchor the daily changing menu, but it's the reasonably priced pastas, pizzas, and tapas that offer the most tang for your buck.

MODERATE

Bay Wolf. 3853 Piedmont Ave. (off Broadway between 40th St. and MacArthur Blvd.). ☎ **510/655-6004.** Reservations accepted. Main courses $14–$18. MC, V. Mon–Fri 11:30am–2pm, 5:30–9pm, Sat–Sun 5:30–9pm. CALIFORNIA

The life span of most Bay Area restaurants is about one year; Bay Wolf, one of Oakland's most venerable and revered restaurants, has been going strong for nearly two decades. This converted brown Victorian is a comfortably familiar sight for most East Bay diners, who have been coming here for years to let chef/owner Michael Wilds do the cooking. Though the menu changes every few weeks, Wild's signature duck has earned tenure on the menu—the latest version was a Liberty Ranch quacker, grilled to perfection and served with duck sausage, French lentils, chard, and a tangy blood orange sauce. Simple yet sagacious preparations—peppered yellowtail, rabbit lasagna, grilled rib-eye—and generous portions are Bay Wolf's not-so-secrets for success, along with wonderful service and cozy patio seating on those deliciously warm summer nights that San Franciscans rarely experiences.

Citron. 5484 College Ave. (off the northeastern end of Broadway between Taft and Lawton sts.) ☎ **510/653-5484.** Reservations accepted. Main courses $12–$18. MC, V. Daily 5:30–9:30pm. FRENCH/MEDITERRANEAN

This petite, adorable French bistro was an instant smash when it first opened in 1992, and it continues to draw raves for its small yet enticingly eclectic menu. Chef Craig Thomas draws the flavors of France, Italy, and Spain together with fresh California produce for Chez Panisse-like results. Though the menu changes every few weeks, dishes range from grilled Colorado lamb sirloin with wild mushroom spoon bread and rosemary jus, to white bean and green garlic ravioli with stewed artichokes, spring tomatoes, and sage butter. The fresh salads and Citron "40 clove" chicken are also superb.

2 Berkeley

10 miles NE of San Francisco

Berkeley would be little more than a quaint, sleepy town east of the big city if it weren't for the University of California at Berkeley, which is world-renowned for its first-rate academic standards, 15 Nobel Prize winners (more than any other university), and protests that led to the most renowned student riots in U.S. history. Today, there's still hippie idealism in the air, but the radicals have aged; the sixties are only present in tie-dye and paraphernalia shops, and the students have less angst. Still, it's a charming town teeming with all types of people, a beautiful campus, vast parks, great shopping, and some incredible restaurants.

ESSENTIALS

The Berkeley **BART** station is two blocks from the university. The fare from San Francisco is under $3.

If you are coming **by car** from San Francisco, take the Bay Bridge, follow I-80 east to the University Avenue exit, and follow University until you hit the campus. Parking is tight near the campus, so either leave your car at the Sather Gate parking lot on Telegraph and Durant or expect to fight for a spot.

Berkeley

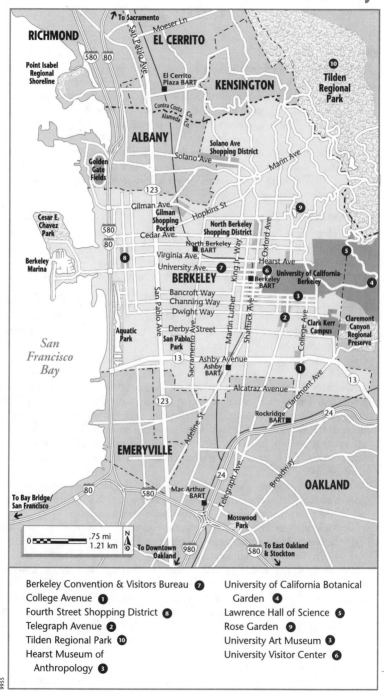

RICHMOND

To Sacramento

Moeser Ln

EL CERRITO

San Pablo Ave

580 80

Point Isabel
Regional
Shoreline

El Cerrito
Plaza BART

KENSINGTON

Contra Costa Co.
Alameda Co.

ALBANY

Solano Ave
Shopping District

Solano Ave.

Marin Ave.

Golden
Gate
Fields

123

Tilden
Regional
Park ⑩

Cesar E.
Chavez
Park

Gilman Ave.
Gilman
Shopping
Pocket

Hopkins St

⑨

580
80

Cedar Ave.

North Berkeley
Shopping District

Oxford Ave

Berkeley
Marina

⑧

Virginia Ave.

North Berkeley
BART

Hearst Ave

⑤

University Ave.

⑦

King Jr. Way

⑥

University of California-
Berkeley

④

BERKELEY

Berkeley
BART

③

San
Francisco
Bay

Bancroft Way
Channing Way
Dwight Way

Martin Luther

Shattuck Ave

②

Clark Kerr
Campus

College Ave

Claremont
Canyon
Regional
Preserve

Aquatic
Park

San Pablo Ave

Derby Street

Sacramento Ave.

San Pablo
Park

13

Ashby Avenue
Ashby
BART

①

Claremont Ave

13

Alcatraz Avenue

123

Adeline St

Rockridge
BART

24

EMERYVILLE

24

Telegraph Ave

Broadway

OAKLAND

To Bay Bridge/
San Francisco
←

80

580

Mac Arthur
BART

Mosswood
Park

0   .75 mi
1.21 km

N

To Downtown
Oakland

980

580

To East Oakland
& Stockton

Berkeley Convention & Visitors Bureau ⑦
College Avenue ①
Fourth Street Shopping District ⑧
Telegraph Avenue ②
Tilden Regional Park ⑩
Hearst Museum of
  Anthropology ③

University of California Botanical
  Garden ④
Lawrence Hall of Science ⑤
Rose Garden ⑨
University Art Museum ③
University Visitor Center ⑥

9955

Phone the **Visitor Hotline** (☎ **510/549-8710**) for automated information on events and happenings in Berkeley.

WHAT TO SEE & DO

Hanging out is the preferred Berkeley pastime, and the best place to do it is on **Telegraph Avenue,** the street that leads to the campus' southern entrance. Most of the action lies between Bancroft Way and Ashby Avenue, where coffeehouses, restaurants, shops, great book and record stores, and craft booths swarm with life. Pretend you're local: Plant yourself at a cafe, sip a latte, and ponder something intellectual or survey the town's unique residents bustling by.

Bibliophiles must stop at **Cody's Books** at 2454 Telegraph Ave., to peruse their gargantuan selection of titles, independent press books, and magazines. The avenue is also packed with street vendors selling everything from T-shirts and jewelry to I Ching and tarot-card readings.

UC BERKELEY CAMPUS

The **University of California at Berkeley** itself is worth a stroll as well. It's a beautiful old campus with plenty of woodsy paths, architecturally noteworthy buildings, and, of course, many of the 31,000 students scurrying to and from classes. Among the architectural highlights of the campus are a number of buildings by Bernard Maybeck, Bakewell and Brown, and John Galen Howard.

Contact the **Visitor Information Center** at 101 University Hall, 2200 University Ave. (at Oxford Street) (☎ **510/642-5215**), to join a free, regularly scheduled campus tour (Monday, Wednesday, and Friday at 10am and 1pm; no tours offered from mid-December to mid-January); or stop by the office and pick up a self-guided walking tour brochure.

You'll find the university's southern entrance at the northern end of Telegraph, at **Bancroft Way.** Walk through the main entrance into Sproul Plaza, and when school is in session you'll encounter the gamut of Berkeley's inhabitants here: colorful street people, rambling political zealots, chanting Hare Krishnas, and ambitious students. You'll also find the **Student Union,** complete with a bookstore, cafes, and an information desk on the second floor where you can pick up a free map of Berkeley, as well as the local student newspaper (also found in dispensers throughout campus).

You might be lucky enough to stumble upon some impromptu musicians or a heated, and sometimes absurd, debate. There's always something going on, so stretch out on the grass for a few minutes and take in the Berkeley vibe.

For viewing more traditional art forms, there are some noteworthy museums here, too. The **Hearst Museum of Anthropology** is open from 10am to 5pm on Wednesday, Friday, Saturday, and Sunday; 10 am to 9pm Thursday. Admission is $2 for adults, $1 for seniors, and 50¢ children under 16. Thursdays are free. The **Lawrence Hall of Science,** offering hands-on science exploration, is open from 10am to 5pm daily and is a wonderful place to watch the sunset. Admission is $6 for adults, $4 for seniors and children 7 to 18, $2 for children three to six. Finally, the **University Art Museum** is open from 11am to 5pm, on Wednesday and Friday through Sunday, Thursday from 11am to 9pm. Admission is $6 for adults, $4 for seniors and children 12 to 17. This museum includes a substantial collection of Hans Hofmann paintings, a sculpture garden, and the Pacific Film Archive.

If you're interested in notable off-campus buildings, contact the **Berkeley Convention and Visitors Bureau** (☎ **510/549-7040**) for an architectural walking tour brochure.

PARKS

Unbeknownst to many travelers, Berkeley has some of the most extensive and beautiful parks around. If you want to wear out the kids or enjoy hiking, swimming, or just getting a breath of California air and sniffing a few roses, jump in your car and make your way to **Tilden Park.** On the way, stop at the colorful terraced **Rose Garden,** located in north Berkeley on Euclid Avenue between Bay View and Eunice Street. Then head high into the Berkeley hills to **Tilden,** where you'll find plenty of flora and fauna, hiking trails, an old steam train and merry-go-round, farm and nature area for kids, and a chilly tree-encircled lake (☎ **510/843-2137** for further information).

Another worthy nature excursion is the **University of California Botanical Garden,** which features a vast collection of herbage ranging from cacti to redwoods (located in Strawberry Canyon on Centennial Drive) (☎ **510/642-3343** for details).

WHERE TO SHOP

If you're itching to exercise your credit cards, head to one of two places. **College Avenue** from Dwight all the way down to the Oakland border is crammed with eclectic boutiques, antique shops, and restaurants. The other option is **Fourth Street,** in west Berkeley just two blocks north of the University Avenue exit. This two-block expanse is the perfect place to go on a sunny morning. Grab a cup of java, read the paper at a patio table, and then hit the **Crate and Barrel Outlet** (where prices are up to 80% off retail) at 1785 Fourth St., between Hearst and Virginia (☎ **510/528-5500**), or any of the small, wonderful stores crammed with imported and locally made housewares. Nearby is **REI,** the Bay Area's favorite outdoor outfitters at 1338 San Pablo Ave., near Gilman Street (☎ **510/527-4140**).

You might also want to visit the factory of **Takara Sake USA,** at 708 Addison St.(☎ **510/540-8250**). Sho Chiku Bai sake, one of this country's most popular brands, is not Japanese; it's made here by America's largest sake maker. Unfortunately, there are no regularly scheduled tours of the plant, but you can learn about sake-making from a slide presentation and taste three different types of rice wine. The tasting room is open daily from noon to 6pm.

WHERE TO STAY

Bed and Breakfast California, P.O. Box 282910, San Francisco, CA 94128 (☎ **415/696-1690** or 800/872-4500; fax 415/696-1699), accommodates visitors in more than 150 private homes and apartments in the San Francisco–Berkeley area. The cost ranges from a reasonable $60 to $150 per night, and there's a two-night minimum. The **Berkeley Convention and Visitor's Bureau,** 1834 University Ave., 1st Floor, Berkeley, CA 94703 (☎ **800/847-4823** or 510/549-8710) is staffed Monday through Friday from 9am to 5pm and can also find accommodations for you, as well as provide free visitors' guides, maps, and area literature.

EXPENSIVE

Claremont Resort & Tennis Club. 41 Tunnel Rd. (at Ashby and Domingo aves.), Berkeley, CA 94705. ☎ **510/843-3000** or 800/551-7266. Fax 510/843-6239. 204 rms, 35 suites. A/C TV TEL. $190–$235 double; from $295 suites. A variety of packages are available, including a one-night package beginning at $159. Breakfast $9.50 extra. AE, DC, MC, V. Parking $8.

You don't have to drive all the way to Wine Country for a spa retreat. The Claremont, one of the most beautiful and elaborate mansions in the East Bay, will pamper you silly—and it's only a half hour drive from the city. Built in 1906 (completed after the earthquake), this majestic all-white Victorian mansion is more like a castle with an exterior so grand, it defines world-class luxury. The 22-acre estate clings to the Berkeley hillside, overlooks the distant San Francisco Bay, and is surrounded by lush, well-tended gardens and an eclectic collection of outdoor sculpture. Rooms, though individually decorated with old-fashioned stateliness, can't contend with their surroundings. Nonetheless, the reason to come here is not to hang out in your room, but rather to pamper yourself at the elaborate spa, which offers five different types of massage, body-care treatments (including a loofah scrub, mud and herbal wrap, aromabath, and Turkish scrub), and a variety of fitness facilities. There's an exercise room, aerobics, yoga, a weight room, two lap pools, and 10 tennis courts. The beauty salon offers a complete range of skin and beauty treatments.

The cuisine is not up to par with that of Sonoma Mission Inn, but does offer nutritionally balanced plates of seafood, salad, and pasta.

MODERATE

Hotel Durant. 2600 Durant Ave., Berkeley, CA 94704. ☎ **800/2-DURANT** or 510/845-8981. Fax 510/486-8336. 140 rms. TV, TEL. $101–$240 double. AAA, AARP, corporate, and government discounts. Continental breakfast included. AE, DC, DISC, MC, V. Parking $5.

Smack dab in the middle of collegiate action, this charming hotel is two blocks from campus and steps from Telegraph Avenue. However, once inside, you're not likely to hear the bellowing fraternity brothers who may be tossing a few back at Henry's, the popular downstairs bar and restaurant. You will, however, find a stately plush lobby that leads to basic, clean Victorian-accented accommodations. While the rooms are nothing special, the prime location and valet parking (only $5!) make this hotel a popular choice.

French Hotel. 1538 Shattuck Ave., Berkeley, CA 94709. ☎ **510/548-9930.** 18 rms. TV TEL. $68–$125 single or double. Government employee, university, and group rates available. Breakfast $4.50 extra. AE, CB, DC, MC, V. Free parking. From I-80 north, take the University Ave. exit and turn left onto Shattuck Ave.; the hotel is six blocks down on your left. BART: Berkeley.

This small hotel is in north Berkeley, the sleepier side of town, and is crawling distance from renowned restaurant **Chez Panisse** (see "Where to Dine," below). Guest rooms are light and airy, decorated in quiet rose, with maroon carpeting and floral-pattern throw cushions; all but three rooms have balconies. In lieu of a dresser, stacked sliding white baskets are provided for your personal things. No-smoking rooms are available.

The downstairs cafe, a casual meeting place with exposed brick walls and outdoor tables, serves espresso, pastries, and other light items—or for lazy folks, many items can be delivered to your room.

Gramma's Rose Garden Inn. 2740 Telegraph Ave., Berkeley, CA 94705. ☎ **510/549-2145.** Fax 510/549-1085. 40 rms, all nonsmoking. TV TEL. $99–$165 double. Rates include breakfast. AE, DC, MC, V. Free parking. Take I-80 north to the Ashby exit and turn left onto Telegraph Ave.; the hotel is located four blocks up. BART: Ashby.

Gramma's restored Tudor-style mansion includes a main house, carriage house, garden house, and the Fay house, with guest rooms furnished in period antiques, floral-print wallpapers, and patchwork quilts. Accommodations in the restored carriage house overlook a garden and have fireplaces and king-size beds.

Guests are served a complimentary breakfast in the downstairs dining room or on the deck overlooking the garden, as well as complimentary wine and cheese in the evening. There's also a bottomless cookie jar and fresh-brewed coffee for any spontaneous sweet tooth. Dinner is served in the Greenhouse Cafe.

INEXPENSIVE

Hillegass House. 2834 Hillegass Ave., Berkeley, CA 94705. ☎ **800/400-5517** or 510/548-5517. 4 rms. TEL. $85–$110 double. Rates include breakfast and sauna use. Extra person $20. AE, MC, V. Free parking.

Built in 1904, this house in a quiet residential neighborhood, a short walk from the university, is furnished with antiques. Guest rooms are outfitted with either king- or queen-size beds, private baths, and voice-mail telephones. There is a sauna on the property, and large, inclusive breakfast is served either indoors or out.

WHERE TO DINE

East Bay dining is a relaxed alternative to the city's gourmet night out—there are plenty of ambitious Berkeley restaurants worth foraging and, unlike San Francisco, plenty of parking.

If you want to do it student-style, eat on campus Monday through Friday. Buy something at any of the sidewalk stands or in the building directly behind the Student Union. The least expensive food is available downstairs in the **Cafeteria,** on Lower Sproul Plaza. There's also the **Bear's Lair Pub and Coffee House,** the **Deli,** the **Ice Creamery,** the **Terrace,** and the **Golden Bear Restaurant.** All the university eateries have both indoor and outdoor seating.

Telegraph Avenue has an array of small, ethnic restaurants, cafes, and sandwich shops. Follow the students: if the place is crowded, it's either good, super cheap, or both.

EXPENSIVE

Chez Panisse. 1517 Shattuck Ave. (between Cedar and Vine) ☎ **510/548-5525.** Fax 510/548-0140. Reservations essential for restaurant—accepted a month in advance; for cafe, accepted for lunch at 9am on the day, not accepted for dinner. Main courses $13–$18; fixed-price dinner $35–$65. AE, CB, DC, MC, V. Restaurant, dinner seatings Mon–Sat at 6–6:30, 8:30–9:15pm. Cafe, Mon–Thurs 11:30am–3pm and 5–10:30pm, Fri–Sat 11:30am–4pm and 5–11:30pm. From I-80 north, take the University exit and turn left onto Shattuck Ave. BART: Berkeley. CALIFORNIA.

California cuisine is so much a product of Waters's genius that all other restaurants following in her wake should be dated "AAW" (After Alice Waters). Read the menus posted outside and you'll understand why. Most of the produce and meat comes from local farms and is organically produced, and after all these years, Alice still attends to her restaurant with great integrity and innovation.

Alice's creations are served in a delightful redwood and stucco cottage with a brick terrace filled with flowering potted plants. There are two separate dining areas—the upstairs cafe and the downstairs restaurant, both offering a Mediterranean-inspired cuisine.

In the upstairs cafe there are displays of pastries and fruit, and large bouquets of fresh flowers adorning an oak bar. At lunch or dinner, a delicately smoked gravlax or a roasted eggplant soup with pesto, followed by lamb ragout garnished with apricots, onions, and spices served with couscous might be featured. Dinner reservations are not taken for the cafe, so there will be a wait, but it's worth it.

The cozy downstairs restaurant, strewn with blossoming floral bouquets, is an appropriately warm environment to indulge in the fixed-price four-course gourmet dinner, which is served Tuesday through Thursday. Friday and Saturday, it's four courses plus an aperitif, and Monday is bargain night with a three-course dinner for $35.

The menu, which changes daily, is posted outside the restaurant each Saturday for the following week. Meals are complemented by an excellent wine list ($20 to $200).

Lalime's. 1329 Gilman St. (between Neilson and Peralta). ☎ **510/527-9838.** Reservations recommended. Main courses $11–$17. MC, V. Mon–Thurs 5:30–9:30pm, Fri–Sat 5:30–10pm, Sun 5–9pm. CALIFORNIA/MEDITERRANEAN.

Banquettes, sponge-painted walls, and colorful art make this a cozy place to stretch out and enjoy a long, flavorful California meal. The menu changes daily but will always feature about a half-dozen fresh dishes and imaginative accompaniments. You might start with baked acorn squash stuffed with Tuscan bean ragout, served with braised fennel and a marinated green-bean salad, or fennel and artichoke salad with crostini topped with salt cod and potato grandade. They're especially known for cooking up darn good lamb—either rack or osso bucco and a savory juniper berry pork chop with french lentil and peppered Seckle pears. The fixed-price menu offers superb value and each course will be accompanied by a particular recommended wine for an extra $10 to $15. Deserts change frequently but may include the popular Saint Paul Dence walnut tart.

MODERATE

Ginger Island. 1820 Fourth St. (between Hearst and Delaware). ☎ **510/644-0444.** Reservations accepted. Main courses $7.50–$17.50. AE, DC, MC, V. Mon–Thurs 11:30am–10pm, Fri–Sat 11:30am–11pm. Sun 10:30am–10pm. CALIFORNIA/ASIAN/POLYNESIAN.

Transport yourself to the tropics at Ginger Island, where you'll dine on island favorites amidst palm trees and an abundance of vegetation. The menu, which changes daily, might offer among 10 or so main courses, including a grilled guava-glazed pork chop with coconut black beans and rum-baked plantains; a revered all-natural hamburger with potato, yam, and taro fries; ginger-roasted chicken with orange-saffron basmati rice; and a savory fresh fish dish.

O Chamé. 1830 Fourth St. (near Hearst). ☎ **510/841-8783.** Reservations necessary Fri–Sat. Main courses $7–$16.50. AE, DC, MC, V. Mon–Fri 11:30am–3pm; Mon–Thurs 5:30–9pm, Fri–Sat 5:30–9:30pm. JAPANESE.

Spare and plain in its decor, with ochre-colored walls marked with etched patterns, this spot has a meditative air to complement the traditional and experimental Japanese-inspired cuisine. The menu, which changes daily, offers meal-in-a bowl dishes (from $7 to $11) that allow a choice of soba or udon noodles in a clear soup with a variety of toppings—from shrimp and wakame seaweed to beef with burdock root and carrot; appetizers and salads, which include a flavorsome melding of grilled shiitake mushrooms and sweet peppers and portobello mushrooms, watercress, and green onion pancakes; a sashimi of the day; and specials that range in price from $10 to $16.50 and always include a delicious roasted salmon.

Rivoli. 1539 Solano. ☎ **510/526-2542.** Reservations recommended. Main courses $10.25–$15 ATM, MC, V. Mon–Thurs 5:30–9:30pm, Fri 5:30–10pm, Sat 5–10pm, Sun 5–9pm. CALIFORNIA.

This small restaurant is one of the favored dinner destinations in the East Bay. It's not the well-appointed atmosphere, floral art, or small garden with magnolias that keeps the locals coming back (though the atmosphere is good); it's the food. If available, start with the portobello mushroom fritters with lemon aioli and shaved Parmesan or the ahi tuna tartare with ginger vinaigrette. Next try the braised pork chile verde with tomatillos, cilantro, chipotle, sour cream, red onion salsa, and corn sticks; the grilled top sirloin with marsala jus, gorgonzola gnocchi, and sauteéed baby spinach; or the chicken breast with currants and red wine finished off with a saffron brioche stuffing. For a finish, opt for the blood-orange granita or the bittersweet chocolate and walnut tart with butterscotch sauce and espresso cream. *Bon appétit.*

INEXPENSIVE

Bette's Oceanview Diner. 1807A Fourth St. ☎ **510/644-3230.** Breakfast $5–7.50. Cash only. Mon–Thurs 6:30am–2:30pm; Fri–Sun 6:30am–4pm. AMERICAN.

Situated in the middle of Berkeley's blooming chi chi shopping area, Bette's may look like an old-style diner, but one glance at the menu and you'll know they've risen to match their surroundings. Sure there are pancakes, eggs, and all the breakfast basics on the menu, but Bette's leaves out the grease and substitutes it with advanced culinary style. Savor any of the fresh house-made morning buns or scones, and surge on with a delightful mound of an omelet filled with fresh ingredients such as roasted red bell pepper with herb cream cheese. Other specialties include soufflé pancakes (banana rum, apple brandy, fresh berry, and chocolate swirl) and grated-to-order potato pancakes.

Blakes. 2367 Telegraph Ave. ☎ **510/848-0886.** Main courses $5–$8. AE, DISC, MC, V. Restaurant daily 11am–10pm; bar daily 11am–2am. AMERICAN.

Known for consistently providing affordable, cheap entertainment, at night there's almost always someone playing music at Blakes, whether it's live or a DJ spinning funk. Three floors provide a variety of entertainment ranging from a pool table and dancing, to an unspectacular but cheap full-service restaurant and bar. The draw here is the music, affordable prices, and down-home atmosphere, not the food.

Blondie's Pizza. 2340 Telegraph Ave. ☎ **510/548-1129.** $7–$14 pizza; $1.50 slice with cheese. No credit cards. Mon–Thurs 10:30am–1am, Fri–Sat 10:30am–2am, Sun noon–midnight. PIZZA.

It may be a law that to live in Berkeley, you must eat at Blondie's. Or at least that's the impression you'll get when you see the swarms of students clamoring for slices. This is no quiet sit-down event, but the portions are big, heavy with toppings, and dirt-cheap. Besides, what's college without pizza?

Blue Nile. 2525 Telegraph Ave. ☎ **510/540-6777.** Reservations needed Fri–Sat. Main courses. $6.50–$7.45 MC, V. Mon–Sat 11:30am–10pm, Sun 5–10pm. ETHIOPIAN.

Step through the beaded curtains into the Blue Nile and the African paintings, and music will summon your appetite to other parts of the world. But the journey doesn't end there—be prepared to savor the flavorful specialties such as doro wat (a spiced stew of beef, lamb, or chicken, served with a fluffy crepe injera) or gomen wat (mustard greens sautéed in cream) with no utensils other than your fingers. Sure, you *could* convince the wait staff to drum up a fork or two, but don't bother. After all, when in Africa . . . . No appetizers are served, but meals come with a small salad.

Cafe Intermezzo. 2422 Telegraph Ave. ☎ **510/849-4592.** Most items $3.25–$5.65. No credit cards. Daily 10:30am–10:30pm. SOUPS/SANDWICHES.

Pay no heed to the line out the door. Counter persons whip up orders with such fervor, you'll be happily munching in five to 10 minutes on what I consider the best and most enormous salads in the Bay Area. The dressings aren't any fancier than Italian or poppy seed, but the salads are literally a trough of fresh greens with kidney and garbanzo beans, sprouts, avocado, egg, and cucumber. One salad is a meal for two, and comes with thick fresh slices of bread and slabs of butter. Soups and sandwiches here are also delicious and one of the best deals around.

People's Park/People's Power

In late 1967, the university demolished an entire block of buildings north of Telegraph Avenue. The destruction, which forced hippies and other "undesirables" from the slum housing that stood there, was done under the guise of university expansion and urban renewal—good liberal causes. But after the lot lay vacant for almost two years, a group of Berkeley radicals whose names read like a who's who of 1960s leftists, including Jerry Rubin, Bobby Seale, and Tom Hayden, decided to take the land for "the people."

On April 29, 1969, hundreds of activists invaded the vacant lot with gardening tools and tamed the muddy ground into a park. One month later, Berkeley's Republican mayor sent 250 police officers into the park, and 4,000 demonstrators materialized to challenge them. A riot ensued, the police fired buckshot at the crowd, and one rioter was killed and another blinded. Gov. Ronald Reagan sent in the National Guard, and for the next 17 days the guardsmen repeatedly gassed innocent students, faculty, and passersby. Berkeley was a war zone, and People's Park became the most important symbol of "people power" during the 1960s.

People's Park once again sparked controversy in 1992 when university officials decided to build volleyball courts there. In August of that year, a park activist broke into the campus home of the university's chancellor. When a police officer arrived, the activist lunged at him with a machete and was shot dead. On the victim's body was a note with the message: "We are willing to die for this land. Are you?" On news of the contemporary radical's death, more than 150 of her supporters rioted. Today you can visit the park and watch the volleyballers self-consciously setting, bumping, and spiking.

Cambodianas. 2156 University Ave. (between Shattuck and Oxford). ☎ **510/843-4630.** Reservations recommended, especially Fri–Sat. Main courses $7.50–$13; fixed-price dinner $10.95. AE, DC, JCB, MC, V. Mon–Fri 11:30am–3pm; nightly 5–10pm. CAMBODIAN.

For those who relish the spicy cuisine of Cambodia, this is quite a find. The decor is as colorful as the fare—amidst brilliant blue, yellow, and green walls with Breuer-style chairs set at tables you can feast on a variety of dishes. Especially tasty is the curry (chicken, beef, and so on) or Naga dishes with a sauce of tamarind, turmeric, lemongrass, shrimp paste, coconut milk galinga, shallot, lemon leaf, sugar, and green chile. This sauce may smother salmon, prawns, chicken, or steak. Another tempting dish is the chicken chaktomuk prepared with pineapple, red peppers, and zucchini in soy and oyster sauce. The three-course, fixed-price dinner is an excellent value.

Jupiter. 2181 Shattuck Ave. ☎ **510/843-8277.** MC, V. No reservations. Mon–Fri 11:30am–1am, Sat noon–1am, Sun noon–midnight. AMERICAN.

Ultra-cool Berkeley hipsters and beer-lovers meet here amidst bronze-colored pressed tin walls to throw back a few of the 39 local microbrews on tap, nasch on wood-fired pizza or a sandwich, and chill to live jazz music (call for schedules). The courtyard "beer garden" seats 150 and is jamming with live music most nights during summer months—heaters are included.

Skates on the Bay. 100 Seawall Drive. ☎ **510/549-1900.** Reservations recommended. Main courses $12–$22. AE, DC, MC, V. Mon–Fri 11:15–3pm, Sat noon–3:30pm, Sun 10:15am–3pm; Mon–Thurs 5–10pm, Fri 5–10:30pm, Sat 4–10:30pm, Sun 4–10pm. AMERICAN.

One of Berkeley's greatest assets is its stunning view of downtown San Francisco shimmering beyond the bay, and Skates is one of the best dining/vista points around. Located on bay-front property, from Skates you can see all three bridges (Bay Bridge, Golden Gate, and Richmond) and from here, the city seems to protrude out of the surrounding water magically, with a fairy-tale mystique much like Dorothy's view of the Emerald City from the poppy field. While true gourmands may want to explore more culinarily revered restaurants in the area, Skates does serve a good dinner. Typical fare includes prime rib, fresh fish, and more exotic dishes such as chicken satay. Try the favored wild Alaskan coho salmon with fresh veggies, rice, and potato, and for dessert, banana cream dream with macadamia-nut, white-chocolate crust.

Triple Rock Brewery & Alehouse. 1920 Shattuck Ave. (at Hearst). ☎ **510/843-2739.** Reservations not accepted. Platters $6–$9. No credit cards. Sun–Wed 11:30am–12:30am, Thurs–Sat 11:30am–1:30am. AMERICAN.

Stop by this Berkeley favorite for a fresh brew piped directly from the glass-enclosed brewery to the bar where sandwiches and chilis are also served. Play a game of shuffleboard or on a sunny afternoon head to the rooftop deck.

3   Angel Island & Tiburon

8 miles N of San Francisco

A federal and state wildlife refuge, **Angel Island** is the largest of the San Francisco Bay's three islets (the others being Alcatraz and Yerba Buena). The island has been, at various times, a prison, a quarantine station for immigrants, a missile base, and even a favorite site for duels. Nowadays, though, most of the people who visit here are content with picnicking on the large green lawn that fronts the docking area; loaded with the appropriate recreational supplies, they claim a barbecue, plop their fannies down on the lush green grass, and while away an afternoon free of phones, televisions, and traffic. Hiking, mountain biking, and guided tram tours are also popular options.

   Tiburon, situated on a peninsula of the same name, looks like a cross between a fishing village and a Hollywood western set—imagine San Francisco reduced to toy dimensions. This seacoast town rambles over a series of green hills and ends up at a spindly, multicolored pier on the waterfront, like a Fisherman's Wharf in miniature. But in reality it's an extremely plush patch of yacht-club suburbia, as you'll see by both the marine craft and the homes of their owners. **Main Street** is lined with ramshackle, color-splashed old frame houses that shelter chic boutiques, souvenir stores, antiques shops, and art galleries. Other roads are narrow, winding, and hilly, and lead up to dramatically situated homes. The view of San Francisco's skyline and the islands in the bay is a good enough reason to pay the precious price to live here.

ESSENTIALS

Ferries of the **Red and White Fleet** (☎ **415/546-2700** or 800/229-2784 in California) leave from Pier 43¹/₂ (Fisherman's Wharf) and travel to both Angel Island and Tiburon. Boats run on a seasonal schedule; phone for departure information. The round-trip fare is $9 to Angel Island, $11 to Tiburon; half price for kids 5 to 11. (*Note:* The Red and White Fleet is slated to be converted into the Blue and Gold Fleet by 1997, but will probably keep the same schedule and fares.)

   By car from San Francisco, take U.S. 101 to the Tiburon/Highway 131 exit, then follow Tiburon Boulevard all the way into downtown, a 40-minute drive from San Francisco. Catch the ferry (☎ **415/435-2131** or 415/388-6770) to Angel Island from the dock located at Tiburon Boulevard and Main Street. The 15-minute round-trip costs $5 adult, $3 children 5 to 11, and $1 for bikes.

WHAT TO SEE & DO ON ANGEL ISLAND

Passengers disembark from the ferry at Ayala Cove, a small marina abutting a huge lawn area equipped with tables, benches, barbecue pits, and restrooms. Also at Ayala Cove is a small store, gift shop, cafe (with surprisingly good grub), and overpriced mountain bike rental shop (helmets included).

Among the 12 miles of Angel Island's hiking and mountain bike trails is the **Perimeter Road,** a partly paved path that circles the island and winds its way past disused troop barracks, former gun emplacements, and other military buildings; several turnoffs lead up to the top of Mount Livermore, 776 feet above the bay. Sometimes referred to as the "Ellis Island of the West," from 1910 to 1940 Angel Island was used as a holding area for Chinese immigrants awaiting their citizenship papers. You can still see some faded Chinese characters on the walls of the barracks where the immigrants were held. During the warmer months you can camp at a limited number of sites; reservations are required.

Also offered at Angel Island are guided sea kayak tours. The all-day trips, which include a catered lunch, combine the thrill of paddling stable one-, two-, or three-person kayaks with an informative, naturalist-led tour that encircles the island (conditions permitting). All equipment is provided, kids are welcome, and no experience is necessary. Rates run about $110 per person. For more information, call **Sea Trek** at **415/488-1000**.

For recorded information about Angel Island State Park, call ☎ **415/435-1915**.

WHAT TO SEE & DO IN TIBURON

The main thing to do in Tiburon is stroll along the waterfront, pop into the stores, and spend an easy $50 on drinks and appetizers before heading back to the city. For a taste of the wine country, stop in at **Windsor Vineyards,** 72 Main St. (☎ **415/435-3113** or 800/214-9463)—their Victorian tasting room dates from 1888. Thirty-five choices are available for a free tasting. Wine accessories and gifts—glasses, cork pullers, gourmet sauces, posters, and maps—are also available. Carry-packs are available (they hold six bottles). Ask about personalized labels for your own selections. The shop is open daily from 10am to 6pm.

WHERE TO DINE IN TIBURON
MODERATE

Guaymas. 5 Main St. ☎ **415/435-6300**. Reservations accepted. Main courses $12–$18. AE, CB, DC, MC, V. Mon–Fri 11:30am–9:30pm, Sat 11:30am–10:30pm, Sun 10:30am–9:30pm Ferry: Walk about 10 paces from the landing. From U.S. 101, exit at Tiburon/Hwy. 131; follow Tiburon Blvd. 5 miles and turn right onto Main St. The restaurant is situated directly behind the bakery. MEXICAN.

Guaymas offers authentic Mexican regional cuisine and a spectacular panoramic view of San Francisco and the Bay. In good weather, the two outdoor patios are almost always packed with diners soaking in the sun and scene. Inside, beige walls are hung with colorful Mexican artwork, illuminated by modern track lighting. Should you be feeling chilled, to the rear of the dining room is a beehive-shaped adobe fireplace.

Guaymas is named after a fishing village on Mexico's Sea of Cortez, and both the town and the restaurant are famous for their camarones (giant shrimp). In addition, the restaurant features ceviche, handmade tamales, and charcoal-grilled beef, seafood, and fowl. Save room for dessert, especially the outrageously scrumptious fritter with "drunken" bananas and ice cream. In addition to a good selection of California wines, the restaurant offers an exceptional variety of tequilas, Mexican beers, and mineral waters flavored with flowers, grains, and fruits.

Sam's Anchor Café. 27 Main St. ☎ **415/435-4527.** Reservations accepted. Main courses $8–$16. AE, MC, V. Mon–Thurs 11am–10pm, Fri 11am–10:30pm, Sat 10am–10:30pm, Sun 9:30am–10pm. Ferry: Walk from the landing. From U.S. 101, exit at Tiburon/Hwy. 131; follow Tiburon Blvd. 4 miles and turn right onto Main St. SEAFOOD.

Summer Sundays are liveliest in Tiburon, when weekend boaters tie up to the docks at waterside restaurants like this one, the kind of place where you and your cronies can take off your shoes and have a fun, relaxed time eating burgers and drinking margaritas outside on the pier. The fare is pretty typical—sandwiches, salads, and seafood such as deep-fried oysters—but the quality and selection of the food is inconsequential: beers, burgers, and a designated driver are all you really need.

INEXPENSIVE

Sweden House Bakery-Café. 35 Main St. ☎ **415/435-9767.** Reservations not accepted. Omelets $6.50–$7; sandwiches $6–$8. MC, V. Mon–Fri 8am–6pm, Sat–Sun 8am–7pm. Ferry: Walk from the landing. From U.S. 101, exit at Tiburon/Belvedere; follow Tiburon Blvd. 5 miles and turn right onto Main St. SWEDISH/AMERICAN.

This small, cozy cafe with gingham-covered walls adorned with copperware and kitchen utensils is a local favorite. On sunny mornings there's no better seat in the Bay Area than on the bakery's terrace, where you can nurse an espresso and pastry while gazing out over the bay. Full breakfasts are served, too, all accompanied by toasted Swedish limpa bread; skip the eggs and bacon routine and go with the tasty Swedish pancakes: lingonberry, blueberry, and apple. At lunch, there's typical American fare plus traditional open-face sandwiches, including avocado and bacon or asparagus tips rolled in Danish ham. Beer and wine are available.

4 Sausalito

5 miles N of San Francisco

Just off the northern end of the Golden Gate Bridge is the eclectic little town of Sausalito, a slightly bohemian, nonchalant, and studiedly quaint adjunct to San Francisco. With approximately 7,500 residents, Sausalito feels rather like St. Tropez on the French Riviera—minus the starlets and the social rat race. It has its quota of paper millionaires, but they rub their permanently suntanned shoulders with a good number of hard-up artists, struggling authors, shipyard workers, and fishers. Next to the swank restaurants, plush bars, and antique shops and galleries, you'll see hamburger joints, beer parlors, and secondhand bookstores. Sausalito's main touring strip is **Bridgeway,** which runs along the water, but those in the know make a quick detour to **Caledonia Street** one block inland; not only is it less congested, there's a far better selection of cafes and shops.

ESSENTIALS

Ferries of the **Red and White Fleet** (☎ **415/546-2700** or 800/229-2784 in California) leave from Pier 43½ (Fisherman's Wharf) and cost $11 round-trip, half price for kids 5 to 11. Boats run on a seasonal schedule; phone for departure information. (*Note:* The Red and White Fleet is slated to be converted into the Blue and Gold Fleet by 1997, but will probably keep the same schedule and fares.)

By car from San Francisco, take U.S. 101 north, then first right after the Golden Gate Bridge (Alexander exit). Alexander becomes Bridgeway in Sausalito.

WHAT TO SEE & DO

Above all, Sausalito has scenery and sunshine, for once you cross the Golden Gate Bridge you're out of the San Francisco fog patch and under blue California sky (we hope). The town's steep hills are covered with houses that overlook a forest of masts on the waters below, but almost all the tourist action, which is almost singularly limited to window shopping and eating, takes place at sea level on Bridgeway.

Bay Model Visitors Center. 2100 Bridgeway. ☎ **415/332-3871.** Free admission. Winter, Tues–Sat 9am–4pm; summer, Tues–Fri 9am–4pm, Sat–Sun 10am–6pm.

The U.S. Army Corps of Engineers uses this high-tech, $1^1/_2$-acre model of San Francisco's bay and delta to resolve problems and observe what impact any changes in water flow will have. The model reproduces (in scale) the rise and fall of tides, the flows and currents of water, the mixing of fresh- and saltwater, and indicates trends in sediment movement. There's a 10-minute film that explains it all and a tour, but the most interesting time to visit is when it's actually being used, so call ahead.

WHERE TO SHOP

Sausalito is a mecca for shoppers seeking handmade, original, and offbeat clothes and footwear, as well as arts and crafts. The town's best shops are found in the alleys, malls, and second-floor boutiques reached by steep, narrow staircases on and off Bridgeway. Additional shops are found on Caledonia Street, which runs parallel to and one block inland from Bridgeway.

Village Fair, at 777 Bridgeway, is Sausalito's closest approximation to a mall. It's a complex of 30 shops, souvenir stores, coffee bars, and gardens. Among them, **Quest Gallery** (☎ **415/332-6832**) features fine ceramics, whimsical chess sets, contemporary glass, hand-painted silks, woven clothing, art jewelry, and graphics. The shop specializes in celebrated California artists, many of whom sell exclusively through this store. The complex is open daily from 10am to 6pm; restaurants stay open later.

Burlwood Gallery. 721 Bridgeway. ☎ **415/332-6550.**

Visit this gallery for one-of-a-kind redwood furniture plus fine jewelry, metal sculptures, hand-blown glass, Oriental rugs, and other interesting gifts. It's well worth browsing. Open daily from 10am to 6pm.

Magnet Madness. 795 Bridgeway. ☎ **415/331-9226.**

Finally, a store that sells something you can afford: refrigerator magnets. Thousands of colorful and creative little gems, from Airedales to Zucchini, are backed with a magnet and stuck to the walls of this irresistibly inviting store. Open daily from 10am to 6pm.

Pegasus Leather Company. 28 Princess St. (off Bridgeway). ☎ **415/332-5624.**

Pegasus is a vendor of beautiful leather clothing and accessories. Along with jackets, coats, skirts, and blouses, there are handsome belts, gloves, and purses made from ultrasoft, richly colored leathers. Clothing can be custom made and altered for a perfect fit at no extra charge. Open daily from 10am to 5:30pm.

The Sausalito Country Store. 789 Bridgeway. ☎ **415/332-7890.**

This place sells oodles of handmade, country-style goods for the home and garden. Many of these items—ceramic, stuffed, and painted-wood animals, aprons, baskets, birdhouses, embossed quilt prints, and lithographs—are made by local artists and artisans. Open daily from 10am to 6pm.

The Marin Headlands

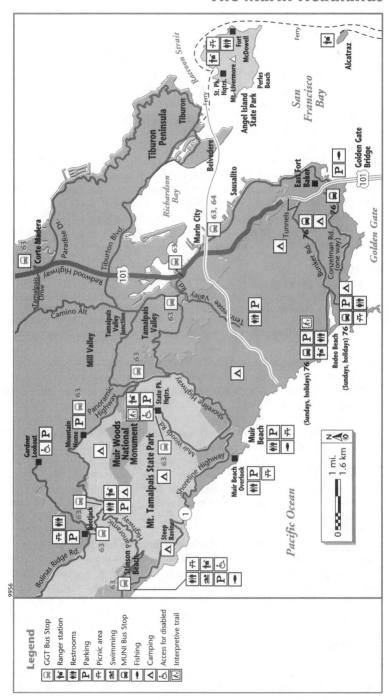

WHERE TO STAY
VERY EXPENSIVE

✪ **Inn Above The Tide.** 30 El Portal (next to the Sausalito Ferry Landing), Sausalito, CA 94965. ☎ **415/332-9535** or 800/893-8433. Fax 415/332-6714. 28 rooms, 2 suites. AC TV TEL. $185–$400 double. Rates include continental breakfast. AE, MC, V.

Perched directly over the bay atop well-grounded pilings, this former luxury apartment complex underwent a $4 million transformation into one of Sausalito's—if not the Bay Area's—finest accommodations. It's the view that clinches it: every room comes with an unparalleled panorama of the San Francisco Bay, including a postcard-quality vista of the city glimmering in the distance. Should you manage to tear yourself away from your private deck (we were tempted to drag our mattress outside), you'll find that your sumptuously appointed room sports a romantic little fireplace, a vast sunken tub with Jacuzzi jets, remote-control air-conditioning, and wondrously comfortable queen- or king-size beds. Soothing shades of pale green and blue highlight the decor, which blends in well with the bayscape outside. Be sure to request that your breakfast and newspaper be delivered to your deck, then cancel your early appointments: on sunny mornings, nobody checks out early.

MODERATE

Casa Madrona. 801 Bridgeway, Sausalito, CA 94965. ☎ **415/332-0502** or 800/567-9524. Fax 415/332-2537. 34 rms, 1 suite. MINIBAR TEL. $105–$245 double; $435 Madrona Villa suite. Extra person $10. Breakfast free from 7:30–9:30am. Two-night minimum stay on weekends. AE, MC, V. Parking $5. Ferry: Walk across the street from the landing. From U.S. 101 north, take the first right after the Golden Gate Bridge (Alexander exit); Alexander becomes Bridgeway in Sausalito.

Sooner or later most visitors to Sausalito look up and wonder at the ornate mansion on the hill. It's part of Casa Madrona, a hideaway by the bay built in 1885 by a wealthy lumber baron. The epitome of luxury in its day, the mansion had slipped into decay when it was saved by Henri Deschamps and converted into a hotel and restaurant. Successive renovations and extensions have added a rambling, New England–style building to the hillside below the main house. Now a certified historic landmark, the hotel offers rooms, suites, and cottages. The 16 newest units are each uniquely decorated by different local designers. The "1,000 Cranes" is Asian in theme, with lots of ash and lacquer. "Artist's Loft" is reminiscent of a rustic Parisian artist's studio. "Summer House" is decked out in white wicker. Other rooms in the mansion are also decorated in a variety of styles; some have Jacuzzis, while others have fireplaces. The newest rooms are located on the water with panoramic views of the San Francisco skyline and bay.

Within the Casa Madrona is **Mikayla Restaurant** (☎ 415/331-5888), which serves superb California cuisine—sautéed wild sturgeon, charred prime sirloin, barbecue glazed quail—in an unbelievably beautiful setting overlooking the bay and San Francisco skyline. It's open for lunch Monday through Friday and for Sunday brunch and for dinner nightly.

WHERE TO DINE
MODERATE

Guernica. 2009 Bridgeway. ☎ **415/332-1512.** Reservations recommended. Main courses $10–$17. AE, MC, V. Daily 5–10pm. From U.S. 101 north, take the first right after the Golden Gate Bridge (Alexander exit); Alexander becomes Bridgeway in Sausalito. FRENCH/BASQUE.

Established in 1976, Guernica is one of those funky old kinds of restaurants that you'd probably pass up for something more chic and modern down the street if you didn't know better. What? You don't know about Guernica's legendary Paella Valenciana? Well now you do, so be sure to call ahead and order it in advance, and bring a partner cause it's served for two but will feed three. Begin with an appetizer of artichoke hearts or escargots, and be sure to try the wonderful homemade bread. Other main courses are grilled rabbit with a spicy red diablo sauce, a hearty Rack of Lamb Guernica, and medallions of pork loin with baked apples and Calvados. Rich desserts include such in-season specialties as strawberry tart and peach Melba.

Horizons. 558 Brideway. ☎ **415/331-3232.** Reservations accepted weekdays only. Main courses $9–$15, salads and sandwiches $6–$8. AE, MC, V. Mon–Fri 11am–11pm, Sat–Sun 10am–11pm. SEAFOOD/AMERICAN.

Eventually, every San Franciscan ends up at Horizons to meet a friend for Sunday Bloody Marys. It's not much to look at from the outside, but it gets better as you head past the funky dark wood interior toward the waterside terrace. On warm days it's worth the wait for alfresco seating if only to watch dreamy sailboats glide past San Francisco's distant skyline. The food here can't touch the view, but it's well portioned and satisfying enough. Seafood dishes are the main items, including steamed clams and mussels, freshly shucked oysters, and a variety of seafood pastas. In fine Marin tradition, Horizons has an "herb tea and espresso" bar, and is a totally nonsmoking restaurant.

INEXPENSIVE

Feng Nian Chinese Restaurant. 2650 Bridgeway. ☎ **415/331-5300.** Reservations accepted. Lunch specials $4–$5.50; main courses $6.55–$14. AE, DISC, MC, V. Mon and Wed–Thur 11:30am–9:30pm, Fri–Sat 11:30am–10pm, Sun 12:30–9:30pm. From U.S. 101 north, take the first right after the Golden Gate Bridge (Alexander exit); Alexander becomes Bridgeway in Sausalito. The restaurant is located near the intersection of Bridgeway and Harbor Drive, before downtown Sausalito. CHINESE.

A pretty restaurant serving fine quality Chinese food, Feng Nian has such a wide selection of appetizers that a combination of several would make a delicious meal in itself. The crispy roast duck is a personal favorite, but if you'd like an assortment, try the flaming combination (enough for two) that includes egg roll, fried prawn, paper-wrapped chicken, barbecued ribs, fried chicken, and teriyaki. There are nine soups, including a truly exceptional, rich crabmeat/shark's-fin soup with shredded crab-leg meat.

Choosing one of the chef's suggestions isn't easy. The Peking duck requires about a half hour of preparation, but it's always delectable. If you enjoy seafood, try the twice sizzling seafood, with prawns, scallops, squid, and fresh vegetables in oyster sauce; it's prepared at your table. Beef dishes are prepared in a variety of ways: Mongolian, Szechuan, Hunan, Mandarin; with ginger, curry, and broccoli, just to name a few. The restaurant offers more than 90 main dishes, including a number of main courses for vegetarians.

PICNIC FARE & WHERE TO EAT IT

Even Sausalito's naysayers have to admit that it's hard not to enjoy eating your way down Bridgeway on a warm, sunny day. If the crowds are too much or the prices too steep at the bay-side restaurants, grab a bite to go for an impromptu picnic in the park fronting the marina.

Café Soleil. 37 Caledonia St. ☎ **415/331-9355.** No credit cards. Daily 7am–6:30pm.

Small, clean, cute, and cheap, Café Soleil whips up some good soups, salads, and sandwiches along with killer smoothies. Order to go at the counter, then take your goods a block over to the marina for a dock-side lunch.

Caledonia Kitchen. 400 Caledonia St. ☎ **415/331-0220.** No credit cards. Daily 8am–8pm.

Caledonia Kitchen is the sort of place you wish were just around the corner from your house—a beautiful little cafe serving a huge assortment of fresh salads, soups, chili, sandwiches, and inexpensive entrées like herbed roast chicken or vegetarian lasagna for only $4.95. Continental-style breakfast items and good coffee and espresso drinks are also on the menu.

Hamburgers. 737 Bridgeway ☎ **415/332-9471.** No credit cards. Daily 11am–5pm.

Like the name says, the specialty at this tiny, narrow cafe is juicy flame-broiled hamburgers, arguably Marin County's best. Look for the rotating grill in the window off Bridgeway, then stand in line and salivate with the rest (chicken burgers are a slightly healthier option). Order a side of fries, grab a bunch of napkins, then head over to the park across the street.

The Stuffed Croissant, Etc. 43 Caledonia St. ☎ **415/332-7103.** No credit cards. Mon–Wed 6:45am–9pm, Thurs–Sat 6:45am–10pm, Sun 7:30am–8pm.

You can get anything here from a snack to a meal. There are all sorts of gourmet croissants, including those filled with almond-chicken salad or Italian pizza, as well as bagels, soups, and stews. Hot, cheap meals such as chicken curry with rice are also popular. For dessert there's carrot cake, pecan bars, fudge and peanut brownies, and more.

Venice Gourmet Delicatessen. 625 Bridgeway. ☎ **415/332-3544.** AE, DC, DISC, MC, V. Daily 9am–6pm.

This classic old deli has all the makings for a superb picnic: wines, cheese, fruits, stuffed vine leaves, mushroom and artichoke salad, quiche, delicious sandwiches (made to order on sourdough bread), olives, and fresh-baked pastries.

5 Muir Woods & Mount Tamalpais

20 miles N of San Francisco

While the rest of Marin County's redwood forests were being devoured to feed the building spree in San Francisco around the turn of the century, the trees of Muir Woods, in a remote ravine on the flanks of Mount Tamalpais, escaped destruction in favor of easier pickings.

To get to **Mount Tamalpais by car,** drive across the Golden Gate Bridge and take the exit for Calif. 1/Mount Tamalpais. Follow the shoreline highway about 2 1/2 miles and turn onto the Panoramic Highway. After about 5 1/2 miles, turn onto Pantoll Road and continue for about a mile to Ridgecrest Boulevard. Ridgecrest winds to a parking lot below East Peak. From there, it's a 15-minute hike up to the top.

To get to **Muir Woods,** follow the Mount Tamalpais directions to the panoramic highway. After about a mile, take the signed turnoff and follow successive signs.

Although the magnificent California redwoods have been successfully transplanted to five continents, their homeland is a 500-mile strip along the mountainous coast of southwestern Oregon and northern California.

The coast redwood, or *Sequoia sempervirens,* is the tallest tree in the immediate region, and the largest-known specimen towers 367.8 feet. It has an even larger relative, the *Sequoiadendron giganteum* of the California Sierra Nevada, but the coastal variety is stunning enough. Soaring toward the sky like a wooden cathedral, it is unlike any other forest in the world.

You can drive the 2,600 feet to the top of Mount Tam, as the locals call it, or hike along one of two clearly marked trails (one gentle, the other fairly rough) to the

John Muir: Savior of Yosemite

John Muir was born in Dunbar, Scotland in 1838 and came to the United States in 1848. After a couple of years studying at the University of Wisconsin at Madison, he dropped out and began a 1,000-mile long walk from Indiana to the Gulf of Mexico, carrying a plant press on his back. From Florida, he took a steamer via Panama to San Francisco in 1868. On his arrival, he asked a passerby for the nearest way out of town. The passerby asked him where he wanted to go, and he replied, "To anywhere that is wild." And so he was directed to the Oakland ferry and a journey that brought him to the Sierra, where he worked for a time as a shepherd, living simply in the wilderness, maintaining a diary and writing about nature and the Yosemite Valley in particular.

In the 1940s he married Louise Streutzel, and they lived in Martinez from 1880 to 1890. He worked as a fruit rancher, eventually becoming wealthy enough to devote his time and energy to what he loved: the wilderness. In 1892, he founded the Sierra Club. Muir wrote passionately about conservation and education and enlisted the help of others (including President Theodore Roosevelt, with whom he embarked on a famous series of camping trips in 1903) to establish a system of national parks that would protect the wilderness for future generations. He saved Yosemite, but he lost the battle to save Hetch Hetchy, which many say caused him to die of a broken heart in 1914. To secure its water supply, San Francisco proceeded with plans to dam the Tuolumne River, thereby denying future generations access to another valley as beautiful as Yosemite. Two years after Muir's death, the National Parks Service was created, securing the park's preservation forever. Today, the efforts to return Hetch Hetchy to its original state continue. Throughout the United States, and especially in Northern California, the torch of this great conservationist still burns bright. Muir Woods was named in his memory.

summit. The mountain offers a special picnic area and miles of trails. And from the peak you get a 100-mile sweep in all directions, from the foothills of the Sierra to the western horizon.

6 Point Reyes National Seashore

35 miles N of San Francisco

The national seashore system was created to protect rural and undeveloped stretches of the coast from the pressures brought on by soaring real estate values and increasing population. Nowhere is the success of the system more evident that at Point Reyes. Comprised primarily of sand beach and scrubland, it's home to birds, sea lions, and a variety of tide pool creatures.

ESSENTIALS

From San Francisco, cross the Golden Gate Bridge and stay on U.S. 101 north. Shortly before Corte Madera, turn left onto Sir Francis Drake Boulevard and drive 20 miles to Bear Valley Road. The information center is half a mile down Bear Valley Road. To get to the infamous Point Reyes Lighthouse, return to Sir Francis Drake Boulevard and continue to its end at a parking lot. The lighthouse is a half-mile walk down a paved road.

In November 1995, the Bay Area suffered a great loss when 12,354 acres of Point Reyes burned in an uncontrollable brush fire. However, there's still plenty of pristine property in this 65,000-acre park and even the areas that suffered the worst are quickly replenishing themselves. The park encompasses several surf-pounded beaches, bird estuaries, open swaths of land with roaming elk, and the Point Reyes lighthouse—a favorite among visitors who are awestruck by the spectacular views of the coast, gray whales (when in season), and wildflowers. Call the **visitor center** (☎ **415/669-1534**) for further information on hours, parking, and whale-watching schedules.

WHAT TO SEE & DO

When headed out to any part of the Point Reyes coast, expect to spend the day surrounded by nature at its finest. But bear in mind that as beautiful as the wilderness can be, it's also untamed. Waters in these areas are not only bone-chilling and home to a vast array of sea life, including sharks, but are also unpredictable and dangerous. There are no lifeguards on duty and waves and riptides make swimming strongly discouraged. Pets are also not permitted on any of the area's trails.

North and South **Point Reyes Beach** face the Pacific and withstand the full brunt of ocean tides and winds—so much so that the water is much too rough for even wading. Until a few years ago, entering the water was actually illegal, but persistent surfers went to court for their right to shred the mighty waves. Today, the park service strongly advises against taking on the tides, so play it safe and stroll the coastline.

Along the south coast **Drake's Beach's** waters can be as tranquil and serene as Point Reyes's are turbulent. Locals come here to sun and picnic and occasionally a hearty soul ventures into the cold waters of Drake's Bay. But keep in mind that storms generally come inland from the south and almost always hit Drake's before moving north or south. A powerful weather front can turn wispy waves into torrential tides.

The main road of the park, Sir Francis Drake Boulevard, which passes by Point Reyes Beach and branches off to reach Drake's Beach, leads right out to Point Reyes itself.

The **Point Reyes Lighthouse** juts out almost 10 miles from the mainland and is one of the best places on the West Coast to watch **gray whales** on their journeys between Alaska and Baja. The annual round-trip is 10,000 miles—one of the longest mammal migrations known. The whales head south in December and January, and return north in March.

If you plan to drive out to the lighthouse to whale-watch, arrive early because parking is limited. If possible, come on a weekday. On a weekend or holiday it's wise to park at the Drake's Beach Visitor Center and take the free shuttle bus to the lighthouse. Dress warmly—it's often quite cold and windy—and bring binoculars.

Whale-watching is far from being the only activity offered at the Point Reyes National Seashore. Rangers conduct many different tours: You can walk along the **Bear Valley Trail,** spotting the wildlife at the ocean's edge; see the waterfowl at **Fivebrooks Pond;** explore tide pools; view some of North America's most beautiful ducks in the wetlands of **Limantour;** hike to the promontory overlooking **Chimney Rock** to see the sea lions, harbor seals, and sea birds; or take a guided walk along the **San Andreas fault** to observe the site of the epicenter of the 1906 earthquake and learn about the regional geology. And this is just a sampling. Since tours vary seasonally, you can either call the ranger station (☎ **415/663-1092**) or request a copy of *Park Paper*, which includes a schedule of activities and other useful information. Many of the tours are suitable for the disabled.

WHERE TO DINE
MODERATE

Station House Café. Main Street, Point Reyes Station. ☎ **415/663-1515.** Reservations recommended. Breakfast $4.45–$7.50; main courses $9–$17.50. DISC, MC, V. Sun–Thurs 8am–9pm, Fri–Sat 8am–10pm. AMERICAN.

This is a favorite local cafe because of its superb food and atmospheric setting. Its many virtues include a fireplace, an open-to-view kitchen, garden dining, and live music on weekends. Breakfast dishes range from bread pudding with stewed fruit compote to a frittata with asparagus, goat cheese, and olives. Luncheon specials might include fettuccine with fresh, local mussels steamed in white wine and butter sauce, or two-cheese polenta served with fresh spinach sauté and grilled garlic-buttered tomato. Organically grown local beef is always on the menu. Rounding out the menu are homemade chili, steamed clams, fresh soup made daily, and fish and chips. The cafe has an extensive list of fine California wines, plus local imported beers. Live entertainment on weekends.

WHERE TO STAY

Inns of Marin, P.O. Box 547, Point Reyes Station, CA 94956 (☎ **800/887-2880** or 415/663-2000) is a service that will help you to find accommodations ranging from one-room cottages to inns and complete vacation homes. Keep in mind that many places here have a two-night minimum, though in slow season they may make an exception.

MODERATE

Point Reyes Country Inn & Stables. P.O. Box 501, 12050 Highway One, Point Reyes Station, California, 94956. ☎ **415/663-9696.** $85–$105, $25 additional human guest, $10–$15 per horse. Rates include breakfast.

Dreaming of a country getaway between the Point Reyes National Seashore and the Tomales Bay State Park—and you want to bring your horse? The Country Inn is a five-bedroom, ranch-style home on four acres that offers pastoral accommodations for two- and four-legged guests (horses only). Each room has a private bath and either a balcony or a garden and there's plenty of hiking. Breakfast is included.

7 Marine World Africa USA

30 miles NE of San Francisco, 10 miles S of Napa

Marine World Africa USA, on Marine World Parkway in Vallejo (☎ **707/643-6722**), is a kind of Disney-meets-Wild-Kingdom theme park, offering aquatic and other trained animal performances.

The **Blue and Gold Fleet** (☎ **415/705-5555**) operates a high-speed **ferries service** from Pier 41 at Fisherman's Wharf. The scenic cruise, passing Alcatraz and the Golden Gate Bridge, takes 80 minutes, plus a brief bus ride. The round trip, including park admission, is $39 for adults, $32 for seniors 62 and over and students 13 to 18, and $23.50 for kids 4 to 12. Service is limited; call for departure times.

By car from San Francisco, take I-80 north to Calif. 37 and follow the signs to the park; it's less than an hour's drive.

WHAT YOU WILL FIND THERE

A variety of events are scheduled continuously throughout the day. There's a **Killer Whale and Dolphin Show,** where the front seven rows of seats are saved for guests who want a thorough drenching. **Shark Experience,** a moving walkway through a clear acrylic tunnel, brings visitors through a 300,000-gallon tropical shark-filled tank.

Cross a bridge over a waterfall, past the flamingos, and you enter **"Africa USA."** Here you'll find **Elephant Encounter,** where visitors can meet (and pet!) some of the park's 11 Asian and African elephants. In addition to shows, you can get more up close and personal at the elephant ride ($3) or the giraffe feeding (50¢). At **Tiger Island,** you can see trainers and Bengal tigers playing and swimming together. An informative show about the park's exotic and endangered animals is performed in the **Wildlife Theater.**

Hawks and other feathered friends swoop overhead and onto the stage at the **Bird Show.** There's also an enclosed **Butterfly World** where one of the many beautiful inhabitants may happen to land on you (don't touch them, though!); a **Small Animal Petting Kraal** (with llamas); **Walrus Experience,** where the adorably chubby and curious creatures splash about and look you in the eye; **Walkabout! An Australian Adventure,** where kangaroos, wallabies, and emu hop freely and koalas hang out in nearby trees; and **Gentle Jungle,** a playground that combines education, fun, and adventure. Here, inside the Prairie Crawl, children can crawl through burrows in the prairie dog village and pop up into Plexiglas domes so they can see the world from these animals' point of view.

A 55-acre lake is the stage for a **Water Ski and Boat Show** April through October. Daredevil athletes jump, spin, and even create a human pyramid while wearing water-skis. In winter, kids throw on their ski clothes and spend the day sledding at **Snow World.**

A wide variety of reasonably priced fast food is available at **Lakeside Plaza.** There's also a restaurant, or you can bring your own picnic—there are barbecue facilities on the grounds. The best way to see the park is to get there early, plot your own itinerary from the leaflet and map given to you at the entrance, and then stick to it. Otherwise, you'll find yourself missing parts of each presentation and feeling frustrated.

Admission is $25.95 for adults, $17.95 for kids four to 12, and $21.95 for seniors over 60, free for children under four. Carte Blanche, Diners Club, MasterCard, and Visa are accepted. The park is open from Memorial Day through Labor Day, daily from 9:30am to 6pm; the rest of the year, Wednesday through Sunday from 9:30am to 5pm.

8 The Wine Country: Napa Valley

55 miles N of San Francisco

Most people don't realize that an afternoon amidst acres of vineyards, the world's best wines, and pastoral splendor is close to an hour away from the city. But after a few days scurrying around downtown, what could be better than fresh country air, beautiful sunny weather, and mountains that dip into a valley gushing with the fruit of the gods?

ESSENTIALS

From San Francisco, cross the Golden Gate Bridge and continue north on U.S. 101. Turn east on Calif. 37, then north on Calif. 29, the main road through the wine country.

California Highway 29 runs the length of Napa Valley, which is just 35 miles long. You really can't get lost—there's just one north-south road, on which most of the wineries, hotels, shops, and restaurants are located.

The Wine Country

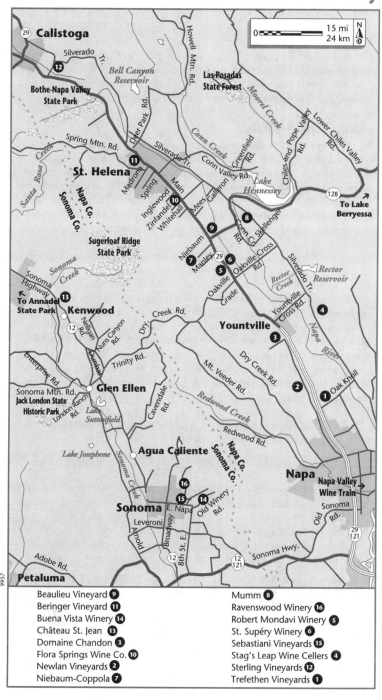

Beaulieu Vineyard **9**
Beringer Vineyard **11**
Buena Vista Winery **14**
Château St. Jean **13**
Domaine Chandon **3**
Flora Springs Wine Co. **10**
Newlan Vineyards **2**
Niebaum-Coppola **7**

Mumm **8**
Ravenswood Winery **16**
Robert Mondavi Winery **5**
St. Supéry Winery **6**
Sebastiani Vineyards **15**
Stag's Leap Wine Cellers **4**
Sterling Vineyards **12**
Trefethen Vineyards **1**

Get wine country maps and brochures from the **Wine Institute** at 425 Market St., Suite 1000, San Francisco, CA 94105 (☎ **415/512-0151**). Once in the Napa Valley, stop first at the **Napa Valley Conference and Visitors Bureau,** 1310 Town Center Mall, off First Street, Napa, CA 94559 (☎ **707/226-7455**) for a variety of local information. All over Napa and Sonoma, you can pick up a very informative (and free) weekly publication called *Wine Country Review.* It will give you the most up-to-date information on wineries and related area events.

TOURING THE WINERIES

Napa Valley is home to more than 250 wineries and an exceptional selection of restaurants and hostelries at all price levels. If you can, plan on spending more than a day here if you'd like to tour even a small segment of the valley and its wineries. The valley is just 35 miles long, so whether you stay in Napa, Yountville, Rutherford, or St. Helena, you can dine, wine, shop, and sightsee without traveling very far.

The beauty of the valley is striking any time of the year, but is most memorable in September and October when the grapes are being pressed and the air in the valley is intoxicating with color and scent.

Touring the Wine Country takes a little planning. With more than 250 wineries each offering a distinct wine, atmosphere, and experience, the best thing you can do is decide what you're most interested in and chart your path from there. Is it a specific wine you want to taste? A tour that interests you? Maybe it's the adjoining restaurant, picnic tables, or art collection that piques your interest. Whatever you do, plan to visit no more than four wineries in one day, ask locals which vintners have the type of experience you're looking for, and take it slow. Wine Country should never be rushed, but like a great glass of wine, should be savored.

Most wineries offer tours daily from 10am to 5pm. Depending on the winery, the tour will chart the process of wine making from the grafting and harvesting of the vines to the pressing, blending, and aging of the wines in oak casks. Most tours are free.

Wineries and towns listed below are organized geographically, from south to north along Calif. 29, beginning in Napa village.

Newlan Vineyards. 5225 Solano Ave., Napa, CA 94558. ☎ **707/257-2399.** Daily from 9am to 5pm.

This small, family-owned winery produces only about 10,000 cases a year. It began in 1967 when physicist Bruce Newlan planted 11 acres of cabernet sauvignon along Dry Creek. Three years later, 16 more acres were planted, and in five years Bruce and his wife, Jonette, had a winery. Cabernet sauvignon, pinot noir, chardonnay, zinfandel, and late harvest Johannesburg Riesling are produced. Tours are offered by appointment only, but you can stop for free wine tasting anytime during open hours.

Trefethen Vineyards. 1160 Oak Knoll Ave. (P.O. Box 2460), Napa, CA 94558. ☎ **707/255-7700.** Daily 10am–4:30pm; tours by appointment year-round. To reach Trefethen Vineyards from Calif. 29, take Oak Knoll Ave. East.

Listed on the National Register of Historical Places, the vineyard's main building was built in 1886, and remains Napa's only wooden, gravity-powered winery. The bucolic brick courtyard is surrounded with oak and cork trees and free wine samples are distributed in the brick-floored and wood-beamed tasting room. Although Trefethen is one of the valley's oldest wineries, it did not produce its first chardonnay until 1973—but thank goodness it did. Their whites and reds are both award-winners and a pleasure to the palate. Tours are offered by appointment only.

Stag's Leap Wine Cellars. 5766 Silverado Trail, Napa, CA 94558. ☎ **707/944-2020.** Sales and tasting daily 10am–4pm; tours by appointment only. Silverado Trail parallels Calif. 29, and you can get there by going east on Trancas St. or Oak Knoll Ave., then north to the cellars.

Founded in 1972, Napa's Stag's Leap Wine Cellars shocked the oenological world in 1976 when its 1973 cabernet won first place over French wines in a Parisian blind tasting. For $3 per person, you can be the judge of the winery's current releases, or you can fork over the big bucks for one of Stag's Leaps's best-known wines, Cabernet Sauvignon Cask 23.

Mumm. P.O. Drawer 500, 8445 Silverado Trail, Rutherford, CA 94573 ☎ **707/942-3434.** Apr–Sept daily, 10:30am–6pm; Oct–Mar daily 10:30am–5pm.

At first glance Mumm, housed in a big redwood barn, looks almost humble. But once you're in the front door, you'll know they mean big business. Just inside the entrance there's an extensive gift shop with champagne buckets, bottles of bubbly, and all sorts of namesake mementos. Beyond is the tasting room, where guests can purchase sparkling wine by the glass (ranging from $3.50 to $6) and take in the breathtaking vineyard and Mayacamas Mountain views. Unfortunately, there's no food or picnicking here, but during warm weather, with the open patio and a glass of champagne, you'll forget all about nibbling (watch out for that champagne kick!). Mumm also offers a 45-minute educational tour every hour from between 11am and 3pm daily as well as an art gallery that smells of crushed grapes and exhibits Ansel Adams photographs of the wine country.

Domaine Chandon. California Dr., at Calif. 29 (P.O. Box 2470), Yountville, CA 94599. ☎ **707/944-2280.** Nov–Apr, Wed–Sun 11am–6pm; May–Oct, daily 11am–6pm.

The valley's most renowned sparkling winery was founded in 1973 by French champagne house Möet et Chandon. The grounds are sculptured perfectly to match the opulent reputation of sparkling wines—it's the kind of place where the world's wealthy might stroll the beautifully manicured gardens under the shade of a delicate parasol, stop for sips of sparkling wine at the outdoor patio, then glide into the dining room for a world-class luncheon.

If you can pull yourself away from the bubbly (sold by the glass and served with complimentary hors d'oeuvres), there's a comprehensive tour of the facilities that's worth the stroll. At the gift shop you can pick up a bottle of Chandon Brut Cuvée, Carneros Blanc de Noirs, Chandon Réserve, and Etoile. There's also a small gallery housing artifacts from the vineyard's parent company, Möet et Chandon, depicting the history of champagnes. The Domaine Chandon restaurant is one of the best in the valley (see "Yountville," below, for complete information).

Robert Mondavi Winery. 7801 St. Helena Hwy. (Calif. 29) (P.O. Box 106), Oakville, CA 94562. ☎ **707/226-1395** or 800/MONDAVI. May–Oct, daily 9:30am–5:30pm; Nov–Apr, daily 9:30am–4:30pm.

If you continue on Calif. 29 up to Oakville, you'll arrive at the Robert Mondavi Winery. This is the ultimate high-tech Napa Valley winery, housed in a magnificent mission-style facility. Almost every processing variable in their wine making is computer controlled and absolutely fascinating to watch.

Reservations are recommended for the guided tour. It's wise to make them one to two weeks in advance, especially if you plan to go on a weekend. After the guided tour, you can taste the results of all this attention to detail with selected current wines. The Vineyard Room usually features an art show, and you'll find some exceptional antiques in the reception hall. During the summer the winery hosts some great outdoor jazz concerts.

St. Supéry Winery. P.O. Box 38, Rutherford, CA 94573. ☎ **707/963-4526** or 800/942-0809. Daily 9:30am–4:30pm.

The outside may look like a modern corporate office building, but inside is a functional and welcoming winery that encourages first-time wine tasters to learn more about oenology. On the self-guided tour, you can wander through the demonstration vineyard where you'll learn about growing techniques. Inside, kids gravitate toward "SmellaVision," an interactive display about how to identify different wine ingredients. Adjoining is the Atkinson House, a Queen Anne Victorian that houses more than 100 years of wine-making history. Tours and tasting are held daily throughout the year. For $2.50 you'll get lifetime tasting privileges, and though they probably won't be pouring their ever-popular Moscato dessert wine, the sauvignon blanc and chardonnay flow freely.

Beaulieu Vineyard. 1960 St. Helena Hwy. (Calif. 29), Rutherford, CA 94573. ☎ **707/963-2411.** Daily 10am–5pm; tours, daily 11am–4pm.

Bordeaux native Georges de Latour founded the third-oldest continuously operating winery in Napa Valley in 1900, and with the help of legendary oenologist André Tchelistcheff, produced world-class award-winning wines that have been served by every president of the United States since Roosevelt. The brick and redwood tasting room is not much to look at, but with Beaulieu's (say BOWL-YOU) stellar reputation, they have no need to visually impress. They do, however, offer you a complimentary glass of chardonnay the minute you walk through the door. The Private Reserve Tasting Room nearby offers tastes of reserve wines for a small fee. A free tour explains the wine-making process and the vineyard's history.

Niebaum-Coppola. 1991 St. Helena Hwy., Rutherford, CA 94573. ☎ **707/963-9099.** Daily 10am–5pm.

In March 1995, Hollywood met Napa Valley when filmmaker Francis Ford Coppola bought historic Inglenook Vineyards. Although Coppola has been dabbling in wine production for years, this is his biggest endeavor. He's plunked down millions to renovate the beautiful 1880s ivy-draped stone winery (purchased for somewhere between $8 and $10 million). Thankfully plans are to restore the entire property to its historic dimension, but it will, of course be combined with the glitz you'd expect from Tinsletown. On display are authentic academy awards, a 1948 Tucker automobile, props from *The Godfather,* and costumes from *Bram Stoker's Dracula.* More traditional vineyard memorabilia is showcased in the Centennial Museum, which chronicles the history of the estate and its wine making, and through a 15-minute film called *A Century of Taste.* Throughout all the Hollywood hullabaloo, wine is not forgotten, however. The goal is to produce 75,000 cases a year of quality wine made from organically grown grapes (wine tasting is $5). If you've had enough wine for the day, perk yourself up at the cappuccino bar. Aside from wine, you can buy Coppola movie memorabilia (surprise, surprise) or have a picnic at any of the designated (and beautiful) garden sites.

Flora Springs Wine Co. 1978 W. Zinfandel Lane, off Calif. 29, St. Helena, CA 94574. ☎ **707/963-5711.** By reservation only; call ahead or write.

While this handsome stone winery dates from Napa Valley's early days, the Flora Springs label first appeared in 1978 and is well known for its barrel-fermented chardonnay, a cabernet sauvignon, and Trilogy, a Bordeaux-style blend.

Flora Springs offers an excellent one-hour tour tailored to all levels of wine enthusiasts. Limited to groups of 10, the course is held Monday through Saturday by appointment only. The program begins in the vineyards, where you'll see a good-growing vine and taste the grapes. While the grapes are being crushed, you taste the must (just-pressed juice) and ultimately see how it becomes a beautiful, clear wine. Then you are taught how to evaluate wines and pair them with different foods.

Beringer Vineyards. 2000 Main St. (P.O. Box 111), St. Helena, CA 94574. ☎ **707/ 963-7115.** Daily 9:30am–5pm.

Follow the line of tourist cars just north of St. Helena's business district to Beringer Vineyards, where everyone stops at the remarkable Rhine House to taste wine and view the hand-dug tunnels carved out of the mountainside. Founded in 1876 by brothers Jacob and Frederick, the Beringer family owned it until 1971, when it was purchased by the Swiss firm of Nestlé. It is the oldest continuously operating winery in the Napa Valley, open even during Prohibition, when Beringer kept afloat by making "sacramental" wines.

Tasting of current vintages is conducted during sales hours in the Rhine House; reserve wines are available in the Founders' Room (upstairs) and a modest fee is charged per taste.

Sterling Vineyards. 1111 Dunaweal Lane, $^1/_2$ mile east of Calif. 29 (P.O. Box 365), Calistoga, CA 94515. ☎ **707/942-3344** or 800/726-6136. Sales and tasting, daily 10:30am–4:30pm. $6 per person.

No, you don't need climbing shoes to reach the grandiose Mediterranean-style Sterling Vineyards perched 300 feet up on a rocky knoll. The way to get to Sterling is scenic, but painless; just fork over $6 and you'll arrive via aerial tram, which offers exceptional views along the way. Once on land, follow the self-guided tour, which will take you through the fermenters, then down to the aging cellar, and farther down still to the final aging cellar. The winery, currently owned by the Seagram Classics Wine Company, produces more than 200,000 cases per year. Samples at the panoramic tasting room are included with tram fare.

NAPA

55 miles from San Francisco

Driving into Napa, you might wonder why you spent more than an hour in the car, only to find the Wine Country is really just a long strip of industrial spaces, motels, and cheesy discount stores. But have no fear; the town of Napa is the commercial center of the wine country and though it has more than its share of industry, thorough exploration will lead you to the rich country, terrain that justifiably makes this area one of California's most popular destinations.

WHAT TO SEE & DO

Napa Valley Wine Train. 1275 McKinstry St. (near First St. and Soscol Ave.). ☎ **707/ 253-2111** or 800/427-4124. Train fare without meals, $30 for daytime rides, $22 for evening rides. Supplement for brunch $22; supplement for lunch $25; supplement for dinner $39.50. Departures Sat–Sun and holidays at 8:30am; Mon–Fri at 11:30am, Sat–Sun and holidays at noon; Tues–Sun and holidays at 6pm. Reduced departure schedule Jan–Feb.

You don't have to worry about drinking and driving if you do the Wine Country aboard the Wine Train, a rolling restaurant that makes a three-hour, 36-mile journey through the vineyards of Napa, Yountville, Oakville, Rutherford, and St. Helena. The vintage-style cars—finished with polished Honduran mahogany paneling and etched-glass partitions—roll you back to opulent sophistication of the 1920s and 1930s. Gourmet meals are served by an attentive staff, complete with all the appropriate details: damask linen, bone china, silver flatware, and etched crystal. Menus are fixed, consisting of three or four courses, which might include poached

Norwegian salmon court bouillon or Black Angus filet mignon served with a cabernet and Roquefort sauce.

In addition to the dining rooms, the train pulls a wine-tasting car, a deli car, and three 50-passenger lounges.

Chardonnay Club. Calif. 12. ☎ **707/257-8950.** Greens fees $60 Mon–Thur, $80 Fri–Sun (includes mandatory cart and practice balls); at 1pm fees go down to $45 and $55 respectively. Course open daily, year-round.

South of downtown Napa, 1.3 miles east of Calif. 29, is a challenging 36-hole land-links golf complex with first-class service. You pay just one fee, which makes you a member for the day. Privileges include the use of a golf cart, the practice range (including a bucket of balls), and services usually found only at a private club. The day that we played, a snack cart came by on the course with a full complement of sandwiches and soft drinks. And at the end of the round, our clubs were cleaned. The course ambles through and around 325 acres of vineyards, hills, creeks, canyons, and rock ridges. There are three nines of similar challenge, all leaving from the clubhouse so that you can play the 18 of your choice. Five sets of tees provide you with a course measuring from 5,300 yards to a healthy 7,100. Starting times can be reserved up to two weeks in advance.

Chardonnay Club services include the golf shop, locker rooms, and a restaurant and grill.

WHERE TO STAY

If you need help organizing your Wine Country vacation, contact **Wine Country Referrals** at P.O. Box 543 Calistoga, CA 94515 (☎ **707/942-2186**). Fax 707/942-4681. It's a knowledgeable company that specializes in the area and offers extensive rental information on inns, hotels, motels, resorts, and vacation homes, as well as wineries, limousine tours, restaurants, spas, ballooning, gliders and train rides.

Expensive

Silverado Country Club & Resort. 1600 Atlas Peak Rd., Napa, CA 94558. ☎ **707/257-0200** or 800/532-0500. Fax 707/257-2867. 281 rms, 28 suites. A/C MINIBAR TV TEL. $195 studio; $255 one-bedroom suite; $365–$470 two- or three-bedroom suite. Golf and promotional packages available. Breakfast $8.50 extra. AE, CB, DC, MC, V. Free parking. Drive north on Calif. 29 to Trancas St.; then turn east to Atlas Peak Rd.

If you long for the opulence of an East Coast country club, bring your racket and golf clubs and fork over big dollars to play at Silverado, a 1,200-acre resort in the wine country foothills. The focus here is on the sporting life, and accommodations are up to par, featuring spacious accommodations ranging from very large studios with a king-size bed, kitchenette, and a roomy, well-appointed bath, to one-, two- or three-bedroom cottage suites, each with a wood-burning fireplace. Cottage suites are in private, low-rise groupings, each sharing tucked-away courtyards and peaceful walkways. All rooms are individually decorated with country home–style furnishings and an atmosphere of privacy.

Dining/Entertainment: The Royal Oak is the quintessential steak and seafood restaurant. Vintner's Court offers superb California and Pacific Rim cuisine with a view of the surrounding eucalyptus and well-tended flower beds. The Silverado Bar and Grill is a large indoor terrace/bar and outdoor deck that serves breakfast, lunch, and cocktails.

Services: Room service, concierge, laundry.

Facilities: The hotel's two golf courses are very cleverly designed by Robert Trent Jones Jr. The South Course is 6,500 yards, with a dozen water crossings; the North

Course is 6,700 yards, somewhat longer but a bit more forgiving. There is a staff of pros on hand. Greens fee is $105 for 18 holes on either course, including a mandatory cart. There are also tennis courts and several swimming pools, as well as a tour desk. No-smoking rooms are available.

Moderate

Cedar Gables Inn. 486 Coombs St., Napa, CA 94559. ☎ **707/224-7969** or 800/309-7969. Fax 707/224-4838. 6 rms. $109–$169 double ($10 less in winter). Rates include breakfast. AE, MC, V. From Calif. 29 north, exit onto First St. and follow signs to "Downtown." The house is at the corner of Oak St.

Innkeepers Margaret and Craig Snasdell have developed quite a following with their cozy, romantic getaway in Old Town Napa. A Victorian bed and breakfast, Cedar Gables was built in 1892, and rooms reflect the era with tapestries and antiques, which are gilded in rich old-world colors. Some accommodations have fireplaces; four have whirlpool tubs; and all feature queen-size elaborate brass, wood, or iron beds. Guests meet each evening in front of the roaring fireplace in the ground-floor sunken family room for complimentary wine and cheese. At other times, it's a perfect place to cuddle up and watch the large-screen television.

Château Hotel. 4195 Solano Ave., Napa, CA 94558. ☎ **707/253-9300** or 800/253-6272 in California. Fax 707/253-0906. 115 rms, 6 suites. A/C TV TEL. Nov–Mar, $100 double; Apr–Oct, $115 double. Rates include buffet breakfast. AE, CB, DC, MC, V. Free parking. From Calif. 29 north, turn left just past Trower Ave., at the entrance to the Napa Valley wine region.

The Château is a contemporary, two-story hotel complex. Rooms are spacious, have individually controlled heating and air-conditioning, and are furnished with oversized beds. Most have refrigerators, and 10 rooms are especially designed for disabled guests. The bath is well sized and comes with a separate vanity/dressing area. Rates include breakfast and a daily newspaper.

If you're used to a daily swim, the Château has a heated pool and spa.

Tall Timbers Chalets. 1012 Darms Lane, Napa, CA 94558. ☎ **707/252-7810.** 8 cottages. A/C MINIBAR TV. Dec–Feb, Sun–Thurs $75 double, Fri–Sat and holidays $90–$105 double; Mar–Nov, Sun–Thurs $80–$95 double, Fri–Sat and holidays $95–$125 double. Extra person $10. AE, MC, V. Free parking. From Calif. 29 north, turn left onto Darms Lane before you reach Yountville.

While many hotels' prices skyrocket during the high season, Tall Timbers—a group of eight whitewashed, roomy cottages surrounded by pines and eucalyptus—remains a cute, centrally located, and affordable option.

Each cottage is nicely decorated and includes a toaster oven and coffeemaker, as well as a basket of fresh fruit waiting for you upon your arrival. Other sweet touches include breakfast treats in the refrigerator and a complimentary bottle of champagne. To maximize the getaway atmosphere, there are no phones in the cottages, but you can always use the one in the main office. Each sleeps up to four (there's a bedroom plus a queen-size sofa bed in the living room) and several have sundecks. Smokers take heed: no inhaling (or faking it) allowed.

Tall Timbers Chalets is not particularly difficult to find, but to be one the safe side, ask for specific directions.

Inexpensive

Napa Valley Budget Inn. 3380 Solano Ave., Napa, CA 94558. ☎ **707/257-6111.** 58 rms. A/C TV TEL. $56–$79 double. AE, DC, DISC, MC, V. Free parking. From Calif. 29 north, turn left onto the Redwood Rd. turnoff and go one block to Solano Ave.; then turn left and go half a block to the motel.

The location of this no-frills lodging is excellent: close to Calif. 29. Rooms are simple, clean, and comfortable. Local calls are free, and there is a small heated pool on the premises. No breakfast is served.

WHERE TO DINE
Moderate
The Red Hen Cantina. 5091 St. Helena Hwy., Napa. ☎ **707/255-8125.** Reservations for large parties only. Lunches $4–$9; main courses $8–$14. AE, DC, MC, V. Sun–Thurs 11am–9pm, Fri–Sat 11am–10pm. MEXICAN.

This is a popular taqueria serving moderately priced food. Seafood dishes supplement the traditional Mexican burritos, tacos, and pollo Mexicano (chicken strips sautéed in white wine, onion, mushrooms, and tomatoes).

YOUNTVILLE
70 miles from San Francisco

Of less historical interest than St. Helena or Calistoga, Yountville is nonetheless an excellent jumping-off point for a wineries tour or for the simple enjoyment of the beauty of the valley. It also has several worthwhile places to stay, interesting shops, and excellent restaurants at various price levels.

At the center of the village is **Vintage 1870** (☎ 707/944-2451), once a winery (from 1871 to 1955) and now a gallery with specialty shops selling antiques, wine accessories, country collectibles, and more. It is also home to three restaurants.

Tired of driving through and tasting the results of the Napa Valley grapevines? Try a different perspective: Balloon over them. **Adventures Aloft,** Vintage 1870 (P.O. Box 2500), Yountville, CA 94599 (☎ **707/944-4408** or 800/944-4408), is Napa Valley's oldest hot-air balloon company, with full-time professional pilots. Groups are small and flights last about an hour. Like all ballooneries, Adventures Aloft flies in the early morning, when the winds are gentle and the air is cool. The cost includes a preflight continental breakfast, a postflight champagne brunch, and a framed first-flight certificate. The cost is $185 per person.

WHERE TO STAY
Expensive
Vintage Inn. 6541 Washington St., Yountville, CA 94599. ☎ **707/944-1112** or 800/ 351-1133. Fax 707/944-1617. 72 rms, 8 minisuites. A/C TV TEL. $150–$275 double; $240–$325 minisuites and villas. Extra person $25. Rates include continental breakfast. AE, CB, DC, MC, V. Free parking. From Calif. 29 north, take the Yountville exit and turn left onto Washington St.

Built on an old 23-acre winery estate in the center of town, Vintage Inn is a contemporary-style, country-French luxury inn in the heart of adorable Yountville. Rooms are bright and cozy, each containing a fireplace or private verandah, oversize beds, and a coffeemaker, plus tubs with Jacuzzi jets and plush bathrobes. If you're looking for a workout, you may rent a bike, reserve one of the two tennis courts, or take a dip. Don't worry because swimming is not seasonal here—the 60-foot swimming pool and outdoor whirlpool are heated year-round. A California continental champagne breakfast (cereals, yogurt, pastries, egg salad, and fruit) and afternoon tea are included and served daily in the Vintage Club. Services include concierge and laundry/valet.

Moderate
Burgundy House Country Inn. 6711 Washington St. (P.O. Box 3156), Yountville, CA 94599. ☎ **707/944-0889.** 5 rms (all with bath). A/C. $125 double. Rates include breakfast. MC, V. Free parking. From Calif. 29 north, take the Yountville exit and turn left onto Washington St.

This distinctly French country inn, built in the early 1890s of local fieldstone and river rock, is tiny yet impressive. Originally built as a brandy distillery, the interior still features thick stone walls and hand-hewn post and lintel beams, enhanced today by antique country furnishings. Each of the five cozy guest rooms has colorful quilted spreads and comfortable beds. All are no-smoking rooms. Delightful touches include fresh flowers in each of the rooms and a complimentary decanter of local white wine. The full breakfast can be taken inside or outdoors in the inn's pretty garden.

Napa Valley Lodge. 2230 Madison St, Yountville, CA 94599 ☎ **707/944-2468** or 800/368-2468. Fax 707/944-9362. 55 rms. $120–$210 double. Rates include continental breakfast. MC, V.

If you don't mind the corporate feel or a view of the highway beyond the swimming pool, the Napa Valley Lodge offers ultraclean, good-size accommodations. Rooms are better appointed than many in the area, and many have vaulted ceilings and fireplaces. All come with a king- or queen-size bed, wicker furnishings, coffeemakers, and either a private balcony or a patio. The cheapest rooms are darker, motel-style, and ground-level, but if you don't want to hang out there, you can always head to the swimming pool, garden spa, sauna, or fitness center. Extras include concierge, complimentary extended continental breakfast buffet, on-command video, afternoon tea and cookies in the lobby, and Friday evening wine tasting in the library. With all the extras, it's no wonder AAA gave the Napa Valley Lodge the four-diamond award for excellence. Ask about winter discounts—they can be up to 30%.

WHERE TO DINE

Expensive

Domaine Chandon. One California Dr. ☎ **707/944-2892.** Reservations required. Main courses $13–$17 at lunch, $24–$28 at dinner. AE, DC, MC, V. Summer, daily 11:30am–2:30pm; Wed–Sun 6–9:30pm. Winter, Wed–Sun 11:30am–2:30pm and 6–9:30pm. Closed first three weeks of Jan. From Calif. 29 north, take the Yountville exit; the restaurant is on the west side of the highway. CALIFORNIA/FRENCH.

There may be no experience more extravagant than a meal at Domaine Chandon. Before even seeing the dining room you'll know you're in the lap of luxury when you see the grounds—ponds, foot bridges, swans, rose gardens, and all. In a word, it's magnificent. Inside isn't shabby either, with a formal dining area encased in large glass windows looking onto the greenery beyond and a wait staff so attentive you're never in need of anything. Tables are dispersed throughout the multilevel interior with arched, fir-paneled ceilings, or on warmer days you can dine outdoors overlooking the vineyards. You must, of course, start with champagne. As for the food menu, just listen for the "mmmmms" and "aaaaaahs" from the surrounding tables and anticipate chiming in when you savor the renowned cream of tomato soup in puff pastry; the caramelized sea scallops with carrots, white corn, and crispy onion rings; or double-cut pork chop with garlic-roasted potatoes, cipollini onions, and caramelized shallot sauce. No matter how much you love every bite of your meal, don't under any circumstances fill up before dessert. End the ultimate of indulgences with any of the sweets, which might include a "Floating Island" with caramel, almonds, and vanilla custard; or the hot and gooey chocolate cake with vanilla ice cream.

Moderate

Mark Allen. 6795 Washington St. ☎ **707/944-0168.** Main courses $12.95–$18.95. AE, MC, V. Daily 11:30–3; dinner 5pm–10pm. CALIFORNIA.

Pacific Rim–influenced California food has made its way up to the Wine Country at Mark Allen, a quaint, airy restaurant that opened in summer of 1995 in the heart of Yountville. Following the Wine Country trend, chef and owner Mark Allen (formerly presiding at San Francisco's Inn at the Opera) styled his restaurant and cafe in a casually sophisticated fashion, with ceramic and tile Mediterranean floors and modern formal table settings. The food is equally as interesting, with such choices as tempura-battered prawns with a spicy bean sprout salad in a soy-mustard vinaigrette starter, or main courses like grilled pork chop with butternut squash raviolis topped with maple/sun-dried–cherry sauce. Word around town is that Mark Allen is a great new choice in Napa Valley.

Mustards Grill. 7399 St. Helena Hwy. (Calif. 29). ☎ **707/944-2424.** Reservations recommended. Main courses $11–$17. CB, DC, MC, V. Apr–Oct, daily 11:30am–10pm; Nov–Mar, daily 11:30am–9pm. CALIFORNIA.

It's always a pleasant surprise to find a serious restaurant with a strong sense of humor. Mustards is one of those places. The minute we sat down here and glanced at the menu, it immediately advised us: "Have a glass of wine," which we did. We were left alone long enough to notice that Mustards is a convivial space—a barn-style restaurant is encased in dark wood and windows with a marble checkerboard floor—before the jovial waiter pointed out the ambitious chalkboard list of specials. Following California's most recent trend, we started out with a wonderfully light seared ahi tuna appetizer that melted in our mouths the way ahi should, and that was served with delicious little crackers. Although the slow smoked barbecue pork ("ooo-eee!" says the menu) and the grilled rabbit with roasted squash polenta and piquant sauce were tempting, we opted for a moist and perfectly flavored grilled chicken breast with mashed potatoes and fresh herbs. We topped off our meal with a startling lemon meringue pie that was topped with the tallest, most perfectly browned meringue we've ever seen. The menu may joke and include such items as wine openers and T-shirts, but on a more serious note, it also includes something for every type of eater, from gourmands and vegetarians to good old burger lovers. Order from the six-page wine list that reads like the who's who in the industry, or you can indulge by the glass for $3.50 to $7.

Napa Valley Grille. 6795 Washington St. ☎ **707/944-8686.** Reservations accepted. Main courses $12–$22; lunch $7–$14. AE, DISC, MC, V. Mon–Thurs 11:30am–9:30pm, Fri–Sat 11:30am–10pm, Sun 10am–9:30pm. The restaurant is located directly on Highway 29 at Madison St. CALIFORNIA/MEDITERRANEAN.

In case you've forgotten that you're in the thick of the vineyard region, the Grille's grape motif woven into tapestries, the wine rack room dividers, and the Napa Valley art on the walls will undoubtedly remind you. The menu synchronizes with its "Wine Country cuisine" prepared with fresh, local ingredients and served against a backdrop of Napa's vineyards. The Grille also offers an extensive wine list featuring, you guessed it, Napa Valley wines. On sunny afternoons, most opt for the umbrella-shaded patio, but inside you can watch the swirl of activity in the exhibition kitchen. The menu offers an array of dishes: smoked duck or hickory-roasted game hen or a pasta such as black spaghetti with rock shrimp, scallops, calamari, enoki mushrooms, and a white wine sauce. Lunches feature a long list of salads to cool you off from the summer heat (in addition to a well-rounded selection of other dishes), and brunch always offers myriad morning munchies, including a smoked-salmon omelet with roasted peppers and herbed cream, or Dungeness crab cakes with poached eggs and Cajun hollandaise.

Inexpensive

The Diner. 6476 Washington St. ☎ **707/944-2626.** Reservations not accepted. Breakfast $4–$8; lunch $6–$10; dinner $8–$13.25. No credit cards. Tues–Sun 8am–3pm and 5:30–9pm.

From Calif. 29 north, take the Yountville exit and turn left onto Washington St. AMERICAN/
MEXICAN.

Funky California meets traditional roadside eatery at this diner that features a func-
tioning Irish Waterford wood stove, a collection of vintage diner water pitchers, and
an art exhibit that changes monthly.

Though named appropriately after its appearance, the Diner's fare is far from that
of a regular greasy spoon; here the menu is extensive, portions are huge, and the
food is very good. Breakfasts feature good old-fashioned omelets, French toast, and
German potato pancakes.

Lunch and dinner dishes include a host of Mexican and American dishes such as
tamari-basted chicken breast salad on baby greens, grilled fresh fish, giant burritos,
and thick sandwiches made with house-roasted meats and homemade bread.

Mark Allen Cafe. 6795 Washington St. ☎ **707/944-0148.** Main courses $4.75–$7.25.
AE, MC, V. Daily 7am–7pm; winter 7am–5pm. CALIFORNIA.

Next door to Mark Allen's upscale dining room, his casual, bright cafe features gourmet deli selections. Sandwiches, served on homemade focaccia, come piled high with
smoked chicken with cheddar, cured salmon and pancetta, or grilled portobello
mushrooms and prosciutto with roasted garlic. Focaccia pizzas are sprinkled with
upscale toppings like duck or goat cheese and salads, pastries, and desserts are equally
as tantalizing.

OAKVILLE & RUTHERFORD

68 miles from San Francisco

Driving farther north on the St. Helena Highway (Calif. 29) brings you to the
Oakville Cross Road and the ✪ **Oakville Grocery Co.,** 7856 St. Helena Hwy., in
Oakville (☎ **707/944-8802**), one of the finest gourmet food stores this side of New
York's Dean and Deluca. Here you can put together the provisions for a memorable
picnic or for a very special custom gift basket. You'll find the best breads and the
choicest selection of cheeses in the northern Bay Area, as well as pâtés, fresh foie gras
(domestic and French, seasonally), smoked Norwegian salmon, smoked sturgeon and
smoked pheasant (by special order), fresh caviar (Beluga, Sevruga, Osetra), and an
exceptional selection of California wines, of course. The grocery will prepare a picnic basket for you themselves with 24-hours' notice. Delivery service is available to
some areas. It's open daily from 10am to 6pm.

WHERE TO STAY

Expensive

✪ **Auberge du Soleil.** 180 Rutherford Hill Rd., Rutherford, CA 94573. ☎ **707/963-1211.**
Fax 707/963-8764. 50 rms and suites. A/C TV TEL MINIBAR. Weekdays $175–$750 double;
weekends $250–$850 double from April to November. Rates are discounted from Dec–Mar.
AE, DC, DISC, MC, V. From Rutherford turn right on 128 and go 3 miles to the Silverado Trail.
Turn left and head north about 200 yards to Rutherford Hill Rd. Turn right.

Auberge du Soliel is the kind of place you'd imagine movie stars would frequent for
a clandestine affair or a weekend retreat. It's set high above the Napa Valley in a
33-acre olive grove (as you stroll the terraced pathways to your private cottage, you
may find a groundsworker gathering sun-ripened olives in baskets), and each accommodation is quiet, indulgent, and luxuriously romantic. The Mediterranean-style
rooms are large enough to get lost in—and you might want to once you discover all
the amenities. The bathtub alone, an enormous hot tub complete with bath salts and
a skylight overhead, will entice you to grab a glass of California red and settle in for
a while. A wood-burning fireplace is surrounded by oversized, cushy furniture with

bright, playfully pink pillows. Fresh flowers and original art, combined with terra-cotta floors and natural wood and leather furnishings, whisk you out of the Wine Country and into the Southwest, but once you step out onto the private balcony, you'll know you've left this planet and gone straight to heaven. Views of the valley are nothing less than spectacular, and each sun-washed deck is entirely exclusive. Auberge du Soleil, or "inn of the sun," also has a celestial swimming pool and work-out room with one of the grandest views around. All in all, it's one of the best places we've ever stayed.

Dining: See separate listing.

Services: 24-hour room service, twice-daily maid service, laundry/valet, compli-mentary shoeshine.

Facilities: Outdoor pool with sundeck, massage rooms, 3 tennis courts, exercise room, beauty salon. Sculpture and nature trail with picnic areas that crisscross the property.

Rancho Caymus. 1140 Rutherford Rd. (P.O. Box 78), Rutherford, CA 94573. ☎ **707/963-1777** or 800/845-1777. Fax 707/963-5387. 26 suites. A/C MINIBAR TV TEL. $125–$155 double, from $235 Master Suite, $295 two-bedroom suite. Rates include continental breakfast. AE, DC, MC, V. From Calif. 29 north, turn right onto Rutherford Rd./128 East; the hotel is ahead on your left.

This Spanish-style hacienda inn was the creation of sculptor Mary Tilden Morton (of Morton Salt). Her family originally constructed this $4 million retreat, with two floors opening onto wisteria-covered balconies. Morton wanted each room in the

Wine Country to Go

Stop wining for a few minutes and take some time to explore a variety of small shops offering alternative Napa Valley mementos. There are dozens of roadside retailers selling handcrafted, collected, and imported items. Here are a few of our favorites:

Want to bring home an unusual and beautiful handcrafted decoration for your home or yard? Seek out **Napa Valley Grapevine Wreath Company,** which weaves big and small indoor or outdoor sculptures made out of little more than cabernet grapevines. Options range from a basic wreath to a star or a full-scale reindeer and all are priced competitively. Call for directions—this tiny shack of a shop is hidden on a side road between Rutherford's vineyards at P.O. Box 67, Rutherford, CA 94573 (☎ **707/963-8893**). Hours vary during winter but are generally Wednes-day through Monday from 10:30am to 5:30pm.

Don't bother forking over big bucks at a gift shop for fancy bottles of olive oil. **Napa Valley Olive Oil Manufacturing Company,** located at the end of Charter Oak Road behind St. Helena's Tra Vigne restaurant, presses and bottles its own oil and sells it at a fraction of the price you'll pay elsewhere. They also have an exten-sive selection of Italian cooking ingredients, imported snacks, and the best deals on exotic mushrooms we've ever seen. It is located at 835 Charter Oak, St. Helena (☎ **707/963-4173**).

Looking for a trinket but don't know quite what you want? Plan to spend at least an hour strolling **Red Hen's** co-op collection of antiques. There's everything here from baseball cards to living room sets, and prices are remarkably affordable. You can't miss this enormous red, barn-style building on Highway 129, at 5091 St. Helena Hwy. (at Oak Knoll Avenue West), Napa, CA 94558 (☎ **415/707/257-0822**). It's open daily from 10am to 5:30pm.

hacienda to be a work of art, hiring the most skilled craftspeople of her day. She designed the adobe fireplaces herself, based on old designs, and wandered through Mexico and South America purchasing artifacts for the property.

Guest rooms are situated around a whimsical garden courtyard adorned with wrought-iron patio furniture and an enormous outdoor fireplace. Decor inside is on the funky side: mixed and matched, overly varnished dark wood furnishings, braided rugs—kind of like a visit to Grandma's house. It is cozy, however, and rooms are decent sized, split-level suites with queen-size beds. Other amenities include a wet bar, a sofa bed in the sitting area, and a small private patio. Twenty-two of the rooms have wood-burning fireplaces, and five have kitchenettes and whirlpool tubs. The rooms and public areas are full of character with hand-carved, black walnut furniture, stained-glass windows, and wall hangings woven by Ecuadorian Otavalon Indians.

Dining: Breakfast, which includes fresh fruit and breads and is included in the rates, is served in the inn's Mont St. John restaurant.

WHERE TO DINE
Expensive

Auberge du Soleil. 180 Rutherford Hill Rd., Rutherford. ☎ **707/963-1211.** Reservations recommended. Main courses $25–$30 dinner; fixed-price dinner $60. AE, DISC, MC, V. Daily 7–11am, 11:30am–2:30pm, and 6–9:30pm. WINE COUNTRY CUISINE.

Auberge du Soleil may be better known for its inn, but it was the restaurant that started all the fuss about this world-class resort. Frenchman Claude Rouas spent $1.5 million (an unheard amount for a Wine Country restaurant at the time) building the restaurant in 1981, and it became such an instant success that the inn soon followed.

Alfresco dining is taken to an entirely new level here, particularly on warm summer nights when diners are rewarded with a gorgeous view of the Mayacamas Mountains fading with the sunset. Inside, a magnificent fireplace, huge wood pillars, and fresh flowers combine to create a warm, rustic ambiance. Chef Andrew Sutton characterizes his cuisine as "Wine Country," a reflection of the region's produce and international influence: Pacific Rim, southwestern, and Mediterranean styles predominate. Your potato-crusted Chilean sea bass, for example, may come with caraway-savoy cabbage and truffled beet relish. Signature dishes include roasted lobster sausage with fennel salad and mustard seed vinaigrette, and grapevine-smoked salmon with walnut wheat croutons and roasted shallot-capers relish. Regardless of what you order, be sure to arrive before sunset and beg for terrace seating.

ST. HELENA
73 miles from San Francisco

Located 17 miles north of Napa on Highway 29, this former Seventh Day Adventist village manages to maintain a pseudo Old West feel while simultaneously catering to upscale shoppers with deep pockets—hence the **Vanderbilt's,** purveyor of fine housewares, at 1429 Main Street. It's a quiet, attractive little town hosting a slew of beautiful old homes and first-rate restaurants and accommodations.

WHAT TO SEE & DO BEYOND THE WINERIES

Literary buffs and other romantics will want to visit the **Silverado Museum** at 1490 Library Lane (☎ **707/963-3757**), which is devoted to the life and works of Robert Louis Stevenson, who honeymooned here in 1880 in an abandoned Silverado Mine bunkhouse. More than 8,000 museum items include original manuscripts, letters, photographs, and portraits, plus the desk he used in Samoa. It's open Tuesday through Sunday from noon to 4pm; admission is free.

The quieter northern end of the valley is an ideal place to rent a bicycle and ride the Silverado Trail. **St. Helena Cyclery,** at 1156 Main St. (☎ **707/963-7736**), rents bikes for $7 per hour or $25 a day, including rear rack and picnic bag.

WHERE TO STAY
Very Expensive

Meadowood Resort. 900 Meadowood Lane, St. Helena, CA 94574 ☎ **707/458-8080.** Fax 707/963-3532. 85 rms. A/C, MINIBAR, TV, TEL. rooms $320–$465; 1-bedroom lodge from $540; 2-bedroom from $830; 3-bedroom from $1,180; 4-bedroom from $1,520. Ask about promotional offers and off-season rates. Two-night minimum. AE, DISC, DC, MC, V.

Less reclusive than Auberge du Soliel, Meadowood is the wealthy grown-ups' summer camp. The resort, tucked away on 250 acres of pristine mountainside amidst a forest of madrone and oak trees, is quiet and exclusive enough to make you forget that busy wineries are 10 minutes away. Many rooms are individual suite-lodges so far removed from the common areas, you must drive to get to them (lazier folks can opt for more centrally located accommodations). Inside, abodes are decorated with American country classics, have beamed ceilings, private patios, stone fireplaces, and wilderness views. Guests spend their days playing on the nine-hole golf course, tennis courts, croquet lawns, swimming pools, health spa, or hiking the surrounding areas. Those who actually want to leave here to do some wine tasting can check in with John Thoreen, the hotel wine tutor, whose sole purpose is to help guests better understand and enjoy Napa Valley's "liquid poetry." Each year the Napa Valley wine auction is held here in June.

Dining: See "Where to Dine," below.

Facilities: Golf, croquet, two outdoor pools with sundeck, massage rooms, 7 tennis courts, exercise room, hiking trails, and an executive conference center.

Harvest Inn. 1 Main St., St. Helena, CA 94574. ☎ **707/963-9463** or 800/950-8466. 54 rms. A/C TV TEL. $185–$220 double. AE, DC, DISC, MC, V.

If you like your accommodations loaded with 20th-Century luxuries yet reminiscent of an Old English inn, you'll like the Harvest Inn. Ornate brick walkways pass through the beautifully landscaped grounds to this Tudor-style inn. Each of the immaculate rooms—with names like "The Earl of Ecstasy" and "Camelot"—are furnished in dark Tudor style with oak beds and dressers, black leather chairs, and antique furnishings; most have brick fireplaces, wet bars, and refrigerators. Facilities include a wine bar, heated swimming pools, and outdoor spas.

Hotel St. Helena. 1309 Main St., St. Helena, CA 94574. ☎ **707/963-4388.** 17 rms (14 with private bath), 1 suite. A/C TEL. $140 double without bath; $190 double with bath; $250 suite. Rates include continental breakfast. AE, DC, MC, V.

This downtown hotel occupies a historic 1881 building, the oldest wooden structure in St. Helena. The hotel keepers celebrated the building's 100th birthday with a much-needed renovation; now, it's more comfortable than ever. The hallways are cluttered with stuffed animals, wicker strollers, and other memorabilia. Most of the rooms have been similarly decorated, with brass beds, wall-to-wall burgundy carpeting, and oak or maple furnishings. There's a garden patio and wine bar. TVs are available upon request. Smoking is discouraged.

The Inn at Southbridge. 1020 Main St., St. Helena, CA 94574. ☎ **707/967-9400** or 800/520-6800. Fax 707/967-9486. MINIBAR TV TEL. $175–$225 double. AE, DC, DISC, JCB, MC, V.

Inspired by small town squares of Europe, The Inn at Southbridge is a welcomed new addition to St. Helena's hotels. It's right next door to **Tra Vigne** (see "Where to

Dine," below), so you can crawl home after stuffing yourself. It's brand new so everything's immaculate, and it's run by the same company that owns Meadowood Resort—they know about style. Rooms are located in adjoining buildings and have vaulted ceilings, fireplaces, bathroom skylights, down comforters, and terry-cloth robes; many have private balconies. Decor is upscale Pottery Barn trendy, which from our point of view is a welcome upgrade from traditional hotel-style stuff; and the rooms have cute and functional touches such as umbrellas, voice mail, and fax modems. On the premises is brand-new restaurant, **Tomatina,** which is owned and run by owners of Tra Vigne. Services include concierge and guest privileges at sister resort Meadowood (for golf, tennis, croquet, spa and fitness swimming).

Expensive

Bartels Ranch & Country Inn. 1200 Conn Valley Rd., St. Helena, CA 94574. ☎ **707/ 963-4001.** Fax 707/963-5100. 4 rms. A/C TV TEL. $135–$315 double. AE, DC, DISC, MC, JCB, V. From downtown St. Helena, turn east on Pope St., cross Silverado Trail and continue onto Howell Mountain Rd. Bear right onto Conn Valley Rd.; the inn is 2 miles ahead on the left.

This palatial retreat, perched on 60 acres of rolling meadows studded with fig trees, cypress, and old oaks, is run by ebullient innkeeper Jamie Bartels, who designed the 7,000-square-foot stone ranch house and has decorated it with her own collection of butterflies and other mementos. The four individually decorated rooms provide every conceivable comfort—fireplaces, VCRs, balconies—plus conveniences like ironing boards, hair dryers, and private baths. The champagne suite has a heart-shaped Jacuzzi in the bathroom, while the Blue Valley room has a private deck and Jacuzzi. The house has a communal sundeck and pool, as well as a game room filled with books, a pool and Ping-Pong table, and a stereo. The bountiful breakfasts consist of fresh fruits, breads, and egg dishes; complimentary wine, fruit and cheese are served each afternoon. Forever aiming to please, Jamie can provide her guests with picnic supplies, lend bicycles, and arrange massages or wine-country tours. A bocce ball court, croquet grounds, and access to horseback riding and tennis courts are other outdoor options.

Wine Country Inn. 1152 Lodi Lane, St. Helena, CA 94574. ☎ **707/963-7077.** Fax 707/ 963-9018. 24 rms. A/C TEL. $115–$248 double. Rates include breakfast. MC, V.

Just off the highway behind Freemark Abbey Vineyard, this attractive wood-and-stone inn, complete with a French-style mansard roof and turret, overlooks a pastoral landscape of Napa Valley vineyards. The rooms are furnished with iron or brass beds and pine country furnishings; most have fireplaces and private terraces overlooking the valley, while others have private hot tubs. One of the inn's best features, besides the absence of televisions, is the outdoor pool, which is attractively landscaped into the hillside.

Moderate

✪ **El Bonita Motel.** 195 Main St. (at El Bonita Ave.), St. Helena, CA 94574. ☎ **707/ 963-3216** or 800/541-3284. 26 rms. A/C MINIBAR TV TEL. $79–$120 double. AE, DC, MC, V.

This 1930s art deco motel is set in $2^1/2$ acres of beautifully landscaped gardens. The rooms are decorated in typical modern style and contain amenities such as microwave ovens and coffeemakers; some have kitchens or whirlpool baths. Families, attracted to the bungalows with kitchenettes, often consider El Bonita one of the best values in Napa Valley, especially considering that the motel comes with a heated outdoor pool, Jacuzzi, sauna, and new massage facility.

WHERE TO DINE

Expensive

Restaurant at Meadowood. At the Meadowood Resort, 900 Meadowood Lane, St. Helena, CA 94574. ☎ 707/963-3646. Reservations recommended. Price-fixed $45; vegetarian $39. AE, DISC, DC, MC, V. Daily 6–10pm. AMERICAN/FRENCH.

One of Napa's more ambitious four-course dinners is served at Meadowood, a top-rated resort with a gazebo-style clubhouse dining room overlooking the golf course. Chef Roy Breiman brought his Southern-French influenced menu to the restaurant a few years back after leaving renowned Ernie's of San Francisco. He's obviously comfortable in his new kitchen because every course we had was well balanced and delicious. Dinner started with a heavy and flavorful warm quail salad with smoky lentils and soy sauce, which was robust but not too heavy. Next came a crispy skinned salmon trout served with exotic mushrooms and truffle oil—superb. The main-course roast moscovy duck flavored with cinnamon star anise and orange was not only impressive in presentation, but also was cooked the way we like it, with the fat well-cooked off the skin. Caramelized banana with currants and vanilla ice cream finished the evening, thank goodness, because we couldn't eat another bite. Though we didn't have room to taste it, the vegetarian four-course meal sounded just as tasty and featured couscous served with layered zucchini flavored with anise seeds and crispy strudel with artichokes, onions, and wild mushrooms. Take a little stroll around the tranquil grounds afterward.

✪ **Terra.** 1345 Railroad Ave. (between Adams and Hunt sts.). ☎ **707/963-8931.** Reservations recommended. Main courses $14–$23. DC, MC, V. Sun–Thur 6–9pm, Fri–Sat 6–10pm. CONTEMPORARY AMERICAN

St. Helena's restaurant of choice, Terra is the creation of Lissa Doumani and her husband, Hiro Sone, a master chef who hails from Japan and once worked with Wolfgang Puck at Spago. Sone makes full use of the region's bounty; he seems to know how to coax every nuance of flavor from his fine local ingredients. The simple dining room is a perfect foil for Sone's extraordinary food. Among the appetizers, the terrine of foie gras with apple, walnut, and endive salad and the home-smoked salmon with cucumber dill salad, caviar, and sour cream are the stars of the show. The main dishes successfully fuse different cooking styles: Try the grilled salmon with Thai red-curry sauce or the sake-marinated sea bass with shrimp dumplings in shiso broth. A recommended finale? The apple crostata with vanilla bean ice cream and cinnamon apple cider sauce.

✪ **Tra Vigne Restaurant & Cantinetta.** 1050 Charter Oak Ave., St. Helena. ☎ **707/963-4444,** 707/963-8888 for the cantinetta. Reservations recommended. Main courses $12.50–$16; cantinetta $4–$8. CB, DC, DISC, MC, V. Daily 11:30am–9:30pm; cantinetta daily 11:30am–6pm. ITALIAN.

If you can only dine at one restaurant while visiting the Wine Country, make it at Tra Vigne. Sure, there are a few fancier places in town, but there's no restaurant that measures up to the combined qualities of this restaurant's atmosphere, food, and pricing. The enormous dining room, with 30-foot ceilings, a hand-carved bar, and ultramodern Italian light fixtures, packs 'em in every night. And whether diners are seated next to the immense curved windows that open onto a large veranda, on the veranda itself (heated during cold nights), or in the center of the bustling scene, they're usually thrilled just to have gotten a seat. Even though it's tempting, don't fill up on the wonderful bread served with house-made flavored olive oils (sold at the adjoining Cantinetta); instead, save plenty of room for the robust California dishes cooked with Italian style that's made this place everyone's favorite.

The menu features about seven or so pizzas, including a succulent version with caramelized onions, thyme, and gorgonzola. The dishes of the day might include a grilled and cedar-planked tuna with herb salad and roasted tomato vinaigrette or a grilled Sonoma rabbit with teleme-layered potatoes, oven-dried tomatoes, and mustard pan sauce, and a dozen or so antipasti. Pastas are equally tempting, including ceppo with sausage, spinach, potatoes, sun-dried tomatoes, and Pecorino. Desserts are delicious and might include warm apple tart with candied walnut crust, sweet gorgonzola, and caramel sauce.

The restaurant's adjoining cafe, called the Cantinetta, offers a small selection of sandwiches, pizzas, and lighter meals (we've never had a better focaccia in our lives!). They also pack picnics, and sell about 20 flavored olive oils infused with everything from roasted garlic to lavender, as well as other creative cooking ingredients.

✪ **Trilogy.** 1234 Main St. (at Hunt Ave.). ☎ **707/963-5507.** Reservations required. Main courses $14.50–$20; fixed-price menu $48. DC, MC, V. Tues–Fri noon–2pm; Tues–Sat 5–9pm. Closed 3 weeks in Dec. CALIFORNIA/FRENCH.

The creation of Diane Pariseau, this small, low-key restaurant is a favorite of Wine Country moguls, with a wine list that is probably second to none in the valley. Pariseau and her assistant do virtually everything themselves, turning out exceptionally fresh food prepared with a fine-honed technique. Though a standard à la carte menu is available, the real treat here is the $48 four-course fixed-price menu, with each course accompanied by the appropriate glass of superior quality wine ("The best deal around," says Pariseau). The menu changes daily, but such delectable cuisine as fresh corn crepes or a wild mushroom ragout are typical of the offerings here. Other selections may include goat cheese gnocchi with sun-dried tomato and roast garlic sauce, or pan-roasted monkfish wrapped in smoked bacon with braised cabbage (accompanied by a peppery '93 Jade Mountain Syrah, of course).

Moderate

Brava Terrace. 3010 St. Helena Hwy. ☎ **707/963-9300.** Reservations recommended. Main courses $8–$15. AE, DC, DISC, MC, V. Thur–Tue noon–9pm. CALIFORNIA/MEDITERRANEAN.

Fred Halpert earned acclaim as the head chef at the Portman Hotel in San Francisco; in 1991, he struck out on his own, setting up his shop in the Wine Country, where he became a hit almost at once. The main dining room has an open kitchen and handsome stone fireplace; there's also a glass-enclosed area and a large terrace with umbrella-covered tables. Halpert is always searching for new taste sensations. Fortunately, that experimentation is backed up by a thorough training in the flavors and zest of Provence and other culinary locales.

The food is both good and reasonably priced. You can order a simple sandwich of grilled portobello mushrooms with mozzarella, red onions, and rosemary aioli, or go whole hog for such main courses as coq au vin or a grilled pork chop with barbecue sauce. There's always a fish, a pasta, and a risotto of the day. Be sure to try the spicy fries (a heartburn special) or the garlic-"smashed" potatoes. If your stomach can handle this wild and robust mixture of flavors and food, finish your meal with the chocolate chip crème brûlée. A dozen selections of wine by the glass are available. Beware: Service can be slow on weekends.

CALISTOGA

81 miles from San Francisco

Sam Brannan, entrepreneur extraordinaire and California's first millionaire, made his first bundle by supplying miners during the gold rush. Flushed with success, he went on to take advantage of the natural geothermal springs at the north end of the Napa

Find the New You: Take a Calistoga Mud Bath

The one thing you should do while you're in Calisoga is what people have been doing here for the last 150 years: Take a mud bath. The natural baths are composed of local volcanic ash, imported peat, and naturally boiling mineral hot-springs water, all mulled together to produce a thick mud that simmers at a temperature of about 104°F.

Once you overcome the hurdle of deciding how best to place your naked body into the mushy stone tub, the rest is pure relaxation—you soak with surprising buoyancy for about 10 to 12 minutes. A warm mineral-water shower, a mineral-water whirlpool bath, and a mineral-water steam room visit follow. Afterward, a relaxing blanket-wrap will slowly cool down your delighted body. All of this takes about 1¹/₂ hours and costs about $45; with a massage, add another half hour and $20 (we recommend a full hour). The outcome is a rejuvenated, revitalized, squeaky-clean you. Mud baths aren't recommended for those who are pregnant or have high blood pressure.

The spas also offer a variety of other treatments, such as hand and foot massages, herbal wraps, acupressure face-lifts, skin rubs, and herbal facials. Prices range from $35 to $125, and appointments are necessary for all services; call at least a week in advance.

Indulge yourself at any of these Calistoga spas: **Dr. Wilkinson's Hot Springs,** 1507 Lincoln Ave. (☎ **707/942-4102**); **Lincoln Avenue Spa,** 1339 Lincoln Ave. (☎ **707/942-5296**); **Golden Haven Hot Springs Spa,** 1713 Lake St. (☎ **707/ 942-6793**); and **Calistoga Spa Hot Springs,** 1006 Washington St. (☎ **707/ 942-6269**).

Valley by building a hotel and spa here in 1859. Flubbing up a speech comparing this natural California wonder to the Saratoga Springs resort on the East Coast, he serendipitously coined the term Calistoga and it stuck.

This small, simple resort town remains popular and uncomplicated today, particularly with city folk who come here to unwind. Calistoga's main street is still only about six blocks long, and no building is higher than two stories. It's a great place to relax and indulge in mineral waters, mud baths, Jacuzzis, massages, and, of course, wine.

WHAT TO SEE & DO BEYOND THE WINERIES

There's plenty to do in Calistoga even beyond the world-famous mud baths (see the sidebar) and aforementioned wineries.

Calistoga Depot, at 1458 Lincoln Ave. (on the site of Calistoga's original 1868 railroad station), now houses a variety of shops, some of which are housed in six restored passenger cars dating from 1916.

Old Faithful Geyser of California, at 1299 Tubbs Lane (☎ 707/942-6463), is one of only three "old faithful" geysers in the world. It's been blowing off steam at regular intervals for as long as anyone can remember. The 350°F water spews out to a height of about 60 feet (20 meters) every 40 minutes or so, day and night (varying with natural influences such as barometric pressure, the moon, tides, and tectonic stresses). The performance lasts about three minutes. You'll learn a lot about the origins of geothermal steam on your visit. You can bring a picnic lunch with you and catch the show as many times as you wish. An exhibit hall, gift shop, and snack bar are open every day.

Admission is $5 for adults, $4 for seniors, $2 for children ages six to 12, and free for children under six. Open summer, daily from 9am to 6pm; winter, daily 9am to 5pm. To get there, follow the signs from downtown Calistoga; it's between Calif. 29 and Calif. 128.

You won't see thousands of trees turned into stone, but you'll still find many interesting petrified specimens at the **Petrified Forest,** 4100 Petrified Forest Rd. (☎ **707/942-6667**). Volcanic ash blanketed this area after the eruption of Mount St. Helena three million years ago. As a result, you'll find redwoods that have turned to rock through the slow infiltration of silicas and other minerals, as well as petrified seashells, clams, and marine life indicating that water covered this area even before the redwood forest. Admission is $3 for adults, $1 for children four to 11, free for children under four. Open daily during the summer from 10am to 5:30pm; in winter, daily from 10am to 4:30pm. To get there from Calif. 128, turn right onto Petrified Forest Road, just past Lincoln Avenue.

BICYCLING

Cycling enthusiasts can rent bikes from **Getaway Bikes,** 1117 Lincoln Ave. (☎ **707/ 942-0332** or 800/499-BIKE). Full day tours ($89), which include lunch and a visit to three or four wineries, are available, as are downhill cruises ($39) for people who hate to pedal. On weekdays they'll even deliver bikes to you.

GLIDER RIDES

Calistoga offers a unique way of seeing its vineyard-filled valleys—from a glider. These quiet "birds" leave from the **Calistoga Gliderport,** 1546 Lincoln Ave., Calistoga, CA 94515 (☎ **707/942-5000**). Twenty-minute rides are $79 for one, $110 for two (weight limits apply). Thirty-minute rides are also available.

WHERE TO STAY
Expensive

Brannan Cottage Inn. 109 Wapoo Ave. (at Lincoln Ave.), Calistoga, CA 94515. ☎ **707/ 942-4200.** 6 rms. $160 double. Rates include full breakfast. MC, V.

At the east end of town, behind a picket fence on a side street facing a trailer park, stands this ornately decorated 1860 cottage. It's one of Sam Brannan's original resort cottages, as well as the only structure left remaining at its original location. Now listed on the National Register of Historic Places, the cottage was massively restored through a community effort to salvage an important piece of Calistoga's heritage. The six spacious, cozy rooms are decorated with country-style antiques, down comforters, and white lace curtains. More importantly, each room also has an air-conditioner, ceiling fan, private bath, and its own entrance. There's a comfortable parlor with reproduction wingback chairs and a pleasant brick terrace furnished with umbrella tables. A full buffet-style breakfast is served in the outdoor garden, weather permitting.

Mount View Hotel. 1457 Lincoln Ave. (on Calif. 29, near Fairway St.), Calistoga, CA 94515. ☎ **707/942-6877.** Fax 707/942-6904. 22 rms, 8 suites, 3 cottages. A/C TV TEL. $110–$140 double; $155–$200 suite, $200 cottage. Packages available. AE, MC, V.

Located on the main highway, near Fairway Street in the middle of Calistoga, the Mount View Hotel is one of the sweetest options in town. Rooms are in the best of taste, decorated in either Victorian or art deco styles, and are adorned with beautiful, hand-painted accents. There are also three self-contained cottages—with queen-size bed, wet bar, private deck, and hot tub—and eight suites. Almost everything in town is within walking distance, although once you settle in, you might not want to leave the quiet and sunny swimming area (the pool is heated). If swimming isn't your idea of relaxation, try the European spa or Jacuzzi. The hotel doesn't serve breakfast, but there are plenty of cafes on the block. Or you might wish to try the hotel's restaurant, **Catahoula,** serving tasty Cajun/Creole cuisine for lunch and dinner Wednesday through Monday (see its separate listing under "Where to Dine," below). Be forewarned: There's a two-night minimum during the high-season weekends.

Moderate

Dr. Wilkinson's Hot Springs. 1507 Lincoln Ave. (Calif. 29, between Fairway and Stevenson aves.), Calistoga, CA 94515. ☎ **707/942-4102.** 42 rms. A/C MINIBAR TV TEL. Winter, $59–$119 double; Summer, $79–$119 double. Weekly discounts and packages available. AE, MC, V.

This spa/resort was originally established by "Doc" Wilkinson, who arrived in Napa Valley just after World War II. Today, it's a typical motel, distinguished by the mud and mineral baths on the premises. Rooms range from Victorian-style units with sundecks and garden patios to rather basic and functional motel-like rooms, not unlike Janet Leigh's room in *Psycho.* All rooms have drip coffeemakers and refrigerators; some have kitchens. No-smoking rooms are available. Facilities include three mineral water pools (two outdoor and one indoor), Jacuzzi, steam room, and a health club. Facials and all kinds of body treatments are available in the salon.

WHERE TO DINE

Expensive

All Seasons Café. 1400 Lincoln Ave. (at Washington St.). ☎ **707/942-9111.** Reservations recommended on weekends. Main courses $13–$19 at dinner. MC, V. Thurs–Tues, 11am–3pm and 5:30–10pm; brunch Sat–Sun 9am–noon (wine shop, Thurs–Tues 11am–8pm). CALIFORNIA.

For a delightful meal, wend your way to the All Seasons Café in downtown Calistoga. Wine Country devotees put this place on the map because of its extensive wine list and knowledgeable staff. The trick here is to buy a bottle of wine from the cafe's wine shop, then bring it to your table; the cafe adds a corkage fee of around $8 instead of tripling the price of the bottle (as they do at most restaurants). The menu is diverse, ranging from pizzas and pastas to such main courses as braised lamb shank "osso bucco" in an orange, Madeira, and tomato sauce. Anything with the house-smoked salmon or spiced sausages is also a safe bet. Chef John Coss saves his guests from any major faux pas by matching wines to his dishes on the menu, so you know what's just right for his grilled duck breast or duck confit pizza.

✪ **Catahoula.** 1457 Lincoln Ave. ☎ **707/942-2275.** Reservations recommended. Main courses $11–$20. MC, V. Mon, Wed–Fri noon–2:30pm, Sat–Sun noon–3:30pm; Mon, Wed–Thurs, and Sun 5:30–10pm, Fri and Sat 5:30–10:30pm. AMERICAN/SOUTHERN.

Named after the official hound of the state of Louisiana, the Catahoula features the beloved dog everywhere: on the metal sculptures over the bar and in the photos in the restaurant and the saloon. The domain of chef Jan Birnbaum, formerly of New York's Quilted Giraffe and San Francisco's Campton Place, this restaurant is the current favorite in town. And with good reason: It's the only place in Napa where you can get a decent rooster gumbo. You'd have to travel all over Louisiana to find another pan-fried jalapeño-pecan catfish like this one. Catahoula's funky and fun, and the food that comes out of the wood-burning oven—like the roast duck with chili cilantro potatoes or the whole roasted fish with lemon broth, orzo, and escarole—is exciting. Start with the spicy gumbo ya ya with andouille sausage, and finish with what may be a first for many non-Southerners: buttermilk ice cream.

Moderate

Wappo Bar & Bistro. 1226B Washington St. (off Lincoln Ave.). ☎ **707/942-4712.** Main courses $8.50–$14.50. AE, DC, MC, V. Wed–Mon 11:30am–2:30pm; Thurs–Mon 6–9:30pm. INTERNATIONAL.

The best alfresco seat in (or, rather, out of) the house is under the honeysuckle- and vine-covered arbor by the fountain. You'll be comfortable inside this small bistro, too, at one of the well-spaced, well-polished tables. The menu offers a wide range of choices: roast vegetables with polenta, rabbit pie with wild mushrooms and puff pastry, and chicken with morels served with a side of chive mashed potatoes might give you an idea of what's going on here. The desserts of choice are the black-bottom coconut cream pie or the strawberry rhubarb pie.

9 The Wine Country: Sonoma County

54 miles from San Francisco

Sonoma is often thought of as the "other" Wine Country, forever in the shadow of Napa Valley. Truth is, even though there are far fewer wineries here (and far, far fewer tourists), its wines have actually won more awards than Napa's. Sonoma County, which stretches west to the coast, is more rural and less traveled than its neighbor to the east. Small, family owned wineries are its mainstay, just like back in the old days of wine-making, when everyone started with the intention of going broke and loved every minute of it. As opposed to the corporate-run tours most Napa Valley wineries run, tastings on the west side of the Mayacamas Mountains are usually free, low key, and come with plenty of friendly banter between the winemakers and their guests.

ESSENTIALS

GETTING THERE   From San Francisco, cross the Golden Gate Bridge and stay on U.S. 101 north. Exit at Calif. 37; after 10 miles, turn north onto Calif. 121. After another 10 miles, turn north onto Calif. 12 (Broadway), which will take you into town. From the town of Napa, take Calif. 121 south to Calif. 12. Don't worry, the roads are well marked with directional signs.

VISITOR INFORMATION   Before you begin your explorations of the area, visit the **Sonoma Valley Visitors Bureau,** 453 First St. East, Sonoma, CA 95476 (☎ **707/996-1090;** fax 707/996-9212). The office, located right on the plaza in the town of Sonoma, offers free maps and brochures about local happenings. It's open daily from in 9am to 5pm in the winter and 9am to 7pm in the summer. An additional office has been added a few miles south of Sonoma at 25200 Arnold Dr. (Hwy. 121; ☎ **707/996-1090**); it's open daily from 9am to 5pm.

The **Sonoma County Convention and Visitors Bureau,** 5000 Roberts Lake Rd., Rohnert Park, CA 94928 (☎ **707/586-8100** or 800/326-7666; fax 707/586-8111), offers a free visitors guide, with information about the whole county. They're also happy to provide lots of specialized information. Write as far in advance as possible.

WHEN TO GO   The best time to visit California's Wine Country is during the autumn harvest seasons when the grapes have ripened and all the wineries are in full production; it's quite a show. Spring has its own rewards: The entire valley is blanketed in wildflowers. Summer? Say hello to hot weather and heavy traffic.

TOURING THE WINERIES

Like its sister valley, Napa, the Sonoma Valley produces some of the finest wines in the United States. What makes a trip to Sonoma so pleasant is the intimate quality of so many of its vineyards; most of the wineries here are still family-owned. California's first winery, Buena Vista, was founded in the Sonoma Valley in 1857; it's still in operation today (see below). Today, Sonoma is home to about 35 wineries and 13,000 acres of vineyards. Chardonnay is the variety for which Sonoma is most noted; it represents almost one-quarter of the valley's acreage in vines.

The wineries here tend to be a little more spread out than they are in Napa, but they're still easy to find. The visitors bureaus listed above will provide you with maps to the valley's wineries. We've listed our favorite ones below; they, and the towns that follow, are listed roughly from south to north.

Ravenswood Winery. 18701 Gehricke Rd., Sonoma. ☎ **707/938-1960.** Fax 707/938-9459. Daily 10am–4:30pm. Reservations required for tours.

This small, traditional winery in the Sonoma Hills, built right into the hillside to keep it cool inside, crushed its first grapes in 1976 for its inaugural zinfandel. The winery is best known for its reds, especially its big, bold zinfandels, but it also produces a merlot, a cabernet sauvignon, and some whites. You'll be able to taste these as well as some younger blends, which are less expensive than the older vintages. Tours follow the wine-making process from grape to glass, and include the oak-barrel aging rooms. A "Barbeque in the Vineyards" is held each weekend from Memorial Day through the end of September (call for details).

Sebastiani Vineyards Winery. 389 Fourth St. E., Sonoma. ☎ **707/938-5532** or 800/888-5532. Daily 10am–5pm (last tour begins at 4pm).

Although Sebastiani doesn't occupy the most scenic setting or structures in Sonoma Valley, its place in the history and development of the region is unique, and it does offer an interesting and informative guided tour. The 25-minute tour, through aging stone cellars containing more than 300 carved casks, is well worth the time. You can see the winery's original turn-of-the-century crusher and press, as well as a large collection of oak-barrel carvings. If you don't want to take the tour, go straight to the tasting room, where you can sample an extensive selection of wines. A picnic area is adjacent to the cellars.

Buena Vista. 18000 Old Winery Rd. (P.O. Box 1842), Sonoma, CA 95476. ☎ **707/938-1266.** Daily 10:30am–4:30pm.

Buena Vista, the patriarch of California wineries, is located slightly northeast of the town of Sonoma. It was founded in 1857 by Count Agoston Haraszthy, the Hungarian émigré who is called the father of the California wine industry. A close friend of General Vallejo, Haraszthy returned from Europe in 1861 with 100,000 of the finest vine cuttings, which he made available to all wine growers. Although Buena Vista's wine-making now takes place in an ultramodern facility outside Sonoma, the winery still maintains a complimentary tasting room here, inside the restored 1862 Press House. There's also a self-guided tour that you can follow anytime during operating hours and a guided tour 2pm daily.

Château St. Jean. 8555 Sonoma Hwy. (Calif. 12), Kenwood. ☎ **707/833-4134.** Self-guided tours, daily 10am–4pm; tasting room, daily 10am–4:30pm.

This winery, founded in 1973, is at the foot of Sugarloaf Ridge, just north of Kenwood and east of Calif. 12. A private drive takes you to what was once a 250-acre country retreat, built in 1920. Château St. Jean is notable for its exceptionally beautiful buildings, well-landscaped grounds, and elegant tasting room. A well-manicured lawn is now a picnic area, complete with a fountain and benches.

There's a self-guided tour with detailed and photographic descriptions of the winemaking process. When you're done with it, be sure to walk up to the top of the tower for a view of the valley. Back in the tasting room, Château St. Jean offers several chardonnays, a cabernet sauvignon, a fumé blanc, a merlot, a riesling, and a gewürztraminer. Since 1984, the winery has been part of the Suntory family of premium wineries.

The toll-free, interactive **Château St. Jean "wine line"** (☎ **800/332-WINE**) offers free recorded reports on the Sonoma Wine Country, including updated information on vineyard conditions, interviews with winemakers and growers, what's happening at the winery, and descriptions of currently available wines.

SONOMA

54 miles from San Francisco

Sonoma owes much of its appeal to Mexican Gen. Mariano Guadalupe Vallejo, who fashioned this pleasant, slow-paced town after a typical Mexican village—right down to central plaza, Sonoma's geographical and commercial center. The Plaza sits at the top of a "T" formed by Broadway (Calif. 12) and Napa Street. Most of the surrounding streets form a grid pattern around this axis, making Sonoma easy to negotiate. The plaza's Bear Flag Monument marks the spot where the crude Bear Flag was raised in 1846, signaling the end of Mexican rule; the symbol was later adopted by the state of California. The eight-acre park at the center of the plaza, with two ponds frequented by ducks and geese, is perfect for an afternoon siesta in the cool shade.

WHAT TO SEE & DO BEYOND THE WINERIES

The best way to see the town of Sonoma is to follow the **Sonoma Walking Tour,** available from the Sonoma Valley Visitors Bureau (see "Visitor Information," above). Highlights include General Vallejo's 1852 Victorian-style home; Sonoma Barracks, erected in 1836 to house Mexican army troops; and the Blue Wing Inn, an 1840 hostelry built to accommodate tourists and new settlers while they erected homes in Sonoma—John Frémont, Kit Carson, and Ulysses S. Grant were all guests.

The **Mission San Francisco Solano de Sonoma,** on Sonoma Plaza at the corner of First Street East and Spain Street (☎ **707/938-1519**), was founded in 1823. It was the northernmost, and last, mission built in California. It was also the only one established on the northern coast by the Mexican rulers, who wished to protect their territory against expansionist Russian fur traders. It's now part of Sonoma State Historic Park. Admission is $2 for adults, $1 for children six to 12, free for children under six. Open daily 10am to 5pm except Thanksgiving, Christmas, and New Year's.

The **Arts Guild of Sonoma,** 140 E. Napa Street (☎ **707/996-3115**), showcases the works of local artists. Exhibits change frequently and include a wide variety of styles and media. Admission is free. Open Wednesday through Monday 11am to 5pm.

SHOPPING

Most of the town's shops, which offer everything from food and wines to clothing and books, are located around the plaza, including **The Mercado,** a small shopping center at 452 First St. E. that houses several good stores selling unusual wares.

BICYCLING

You can rent a bike at the **Goodtime Bicycle Company,** 18503 Hwy. 12 (☎ **707/938-0453**). They'll happily point you to easy bike trails. They also provide a picnic on request. Bikes cost $25 a day, $5 per hour. Bikes are also available from **Sonoma Valley Cyclery,** 20093 Broadway (☎ **707/935-3377**), for $20 a day, $6 per hour.

For biking information in Sonoma County, contact, call the friendly folks at **Dave's Bikes Sport,** 353 College Ave., Santa Rosa, CA 95402 (☎ **707/528-3283**).

WHERE TO STAY

Very Expensive

Sonoma Mission Inn & Spa. 18140 Calif. 12, Boyes Hot Springs, CA 94576. ☎ **707/938-9000** or 800/862-4945. Fax 707/938-4250. 170 rms, 3 suites. A/C MINIBAR TV TEL. Nov–Apr, $110–$250 Historic Inn room; $155–$350 Wine Country room. May–Oct, $140–$285 Historic Inn room; $180–$365 Wine Country room. Year-round, suites from $325. AE, DC, MC, V. From central Sonoma, drive 3 miles north on Calif. 12.

More than 30 years ago the lifeblood of this historic resort—a natural spring of hot mineral water—ran dry, and it wasn't until 1991 that they discovered a new source of liquid inspiration 1,100 feet directly beneath the inn: 127°F natural artesian mineral water, piped directly into the world-class spa's two pools and whirlpools.

The Sonoma Mission Inn and Spa is a 1920s-era resort, housed in a three-story pink Mediterranean-style structure, complete with mission towers, and set on eight landscaped acres of well-groomed lawns, bougainvillea, pine, and eucalyptus. The mission theme reappears in the lobby, with its beamed ceiling and large fireplace. While Clara Bow or Mary Pickford would have felt at home here, you're more likely to see Barbra Streisand or Harrison Ford strolling around in their aquatic skivvies.

The standardized rooms are furnished in a modern style with framed watercolors, ceiling fans, and such extra amenities as bathroom scales, hairdryers, and oversize bath towels. The larger Wine Country rooms are in a newer building and furnished with king-size beds, down comforters, desks, and refrigerators; some offer fireplaces, and many have balconies. The older Historic Inn Rooms are slightly smaller; most are furnished with queen-size beds. All rooms have VCRs and come with a complimentary bottle of wine. The rooms are well equipped and comfortable, but short on style.

Dining: The Grille, run by chef Toni Sakaguchi, is known for its low-calorie, sodium, and cholesterol California cuisine and its 200 varieties of Napa and Sonoma wines. The casual cafe, serving Italian cuisine at lunch, is renowned for its bountiful all-American breakfasts.

Services: Room service, concierge, laundry.

Facilities: Full spa facilities with a full range of treatments and nutritional consultation; health club; tennis courts. The tariff for individual spa and salon services ranges from $35 to $199. The use of the spa's bathhouse, which includes a sauna, steam room, whirlpool, outdoor exercise pool, and gym with weight equipment, costs $10 weekdays, $20 weekends, but is complimentary with any spa service. Guests have use of the nearby 18-hole Sonoma Golf Club.

Moderate

El Dorado Hotel. 405 First St. W., Sonoma, CA 95476. ☎ **707/996-3030** or 800/289-3031. Fax 707/996-3148. 27 rms. A/C TV TEL. Winter $85–$110 double, summer $105–$145 double. Rates include continental breakfast, split of wine. AE, MC, V.

If sleeping on a rickety antique bed and bathing in a cramped claw-foot tub isn't exactly your idea of a good time, consider the El Dorado Hotel. It may look like another old timer from the front, but inside it's all 20th-century deluxe. Each modern, handsomely appointed guest room—designed by the same folks who put together Auberge du Soleil—has French windows and small terraces; some offer lovely views of the Town Square, others overlook the hotel's private courtyard and heated pool. Each guest room has a canopy bed and a private bath with plush towels and hair dryers. All rooms (except those for the disabled) are on the second floor. The two rooms on the ground floor are off the private courtyard; each has its own partially enclosed patio. Services include concierge, laundry, in-room massage, bicycle rental, and access to a nearby health club.

Breakfast, served either inside or out, includes coffee, fruits, and freshly baked breads and pastries. The regional Italian cuisine at the highly acclaimed **Ristorante Piatti** (☎ **707/996-2351**) is prepared in an open, wood-burning oven (see "Where to Dine," below).

✪ **Sonoma Chalet.** 18935 Fifth St. West, Sonoma, CA 95476. ☎ **707/938-3129.** 3 rms, 3 cottages, 1 suite. Apr–Oct $95–$140 double; Nov–Mar $80–$130 double. Rates include continental breakfast. AE, MC, V.

This is one of the few accommodations in Sonoma that is truly secluded; it's a bit out of town, in a peaceful country setting overlooking a 200-acre ranch. Accommodations are in a Swiss-style farmhouse and several cottages, but they're by no means rustic—all were delightfully decorated by someone with an eye for color and a concern for comfort. They have claw-foot tubs, beds covered with country quilts, oriental carpets, comfortable furnishings, and private decks; some have woodstoves. A breakfast of fruit, yogurt, pastries, and cereal is served either in the country kitchen or in your room (and the gaggles of ducks, chickens, and ornery geese will be glad to help you finish off the crumbs).

Sonoma Hotel. 110 W. Spain St., Sonoma, CA 94576. ☎ **707/996-2996** or 800/468-6016. Fax 707/996-7014. 17 rms (5 with bath). Winter, Sun–Thur $65 double without bath, $95 double with bath; Fri–Sat $75 double without bath, $115–$125 double with bath. Summer, $75–$85 double without bath, $115–$125 double with bath. Rates include continental breakfast. AE, MC, V. Free parking.

This cute, little historic hotel on Sonoma's tree-lined Town Square still retains the same ambiance as it did over a century ago when it first opened. With an emphasis on European-style elegance and comfort, each room is decorated in an early California style, with antique furnishings, fine woods, and floral-print wallpapers. Some of the rooms feature brass beds, and all are blissfully devoid of phones and TVs. Five of the third-floor rooms share immaculate baths (and significantly reduced rates), while rooms with private baths have deep claw-foot tubs with overhead showers. Perks include nightly turndown, continental breakfast, and a bottle of wine on arrival. Also within the hotel is small restaurant and bar.

Inexpensive

✪ **El Pueblo Inn.** 896 W. Napa St., Sonoma, CA 94576. ☎ **707/996-3651** or 800/900-8844. 38 rms. A/C TEL. May–Oct $70–$80 double; Mar–Apr and Nov $60–$70, Dec–Feb $59 except during holidays when rates are higher. AE, DISC, MC, JCB, V.

This ain't Sonoma's fanciest hotel, but it offers some of the best-priced accommodations around. Located on Sonoma's main east-west street eight blocks from the center of town, the rooms here are pleasant enough, with post-and-beam construction, exposed brick walls, light wood furniture, and geometric prints. A drip coffee machine with packets of coffee should be a comfort to early risers. An outdoor heated pool will cool you off in hot weather. If possible, reservations should be made at least a month in advance for the spring and summer months.

WHERE TO DINE
Moderate

Depot Hotel Restaurant & Garden. 241 First St. W. (off Spain St.). ☎ **707/938-2980.** Reservations recommended. Main courses $7–$16 at dinner. AE, DC, DISC, MC, V. Wed–Fri 11:30am–2pm; Wed–Sun 5–on. NORTHERN ITALIAN.

Michael Ghilarducci has been the chef and owner here for the past 11 years, so you know he's either independently wealthy or a good cook. Fortunately, it's the latter. Located one block north of the Plaza in a handsome and historic 1870 stone building, the Depot Hotel offers pleasant outdoor dining in the Italian garden complete with central reflection pool and cascading Roman fountain. The menu is unwaveringly Italian, filled with a plethora of classic dishes such as spaghetti Bolognese and veal alla parmigiana. Start with the bounteous antipasto misto and end the feast with a dish of Michael's handmade Italian ice cream and fresh fruit sorbets.

✪ Eastside Oyster Bar & Grill. 133 East Napa St. ☎ **707/939-1266.** Reservations recommended. Main courses $9–$15. AE, DC, MC, V. Mon–Sat 11:30am–2:30pm, 5:30–9:30pm; Sun noon–9:30pm. Closed Tue–Wed in winter. INTERNATIONAL.

This is one of Sonoma's most popular restaurants, opened in 1992 by Charles Saunders, who gained fame and a following at the Sonoma Mission Inn and Spa. If possible, dine on the vine-entwined brick patio, which is warmed on cool nights

---

Where to Stock Up for a Gourmet Picnic, Sonoma Style

Sonoma has plenty of restaurants but, on a sunny day, the Wine Country is really the place to picnic. Sonoma's Plaza Park is a perfect place to set up a gourmet spread; there are even picnic tables available. Below are Sonoma's top spots for stocking up for such an alfresco fete.

If you want to pick up some specialty fare on your way into town, stop at **Angelo's Wine Country Deli,** 23400 Arnold Dr. (☎ 707/938-3688). Angelo's sells all types of smoked meats, special salsas, and homemade mustards. The deli is known for its half-dozen types of homemade beef jerky. It's open daily from 9am to 6pm.

The Sonoma Cheese Factory, on the Plaza at 2 Spain Street (☎ **707/996-1000**), offers an extraordinary variety of imported meats and cheeses; a few are set out for tasting every day. The factory also sells caviar, gourmet salads, pâté, and homemade Sonoma Jack cheese. Sandwiches are available, too. While you're there, you can watch a narrated slide show about cheesemaking. The factory is open weekdays from 8:30am to 5:30pm and weekends from 8:30am to 6pm.

At 315 Second Street East, one block north of East Spain Street is the **Vella Cheese Company** (☎ 707/938-3232 or 800/848-0505). Established in 1931, the folks at Vella pride themselves on making cheese into an award-winning science, their most recent victory being "U.S. Cheese Championship 1995–96" for their Monterey Dry Jack. Other cheeses range from flavorful High Moisture Jack to a mild Daisy and a razor-sharp Raw Milk Cheddar. Among other cheeses for which Vella has become famous is Oregon Blue, made at Vella's southern Oregon factory—rich, buttery, and even spreadable, one of the few premier blues produced in this country. Any of these fine handmade, all-natural cheeses can be shipped directly from the store. Vella Cheese Co. is open Monday to Saturday 9am to 6pm, and Sunday 10am to 5pm.

Of course, you're going to need something to wash down all of this gourmet fare. Head to the **Wine Exchange,** at the Mercado, 452 First St. East (☎ 707/938-1794), which carries more than 600 domestic wines and has a full wine-tasting bar. The beer connoisseur who's feeling displaced in the Wine Country will be happy to find more than 280 beers from around the world here too, including a number of exceptional domestic beers. There are wine and beer tastings daily. Open daily from 10am to 6pm.

by a fire. Saunders is blessed with an unerring sense of proportion and flavor; he knows how to keep both the visiting and local foodies coming back for more. The emphasis is on seafood, although there will certainly be a local bird of the day—perhaps a pheasant or a local chicken—as well as sandwiches. Our favorite dishes are the drunken Manila clam linguini dunked in garlic, smoked chile peppers, Spanish chorizo sausage, oregano, and a splash of golden tequila. Top it all off with the New Orleans–style praline-meringue layered with chocolate ganache in a pool of bourbon spiked crème anglaise—wow!

Piatti. 405 First St. W. ☎ **707/996-2351.** Reservations recommended. Main courses $7–$12. AE, MC, V. Mon–Thurs 11:30am–2:30pm and 5–10pm, Fri–Sat 11:30am–11pm, Sun 11:30am–10pm. ITALIAN.

This local favorite is known for serving reasonably priced food in a rustic Italian-style setting with delightful patio seating. The restaurant occupies the ground floor of the rejuvenated El Dorado Hotel, a 19th-century landmark. Good-tasting pizzas emerge from a wood-burning oven. There are also satisfying pastas, such as lasagna al pesto and spaghetti con agnello (with fresh mushrooms and lamb ragout). Other dishes include a wonderful roast vegetable appetizer, rotisserie chicken with creamy mashed potatoes, and a good scaloppini Pizzaiola. Granted, there are far fancier restaurants in the area, but not many that can fill you up at these prices.

Swiss Hotel. 18 W. Spain St. ☎ **707/938-2884.** Reservations recommended. Main courses $8–$16. MC, V. Daily 11am–2:30pm, 5–9:30pm. Bar daily 11am–2am. CONTINENTAL/NORTHERN ITALIAN.

The historic Swiss Hotel, located right in the town center, is a Sonoma landmark, complete with slanting floors and aged beamed ceilings. The turn-of-the-century long oak bar at the left of the entrance is adorned with black-and-white photos of pioneering Sonomans. The bright white dining room and rear dining patio are pleasant spots to enjoy lunch specials like penne with chicken and mushrooms, sandwiches, and California-style pizzas fired in a wood-burning oven. Dinner might start with a warm winter salad of pears, walnuts, radicchio, and blue cheese. Main courses run the gamut; we like the linguine with a spicy tomato sauce, the filet mignon wrapped in a cheese crust, and the duck in a red wine sauce.

Inexpensive

La Casa. 121 E. Spain St. ☎ **707/996-3406.** Reservations recommended on weekends and summer evenings. Main courses $6–$11. AE, CB, DC, DISC, MC, V. Daily 11:30am–10pm. MEXICAN.

This no-nonsense Mexican restaurant, on the Sonoma Town Square across from the mission, serves great enchiladas, fajitas, and chimichangas. To start, try the black bean soup or the ceviche made of fresh snapper, marinated in lime juice with cilantro and salsa, and served on crispy tortillas. Follow that with tamales prepared with corn husks spread with corn masa, stuffed with chicken filling, and topped with a mild red chile sauce. Or, you might opt for the delicious Suiza—deep-dish chicken enchiladas, or the fresh snapper Veracruz if it's available. Wine and beer are available.

Feed Store Café & Bakery. 529 First St. W. (at Napa St.). ☎ **707/938-2122.** Reservations accepted; recommended Sun. Main courses $5–$9. MC, V. Daily 7am–4pm. CALIFORNIA.

This attractive, airy restaurant has a small fountain-cooled courtyard, a helpful staff, and first-rate, reasonably priced food served in bountiful portions. For breakfast, there are more varieties of eggs than you can imagine. For lunch, quesadillas, burgers, and the crowd-pleasing Jalisco club sandwich (a grilled chicken-breast Mexican burrito) are all good choices. Under the same roof is the Bakery at the Feed Store.

Index

FROMMER'S COMPLETE TRAVEL GUIDES

(Comprehensive guides to destinations around the world, with selections in all price ranges—from deluxe to budget)

Acapulco/Ixtapa/Taxco
Alaska
Amsterdam
Arizona
Atlanta
Australia
Austria
Bahamas
Bangkok
Barcelona, Madrid & Seville
Belgium, Holland & Luxembourg
Berlin
Bermuda
Boston
Budapest & the Best of Hungary
California
Canada
Cancún, Cozumel & the Yucatán
Caribbean
Caribbean Cruises & Ports of Call
Caribbean Ports of Call
Carolinas & Georgia
Chicago
Colorado
Costa Rica
Denver, Boulder & Colorado Springs
Dublin
England
Florida
France
Germany
Greece
Hawaii
Hong Kong
Honolulu/Waikiki/Oahu
Ireland
Italy
Jamaica/Barbados
Japan
Las Vegas
London
Los Angeles
Maryland & Delaware
Maui

Mexico
Mexico City
Miami & the Keys
Montana & Wyoming
Montréal & Québec City
Munich & the Bavarian Alps
Nashville & Memphis
Nepal
New England
New Mexico
New Orleans
New York City
Northern New England
Nova Scotia, New Brunswick & Prince
  Edward Island
Paris
Philadelphia & the Amish Country
Portugal
Prague & the Best of the Czech Republic
Puerto Rico
Puerto Vallarta, Manzanillo & Guadalajara
Rome
San Antonio & Austin
San Diego
San Francisco
Santa Fe, Taos & Albuquerque
Scandinavia
Scotland
Seattle & Portland
South Pacific
Spain
Switzerland
Thailand
Tokyo
Toronto
U.S.A.
Utah
Vancouver & Victoria
Vienna
Virgin Islands
Virginia
Walt Disney World & Orlando
Washington, D.C.
Washington & Oregon

FROMMER'S FRUGAL TRAVELER'S GUIDES
(The grown-up guides to budget travel, offering dream vacations at down-to-earth prices)

Australia from $45 a Day

Berlin from $50 a Day

California from $60 a Day

Caribbean from $60 a Day

Costa Rica & Belize from $35 a Day

Eastern Europe from $30 a Day

England from $50 a Day

Europe from $50 a Day

Florida from $50 a Day

Greece from $45 a Day

Hawaii from $60 a Day

India from $40 a Day

Ireland from $45 a Day

Italy from $50 a Day

Israel from $45 a Day

London from $60 a Day

Mexico from $35 a Day

New York from $70 a Day

New Zealand from $45 a Day

Paris from $65 a Day

Washington, D.C. from $50 a Day

FROMMER'S PORTABLE GUIDES
(Pocket-size guides for travelers who want everything in a nutshell)

Charleston & Savannah

Las Vegas

New Orleans

San Francisco

FROMMER'S FAMILY GUIDES
(The complete guides for successful family vacations)

California with Kids

Los Angeles with Kids

New England with Kids

New York City with Kids

San Francisco with Kids

Washington, D.C. with Kids

FROMMER'S AMERICA ON WHEELS
(Everything you need for a successful road trip, including full-color road maps and ratings for every hotel)

California & Nevada

Florida

Mid-Atlantic

Midwest & the Great Lakes

New England & New York

Northwest & Great Plains

South Central & Texas

Southeast

Southwest

FROMMER'S WALKING TOURS
(Memorable neighborhood strolls through the world's great cities)

Berlin

Chicago

England's Favorite Cities

London

Montréal & Québec City

New York

Paris

San Francisco

Spain's Favorite Cities

Tokyo

Venice

Washington, D.C.

SPECIAL-INTEREST TITLES

Arthur Frommer's Branson!

Arthur Frommer's New World of Travel

The Civil War Trust's Official Guide to the
Civil War Discovery Trail

Frommer's America's 100 Best-Loved State
Parks

Frommer's Caribbean Hideaways

Frommer's Complete Hostel Vacation Guide
to England, Scotland & Wales

Frommer's Food Lover's Companion to
France

Frommer's Food Lover's Companion to Italy

Frommer's National Park Guide

Outside Magazine's Adventure Guide to
New England

Outside Magazine's Adventure Guide to
Northern California

Places Rated Almanac

Retirement Places Rated

USA Sports Traveler's and TV Viewer's
Golf Tournament Guide

USA Sports Minor League Baseball Book

USA Today Golf Atlas

Wonderful Weekends from NYC

FROMMER'S IRREVERENT GUIDES
(Wickedly honest guides for sophisticated travelers)

Amsterdam	Miami	Santa Fe
Chicago	New Orleans	U.S. Virgin Islands
London	Paris	Walt Disney World
Manhattan	San Francisco	Washington, D.C.

BAEDEKER
(With four-color photographs and a free pull-out map)

Amsterdam	Greece	San Francisco
Athens	Greek Islands	St. Petersburg
Austria	Hawaii	Scandinavia
Bali	Hong Kong	Scotland
Belgium	Israel	Singapore
Budapest	Italy	South Africa
California	Lisbon	Spain
Canada	London	Switzerland
Caribbean	Mexico	Venice
Copenhagen	New York	Vienna
Crete	Paris	Tokyo
Florence	Prague	Tuscany
Florida	Provence	
Germany	Rome	

FROMMER'S BY NIGHT GUIDES
(The series for those who know that life begins after dark)

Amsterdam	Los Angeles	New York
Chicago	Miami	Paris
Las Vegas	New Orleans	San Francisco
London		

FROMMER'S BEST BEACH VACATIONS

(The top places to sun, stroll, shop, stay, play, party, and swim, with ratings for each beach)

California
Carolinas & Georgia
Florida
Hawaii

Mid-Atlantic (from New York to Washington, D.C.)
New England

FROMMER'S BED & BREAKFAST GUIDES

(Selective guides with four-color photos and full descriptions of the best inns in each region)

California
Caribbean
Great American Cities
Hawaii

Mid-Atlantic
New England
Pacific Northwest

Rockies
Southeast
Southwest

FROMMER'S DRIVING TOURS

(Four-color photos and detailed maps outlining spectacular scenic driving routes)

Australia
Austria
Britain
Florida
France

Germany
Ireland
Italy
Scandinavia

Scotland
Spain
Switzerland
U.S.A.

FROMMER'S BORN TO SHOP

(The ultimate guides for travelers who love to shop)

France
Great Britain

Hong Kong
London

Mexico
New York

TRAVEL & LEISURE GUIDES

(Sophisticated pocket-size guides for discriminating travelers)

Amsterdam
Boston
Hong Kong

London
New York
Paris

San Francisco
Washington, D.C.

UNOFFICIAL GUIDES

(Get the unbiased truth from these candid, value-conscious guides)

Atlanta
Branson, Missouri
Chicago
Cruises
Disneyland

Euro Disneyland
The Great Smoky & Blue
     Ridge Mountains
Las Vegas
Miami & the Keys

Skiing in the West
Walt Disney World
Washington, D.C.